P9-CEN-062

That the People Might Live

That the People Might Live

Native American Literatures and Native American Community

JACE WEAVER

New York   Oxford
Oxford University Press
1997

Oxford University Press

Oxford   New York
Athens   Auckland   Bangkok   Bogota   Bombay   Buenos Aires
Calcutta   Cape Town   Dar es Salaam   Delhi   Florence   Hong Kong
Istanbul   Karachi   Kuala Lumpur   Madras   Madrid   Melbourne
Mexico City   Nairobi   Paris   Singapore   Taipei   Tokyo   Toronto   Warsaw

and associated companies in
Berlin   Ibadan

Copyright © 1997 by Jace Weaver

Published by Oxford University Press, Inc.
198 Madison Avenue, New York, New York 10016

Oxford is a registered trademark of Oxford University Press

All rights reserved. No part of this publication may be reproduced,
stored in a retrieval system, or transmitted, in any form or by any means,
electronic, mechanical, photocopying, recording, or otherwise,
without the prior permission of Oxford University Press.

Library of Congress Cataloging-in-Publication Data
Weaver, Jace, 1957–
   That the people might live : Native American literatures and
Native American community / Jace Weaver.
      p.   cm.
   Includes bibliographical references and index.
   ISBN 0-19-511852-9 (cloth); ISBN 0-19-512037-X (paper)
   1. Indian literature—United States—History and criticism.
2. American literature—Indian authors—History and criticism.
3. Indians of North America—Religion.   4. Indians of North America—
Ethnic identity.   I. Title.
PM157.W43   1997
810.9'897—dc21   97-3273

Sherman Alexie, "Introduction to Native American Literature." Reprinted with permission of
Caliban.

Louis Littlecoon Oliver, "Salute to Alexander Posey," in *Chasers of the Sun*. Reprinted with permission of The Greenfield Review Press.

Simon Ortiz, *The People Shall Continue.* © 1988. Reprinted with permission of
Children's Book Press, San Francisco, California.

Lynn Riggs, "The Hollow," in *The Iron Dish.* © 1930 Lynn Riggs. Reprinted with permission of
Doubleday, a division of Bantam Doubleday Dell Publishing Group, Inc.

9 8 7 6 5 4 3 2 1

Printed in the United States of America
on acid-free paper

Somewhere in America a television ex-
     plodes

& here you are again (again)
asking me to explain broken glass.

You scour the reservation landfill
through the debris of so many lives:
old guitar, basketball on fire, pair of
     shoes.
All you bring me is an empty bottle.

Am I the garbageman of your dreams?

*

Listen:

it will not save you
or talk you down from the ledge
of a personal building.

It will not kill you
or throw you facedown to the floor
& pull the trigger twice.

It believes a roomful of monkeys
in a roomful of typewriters
would eventually produce a roomful
of poetry about missing the jungle.

You will forget
more than you remember:
that is why we all dream slowly.
Often you need a change of scenery.
It will give you one black & white photo-
     graph.

Sometimes it whispers
into anonymous corner bars
& talks too much about the color
of its eyes & skin & hair.

It believes a piece of coal
shoved up its own ass
will emerge years later
as a perfectly imperfect diamond.

Sometimes it screams
the English language near freeways
until trucks jackknife & stop all traffic
while the city runs over itself.

Often, you ask forgiveness.
It will give you a 10% discount.

*

Because you have seen the color of my
     bare skin
does not mean you have memorized the
     shape of my ribcage.

Because you have seen the spine of the
     mountain
does not mean you made the climb.

Because you stood waist-deep in the
     changing river
does not mean you were equal to MC^2.

Because you gave something a name
does not mean your name is
     important.

Because you sleep
does not mean you see into my dreams.

*

Send it a letter: the address will keep
     changing.
Give it a phone call: busy signal.
Knock on its door: you'll hear voices.
Look in its windows: shadows dance
     through blinds.

In the end, it will pick you up from the
     pavement
& take you to the tribal cafe for breakfast.

It will read you the menu.
It will not pay your half of the bill.

—Sherman Alexie (Spokane/Coeur d'Alene),
"Introduction to Native American Literature"

Preface

Doing theology is a decidedly non-Indian enterprise. William Baldridge (Cherokee) writes, "When I talk about Native American theology to many of my Indian friends, most of them just smile and act as if I hadn't said anything. And I'm pretty sure that as far as they are concerned I truly hadn't said anything."[1] Similarly, Jack Forbes (Powhatan/Lenape/Saponi) notes that Natives "tend to avoid theology."[2] In part, no doubt, this is because traditional Native religions are not primarily religions of theology but, as Tom Driver points out of Shinto, religions of "ritual observance."[3] Forbes, however, cites two further but related reasons. First, "the study of God" is thought to be impossible or at least presumptuous, and second, "such a study leaves the problems of this life still to be solved for each individual."[4]

Traditional Native religions are integrated totally into daily activity. They are ways of life and not sets of principles or credal formulations. As Charles Eastman (Santee Dakota) observed, "Every act of [an Indian's] life is, in a very real sense, a religious act."[5] To speak in terms of "religion," as normally conceptualized in Western thought, and Native community and traditions is, in fact, to be engaged in a kind of incommensurate discourse. Native "religion" does not concern itself—does not try to know or explain—"what happens in the other world."[6] Native languages do not even have words for "religion" or "theology" or "philosophy." Instead, for example, "Hopi" designates both tribe and religious practice. The Navajo call themselves Diyin dine' é (Children of the Holy

People). The name Cherokee may derive from *cheera tahge,* the term for wise ones, meaning "possessors of the divine fire." And the word in Cherokee usually translated as "religion," *eloh*, also means, at one and the same time, land, history, law, and culture. Forbes has speculated sarcastically that there may be no need for a word for religion until a people no longer have religion.[7] Perhaps there is no need for theology until these things have been lost as well.

Bill Baldridge highlights the potential pitfalls of Natives attempting to do theology, writing, "When Indians theologize they must place one foot into the Euro-American culture; and if they are not careful they will soon have both feet outside their own culture. There is also a difference between Native American theology and Native Americans doing theology, as any Native American student in theological training soon finds out."[8] These dangers are especially acute for a Cherokee. Around the time of first White contact, according to legend, the Cherokee revolted against their priests, killing them all and overthrowing and disestablishing the priestly class.

This is not, however, a volume of theology but a work in religious studies (though the two disciplines are closer than practitioners of the latter would like to admit) and in literary criticism and theory. It seeks to dialogue not only with the 10–25 percent of American Natives who are Christian but also with the vast majority who are not. Because of the intimate connection between Native religion and Native culture and community, Christianity has been unable to displace traditional religious practice and belief, despite more than 500 years of ongoing colonialist attempts to do so. In fact, today the survival not of traditional spirituality but of Christianity in Indian country is an open question. Even among Natives who consider themselves Christian, traditional ways are often still important and honored. Many practice syncretism and religious dimorphism.

Traditional religions are, fundamentally, "a not-easily-accessible inner reality which is first experienced on the level of tribe, clan and extended family."[9] There is no practice of Native religions for personal empowerment. They are communal and communitarian.

This book is also not, however, about Native religion or Native peoples per se. Dennis McPherson (Anishinaabe) and Douglas Rabb are correct when they declare that Indians have been "studied to death."[10] Rather, this volume is about Native community. It takes as both its lens and its focus Native American literature. In communities deeply fractured by the continuing impact of invasion and colonialism, this literary output is both a reflection and a shaper of community values. It has assumed an important role for modern-day Native peoples, especially urban Natives separated from their tribal lands and often from their cultures and religions as well.

Scope and Contribution

It is my hope that this work will engage contemporary American Indian intellectuals and challenge them to do more extensive critical work of our own intellectual traditions and will provide a methodological and theoretical framework for doing so. This kind of work is crucial in the area of religious studies. Traditional religions, Christianity, and syncretic movements have created in American Indian communities a religious pluralism that produces communal tensions and misunderstandings that undermine the work of community organizing. Thus, critical assessment of Native literature, which speaks across these divisions, is of vital importance. Until recently, most analysis of Native literary production has been left to non-Native scholars. Now, however, a small number of critical voices is being raised among Natives, but much more work needs to be done from Native perspectives.

This book examines, extends, and critiques the emerging critical approaches to Native literature offered by Native scholars such as Gerald Vizenor (Anishinaabe), Louis Owens (Choctaw/Cherokee), Georges Sioui (Huron), Robert Warrior (Osage), and others. It explores what, if anything, distinguishes written product by Natives from that of non-Natives. In so doing, it discusses the work done on worldviews by Native scholars such as Owens, McPherson, and Donald Fixico (Shawnee/Sac and Fox/Creek/Seminole) and by non-Natives such as Åke Hultkrantz and Calvin Martin. It is my hypothesis that Native literature both reflects and shapes contemporary Native identity and community and that what distinguishes it and makes it a valuable resource is what I term in this study "communitism."

Examining this hypothesis involves a broad reading across Native literature. In such a reading, my approach is similar to that followed by the Dutch/Indonesian writer and critic Rob Nieuwenhuys in his study of Dutch colonial literature, *Mirror of the Indies*. Like Nieuwenhuys, I define literature broadly as the total written output of a people. Even biographies, autobiographies, and tribal histories would come under such a definition, because to impress form on the relative formlessness of a life or a culture, to exercise selectivity over what is to be included and what excluded, is an act of literary creation. This approach is supported by the work of A. LaVonne Brown Ruoff and Paula Gunn Allen (Laguna/Sioux), among others. Ruoff includes in her monograph *American Indian Literatures* sermons, biographies, autobiographies, tribal histories, and travel accounts among other written works. Allen notes that nonfiction has influenced Native fiction "at least as thoroughly as have more exotic folk and ceremonial traditions" and that therefore its inclusion in any discussion is necessary "to a proper, full-bodied representation of Native literature." In similar fashion, Penny Petrone subsumes a variety of forms, including speeches, letters, reports, petitions, diary entries, essays, history, protest literature, journals, and journalism, under the definition of literature in *Native Literature in Canada*.[11] In so doing, she deliberately forgoes "the purist attitude of Western literary critics toward literature that does not conform totally to their aesthetic criteria."[12] Not to do so, she argues, leads to neglect of Native literary output. I have, however, in deference to literary purists, adopted the formulation of "literatures," in the plural, to avoid any confusion. Such an expansive definition has the advantage of covering the full spectrum of whatever Natives have produced. For too many non-Native scholars like Arnold Krupat and John Bierhorst, the only "genuine" Indian literature consists of oral myths. It ceases to be Indian when it employs Western forms such as the short story or the novel. Yet is this really true, or does something about it remain somehow Indian despite its form? What real difference is there between the "rant and roll" poetry of John Trudell (Santee Dakota), the religio-political writings of Vine Deloria Jr. (Standing Rock Sioux), the untutored letters of Richard Fields (Cherokee), the postmodernist novels of Gerald Vizenor, or the Broadway theatricals of Lynn Riggs (Cherokee) if they speak to and for Indian peoples and reflect and shape them as persons?

Also, following Nieuwenhuys, I discuss these literatures without regard to quality. This obviates the temptation to discuss what is worth reading, what is worthy of being in the canon. As will be noted, this Eurocentric trap in non-Native criticism has led, albeit perhaps by inadvertence and with honorable intentions, to a denial of Native personhood and damage to Native subjectivity. To avoid questions of quality also prevents Eurocentric comparisons, such as that which asks with a plaintive arrogance, "Where is the African Proust?" or that of Albert Schweitzer, who dubbed South Asian Nobel laureate Rabindrinath Tagore "the Indian Goethe." In each case there is the clear implication that persons who need the adjectival modifier are something less than their Western counterparts, the "actual" Proust or the "real" Goethe.

What emerges is a reading that is deeply experiential and narrative rather than simply theoretical. It is also profoundly cultural. Culture embodies those moral, ethical, and aesthetic values—what Ngugi wa Thiong'o calls "the set of spiritual eyeglasses"—through which a people come to view themselves and their place in the universe. As Ngugi notes, values are the basis of a people's identity and their sense of particularity as members of the human race. And as both Ngugi and Inés Talamantez (Mescalero Apache) remind us, all this is carried in language. Story and literature are the primary means by which it does its work.

Limitations

While I must undertake a broad reading across Native literatures in order to illustrate what I believe to be the utility of the concept of communitism, such a reading must also be limited. I have tried to be suggestive rather than exhaustive. I want to work through my idea on a large scale in the hope that it may become part of the ongoing discussion of both Native literature and Native religious traditions. My goal is merely to provide what I believe to be a useful analytic tool and illustrate its use. In this I resonate with Robert Warrior, who in his dissertation and, later, book *Tribal Secrets* declared that he was "laying a groundwork rather than erecting structures."[13] As he does for his notion of "intellectual sovereignty," I suggest that Native peoples must realize what is, I believe, a traditional commitment to communitism and "allow the definition and articulation of what that means to emerge as we critically reflect" on that commitment.[14]

All of this is to say that this work makes no claim to being definitive. Native peoples have never recognized the arbitrarily drawn borders that demarcate the modern nation-states of the Americas. Critics like Forbes, Ruoff, and Geary Hobson (Cherokee/Chickasaw) have argued for a "borderless" Native literature, hemispheric in scope and regarding the Americas as a single unit for literary study.[15] Still other Native intellectuals conceptualize a "Fourth World," comprising all indigenous peoples around the globe, or an "indigenism" that takes the rights of all such persons as its highest priority.[16] While I agree with many of these scholars, I have out of deference to the sheer volume of material involved limited my reading to authors and writings from the territory comprised by the United States. I do not discuss Canadian Natives, excluding in the process many fine writers who could usefully be brought into the dialogue—for example, Tomson Highway (Cree), Ruby Slipperjack (Anishinaabe), Jordan Wheeler (Cree/Anishinaabe), Howard Adams (Métis). I have omitted any discussion of important mestizo writers, like Rudolfo Anaya and Miguel Méndez, from the United States and Mexico.[17] Finally, though Native Hawaiian writers, such as Dana Naone, express themes and concerns similar to those of other indigenous peoples in the United States, they too have been excluded.[18] Even then, not all American Native writers can be analyzed. Some of those discussed are well-known. Others are rather obscure and have received little critical attention. There are no doubt many loose ends, and I am sure that I have left undone things that might—indeed should—have been done. I hope, however, that should the idea prove fruitful for discussion, other Native critics will take it up, develop it further, and apply its precepts to other writers.

I can imagine that I will be criticized both by non-Native scholars who look back on a supposedly pristine orature as the only legitimate Indian literature and by Natives who might object that I use critical resources by those other than American Indians. Warrior, in particular, is stringent in his demand in *Tribal Secrets* that we employ only internal Native criticism and scholarship in our work.[19] I agree that we must drink from our own wells and, in the case of religious studies and literary criticism, indeed, first sink wells from which to drink. I nonetheless have been more willing in this present work to engage White scholars, not because we should be put constantly in the position (as we so often are) of answering Whites and thus allowing them to continue to set the agenda of the discourse but because I believe that it is important to stake out our own territory contrapuntally to those non-Native voices that have been heard almost exclusively heretofore. I also have employed the work of numerous postcolonial theorists and critics from whom I believe we have much to learn in our own intellectual and political struggles. Beyond Nieuwenhuys, those working in an anticolonial or postcolonial vein by whom I have been most influenced include Frantz Fanon, Ngugi wa Thiong'o, Edward Said, G. C. Spivak, Homi K. Bhabha, Albert Memmi, and Ashis Nandy (whose work itself is largely derivative of Memmi's two decades earlier). I hope that in bringing such scholars to the table, even though I still privilege Native voices, I am not violating Warrior's intellectual sovereignty. I take some solace from the fact that others, including Owens and Vizenor, rely on a wide variety of resources, Native and non-Native, and that the works of Warrior's two exemplary cases, Deloria and John Joseph Mathews (Osage), also were the products of wide-ranging influences, from Lord Byron to Pierre Teilhard de Chardin to Marshall McLuhan. Warrior himself notes that "we can further humanize ourselves and our works by engaging our particular question in the context of other Others around the world who face similar situations. Whether such engagement is fruitful is not so important as is opening ourselves, from the standpoint of intellectual sovereignty, to a wide range of perspectives."[20] Through communitism, by proclaiming and living our commitment to Native community and values, we would set our scholarly work and our literatures in the stream of history to which they belong and thus be better understood and appreciated, and, on the other hand, we would be better able to embrace and assimilate the thoughts of other Others and of the dominating culture without losing our roots.[21]

Terminology

Central to this study is the concept of communitism. I offer it as a term not without some genuine trepidation. It runs the risk of being merely one more obscure bit of technical vocabulary in an academia that currently seems in love with jargon to the extent that much of so-called postmodernist scholarship is comprehensible only to the cognoscenti (and often not even then). Further, Indians have indeed been "studied to death." As Gerald Vizenor notes, "Foundational theories have overburdened tribal imagination, memories, and the coherence of natural reason with simulations and the cruelties of paracolonial historicism."[22] Communitism is related to Vizenor's "survivance," Warrior's "intellectual sovereignty," and Georges Sioui's "autohistory." Its coining, however, is nevertheless necessary because none of these terms from Native intellectuals nor any word from the Latin root *communitas* carries the exact sense implied by this neologism. It is formed by a combination of the words "community" and "activism." Literature is communitist to the extent that it has a proactive commitment to Native community, including what I term the "wider community" of Creation itself. In communities that have too often been fractured and rendered dysfunctional by the effects of more than 500 years of colonialism, to promote communitist values means to participate in the healing of the grief and sense of exile felt by Native communities and the pained individuals in them.

A few other notes with regard to terminology employed herein need to be made. Much of postcolonial discourse reflects on the relationship between the colony/former colony and the colonial center, that place from which the colonizers came. That center is usually called the "metropolis." For reasons of clarity and personal preference, I employ the French term for the colonial mother country, *métropole*.[23] For non-Natives, what is the preferred term for America's indigenous peoples has been a source of some minor confusion. To use either "Indian" or "Native American" to describe persons or a literature is to employ a term with a built-in contradiction. To use such terms is to ignore the traditional self-definition of American indigenes as first and foremost tribal in identity. Despite a growing pan-Indian discourse, a Native person's primary self-identification remains that of his or her own tribe. In the first instance, I have whenever possible and appropriate employed such a designation. Otherwise, I have used the terms "Native American," "American Indian," "Indian," and "Native" more or less interchangeably. White non-Natives are most commonly referred to in print as "Euro-Americans." Louis Owens opts for "Euramerican," a label current among some scholars. I employ the term "Amer-European," which I borrow from John Joseph Mathews.[24] Though the bulk of Mathews's work was done in the 1930s and 1940s before the term Euro-American became popular, his usage reflects more than the lack of a commonly accepted vocabulary. "Euro-American" means an American of European descent. It is thus akin to "African American" or "Asian American." "Amer-European" connotes something very different. They are Europeans who happen to live in America. Mathews's terminology reflects the difference in worldviews between the two peoples, Native and non-Native. Born of and shaped by a different continent, Amer-Europeans will never truly be of this continent, never truly belong here, no matter how many generations they may dwell here.[25]

This is a work about community. Ultimately, no Native scholarship can be produced in isolation. It must be a communal effort. In this work, I stand upon the strong and sophisticated foundations laid by others, particularly Vizenor and Warrior. There are friends, many of them senior Native scholars, I wish to thank for their support and encouragement during my graduate study and who have been kind enough to read and critique this manuscript: William Baldridge, Betty Louise Bell (Cherokee), Elizabeth Cook-Lynn (Sicangu Dakota), Thom Fassett (Seneca), Donald Fixico, Diane Glancy (Cherokee), Mariana Annette Jaimes-Guerrero (Yaqui/Juaneño), Thomas King (Cherokee), Dennis McPherson, Homer Noley (Choctaw), Greg Sarris (Pomo/Coastal Miwok), Andy Smith (Cherokee), and George Tinker (Osage). In his preface to *Tribal Secrets,* Robert Warrior thanks me and characterizes me as his "better self." As flattering as this is, I can honestly say that I owe him more in this current work. Both he and Christopher Jocks (Mohawk) read the manuscript for Oxford University Press and offered useful thoughts. This book began as a doctoral dissertation. I want to thank my dissertation committee: Gerald Vizenor, Inés Talamantez, Delores Williams, and James H. Cone, without all of whom I would never have gotten to this point. Finally, the opportunity to work through these ideas over four years of teaching in the classroom has been an invaluable gift. I want to thank my students, especially my Native students, for their participation in this creative process.

As I have stated, in writing this book I do not intend to merely produce one more superfluous "study" of Indians. What McPherson and Rabb said of philosophy, I would claim for religion: that it can help the People see themselves as people, "as experiencing persons, not as mere objects to be experienced or studied by others."[26] It is my fondest wish that this present work will in some small way contribute to that process by which the People might live. *Wado.*

Oklahoma City, Oklahoma   J. W.
February 1997

Contents

That the People Might Live

Chapter One

Native American Literatures and Communitism

There is something about writing that's like armor to the soul.

—Anonymous

If you can survive in today's society and maintain your *soul* self, and if you can do these things and know who you are as a person, you are a true warrior.

—Murray Stonechild (Cree), "To Be an Indian,"
in Hirschfelder and Singer, *Rising Voices*

We must struggle for our lives.
We must take great care with each other.
We must share our concern with each other.
Nothing is separate from us.
We are all one body of People.
We must struggle to share our human lives with each other.
We must fight against those forces
which will take our humanity from us.
We must ensure that life continues.
We must be responsible to that life.
With that humanity and the strength
which comes from our shared responsibility
for this life, the People shall continue.

—Simon Ortiz (Acoma), *The People Shall Continue*

Leslie Marmon Silko (Laguna) has written, "The following statement, 'All existence is meaningless,' is actually full of meaning; that is the irony of language. The act of stating what *is*, inevitably reminds us of what is *not*. Language forces meaning into existence. All barriers yield to language: distance, oceans, darkness, even time and death itself are easily transcended by language. We hear a story about a beloved ancestor from hundreds of years ago, but as we listen, we begin to feel an intimacy and immediacy of that long ago moment so that our beloved ancestor is very much present with us during the storytelling."[1] Storytelling. At base that is what American Indian authors and poets are doing—storytelling. According to Silko, when we use language to transcend humanly insurmountable barriers, we call that transcendent use art. To the extent that it deals with transcendence, it also involves religion. N. Scott Momaday (Kiowa/Cherokee) states, "We have all been changed by words; we have been hurt, delighted, puzzled, enlightened, filled with wonder. . . ."[2] This power of language to transform has religious implications as well.

To discuss something labeled "Native American literature" is to enter a thicket that would make Brer Rabbit (already an exercise in hybridity and syncreticity, the melding of the Cherokee rabbit-trickster *Jisdu* into the culture of African slaves) envious. Almost immediately, briarlike questions arise. Who or what is a Native American? Louis Owens, at the beginning of his volume *Other Destinies: Understanding the American Indian Novel,* maps out this thicket: "Take one step into this region and we are confronted with difficult questions of authority and ethnicity: What is an Indian? Must one be one-sixteenth Osage, one-eighth Cherokee, one-quarter Blackfoot, or full-blooded Sioux to be Indian? Must one be raised in a traditional 'Indian' culture or speak a native language or be on a tribal roll? To identify as Indian—or mixedblood—and to write about that identity is to confront such questions."[3] In *Tribal Secrets,* as Gregory Gagnon points out, Robert Warrior avers that we often spend far too much time worrying about whether a given writer is "really an Indian."[4] Or as Sherman Alexie states in his satiric poem "Introduction to Native American Literature," "Sometimes, it . . . talks too much about the color of its eyes & skin & hair."[5] Behind this wrangling is the seemingly constant, essentializing attempt by some activists and intellectuals to define "Indianness" while the majority of Indians live their lives as if such definitions were largely irrelevant, living out their own Indianness without a great deal of worry about such contestations over identity.[6] Few concern themselves with the delicate gymnastics of authenticity, such as those of Wub-e-ke-niew (Francis Blake Jr.) (Anishinaabe) who constructs a hierarchy of "Indian" (inauthentic), "Aboriginal Indigenous" (more authentic), and tribal identification (most authentic).[7]

Today, as Geary Hobson points out, there is "no universal agreement" as to who is a Native, a process rendered more dysfunctional by the fact that for many years, for its own colonialist reasons, the United States government intruded itself into the question of definitions, an intrusion that still has a significant impact on Indian identity politics. Thomas King likewise acknowledges the difficulty in knowing who is Indian—and the unspoken irony here is that to back this proposition up he cites Wallace Black Elk, who has been severely criticized by the Native community for peddling traditional spirituality to Amer-Europeans.[8] Persons are defined as Indian based on a variety of often conflicting standards: (1) the tribe's or Native community's judgment, (2) the Amer-European community's judgment, (3) the federal government's (or, in some cases, a state's) judgment, or (4) self-identification.[9] One or more of these categories encompass all Native peoples within the United States, including those A. T. Anderson (Tuscarora/Mohawk), in his report on the American Indian Policy Review Commission, called "the Uncounted": all those other than enrolled members of federally recognized tribes.[10]

In discussing the issue of identity and definition, Dennis McPherson and Douglas Rabb adopt the concept of the "outside view predicate," a notion derived from the Western philosophical schools of British conceptual analysis and European existential phenomenology. Coined by Phyllis Sutton Morris, the term means definitions "which, when applied to ourselves, imply an 'outside view' in either a literal or figurative sense." McPherson and Rabb elaborate:

> However, to apply an outside view predicate to yourself is much more than seeing yourself as others see you, though it is that as well. It is also allowing them to tell you who you are. It is in a sense giving up your freedom, your self determination to others; becoming what they want you to become rather than becoming what you have it within yourself to become. To accept an outside view predicate, such as ugly or ashamed . . . , is to fit into the plans and projects of others, to make it easy for them to manipulate you for their own ends, their own purposes. It is, in a very real and frightening sense, to lose yourself, to become alienated, to become a stranger, an alien to yourself.[11]

As can be seen, categories 2 and 3 in the preceding paragraph are outside view predicates. The need, McPherson and Rabb contend in the title of their volume, is for Natives to see, define, and be "Indian from the Inside."

In an often cited passage from his autobiographical work *The Names: A Memoir,* Scott Momaday, writes of his mother that, though just one-eighth Cherokee, she reawakened her Native background by *imagining* herself Indian. He wrote that "she began to see herself as an Indian. That dim heritage became a fascination and a cause for her, inasmuch, perhaps, as it enabled her to assume an attitude of defiance, an attitude which she assumed with particular style and satisfaction; it became her. She imagined who she was. This act of imagination was, I believe, among the most important events of my mother's early life, as later the same essential act was to be among the most important of my own."[12] American Indian writers help Native readers imagine and re-imagine themselves as Indian from the inside rather than as defined by the dominant society. Gerald Vizenor, especially, has been strident in his denunciation of the imaginary Indians that Natives too often become by capitulation to outside view predicates.

Today, notes Geary Hobson, "[p]eople are classified by their tribe, the family, or the government as 'full-bloods,' 'half-bloods,' 'one-fourths,' 'one-eighth,' and so on. This is the genetic distinction. Culturally, a person is characterized in terms of where he or she is from, who his or her people are and what their ways of life, religion, language are like. Socially (I believe there is a rather fine line between this and the cultural criterion), a person is judged as Native American because of how he or she views the world, his or her views about land, home, family, culture, etc." [13] Acknowledging that there are no easy answers, he goes on to discuss the case of John Ross, the great Principal Chief of the Cherokee Nation who led the tribe on the Trail of Tears and shepherded them through the Oklahoma reconstruction, and John Ridge. Though Ross was only one-eighth Cherokee and Ridge was seven-eighths, the former fought the tribe's dispossession from their homeland, while the latter "collaborated," supported Removal, and was executed for cooperating in the alienation of tribal lands. Concludes Hobson, "Though genetically part Indian, of differing degrees, it was clear to the Cherokee people of the 1830s that John Ross was more 'one of themselves' than was John Ridge." [14] While Hobson is helpful in highlighting the limits of assimilation and the impulse toward Native identity (he could have added the example of Richard Fields, the chief of the Texas Cherokee who, though only one-fourth Cherokee himelf, died leading the band in an abortive rebellion against its White oppressors),[15] his example ultimately does more to obscure than to illuminate: the situation of Ross and Ridge was more complex than he depicts it, and the struggle between their two factions divided the Cherokee Nation for years. I agree with him, however, that simple essentialized identifications based on race are not adequate. Again, Vizenor has struggled against essentialism in notions of blood quantum identification with his coining of the neologism "crossblood" to replace the various "mixed blood" categories delineated by Hobson.

Ultimately, racially based definitions are insufficient; what matters is one's social and cultural milieu, one's way of life.[16] Hobson illustrates this with the case of Hispanic Americans: "While they are undeniably of Indian blood, and genetically Indian, they are nevertheless culturally and socially Spanish. Because of centuries of Catholicism, they are for the most part irrevocably alienated from the Native American portion of their heritage. Thus, to most Native Americans today, it is not merely enough that a person have a justifiable claim to Indian blood, but he or she must also be at least somewhat socially and culturally definable as a Native American." [17] Much the same could be said of most African Americans, many of whom, particularly from the South, have some degree of Native blood but nevertheless identify culturally and socially only as Black. Thomas King goes further, contending that definition on the basis of race is a kind of *dicto simpliciter*. He writes,

> It assumes that the matter of race imparts to the Native writer a tribal understanding of the universe, access to a distinct culture, and a literary perspective unattainable by non-Natives. In our discussions of Native literature, we try to imagine that there is a racial common denominator which full-bloods raised in cities, half-bloods raised on farms, quarter-bloods raised on reservations, Indians adopted and raised by white families, Indians who speak their tribal language, Indians who speak only English, traditionally educated Indians, university-trained Indians, Indians

with little education, and the like all share. We know, of course, that there is not. We know that this is a romantic, mystical, and, in many instances, a self-serving notion that the sheer number of cultural groups in North America, the variety of Native languages, and the varied conditions of the various tribes should immediately belie.[18]

There are, alas, no stories carried in the blood.

In so stating, however, I do not join in the, I believe, erroneous and misguided criticism Arnold Krupat voices of Scott Momaday. Krupat derides Momaday for his use of the phrases "racial memory" and "memory in the blood." He professes ignorance as to precisely what the author meant but states that the evidence from his writing is that it is "overwhemingly if unfortunately" and "absurdly" racist. H. David Brumble III, in his volume *American Indian Autobiography*, states that in Momaday's lexicon the terms are an "evocative synonym for 'culture.' " Given the previously cited statement by Momaday concerning his mother, one is tempted to agree with Brumble. Krupat, however, brushes Brumble's assessment aside as a reflection of his "charitably decent inability to believe that someone as talented and intelligent as Momaday could actually mean" the racist things he says. Paula Gunn Allen also uses the term, however, as for instance in *Spider Woman's Granddaughters,* when she writes, "The workings of racial memory are truly mysterious. No Cherokee can forget the Trail of Tears." One can acknowledge the truth of Allen's statement—and Momaday's—without being "absurdly racist." The Cherokee *can* never forget the Trail of Tears—not because of some genetic determinism but because its importance to heritage and identity are passed down through story from generation to generation. I will always recall the unconveyable disdain and contempt in the voice of my grandmother, expressing a sentiment inherited from my grandfather, when she mentioned the name of Andrew Jackson. I would contend that what writers like Momaday and Allen mean is the multiplicity of cultural codes that are learned and go toward shaping one's identity. As Ngugi points out, "[C]ulture does not just reflect the world in images but actually, through those very images, conditions a child to see the world in a certain way."[19] Such cultural coding exists finally beyond conscious remembering, so deeply engrained and psychologically embedded that one can describe it as being "in the blood."

David Murray, in *Forked Tongues: Speech, Writing and Representation in North American Indian Texts,* states, "The question of whether Indian identity is measured by blood, expressed through kinship and genealogy, or through culture and place, remains a complex problem in Indian writing, reflecting the complexity of arguments over Indians' actual legal and cultural status in America, but in either case it is the problematic relation to the past and the role of the past in memory, personal and tribal, and in self-definition which continues as a major theme."[20] Thomas King succinctly summarizes, "One can become Canadian and a Canadian writer [or American and an American writer], for example, without having been born [there], but one is either born an Indian or one is not."[21] It is part of the distinction drawn by Edward Said between filiation and affiliation.[22] Joseph Conrad can become a part of English letters and Léopold Sédar Senghor a member of the French Academy, but Roger Welsch, for instance, can never become an Indian author.[23]

This is not to imply that Native identity, any more than any other element of Native culture, is forever static. It is important to insist that Native cultures be seen as living, dynamic cultures, "that they are able to adapt to modern life, and to *offer their members the basic values they need to survive in the modern world.*"[24] In this process, as Louis Owens states, Native writers move beyond "ethnostalgia—most common to Euramerican treatments of Native American Indians—toward an affirmation of a syncretic, dynamic, adaptive identity in contemporary America"[25]—part of what Vine Deloria hinted at in the subtitle to his 1970 book, *We Talk, You Listen: New Tribes, New Turf.*[26]

Ultimately, for purposes of this study, I accept Hobson's definition: "Native American writers . . . are those of Native American blood and background who affirm their heritage in their individual ways as do writers of all cultures."[27] Such a definition is admittedly imperfect. It begs the question of what to do with writers who do not affirm such an identity or, more important, who affirm it at different times and in a multiplicity of different ways. It also only hints at the perhaps even thornier definitional question of what "Native American literature" or "literatures" are.[28]

In the Preface, I limned already the necessity and difficulty of including nonfiction in the definition of Native American literatures. Indians have written books about Oliver La Farge, an Amer-European Native Americanist; E. W. Marland, oil tycoon and governor of Oklahoma; even about a non-Native federal judge.[29] Why were these authors drawn to these topics? What makes these writings Indian literature—if they are at all? One is tempted to say, with Tom King, that "[p]erhaps our simple definition that Native literature is literature produced by Natives will suffice for the while providing we resist the temptation of trying to define a Native."[30] Is Indian literature simply any writing produced by an American Indian? Thus, is *Gorky Park,* which deals with a KGB investigation of murders in Moscow, written by Martin Cruz Smith, American Indian literature simply because its author is a Senecu del Sur/Yaqui Indian? Does the fact that Robbie Robertson, musician and songwriter with the folk rock group The Band, is Mohawk make songs like "The Night They Drove Old Dixie Down" or "Up on Cripple Creek" Indian poetry or music? On the other hand, Smith has written works with Indian themes, most notably the anticolonialist alternate history *The Indians Won,* and Robertson has produced the soundtrack for a television documentary series about Natives, in which he employs and adapts traditional chromatics and themes and which he vetted with elders on his reserve in Canada.[31]

Jack Forbes maintains that Native literature is that produced "by persons of Native identity and/or culture." The key question for him "is whether the work is composed or written to be received by a particular people. Is it internal to the culture?" What most fits his criteria, he concludes, is not what would commonly be considered literature at all according to the Western purist standards discussed by Petrone but the discourse in "Indian published periodicals," often topical, occasional, nonfiction writing.[32] Krupat criticizes Forbes's attempt at an internally derived definition, particularly his inclusion of the "identity" of the author as a criterion, as "not only largely useless (e.g., a great many Indians, as a great many others, are persons of mixed racial origins) but obnoxious (e.g., it can tend to distinguish different percentages of 'blood,' ranking each a 'higher' or 'lower' type, depending on the context of concern)."[33] Involved in the gymnastics of authenticity, Krupat's critique is self-contradictory. On one hand, he labels Forbes's definition as offensive because of its potentially essentializing tendencies; on the other, he himself engages in such essentializing when he posits a pure, authentic Native identity counterposed to the "mixed blood" status of many Natives. While I support Forbes's attempt to broaden the definition of Native literature by including nonfictional discourse, I believe the boundaries that he ultimately sets are too restrictive, excluding too much writing by Natives. Reception and ownership within Native communities can serve to bring back much of what Forbes excludes. The issue of audience, as Forbes points out and as will be seen later, is a fundamental one in many respects. The reality of a publishing industry controlled by non-Natives (overwhelmingly Amer-Europeans) and the limited potential for a Native readership (due to economics, small population base, etc.) renders the issue of audience more complex than Forbes acknowledges.

Conversely, LaVonne Ruoff includes within her bibliographic review a wide variety of literatures, both fiction and nonfiction, and states with regard to the author's identity, "Although I have generally accepted writers' designations of themselves as American Indian, I have respected the wishes of those who have indicated that their Indian ancestry was so marginal that they did not feel it appropriate to so define themselves."[34] She includes in her discussion not only the previously mentioned "non-Indian" works by Martin Cruz Smith but also works as diverse as the murder mysteries of Todd Downing (Choctaw), dating from the 1930s and primarily set in Mexico (*Murder in the Tropics, Death under the Moonflower,* etc.) with few or no Indian elements, and Lynn Riggs's screenplay for the Arabian romance, *Garden of Allah.* Amer-European critic Brian Swann concludes, "Native Americans are Native Americans if they say they are, if other Native Americans say they are and accept them, and (possibly) if the values that are held and acted upon are values upheld by the various native peoples who live in the Americas."[35] Perhaps, then, one finally must be left in a sort of intellectual/critical limbo, floating with Tom King, who states that in reality, we know neither what Native American literature is nor who Native writers are. He declares, "What we do have is a collection of literary works by individual authors who are of Native ancestry, and our hope, as writers and critics, is that if we wait long enough, the sheer bulk of this collection, when it reaches some sort of critical mass, will present us with a matrix within which a variety of patterns can be discerned."[36]

In their volume *The Empire Writes Back*, Bill Ashcroft, Gareth Griffiths, and Helen Tiffin attempt to define "postcolonial literature," a category into which, at least arguably, Native American literatures fit. They contend that what all postcolonial literatures share is a certain relationship with the former colonizer, to the *métropole*. These postcolonial literatures have emerged out of the experience of colonization and asserted themselves by foregrounding the tension with the former colonial power and by emphasizing their differences from the assumptions of the colonial *métropole*.[37]

Although some elements of this definition are helpful in coming to an understanding of Indian literature that, in part, asserts itself over and against the dominant culture, it nonetheless falls short in that American Natives are not *post*colonial peoples.[38] Instead, today they remain colonized, suffering from internal colonialism. The term "internal colonialism" was coined to characterize the subordination of the Scots and Welsh by the English and was first applied to the situation of American indigenes by anthropologist Robert Thomas (Cherokee).[39] It differs from classic colonialism in that in classic colonialism, a small minority of colonizers from the *métropole* exerts power over a large indigenous population in an area removed from the "mother country." By contrast, in internal colonialism, the autochthonous population is swamped by a large colonizer group, which, after several generations, no longer has a *métropole* to which to return.[40] The colony and the *métropole* are thus geographically coextensive. In postcolonial discourse, internal colonialism is often referred to as settler colonialism. Ashcroft, Griffiths, and Tiffin define "settler colonies" in contrast to "invaded colonies" as those in which the "land was occupied by European colonists who dispossessed and overwhelmed the Indigenous populations. They established a transplanted civilization which eventually secured political independence while retaining a non-Indigenous language" and worldview.[41] Said recognizes the United States as a settler colony, which he sees as "superimposed on the ruins of considerable native presence."[42] Vizenor calls the phenomenon "paracolonialism."[43] Besides the indigenous peoples of the Americas, others in situations of internal colonialism include Palestinians, Maoris, and Australian Aborigines. For Natives, "the structures of colonialism will remain substantially intact if the institutionalized forms of racism, oppression and discrimination, which, as the solidified legacies of the colonial era, continue to bear uniquely on indigenous populations, are not also disman-tled."[44]

If Indian literatures cannot be considered postcolonial literatures, are they then perhaps anticolonial or resistance literature? The phrase "resistance litera-ture," according to Barbara Harlow in her book of the same name, was devel-oped by Palestinian writer Ghassan Kanafani to describe the literature of that people. It presupposes a people's collective relationship to a common land, a common identity, or a common cause on the basis of which it is possible to distinguish between two modes of existence for the colonized, "occupation" or "exile." This distinction also presupposes an "occupying power" that has either exiled or subjugated—or, in the cases of Palestinians and Native Americans, exiled *and* subjugated—the colonized population and has, in addition, signifi-cantly intervened in the literary and cultural development of the people it has dispossessed and whose land it has occupied. In other words, literature be-comes a critical arena for struggle.[45]

Once again, I believe that this definition is useful in evaluating Native litera-tures. American Indians have been both subjugated and exiled from lands that were sacred to them, numinous landscapes where every mountain and lake held meaning for their identity and their faith. The dominant culture has intervened consequentially in their literature and culture. Today, Indians are indisputably an oppressed minority in the United States. "The result," as sociologist Menno Boldt puts it, "is a cultural crisis manifested by a breakdown of social order in Indian communities."[46] The statistics, which are often repeated, are staggering. The average yearly income is half the poverty level, and over half of all Natives are unemployed. On some reservations, unemployment runs as high as 85–90 percent. Health statistics chronically rank Natives at or near the bottom. Male life expectancy is forty-four years, and female is forty-seven. Infant mortality is twice the national average. Diabetes runs six times the national average; alco-holism five times the national average; and cirrhosis of the liver eighteen times the national average. The worst part is that these statistics have not changed in thirty years. Substance abuse, suicide, crime, and violence are major problems among both urban and reservation populations. Increasingly, violence victim-izes those with the least power—women, children, and the elderly.[47] Sexual abuse and violence against women have increased markedly. These problems did not occur, or occur to this degree, in traditional societies. Again, according to Boldt, "the problem is significantly attributable to cultural degeneration"— that process created by the compounded impact of genocide, colonialism, forced cultural and institutional assimilation, economic dependence, and rac-ism.[48] The situation is not, however, as absolute as many, including some Indi-ans, would suggest. Native survival in the face of internal colonialism and the revitalization of Native traditions attests to the truth of Said's repeated theme that there is always something beyond the reach of dominating systems, no

matter how totally they saturate society, and that it is this part of the oppressed
that the oppressor cannot touch that makes change possible: in "every situation,
no matter how dominated it is, there's always an alternative."[49]

Ashcroft, Griffiths, and Tiffin observe that a distinctive characteristic of settler colonies is the maintenance of a nonautochthonous language following political independence from the *métropole*. They write, "Having no ancestral contact with the land, they [colonizers] dealt with their sense of displacement by
unquestioningly clinging to a belief in the adequacy of the imported language—where mistranslation could not be overlooked it was the land or the
season which was 'wrong'. Yet in all these areas [of the decolonized world]
writers have come, in different ways, to question the appropriateness of imported language to place."[50] Some postcolonial theorists, following Fanon and
Memmi, argue that colonization can only be put behind by achieving "full
independence" of culture, language, and political organization. Thus, for example, Sukarno, realizing that Indonesia could not sever its colonial ties without
ridding itself of Dutch, banned its teaching in all schools.[51] Others, like Guya-
nese Denis Williams, argue "that not only is this impossible but that cultural
syncreticity is a valuable as well as an inescapable and characteristic feature of
all post-colonial societies and indeed is the source of their peculiar strength."[52]
Homi K. Bhabha agrees, averring that the "interstitial passage between fixed
identifications opens up the possibility of a cultural hybridity that entertains
difference without an assumed or imposed hierarchy."[53] Not all are so consistent: Ashis Nandy misguidedly criticizes Fanon (who, after all, averred that one
must decolonize the mind or there was no true freedom) for attacking the West
in French "in the elegant style of Jean-Paul Sartre," even though Nandy himself
writes in English, for which he has "developed a taste" despite the fact that he
forms his thoughts "in my native Bengali and then translate when I have to
put them down on paper."[54]

One postcolonial theorist who has been consistent is Ngugi, who in his slim
volume *Decolonising the Mind: The Politics of Literature in African Literature*
wrote back to the *métropole* in English, the language of his colonizer, to explain
why henceforth he would write only in his native African language. Although
he would unquestionably eschew the characterization, Ngugi skirts the realm
of religion and deals with the intricate web of issues central to this study when
he writes, "Culture embodies those moral, ethical and aesthetic values, the set
of spiritual eyeglasses, through which [a people] come to view themselves and
their place in the universe. Values are the basis of a people's identity, their sense
of particularity as members of the human race. All this is carried by language.
Language as culture is the collective memory bank of a people's experience in
history. Culture is almost indistinguishable from the language that makes possible its genesis, growth, banking, articulation and indeed its transmission from
one generation to the next." Language is both a shaper and a reflection of

culture, and written and oral literatures are the primary means by which it does its work. Ngugi writes, "Language carries culture, and culture carries, particularly through orature and literature, the entire body of values by which we come to perceive ourselves and our place in the world. How people perceive themselves affects how they look at their culture, at their politics and at the social production of wealth, at their entire relationship to nature and to other beings. Language is thus inseparable from ourselves as a community of human beings with a specific form and character, a specific history, a specific relationship to the world."[55] Language as a bearer of culture and worldview is undisputed. In the Native community, Ngugi's words take on concrete form when one considers the Lumbee of North Carolina. With no language and little culture of their own, they borrow from pan-Indianism for their cultural expressions, leading Nick Locklear (Tuscarora), whom the Lumbee claim as one of their own, to state, "There ain't no such thing as a Lumbee. They made this thing up."[56]

The issue of language has been an important one in Native communities. The issue begins with the appellation "Indian," an outside view predicate designed, according to Louis Owens, to impose a distinct alterity on indigenes. He writes, "To be 'Indian' was to be 'not European.' Native cultures—their voices systematically silenced—had no part in the ongoing discourse that evolved over several centuries to define the utterance . . . within the language of the invaders."[57] As part of its attempt at cultural genocide, the concerted assault on Native cultures and personhood, the dominant culture also sought to eradicate tribal languages. The "night of the sword and the bullet was followed by the morning of the chalk and blackboard. The physical violence of the battlefield was followed by the psychological violence of the classroom."[58] Boarding schools banned Native languages. In their place, they hoped to inculcate English, Amer-European values, and Christianity. Students routinely were punished for speaking "Indian." As a result, entire generations were beaten into silence and through language and literature taken farther and farther from their world and themselves. Isabelle Knockwood (Mi'kmaw) describes the process: "When little children first arrived at the school we would see bruises on their throats and cheeks that told us that they'd been caught speaking [their Native language]. Once we saw the bruises begin to fade, we knew they'd stopped talking."[59]

Though Knockwood writes about her experiences in a Canadian residential school, her story could be replicated many times over for boarding schools here in this country. Indians speak of being beaten or having their mouths washed out with yellow cake soap for talking in their own tongues. Jim McKinney (Potawatomi) remembers being put in a dormitory room with three boys from three different tribes in order to force the speaking of English as a common language: the outcome was not that he learned much English but that he learned quite a lot of three other tribal languages. Quanah Tonemah (Kiowa/ Comanche) says that, as a result, he and others became "lost generations," unable to speak their own languages and thus in large measure deracinated. With Tonemah, Knockwood concludes, "The punishment for speaking Mi'kmaw began on our first day at school, but the punishment has continued all our lives as we try to piece together who we are and what the world means to us with a language many of us have had to re-learn as adults."[60]

In light of such history, it is little wonder that, just as many Natives reject Christianity as the imported religion of the colonizer, many also question English (or Spanish or French) as the nonindigenous language of the invaders as well. Luci Tapahonso (Navajo) has written poetry in English but now prefers, like Ngugi, to express herself in the native language that carries her culture and thoughtworld.[61] White critics, too, point to the use of English in their gymnastics of authenticity. David Murray, following Krupat, declares, "[T]o write about Indian experience and be published in English is inevitably to be involved in an ambiguous area of cultural identity [and runs] the risk of becoming yet another second-hand cultural identity." In a bizarre turn indicative of the gymnastics of authenticity that denigrates Native identity in favor of a "universal" humanity, he goes on to claim, "Another way of putting this is to say that modern Indian writers writing in English are not so very different from the white ethnopoets [who appropriate Native expressions and forms], in their relation to Indian cultures."[62]

Yet what is a viable option for Ngugi or Tapahonso is not always so for Native Americans. Publishing opportunities in most Native languages are nonexistent. Many Natives do not speak their tribal languages, and so, as in Jim McKinney's dorm room at boarding school, in written literature the only real alternative is English if one wishes to communicate across the community. Owens writes that "[f]or the Indian author, writing within consciousness of the contextual background of a nonliterate culture, every word written in English represents a collaboration of sorts as well as a reorientation (conscious or unconscious) from the paradigmatic world of oral tradition to the syntagmatic reality of written language."

Ashcroft, Griffiths, and Tiffin, while pointing up the limitations and difficulties in the use of English, note, "This is not to say that the English language is inherently incapable of accounting for post-colonial experience, but that it needs to develop an 'appropriate' usage in order to do so."[63] Thus Joy Harjo (Creek), who acknowledges language as a bearer of culture and worldview and the importance of literary creation in tribal languages for their renewal and revitalization but who does not know Muscogee, speaks of poetry as a means of escaping the limitations and frustrations of English.[64] She now often talks in terms of "reinventing the enemy's language." Gerald Vizenor, who has rewritten a substantial amount of that language through his postmodernist wordplay and coining of neologisms, declares:

> The English language has been the linear tongue of colonial discoveries, racial cruelties, invented names, the simulation of tribal cultures, manifest manners, and the unheard literature of dominance in tribal communities; at the same time, this mother tongue of paracolonialism has been a language of invincible imagination and liberation for many tribal peoples in the postindian world. English, a language of paradoxes, learned under duress by tribal people at mission and federal schools, was one of the languages that carried the vision and shadows of the Ghost Dance, the religion of renewal, from tribe to tribe on the vast plains at the end of the nineteenth century. . . . English, that coercive language of federal boarding schools, has carried some of the best stories of endurance, the shadows of tribal survivance, and now that same language of dominance bears the creative literature of distinguished postindian authors in the cities. The tribal characters dance with tricksters, birds, and animals, a stature that would trace the natural reason, coherent memories, transformations, and shadows in traditional stories. The shadows and language of tribal poets and novelists could be the new ghost dance literature, the shadow literature of liberation that enlivens tribal survivance.[65]

Today, many Native authors (as well as social scientists, historians, etc.) have, according to McPherson and Rabb, learned "to play the language-games of Europe" precisely because they, like Ngugi, "wish to tell *us* [Amer-Europeans] in language *we* will understand that *they* have no desire to become one of *us*, that assimilation is not the solution because they are not the problem. They have had to learn our language games because, with rare exceptions, in our ethnocentric arrogance we have not bothered to try to understand them in their own terms."[66]

Even Ngugi admits that language itself is not enough to bring renewal to a culture if the content of the literature produced in it is not liberative.[67] Every story—every myth—has "a pragmatic character." Every myth serves some purpose or end. The logical question, then, is to ask where a particular myth came from and what and whose purposes and ends it is designed to serve.[68] Traditional Native American tribal myths are communal in character, forming identity, explaining one's place in the cosmos, creating a sense of belonging. They serve as a countermythology to Amer-European myths that serve colonial interests—myths of discovery, conquest, lost tribes, nomadic savages perpetually involved in the chase and then quietly receding into the shadows until vanishing entirely from the stage of the New World Drama. George Tinker describes the matter:

> The Euro-Americans have stories, of course, but they tend to be stories of conquest. For instance, Columbus is the quintessential all-American culture hero, the perfect

exemplar for the righteous empire, the "discoverer" and conqueror who knew no sin. Even Jesus, the most important culture hero of America, has become a conqueror in Western storytelling. The sacrificial cross of Jesus has become a symbol of conquest that seems to encourage more conquest. Thus the myth of Columbus and the stories of conquest continue to play themselves out with disastrous consequences in the lives of modern Indian peoples.[69]

According to Tinker, such myths of conquest are accompanied by myths of "utilitarian rationalization" and by a need to impose themselves on Others, to conquer the myths of Others.[70] The impulse is so patent that even White theologian Achiel Peelman admits, "With respect to this native spirituality, the West is now forced to recognize that, notwithstanding its Judeo-Christian foundations (the Old Testament creation narratives), its true symbols are power (oppression), progress, conquest and individualism,"[71] all the while murmuring in the ear of the Native, "Theft is Holy."[72]

Enrique Dussel links Amer-European myths of conquest of Indians with the metamyth of modernity. He writes,

> The birthdate of modernity is 1492, even though its gestation, like that of the fetus, required a period of intrauterine growth. Whereas modernity gestated in the free, creative medieval European cities, it came to birth in Europe's confrontation with the Other. By controlling, conquering, and violating the Other, Europe defined itself as discoverer, conquistador, and colonizer of an alterity likewise constitutive of modernity. Europe never discovered *(des-cubierto)* this Other as Other but covered over *(encubierto)* the Other as part of the Same: i.e., Europe. Modernity dawned in 1492 and with it the myth of a special kind of sacrificial violence which eventually eclipsed whatever was non-European.[73]

As Owens points out, these myths, which made sense of Amer-European responses to the "New World," had little or nothing to do with the actual inhabitants of the Americas.[74]

Upon discovery, the European's first response was to define the indigenes they found not in terms of alterity but in terms of sameness. March 1493 presented the Church, and therefore European civilization, with a terrible problem. That month Columbus arrived back in Spain with a number of indigenous captives who appeared to be human. At issue was how to account for these "man-like creatures inhabiting the Americas" when the biblical protology clearly spoke of only three continents (Europe, Africa, and Asia), each populated by the progeny of a different son of Noah after the Flood. Though ultimately the dilemma was resolved in 1512 when Pope Julius II declared Natives to be descended from Adam and Eve through the Babylonians, the first response was to postulate that the dark-skinned peoples that met Columbus were the Lost Tribes of Israel. Implicit in such a determination is that no people can achieve any level of civilization, even language, unless they are of the same stock as those already known. They are not Other but Same.[75]

In the myths of conquest, Columbus and those who followed discovered a vast, virginal, primeval wilderness, sparsely inhabited by a few roaming savages with no fixed abode. Amer-European pioneers conquered this land, bending it to their plow and to their will, impressing form on what previously had been formless, taking what had been held in escrow for them from the foundation of the world, becoming in the process a peculiarly chosen people, "God's American Israel," in their battle with the new frontier. This myth pervades the American psyche and was codified in Amer-European law. The reality was starkly different. Contrary to the myopic vision of European colonizers, America was an inhabited place. As historian Francis Jennings summarizes, "The American Land was more like a widow than a virgin. Europeans did not find a wilderness here; rather . . . they made one. . . . The so-called settlement of America was a *re*settlement, a reoccupation of a land made waste by the diseases and demoralization introduced by the newcomers."[76] Jennings conveniently omits that a great many original inhabitants were simply slaughtered as well. In the myths of conquest, Amer-Europeans did not commit such atrocities. When killings did occur, from Mystic Fort to the Marias, from Gnadenhutten to the Washita, they were tragic mistakes never to be replicated, the result of misunderstandings or madmen operating beyond their instructions. The question Natives force upon Amer-European conscience and consciousness is how many such incidents it takes before a pattern can be discerned and they are seen to be, however "tragic," more than "mistakes." Terry Goldie notes that "a strong argument could be made that the white violence is, if not an essential, at least a systemic part of the imperial principle. Any opposition to the system of order imposed by the imperial invasion, an opposition which was inevitable given the different epistemes of the indigenous peoples, required the violent reaction of the white powers."[77]

Of course, even the few rude, scattered tribes could not be allowed to survive in the myths of conquest. To allow their survival would be to pose an impediment to Amer-European designs on the continent. Extinction is a superior means of creating indigeneity. If all the indigenes are dead, there is no one to dispute the claim. In fact, guilt for wrongs done to the indigenous peoples in the past does not allow them to be other than *of* the past.[78] Thus the myth of the Vanishing Indian was born. By the 1870s, D. P. Kidder of Drew Theological Seminary could explain the failure of Christian missions to displace indigenous religious traditions:

In no part of the world have there been greater personal sacrifices or more diligent toil to Christianize savages with results less proportioned to the efforts made. Without enumerating . . . causes, the fact must be recognized that throughout the whole continent the aboriginal races are dying out to an extent that leaves little present prospect of any considerable remnants being perpetuated in the form of permanent Christian communities. Still missions are maintained in the Indian territories and on the reservations, and the government of the United States is effectively cooperating with them to accomplish all that may be done for the Christian civilization of the Indians and Indian tribes that remain.[79]

With the rise of the great rationalizing science of the 19th century, anthropologists rushed to study the remnants of Native cultures that remained. As improbable as it may now seem, until Margaret Mead packed her field kit and set her face toward Samoa in the 20th century, American anthropologists almost exclusively studied Native Americans, motivated by a belief that such societies were dying out. As Joan Mark of the Peabody Museum observes, "It was urgent to record as many of the old ways as possible before the last instance or even last memory of them disappeared completely. The reason it was considered urgent was that cultures represent alternative social arrangements from which we might learn something as well as clusters of irreplaceable historical data. For a culture to die out unrecorded, to become extinct, was analogous to a biological species becoming extinct. In each case it meant an irreparable loss of diversity and of scientific information."[80] By viewing the Indian as vanishing and Indian cultures as disintegrating, it was possible to view 20th-century Indians who refused to vanish as degraded and inauthentic and to contrast them with stereotypes of the "pure," "authentic" *bon sauvage* or *sauvage noble* of the past and thus keep Indians safely in the stasis box of the 19th century. It is a vision of the "Indian as corpse," and the stasis box is only a thinly disguised coffin. An extinct people do not change. Their story is complete.[81] For most of America, the last Indian died on the frozen ground of Wounded Knee in 1890. Epitomizing this view was Henry Luce, publisher of *Time* and *Life,* who during the 1950s and 1960s forbade coverage of Indian stories and issues in his publications because he considered modern-day Natives to be, in his word, "phonies."[82] The closer an indigene is allowed to the coeval, the greater the diminution in Indianness.

Thus, as Dussel makes clear in *The Invention of the Americas,* even the glorification of Natives as Noble Savages, who are not allowed (alone of all minorities) to enter the 20th century, serves colonial interests, just as did the romanticized Arab world of Orientalism limned by Edward Said. It is no accident that one avatar of imperialism, Karl May, chose as his twin subjects of colonial fantasias the American West of the noble Apache Winnetou and the Arabia of Kara-ben-Nemsi. It did not matter that when he wrote of these exotic locales and peoples he had visited neither and, in fact, had spent the period of his purported travels in Germany's Zwickau prison, serving a sentence for fraud. May's colonialist fairy tales, like those of James Fenimore Cooper, were more authentic to White readers than anything dull reportage could offer.[83] By relegating Natives to an increasingly distant, and therefore comfortable, past, Amer-Europeans are freed to pursue their designs and complete their conquest of an ethnically cleansed America unimpeded. They can convince themselves of their own indigeneity. As Vine Deloria writes, however, "Underneath all the conflicting images of the Indian, one fundamental truth emerges: the white man knows that he is alien and he knows that North America is Indian—and he will never let go of the Indian image because he thinks by some clever manipulation he can achieve an authenticity which can never be his."[84] Memmi, Fanon, and Said all elaborate that it is not enough for the colonizer to control the present and the future of the colonized but, in the effort to prove his indigeneity, must also rewrite the past as well. According to Fanon, "Colonialism is not satisfied merely with holding a people in its grip and emptying the native's brain of all form and content. By a kind of perverted logic, it turns to the past of the people, and distorts, disfigures, and destroys it. This work of devaluing pre-colonial history takes on a dialectical significance today."[85] Métis author Howard Adams elaborates on Fanon's observation for American indigenes:

> The native people in a colony are not allowed a valid interpretation of their history, because the conquered do not write their own history. They must endure a history that shames them, destroys their confidence, and causes them to reject their heritage. Those in power command the present and shape the future by controlling the past, particularly for the natives. A fact of imperialism is that it systematically denies native people a dignified history. Whites claim that Métis and Indians have no history or national identity, or, if they do, then it is a disgraceful and pathetic one. When natives renounce their nationalism and deny their Indianness, it is a sure sign that colonizing schemes of inferiorization have been successful.[86]

Myths of conquest must conquer other stories. Speaking of anthropology, the science Claude Lévi-Strauss called the "handmaiden of colonialism," Georges Sioui writes, "Far from bringing benefits to the people whose 'cultural conduct is being studied,' these scientific games have the unhappy effect of overshadowing their socio-economic condition and of dashing their efforts to restore their historic dignity," too often drowning out their attempts at assertion of their own subjectivity in a sea of "scientificity." Johannes Fabian, in his *Time and the Other: How Anthropology Makes Its Object*, agrees, noting the primitivism the discipline imposes on indigenous cultures: "Anthropology contributed above all to the intellectual justification of the colonial enterprise. It gave politics and economics—both concerned with human Time—a firm belief in 'natural', i.e., evolutionary Time. It promoted a scheme in terms of which not only past cultures, but all living societies were placed on a temporal slope, a stream of Time—some upstream, others downstream."[87] Gerald Vizenor declares, "Social science narratives, those unsure reins of final vocabularies and incoherent paracolonialism, overscore the tribal heard as cultural representations. David Carroll argued in *The Subject in Question* that any 'narrative that predetermines all responses or prohibits any counter-narratives puts an end to narrative itself, by making itself its own end and the end of all other narratives.' "

It is not enough, as Albert Memmi reminds, that the colonizer be the master in fact; in order to satisfy his own need for legitimacy, the colonized must accept his status. Its most important arena of domination is "the mental universe of the colonised, the control, through culture, of how people perceived themselves and their relationship to the world. Economic and political control can never be complete or effective without mental control. To control a people's culture is to control their tools of self-definition in relationship to others." The colonized becomes, in a very real sense, self-colonizing. In his book *Missionary Conquest,* George Tinker misconstrues Robert Thomas's concept of internal colonialism to refer to this psychological internalization of oppression (what M. A. Jaimes-Guerrero terms "autogenocide"), writing "The truth is . . . that Indian people have internalized [the illusion of white superiority] just as deeply as white Americans have, and as a result we discover from time to time just how fully we participate in our own oppression. Implicitly, in both thought and action, we too often concede that the illusion of white superiority is an unquestionable factual reality." Yet despite Tinker's claim, there is always something the dominating system cannot touch. As Jean Raphaël (Montagnais/ Mashteuiatsh) maintains, "[T]he Indian will always continue to identify . . . as an Indian." Answering the cant of White superiority, Sioui asserts, "At first both civilizations were sure of their moral superiority. Now, only Amerindian civilization has that certainty." In response to the falsely asserted indigeneity of the Amer-European, Dale Ann Frye Sherman (Yurok/Karok/Tolowa/Hupa) states, "We are of this continent. We were not created elsewhere. We were created here. Our memories are here, and the blood of our ancestors is here. We are made of this continent."[88]

Colonialism succeeds by subverting traditional notions of culture and identity and by imposing social structures and constructs incompatible with traditional society. As part of the captivity of Indians in the 19th century, a doomed and vanishing icon, Western social science and literary criticism have announced the death of the traditional oral literature (orature) of Native peoples. In her autobiographical text *Storyteller,* however, Leslie Silko points out what every Native knows: that the oral tradition is very much alive and imbued with power to create identity and community. She writes, "White ethnologists have reported that the oral tradition among Native American groups has died out because whites have always looked for museum pieces and artifacts when dealing with Native American communities. . . . I grew up at Laguna listening, and I hear the ancient stories, I hear them very clearly in the stories we are telling right now. Most important, I feel the power which the stories still have, to bring us together, especially when there is loss and grief." [89] Yet despite the continued telling, retelling, creation and re-creation of orature among Native peoples, scholars continue to treat it as an artifact.

Denise and John Carmody, in their textbook *Native American Religions,* consistently refer to oral tradition in the past tense and depict Natives as having swapped nature for literacy, of "trad[ing] a vast, wrap-around world of wonders for dry, abstract notations on a page." [90] By contrast, Karl Kroeber, in his volume *Traditional Literatures of the American Indian: Texts and Interpretations,* acknowledges that the Native storytelling tradition "is still being carried forward today," but he identifies the medium of that continuance as "new generations of Native American writers"—like Momaday, Silko, and James Welch. In other words, the oral has moved ineluctably to the written. Elsewhere, Kroeber perpetuates the myths of conquest, the metanarrative of dominance, by (re)presenting the Vanishing Indian. He writes, "In brief, one is confined to translations, and of a kind which create a confluence of troubling questions. . . . Am I misreading this story because I am ignorant of the *vanished culture* in which it originated and which, to some degree, it reflects?" [91] Similarly, Penny Petrone subtitles her study of native literature "From the Oral Tradition to the Present." Though she admits, "Oral traditions have not been static. Their strength lies in their ability to survive through the power of tribal memory and to renew themselves by incorporating new elements," the presentation and general use of verbs in the past tense posits a linear progression in which orality is left behind in the past. [92] Vizenor states, "The notion in the literature of dominance, that the oral advances to the written, is a colonial reduction of natural sound, heard stories, and the tease of shadows in tribal remembrance." [93]

By treating orature as a dead relic and thus valorizing the written over the oral, one renders the written version normative and a representation of a pure, authentic culture and identity over against current degraded Natives. John Bierhorst, for instance, in his collection *Four Masterworks of American Indian Literature,* rules out the possibility of including any Incan stories because the extant orature is "substantially acculturated." [94] An incident included by Kroeber in his introduction to *Traditional Literatures* is illustrative of this tendency to want to fossilize the oral tradition. He tells of listening, as a child, to stories told by Robert Spott (Yurok). When the storyteller deviated from the version Kroeber had "received" from his anthropologist father, the child would "correct" him. He notes that the Indian was "amused by my childish firmness in insisting he adhere exactly to my view of what were 'authentic' versions of his sacred myths." [95] What is amusing and forgivable in a child is far more serious when adopted by an adult scholar. As Vizenor writes, "Native American Indian literatures are tribal discourse, more discourse. The oral and written narratives are language games, comic discourse rather than mere responses to colonial demands or social science theories."[96]

Amer-Europeans have always controlled written literary production through control of publishing outlets, deciding what will be disseminated and thus read. They have also sought to influence what is read through their domination of literary criticism. As in other postcolonial situations where the bulk of literary criticism still comes from the *métropole,* the majority of critical study of American Indian literatures is produced by Amer-European scholars, " 'adding value' to the literary 'raw material' " of Native texts. Historian Larzer Ziff, in *Writing in the New Nation,* said that the literary annihilation of Indians would only be checked when they began representing their own cultures. Yet even as Natives begin to produce internal theory and criticism, "most readers and critics influenced by structuralism, modernism, and the dualism of subject, object, or otherness have more confidence in paracolonial discoveries and representations of tribal literatures." Entangled in the metanarrative of Western dominance, this criticism often has more to do with colonial needs and theories than it does with "the wild memories and rich diversities of tribal and postindian literature."[97]

As with George Tinker's discussion of internalized racism, it is amazing how often we are complicitous in this theoretical domination, either by fetishizing our own cultures and thus leaving our scholarship open to summary dismissal by non-Natives or by remaining preoccupied with questions of identity and authenticity—the very issues most interesting to non-Native critics—in our own criticism. Thus, according to Robert Warrior, "[the] tendency to find in the work of other American Indian writers something worthy either of unmitigated praise or of unbridled criticism stands in the way of sincere disagreement and engagement. This prevents contentious issues of, for instance, gender, sexual orientation, and economic, social, and political privilege from gaining the attention they deserve. Thus, forums in which complex critical problems of audience, reception, and representation are worked through—rather than pronouncing critical judgment—remain few and far between."[98] Rather than challenging the codes and canons of both theory and praxis of literature and dominant literary criticism, such critical stances leave the field wide open to continued domination by non-Natives.[99]

One particular manifestation of this critical and theoretical domination involves attempts to establish a canon of Native literature, or, more often, to subsume it into a national literature and establish its worth within the national canon. Almost always that which is considered for canonization is the traditional orature of the People. Bierhorst, for example, saw his previously mentioned collection of oral literature recorded by non-Natives as a "first step" toward producing a canon of Native American literature, by which he means exclusively oral literature.[100] Similarly, Krupat examines the question of the American canon in *The Voice in the Margin,* hoping to make a case for the inclusion of Native orature, which he considers to be the only genuine Indian literature. In the penultimate chapter of the volume, he states most explicitly what until then he had left only implicit: "So far as the category of an Indian literature—and along with it the general category of local literature—may be useful, it would seem necessary to define it pretty exclusively by reference to the ongoing oral performances of Native peoples."[101]

There is much at work in this discussion of canon and orature. As a starting point, it is worth noting that the academic discipline of English developed in the colonial era, and it should be equally patent that Eurocentric attempts to define a canon since the 19th century have been "less a statement of the superiority of the Western tradition than a vital, active instrument of Western hegemony."[102] Limiting consideration or admission to the canon to orature is a way of continuing colonialism. It once again keeps American Indians from entering the 20th century and denies to Native literary artists who choose other media any legitimate or "authentic" Native identity. In thus limiting Native literature to the oral tradition, non-Native critics and authors may be attempting, as Terry Goldie puts it in his study of Anglocolonial representation of indigenes, *Fear and Temptation,* "to make contact with [an] essential dynamism, a phenomenological presence of life." It is to seek a primitive time when, in Walter Ong's words, language was "a mode of action and not simply a countersign of thought"—when the word was truly performative.[103]

On the other hand, to insist, as Krupat and others do, on a "genuinely heterodox national canon" inclusive of American Indian literature (orature or otherwise) has equally undesirable implications.[104] It becomes equally an instrument of control as Eurocentric standards of judgment are employed to claim into the national canon only those works of which the *métropole* approves, those which best legitimate the existing social order.[105] "Indigenous writing has suffered many of the general historical problems of post-colonial writing, [including] being incorporated into the national literatures of the settler colonies as an 'extension' rather than as a separate discourse."[106] Such incorporation denies Native literature recognition of its distinct existence, specific differences, and independent status as literary production and, as Owens contends, retards consideration of Native works in their own cultural contexts.[107] As I noted earlier, Natives have never been great respecters of national borders. The very fact that Thomas King, E. Pauline Johnson (Mohawk), Peter Jones (Anishinaabe), and George Copway (Anishinaabe)—among others—can be, and have been, claimed at various times and for various purposes as part of the national literatures of both the United States and Canada says that something more important and complex is occurring in Native literature, something that merits special recognition as a separate discourse.[108]

Finally, by bringing Native literature into the canon of the United States, Krupat helps establish the indigeneity of Amer-European settler literature as part of a national literature rooted in the new soil of this continent. This quest for indigeneity has been a constant in settler colonies from their inception: from Hector St. John de Crèvecoeur, boasting of the "new man" being born as colonists tilled the fields of North America, to New Zealand poet Allen Curnow, marveling at "something different, something nobody counted on" resulting from living in the new environment, to Reinhold Niebuhr, observing that in America "all the races of Europe were formed into a new amalgam of races, not quite Anglo-Saxon, but prevailingly European."[109] It validates attempts by Amer-Europeans, such as those of Jerome Rothenberg and the ethnopoetics movement, to incorporate or utilize indigenous forms and aesthetics as part of "an enriching cultural appropriation."[110] Begged, of course, is the question of precisely who is "enriched" and who diminished in the process.

For many non-Native scholars, literature by Indians ceases to be Indian literature when it employs the language of the colonizer and adopts such Western literary forms as the novel, short story, or autobiography. Krupat excludes from Indian literature (which he ultimately defines solely as orature) "writing influenced in very substantial degree by the central forms and genres of Western, or first world literature," thus removing from the category most, if not all, Native authors, including "Momaday, Silko and Forbes." Instead, he labels this "mixed breed literature" *indigenous literature.*[111] Rather than, as we have argued should be the case, bringing all writings under the rubric of Native literature, the creation of this "in between" category fractures Native literary output. Though Krupat argues against essentialism and brings Natives to task for it, such an approach to literature is highly essentializing because in most writing it sees what Vizenor terms "a descent from pure racial simulations."[112] James Ruppert, in his recent volume *Mediation in Contemporary Native American Fiction,* shares Krupat's cultural stasis assumption that the oral tradition forms the only pure Native American literature. Refusing to recognize literature by Indians as Native despite its form or genre, Ruppert writes, "The successful contemporary Native writer can create a text that merges delegitimizing influences while continuing oral tradition and culture. The text is *both substantially Native and substantially Western.*"[113] David Murray, too, follows a Krupatian analysis. However, although he still looks backward to the forms of the oral tradition, he does ask, "How can the forms of white writing, not just autobiography but novels, poems and plays, be used to express and create Indian subjects (in all senses), and what role does the past play in this use?"[114]

Can one fracture Native literature in such a fashion and segregate orature as a more "pristine" Native literary type? Or isn't there still something "Indian" about it regardless of its form or the language in which it speaks? Most Native writers and critics would vociferously disagree with the Krupatian formula. So would Goldie, who writes, "[I]s it possible for the [Native] writer to take a European form such as the novel and use it successfully to describe his or her own people? When this question has been addressed to me my usual reaction has been to attempt to deflect it. Regardless of Arnoldian claims for the freedom of the disinterested liberal critic, I question the right of any person to judge another's representation of his or her own culture."[115]

Poet Simon Ortiz argues against those who would see written literature as less than "authentic" Indian literature, maintaining, importantly, that the goal is what makes the difference. He writes, "The ways and methods have been important, but they are important only because of the reason for the struggle. And it is that reason—the struggle against colonialism—which has given substance to what is authentic. . . . This is the crucial item that has to be understood, that it is entirely possible for a people to retain and maintain their lives through the use of any language. There is not a question of authenticity here; rather it is the way that Indian people have creatively responded to forced colonization."[116] Whereas Paula Gunn Allen argues that novels by Indians are not, after all, Western in form but Native, Ortiz sees no contradiction in being Native and employing Western forms of expression, speaking of "the creative ability of Indian people to gather in many forms of the socio-political colonizing force which beset them and make these forms meaningful in their own terms. . . . They are now Indian because of the creative development that the native people applied to them."[117] In this analysis, Ortiz follows Ngugi, who sees, in the indigenous use of the novel, a way of (re)connecting with the struggles of the people. Ngugi states, "The social or even national basis of the origins of an important discovery or invention is not necessarily a determinant of the use to which it can be put. . . . Perhaps the crucial question is not that of the racial, national, and class origins of the novel, but that of its development and the uses to which it is continually being put."[118]

Thomas King sees this "peculiar hybrid of antithetical cultures" (to use Nieuwenhuys's phrase) as positive. As long as literature was oral and in Native languages it was inherently limited, but bilingualism (allophonia) and writing has opened the process and "has helped to reinforce many of the beliefs that tribes have held individually, beliefs that tribes are now discovering they share mutually. While this has not, as yet, created what might be called a pan-Indian literature, the advent of written Native literature has provided Native writers with common structures, themes, and characters which can effectively express traditional and contemporary concerns about the world and the condition of living things."[119] Contrary to the critical arrogance of Krupat in his attempts at defining Indian written literature out of existence, King declares, "Whatever definition we decide on (if we ever do), the appearance of Native stories in a written form has opened up new worlds of imagination."[120]

Just as North American Natives have been no respecters of nation-state boundaries, says Clifford Trafzer (Wyandot), have they played with the "rules" of Western literary genre. They have "used the written word to extend the boundaries of their own creativity into genres outside Indian oral tradition." According to Penny Petrone, "[N]ative writers have borrowed from Western traditions the forms of autobiography, fiction, drama, and the essay. Their uses, however, judged by Western literary criteria of structure, style, and aesthetics, do not always conform. They are different because form is only the expression of the fabric of experience, and the experience of native writers has been different. Like the archetypal figure, the trickster [celebrated by Vizenor, King, and others], native writers easily adopt a multiplicity of styles and forms to suit their purposes, and in so doing they are giving birth to a new literature." They easily adopt and adapt the alien forms, and that new literature is still Indian without the essentialized need for "beads and feathers."[121]

Murray rightly argues that Leslie Silko, in her novel *Ceremony*, fuses traditional myth with the novelistic form to assert a continuum from oral literature to novels written in English.[122] Paula Gunn Allen notes that contemporary Native American fiction has two sides: the oral tradition and Western fiction and its antecedents. These "interact, as wings of a bird in flight interact. They give shape to our experience. They signify."[123] Tom King labels the product of this interaction "interfusional literature," blending the oral and the written.[124] But as Warrior cautions, "However much these writers are performing an activity somehow continuous with that of storytellers and singers, they are also doing what poetry [for example] has done in its European forms and in other non-European contexts."[125] In the end it is a political issue and it may come down to a question of what Vizenor calls the "literature of dominance" versus the "literature of survivance" and which of these two opposing aesthetics Native writers serve.[126]

What may distinguish any people's literature from that of any other group is that to which I have already alluded: worldview. Although the rich diversity of Native cultures in the Americas makes it impossible to speak in a general, universalizing way about "things Indian," many believe that one can speak broadly of a worldview common to the indigenous peoples of the hemisphere. Several scholars, both Native and non-Native, have attempted to delineate the components of this worldview and discuss its importance both for Native literature and for Native community in general.

Louis Owens, quoting a 1979 observation of Michael Dorris (Modoc), argues that a requisite for Native literature is a reflection of " 'a shared consciousness, an identifiable world-view.' More than a decade later, it seems there is indeed such a thing as Native American literature, and I would argue that it is found most clearly in novels written by Native Americans about the Native American experience. For, in spite of the fact that Indian authors write from very diverse tribal and cultural backgrounds, there is to a remarkable degree a shared consciousness and identifiable worldview reflected in novels by American Indian authors, a consciousness and worldview defined primarily by a quest for identity."[127] In a similar vein, LaVonne Ruoff writes, "Divided into numerous cultural and language groups, native North Americans practiced many different religions and customs. However, there are some perspectives on their place in the universe that many native American groups shared and continue to share. . . . Although individual Indians today vary in the extent to which they follow tribal traditions, their worldviews and values continue to reflect those of their ancestors."[128] Thus, it follows that the literatures they produce would reflect such worldviews and values.

The differences between this supposed, singular Native worldview and that of the West is often cited as a barrier to crosscultural understanding between Natives and Amer-Europeans. Historian Calvin Martin has cautioned modern-day non-Natives not to assume that the worldview of Natives is the same as that produced by the Enlightenment or that Natives operated (or operate) from the same motivations as Amer-Europeans.[129] Likewise, Rosemary Maxey (Creek) writes, "Conveying ideas [to Amer-Europeans] in our common language of English is incomplete and misunderstood because of our differing world views, which remain largely unexplored and foreign to one another."[130] In fact, here, as in all colonial societies, the Indian as subaltern knows quite a lot about the mindset and psychological makeup of those in the dominant culture; only the reverse remains untrue.[131] Achiel Peelman agrees with Maxey but attributes the lack of understanding to more than linguistics, observing, "It is interesting to note . . . that a certain number of anthropologists are now convinced that the lack of studies of the Amerindian religious experience . . . is not related to the linguistic incompetency of the anthropologists, but to their inability to enter into the spiritual universe [i.e., worldview] of the Amerindians."[132]

Those who assert that such a commonly held worldview exists differ markedly, however, on its components and on how precisely it is to be characterized; their description of it more often reflects their own social location and their individual, often highly romantic, perception of Native cultures than any pantribal reality. Deloria rests much of it in the spatial versus temporal orientation of Native peoples and in a view of time that is cyclical rather than linear. Owens refers to the "nonanthropocentric and ecologically oriented world-view of the Indian."[133] Sioui describes the "mentality" of Natives as shaped by the attachment to ancestral values and an "awareness that the cultural habits associated with those values have been suppressed in a completely illogical and unjust manner." For him, "this explains both the Amerindians' singular awareness of their duty to remain, essentially, Amerindian, and the persistence of a particular ideological portrait."[134] James Treat (Creek) refers to "foundational native values such as holism, equality, respect, harmony, and balance."[135] Ruoff lists "emphasis on the importance of living in harmony with the physical and spiritual universe, the power of thought and word to maintain this balance, a

deep reverence for the land, and a strong sense of community."[136] While coun-
seling that it is "difficult to generalize about Native American cultures and
religions," Åke Hultkrantz nevertheless claims, "Four prominent features in
North American Indian religions are a similar worldview, a shared notion of
cosmic harmony, emphasis on experiencing directly powers and visions, and a
common view of the cycle of life and death."[137] The Carmodys suggest "a
mythopoeic mentality, great influence from local physical conditions, a keen
sensitivity to animals and plants, a rich sense of the spiritual world," and a
prediliction for ritual.[138] Blair Schlepp (Standing Rock Sioux) and David
Rausch discuss many of the previously named elements and add "respect for
family, the preciousness of children, honoring the elderly, pride in craftsman-
ship, the value of working for a purpose with one's hands, listening to one's
neighbor, being discreet (especially when another's honor and dignity are concerned), taking time to be introspective and contemplative about the mysteries
of the universe, and valuing oral traditions that engender humbleness, sharing
[sometimes characterized as an ethic of generosity], and laughter."[139] McPherson and Rabb add a belief in the integrity of the person.[140]

While many Natives would affirm some or all of these components, it is
legitimate nonetheless to inquire to what extent they reflect, on the one hand,
generalized emotive and psychological factors held in common by many peoples around the world at one time or another and/or an essentialized Indian
identity on the other. It is indisputable that worldview continues to be important for Natives as a source of personal and collective energy, identity, and
values.[141] Because of the failure of Native cultures to recognize any split between sacred and secular spheres, this worldview remains essentially religious,
involving the Native's deepest sense of self and undergirding tribal life, existence, and identity, just as the Creator undergirds all the created order.[142] However, Native religions—these shapers of worldview and identity—often differ
from one another as drastically as Christianity differs from Buddhism or Juda-
ism from Hinduism. Thus, the worldviews they engender differ as well. It is
not so much incorrect to refer to a single Native worldview as it is imprecise.
M. A. Jaimes-Guerrero admits this when she states that Indian identity is derived from a sense of place—what Vine Deloria Jr. and Jaimes-Guerrero term
"geomythology." Worldview and religion are thus "bioregional," varying with
the natural environment in which they evolved.[143] McPherson and Rabb also
acknowledge this diversity in the title of their pioneering university course,
"Native Canadian World Views" (world*views* in the plural).[144] Regardless, these
differing Native worldviews are different still from that formed by Western Enlightenment thought and values.

According to McPherson and Rabb, some would argue that it is not in the
end "very interesting that different peoples have radically different world views.
Such differences may be of interest to the anthropologist who is studying differ-

ent peoples, but these differences do not cast any light on the nature of ultimate reality."[145] For McPherson and Rabb the most virulent form of such an argument also includes a claim that Christianity (or modern Western science) "has given us the true picture of reality and hence that the primitive beliefs of mere savages (or heathens) ought to be discarded, by the savages themselves if they wish to cease being savages." The two authors refer to this argument with "deliberate disrepect" as the "save-the-savages argument."[146]

Christian missionaries did indeed come to save the savages from their lives of darkness, idolatry, ignorance, and sin. Louis Hall Karaniaktajeh (Mohawk) responds, "The missionaries say they brought God to America. Helpless God. Can't go anywhere by himself. Needs the missionaries to take him here and there. They say they're still bringing God to the jungles of South America and Africa."[147] Indeed, as Karaniaktajeh implies, the process is one shared in common by all colonial societies and, in the case of the American Native, continues to this day. If Native cultures are viewed as inherently heathen and can be "mystified still further as some magical essence of the continent, then clearly there can be no meeting ground, no identity, between the social, historical creatures of Europe and the metaphysical alterity of the Calibans and Ariels [of Bermoothes]. If the difference between Europeans and the natives are so vast, then clearly . . . the process of civilizing the natives can continue indefinitely."[148]

Tinker writes that an illusion with which American Christians live "too comfortably . . . is the historical interpretation of the churches' missionary outreach to the native peoples of this continent."[149] And while most Americans today probably acknowledge at least a part of this unsavory past, many are surprised to find out that Amer-European missionaries are still at work in Indian Country. Bill Baldridge states that he continues "to be impressed by the number of people, active in the life of their various denominations, who are shocked to hear about the realities of current mission programs to Native Americans and who assumed that 'we stopped doing missions like that a hundred years ago.' "[150]

In many locales, missions have *not* changed in a hundred years. Deloria illustrates the truth of this, and the statement of Abdul JanMohamed cited earlier, when he relates a 1967 encounter with a Presbyterian missionary in charge of work among the Shinnecock of Long Island. Deloria asked the clergyman "how long the Presbyterians intended to conduct mission activities among a tribe that had lived as Christians for over three hundred and fifty years." The missionary replied impassively, "Until the job is done."[151] In 1985, Carl Starkloff, a Jesuit priest who has worked among Natives and written extensively on them (and who not so subtly chastised Deloria in 1972)[152,] wrote, "[T]he task of the Church remains missionary, in that as yet there does not exist a self-supporting, self-governing and self-propagating body that is a native Indian Protestant church save in a few local cases—and even fewer in Roman Catholicism."[153]

James Treat, however, says that Starkloff "does not seem to consider the possibility that it may well be the Church's missionary stance which is the only thing *preventing* the widespread establishment and maturation of indigenous Christian bodies."[154]

This ecclesiastical serfdom can be seen at work in the fulfillment theology or, in a post–Vatican II era, "anonymous Christ" theology that is still preached to Native Americans, even though, as comparative religionists Denise and John Carmody point out in the case of Mesoamerica (and it is no less true of North America), "The fulfillment of their people cannot come from Christ and Christianity."[155] It can be seen in the outside view predicate of a White theologian taking it upon himself to articulate a Christology for Native peoples although a growing body of theological writings by Native Christians exists.[156] This vested interest in maintaining the status quo of Amer-European church privilege has led to continued religious oppression of Native peoples, and it is not uncommon for whole Native congregations to remain faithful to the assimilationist, self-hating theology first brought by the missionaries—"even when the denomination [that brought it] has long abandoned that language for a more contemporary articulation of the gospel."[157] While Tinker is willing, at least in the case of historic missions, to give missionaries the benefit of the doubt for their good intentions, even if they confused "the kerygmatic content of [their] faith . . . with the accouterments of [their] cultural experience and behavior," other Native thinkers and theologians are not so generous. Homer Noley (Choctaw) notes that missionaries "did not take the time to understand the culture, history, and needs of the various tribal people" they evangelized, and he states, "On the one hand, church denominations geared themselves up to take the souls of Native American peoples into a brotherhood of love and peace; on the other hand, they were part of a white nationalist movement that geared itself up to take away the land and livelihood of Native American people by treachery and force."[158] Both Noley and McPherson find it inconceivable that missionaries could not have known precisely their culpability in the destruction of Native cultures. This complex history, combined with the congruity of traditional religious beliefs and practices with Native culture and identity, is what leads Treat to declare the concept of a Native Christian identity "both historically and culturally problematic."[159] Speaking more ontologically, Marie Therese Archambault (Hunkpapa Lakota) expresses "the terrible irony" of being both Indian and Christian.[160]

Peelman concedes that non-Natives are mystified by Indians "clinging" to traditional religion while "assimilating" in other ways by borrowing Western technology and other material items. He writes, "They want the Amerindians to be successful in the field of education, politics and commerce, but, at the same time, they spontaneously wish that these 'civilized' Indians would proclaim at the end of the process: 'Now, we have become just like you. Thank you for your civilizing efforts!' But, usually, these 'civilized' Indians don't fall on their knees to thank their western educators."[161] Noley makes clear that genuflection is not an option. Instead, Natives "forcefully express the desire to maintain and to enhance their cultural identity. They claim the right to be Indian *today* as members of the modern world and see the return to their traditional values as the best guarantee for their cultural survival."[162] While this religious resurgence may be "fascinating and disconcerting" to Euro-Christians, it is, "in many ways, a return to the positive content of American Indian identity, the content that makes some sense of the negative discriminatory experience of living as a Native in the U.S. in the late twentieth century." Robert Warrior is not alone in declaring it "one of the most important processes of contemporary American Indian history."[163] In this regard, Peelman again concedes, "Insofar as the suppression of traditional religions was one of the factors that contributed to the social collapse of the exploited and colonized peoples, the revitalization of their traditional religion, in the wake of the growing pressures of secularization and technology, has become an indispensable element in their integral development."[164]

In contrast to the dominant strains of Christianity, the various worldviews of Native cultures and religious tradition do not recognize a radical discontinuity between Creator and creation. As Deloria observes, a primary difference "between Indian tribal religions and Christianity would appear to be in the manner in which deity is popularly conceived. The overwhelming majority of American Indian religions refuse . . . to represent deity anthropomorphically."[165] The biblical witness depicts Yahweh as having inherently human characteristics, even if in the case of the deity these are portrayed as being somehow *more* than human: thus God is spoken of as not only possessing human emotions such as anger, pleasure, and love but is pictured as the personification of love itself. Many Christians have a felt need for a personal relationship with deity, particularly with the second person of the Trinity. Native religious traditions demonstrate no such interest in an intimacy with ultimate reality. There is also no intimation that the Creator has any different or special regard for human beings than with the rest of the created order. Natives cannot imagine a relationship with ultimate reality separate from all their other relationships that constitute personal and communal life. Nothing can stand apart from ultimate reality, and this reality is experienced in community. This is not, however, to divinize community. For Natives, Peelman correctly contends, "We can truly experience the supreme being once we have found our right place in the universe and once we have developed right relationships"—what in Old English theological language would have been called being *rightwised*.[166] This involves right relation not only between the human self and human others but between self and place.

Any discussion of Native theology must take into account these differences between Western and Native worldviews. It must take seriously these differences in concepts of deity, creation, the spatial orientation of Native peoples, and community. It must be inclusive, as Moises Colop (Quiche Mayan) contends, not only of Christians but of the majority of Natives who adhere to either traditional or syncretic faiths, thus seeking to encompass—as much as possible—the entirety of Native community.[167]

In seeking such an expansive construct, the definition of theology itself need not be altered. Like philosophical metaphysics, the subject of theology is ultimate reality. It deals with the noumenal in a Kantian sense, asserting "that there is a dimension other than the material one generally recognized as real."[168] It is, as the etymology of the word suggests, "God talk." As McPherson and Rabb argue concerning metaphysics, "Is it really necessary to change the role of philosophy so drastically in order to show that the aboriginal peoples . . . have their own distinctive philosophy? We think not. . . . We see philosophy as the pursuit of truth, and it is in this more traditional sense of philosophy that we believe that [aboriginal people] have their own distinctive philosophy."[169] So it is with theology. The topic of theology is how humanity relates to ultimate reality. Natives define their identity in terms of community and relate to ultimate reality through that community. Thus a profoundly anthropological theology that takes the imperatives of Native community as its utmost goals is nonetheless theology in the strictest sense. Just as Colop can speak of an ecumenical Mayan theology, so one can speak of an evolving Native American theology.

This is not to say that a Native theology will resemble in many ways its orthodox Western Christian counterpart. According to William Wantland (Seminole), a true Native theology will be "strange, if not alien, to people of European background. It will be something far different from English or Scottish Christianity."[170] Native heritage and experience may require rejection of certain elements of orthodox theology and, in addition, consideration of new paradigms and categories. For instance, many Natives refuse to entertain Christ as the sole salvific revelation of deity. To borrow from Steve Charleston (Choctaw), they have a prior testament, another covenant with the Creator lived long before the advent of Europeans on this continent.[171] Similarly, Christian notions of atonement, sin, and salvation must be reconsidered in light of Native thoughtworlds.[172] Deity itself may need to be reevaluated and room made for new categories, such as Trickster discourse.

Given the diversity of Indian cultures and worldviews, Native theology is what McPherson and Rabb call "polycentric." They explain this methodological approach as follows:

> This perspective, this polycentrism, recognizes that we finite human beings can never obtain a God's eye view, a non-perspectival view, of reality, of philosophical truth. Every view is a view from somewhere. Hence it follows that no one philosophical perspective can ever provide an entirely adequate metaphysical system. But this does not mean . . . that philosophical systems do not point toward truth, that

they have nothing to say about truth. It merely follows that no one perspective can contain the whole truth. Although [Thomas W.] Overholt and [J. Baird] Callicott are on the right track when they say that "no culture's world is privileged in respect to truth," they are wrong to think that this fact leads to relativism. The fact that different cultures can have radically different world views reveals something very interesting not just about cultures, not just about language, but about reality itself and the way in which we can come to know it. Though none is privileged yet each culture's world view, each different metaphysical system, contributes something to the total picture, a picture which is not yet and may never be wholly complete. Such is the polycentric perspective.[173]

Though there can never be a "supercultural platform to which we might repair,"[174] and though no culture's worldview can be privileged in any universal sense, it can and must be privileged *for that particular culture.*

Ultimate reality, which we see through a glass darkly, is like a child's kaleidoscope. How it is perceived depends on how the cylinder is held, even though the bits of glass that form the picture are unchanging. The task must be to learn as much as one can not only about the given pattern but about the individual bits of glass, so that when the cylinder is shaken we can know something about the new image when it forms. In his essay "An American Indian Theological Response to Ecojustice," George Tinker alludes to a story that illustrates the polycentric approach. Imagine two Indian communities who live in close proximity to each other, separated by a mountain. A non-Native visitor arrives at the first community. In the course of the stay, she is informed that the tribe's council fire is the center of the universe and creation myths are told to demonstrate this concept. The following day, the outlander and representatives of the first tribe travel to the other community. The elders of the new tribe declare that their council fire is the center of the universe, and the members of the first tribe nod their assent. Confused, the visitor asks her host, "I thought you said that your fire was the center." The Indian replies, "When we're there, that is the center of the universe. When we are here, this is the center." Tinker concludes, "Sometimes a single truth is not enough to explain the balance of the world around us. . . . Yet we need communal stories that can generate 'functional' mythologies, that will undergird the life of the community (the lives of communities) in new and vibrant ways."[175] We need to examine as many different cultural codes as we can to re-create the structures of human life—self, community, spirit, and the world as we perceive it. Speaking to this point, Goldie quotes Stephen Muecke from *Reading the Country: Introduction to Nomadology:* "Within the issue of Aboriginal sovereignty there is more at stake than the use of lands; there is the right to control the production of [the nation's] mythologies."[176]

Paul Knitter, discussing the work of Sri Lankan thinker Aloysius Pieris, writes, "To *advocates of interreligious dialogue and pluralism,* Pieris voices the

'hermeneutic of suspicion' that perhaps all their conferences, their scholarly and mystico-ritual encounters, might be serving as a holy smoke screen behind which they are avoiding, unconsciously, the harsh realities of poverty, injustice, and exploitation—and perhaps even their own religious complicity in such realities. Is dialogue being practiced on mountaintops by a privileged holy remnant of scholars and mystics, while the masses are left in the valleys to dialogue with malnutrition and disease and lack of land?"[177] I would contend that such questions are even more germane to the ongoing colonial situation of American Natives than they are in Asia. Are we, by our work, merely contributing to the ever accelerating process of creating a rainforest society in which canopy dwellers live a privileged existence in the treetops while others are left scuttling along and fending for themselves on the floor below?

Five centuries of ongoing colonialism, here as in other colonial societies, has led to an erosion of self and community due to the dislocation resulting from cultural denigration, enslavement, forced migration, and fostered dependency.[178] Among Native peoples this has led to a tremendous grief that is not unlike the Korean concept of *han*.[179] Speaking of his conversations on the subject with Jake Swamp (Mohawk), Philip Arnold writes, "[G]rief clogs one's throat with a lump so large that genuine speech is obstructed, grief blocks the ears so hearing is impaired, and clouds one's eyes with tears making vision and future sight blurred." Swamp avers that "with the abolition of grief there will come a clearing of the human heart and mind."[180] In the case of Native Americans, as for Koreans, grief can never be finally "abolished." Any Native scholarship or intellectual work must, however, take the ongoing and continual healing of this grief—what Noley and Mary Churchill (Cherokee) call a sense of exile and others term a consciousness of removal—as both a goal and a starting point.[181] It must expand the definition of liberation to include survival. Natives engaged in literary production participate in this healing process.

It has been suggested that Native writers are primarily engaged in an act of cultural mediation. Treat writes, "These writings [by Native Christian theologians], like many other types of contemporary native literature, cross cultural boundaries in order to facilitate intercultural understanding and respect and to effect structural change; they are cross-cultural epistles to the cross culture."[182] Greg Sarris, in a similar vein, declares:

> My discussions and stories . . . contribute to current discussions regarding reading of American Indian literatures in particular and cross-cultural literatures in general. . . . What makes written literatures cross-cultural depends as much on their content and production as on their being read by a particular reader or community of readers. Many Americans from marginal cultures with specific languages and mores write in a particular variety of English or integrate their culture-specific language with an English that makes their written works accessible in some measure to a large English-speaking readership. These writers mediate not only different languages and narrative forms, but, in the process, the cultural experiences they are

representing, which become the content of their work. Their work represents a dialogue between themselves and different cultural norms and forms and also, within their text, between, say, characters or points of view. This cross-cultural interaction represented by the texts is extended to readers, many of whom are unfamiliar with the writers' particular cultural experiences and who must, in turn, mediate between what they encounter in the texts and what they know from their specific cultural experiences.[183]

This theme of cultural mediation has been taken up by a number of non-Native critics, notably Margaret Connell Szasz, Dorothy R. Parker, James Ruppert, and David Murray.[184] Ruppert, in particular, devotes an entire volume to the topic—*Mediation in Contemporary Native American Fiction*. Defining mediation as "an artistic and conceptual standpoint, constantly flexible, which uses the epistemological frameworks of Native American and Western cultural traditions to illuminate and enrich each other," he declares, "Whether by blood or experience, Native Americans today, especially writers, express a mixed heritage. As old and isolating world views give rise to new ones, the writer acts out his or her role as mediator-creator."[185] Like Ruppert, Murray focuses on mediation in his book *Forked Tongues: Speech, Writing, and Representation in North American Indian Texts*, writing, "By paying attention to the mediator . . . rather than what he is pointing to, or in other words by concentrating on the various forms of cultural and linguistic mediation which are always taking place, we reduce the danger of making the space between the two sides into an unbridgeable chasm or turning differences into Otherness."

The concern with getting rid of "old and isolating world views" and "unbridgeable chasm[s]" has always been more of a concern for Amer-Europeans than for Natives, who do not view their own cultural responses as "old and isolating" and who often express scant interest in bridging their worldview with that of the dominant culture. It becomes another way of asserting Western universalism against Native peoples. Ruppert quotes Vizenor: "Métis earthdivers waver and forbear extinction in two worlds. Métis are the force in the earthdiver metaphor, the tension in the blood and the uncertain word, the imaginative and compassionate trickster on street corners in the cities. When the mixedblood earthdiver summons the white world to dive like the otter and beaver and muskrat in search of earth, and federal funds, he is both animal and trickster, both white and tribal, the uncertain creator in an urban metaphor based on a creation myth that preceded him in two world views and oral traditions."[186] Ruppert's argument is perhaps strongest with regard to Vizenor, who more so than any other Native writer champions mixed-blood (crossblood/Métis) identity. Even so, however, he champions these crossblood people *as Indians*.

According to Ruppert, seeing Native literature as "between cultures" is a romantic and victimist perspective. It is better, he contends, to see them as participating in two cultures. Such a stance ignores, again in a universalizing manner,

the fact that colonized persons, particularly crossbloods, feel themselves in precisely that unstable location, at once limnal and littoral to two ways of being
and knowing. Nieuwenhuys writes of the "emotional confusion" this can engender, describes both himself and others similarly situated as "between two
'homelands,'" and speaks of the "insecurity" shared by those "forced to live
between two worlds."[187] Many North American Natives express this same experience. Leonard Crow Dog (Sicangu Lakota), a traditional and a peyotist, speaks
of the difficulty felt by many Native Christians: "Indian Christians have a very
hard time these days as they are caught between two ways of seeing the
world."[188] Mourning Dove (Okanagan/Colville), writing in the second decade
of this century, describes both herself and her title character in *Cogewea, the
Half-Blood* in extreme terms, wondering if there is any place for the "'breed'!—
the socially ostracized of two races." "[W]e are between two fires," she writes,
"the Red and the White. . . . We are maligned and traduced as no one but we
of the despised 'breeds' can know. If permitted, I would prefer living the white
man's way to that of the reservation Indian, but he hampers me. I appreciate
my meagre education, but I will *never* disown my mother's blood. Why should
I do so? Though my skin is of the tawny hue, I am not ashamed."[189] And
Owens notes that much Indian fiction reflects a "fragmented sense of self . . .
characters who truly find themselves between two realities and wondering
which world and life might be theirs."[190] At the same time, however, Owens
notes, "Repeatedly in Indian fiction . . . we are shown the possibility of recovering a centered sense of personal identity and significance."[191]

Unquestionably, mediation occurs in Native literatures. The need to appeal
and be accessible to a wide readership in order to be published necessitates
this. Likewise, it is also true that a knowledge of the cultural codes of the writer
leads to a fuller understanding. Ruppert writes as an Amer-European about
Native literature, so mediation becomes important to him as an entry point.
But what about the Native reader? Is there not also something much more
intimate going on than cultural mediation? Ruppert is correct that Native authors write for two or three different audiences (local, pan-Indian, metropolitan), but he ignores that in this process they most often privilege the Native
reader. As David Murray notes, in attempting to categorize and critique Indian
literatures, he may be "ignoring the fact that . . . what may be read as derivative Romanticism within a white context may also have stronger and more
complex reverberations within relevant Indian cultures."[192] Vizenor's updated
trickster stories, by Ruppert's own admission, "place Native American perceptions in a modern framework to delight Native audiences."[193] Simon Ortiz says
he writes for "[a]nybody, but maybe Indian people particularly since I always
try to focus upon the relationships among us all."[194] And Paula Gunn Allen,
who is herself both a critic and a novelist, states that Indian writers often
add secondary elements to their intrinsically Native story in order to satisfy a

metropolitan audience who will understand and expect them.[195] Thomas King stakes out a more radical position, claiming, "I really don't care about the white audience. They don't have an understanding of the intricacies of Native life, and I don't think they're much interested in it, quite frankly."[196] Thus the very hybridity of the work, argues Owens, is subversive. The Indian reader becomes the insider, privileged and empowered. The *métropole* is pushed to the periphery, made liminal, at best littoral in the same way that a non-Native town may exist on the border of a reservation.[197]

Non-Native critic Petrone observes:

> The literature of [North America's] native peoples has always been quintessentially political, addressing their persecutions and betrayals and summoning their resources for resistance. The political dimension is an inherent part of their writing because it is an inherent part of their lives. Debasing experiences reflecting new realities of political and social change created by changing contact situations— suicide, alcoholism, self-destructive behaviour, poverty, family violence, disintegration of the extended family, and the breach between generations—are real problems in the lives and tragedies of Indians today all across the [continent]. The presentation of these lives in poetry, short fiction, novel, drama, and memoir constitutes a political comment. Native writers tell what they see, what they have experienced or are experiencing. They tell what it is like to live as an Indian in today's society, increasingly caught between tradition and mainstream culture.[198]

In this way they are active not only on their own behalf but on that of Native people in general.[199]

A feature that cuts across various Native worldviews is the importance of community. The need for collective survival in diverse, often quite harsh, natural environments led to such an emphasis. Such an emphasis, as Deloria points out, means that "Indian tribes are communities in fundamental ways that other American communities or organizations are not. Tribal communities are wholly defined by family relationships, whereas non-Indian communities are defined primary by residence or by agreement with sets of intellectual beliefs."[200] Among the Cherokee, this commitment manifests itself in the Kituwha spirit. Historian William McLoughlin summarizes the elements of Kituwha as "loyalty to each other, concern for the spiritual power in their way of life, and their insistence upon the importance of tribal unity and harmony."[201] D'Arcy McNickle vividly captured this Native sense of community, in *Wind from an Enemy Sky*, in a single brief sentence: "A man by himself was nothing but a shout in the wind."

Although some, like Reinhold Niebuhr, have questioned whether autochthonous cultures possess community, it is, in fact, the highest value to Native peoples, and fidelity to it is a primary responsibility.[202] Although they curiously phrase it in the past tense—once again relegating Natives to a fast-receding history—Carmody and Carmody are nonetheless correct when they write, "Nothing stood higher in native American conception than the well-being of one's people."[203] Thomas King, himself a Cherokee, puts the matter succinctly when he declares that the "most important relationship in Native cultures is the relationship which humans share with each other, a relationship that is embodied within the idea of community. Community, in a Native sense, is not simply a place or a group of people, rather it is, as novelist Louise Erdrich [Anishinaabe] describes it, a place that has been 'inhabited for generations,' where 'the landscape becomes enlivened by a sense of group and family history.' "[204]

This linkage of land and people within the concept of community, reflecting the spatial orientation of Native peoples, is crucial. Warrior terms community and land "central critical categories."[205] As Geary Hobson states, "These are the kinds of relationships we must never forget. Our land is our strength, our people the land, one and the same, as it always has been and always will be."[206] When Natives are removed from their traditional lands, they are robbed of more than territory; they are deprived of numinous landscapes that are central to their faith and their identity, lands populated by their relations, ancestors, animals and beings both physical and mythological. A kind of psychic homicide is committed.

Native religious traditions reflect and reinforce this collectivity and remain a primary factor of social integration in Native community. Whereas Christianity is a metareligion, rooted in a fixed sacred written text, the survival of Native religions depends largely "on the willingness of community members to participate in their ongoing realization. The fact that we now find more and more published studies of Amerindian religions does not change this situation."[207] Historically, this lack of a "book" has led non-Natives to view indigenous religious traditions as "inadequate." David Thompson, writing in the 1840s, stated, "The sacred Scriptures to the Christian; the Koran to the Mohametan give a steady belief to the mind, which is not the case with the Indian, his idea on what passes in this world is tolerable correct so far as his senses and reason can inform him; but after death all is wandering conjecture taken up on tradition, dreams and hopes."[208] Paula Gunn Allen describes it somewhat differently: "The tribes do not celebrate the individual's ability to feel emotion, for they assume that all people are able to do so. One's emotion's are one's own; to suggest that others should imitate them is to impose on the personal integrity of others. The tribes seek—through song, ceremony, legend, sacred stories (myths), and tales—to embody, articulate, and share reality, to bring the isolated, private self into harmony and balance with this reality, to verbalize the sense of majesty and reverent mystery of all things, and to actualize . . . those truths that give to humanity its greatest significance and dignity.[209] As I noted earlier, the closest tribal approximation of "sin" in the Christian lexicon is a failure to fulfill one's responsibilities to the community. Conversely, there is generally no concept of "salvation" beyond the continuance of the community. The Sun Dance, practiced by numerous Plain tribes (and increasingly in a pan-Indian context), is illustrative: it is generally said to be performed "that the People might live."

This is not to say that there is no place for individuation in Native society. McPherson and Rabb refer to the "integrity of person" as an element of their generic Native worldview. The self is the locus where tribal values become concrete. Psychoanalyst Erik Erikson developed his theories of stages in psychosocial development of the individual from his work with the Sioux and Yurok.[210] It is simply, as anthropologist Clifford Geertz reminds us, that "the Western conception of the person as a bounded, unique, more or less integrated motivational and cognitive universe, a dynamic center of awareness, emotion, judgement, and action organized into a distinctive whole and set contrastively both against other such wholes and against its social and natural background, is . . . a rather peculiar idea within the context of the world's cultures."[211] Native societies are synecdochic (part-to-whole), while the more Western conception is metonymic (part-to-part); as Donald Fixico notes, Natives tend to see themselves in terms of "self in society" rather than "self and society."[212] It is what Allen refers to as a "greater self" and McPherson calls an "enlarged sense of self."[213] It is in a profound sense a mentality that declares, "I am We."

This oneness "transcends linear time, life, and death."[214] It encompasses what I term the "wider community" that includes all the created order, which is also characterized in kinship terms. No sharp distinction is drawn between the human and nonhuman persons that make up the community. Thus, the Lakota precatory punctuation *mitakuye oyasin*, translated as "all my relations," includes not only one's family nor even all human beings but also "the web of kinship extending to the animals, to the birds, to the fish, to the plants, to all animate and inanimate forms that can be seen or imagined. More than that, 'all my relations' is an encouragement for us to accept the responsibilities we have within this universal family by living in a harmonious and moral manner (a common admonishment is to say of someone that they act as if they have no relations)."[215]

Such an embrace of the universe stands in marked contrast to the dominant streams of Christianity. Carmody and Carmody declare that "it is hard to deny that Christianity lost something precious when it took over the biblical polemic against the fertility gods of the Canaanites and separated God from the cosmos." Peelman, picking up the theme, delineates, "It is also important to note that the radical separation between God and the cosmos in western thinking is also the origin of a series of other dualisms or separations which have profoundly influenced Roman Catholic and Protestant theology: cosmos-history, nature-grace, body-spirit, profane-sacred, world-church, individual-society, man-woman."[216] Native traditions suffer from no such dualistic thinking and thus have "not become the victim of the . . . reduction which characterizes western theology when it moved from its cosmocentric to its anthropocentric vision of reality."[217]

The necessity of community permeates every aspect of Native life, including epistemology. Christopher Ronwanièn:te Jocks argues, "Knowledge without a supportive community to effect it is useless; it is, in some sense, undefined. Until [one] is surrounded by that supportive community, knowledge is not defined because [the knower] is not defined as a human being. Thus knowledge requires a network of knowers, or more accurately, of actors. Knowledge is something you do; not a preexisting tool independent of the person holding it, nor of the uses to which it might be put."[218] Leslie Silko states the same point somewhat differently when she says, "[S]tory makes . . . community." We must have stories, since that is how "you know; that's how you belong; that's how you know you belong."[219]

The importance of story for Natives cannot be overestimated. As Vizenor writes, "Native American Indian identities are created in stories, and the names are essential to a distinctive personal nature, but memories, visions, and the shadows of heard stories are the paramount verities of a tribal presence. . . . Tribal consciousness would be a minimal existence without active choices, the choices that are heard in stories and mediated in names; otherwise, tribal identities might be read as mere simulations of remembrance."[220] Language and narrative have tremendous power to create community. Indeed, it may be that the People cannot have life outside of stories, their existence contingent upon the telling and hearing of communal stories. Elsewhere, Vizenor quotes Jean-François Lyotard—"the people does not exist as a subject but as a mass of millions of insignificant and serious little stories that sometimes let themselves be collected together to constitute big stories and sometimes disperse into digressive elements."[221] Two examples testify to this tremendous power of story, at once formative and transformative.

Alister McGrath, in *Evangelicalism and the Future of Christianity*, relates attending a lecture by a Kiowa Apache from Oklahoma, who told of learning the story of his people when a young boy. McGrath relates the talk:

> One day, just after dawn, his father woke him and took him to the home of an elderly Kiowa woman. He left him there, promising to return to collect him that afternoon. All that day the woman told this young boy the story of the Kiowa people. She told him of his origins by the Yellowstone River and how they then migrated southward. She told him of the many hardships they faced—the wars with other Native American nations and the great blizzards on the winter plains. She told him of the glories of the life of the Kiowa nation—the great buffalo hunts, the taming of wild horses and the skill of the braves as riders. Finally she told him of the coming of the white man and the humiliation of their once-proud nation at

the hands of the horse soldiers who forced them to move south to Kansas, where they faced starvation and poverty. Her story ended as she told him of their final humiliating confinement within a reservation in Oklahoma. . . . [S]hortly before dark, his father returned to collect him. "When I left that house, I was a Kiowa," he declared. He had learned the story of his people. He knew what his people had been through and what they stood for. Before learning the family history, he had been a Kiowa in name only; now he was a Kiowa in reality.[222]

Barre Toelken similarly relates a conversation he had with Tacheeni Scott (Navajo) about the "sustaining function" of story: "Why tell the stories? 'If my children hear the stories, they will grow up to be good people; if they don't hear them, they will turn out to be bad.' Why tell them to adults? 'Through the stories everything is made possible.' "[223]

Thus, many contemporary Natives "understand clearly that they are part of today's world but that their tribal traditions, languages, ceremonies, and stories create a relationship to this land that is unmatched by others. Their relationship is with each other as a *community* and with places, plants and animals. Their relationship forms a legacy, and they have a future that is based on past experience. Story is the magic that ties all of these themes and ideas together."[224] As Paula Gunn Allen states, "It becomes clear, therefore, that oral literature must be approached from the *religious,* social, and literary traditions that influence them."[225]

Contemporary Native writers continue, supplement, and expand the oral tradition, nourishing it while being nourished by it.[226] They help modern-day Natives apprehend and navigate the modern world just as traditional orature helped their ancestors understand their own. As Clifford Trafzer puts it, "Contemporary Native American writers draw on [the oral] tradition to tell new tales that mirror their survival and continued presence in this country today."[227] They "write out of tribal traditions, and into them."[228] Thus, even as Tom King tells new pan-tribal trickster stories, he acknowledges that he was influenced by traditional storytellers like Harry Robinson (Okanagan).[229] Similarly, Paula Gunn Allen contends that as what she deems the formative period of Native fiction was coming to a close, in 1970, that fiction "came to resemble traditional Native Narrative more and more while the voice, tone, and style ever more closely replicated a communal voice: multiple, integral, and accretive."[230] Native literatures are dialogic texts that both reflect and shape Native identity and community.[231]

The issue of a communal voice is of vital importance. It is undeniably true, as Larzer Ziff declared, that "[t]he process of literary annihilation [a process continuous with, a collaboration conscious or unconscious with, physical extermination] would be checked only when Indian writers began representing their own culture."[232] Narrative is a means that colonized people employ to assert their own existence and identity. The struggle may be land and sovereignty, but it is often reflected, contested, and decided in narrative.[233] Traditional stories, however, are communal. They belong to the People and define the People—the community—as a whole. In contrast to "the heroes of Western literature who exemplify rugged individualism, the culture heroes in [traditional] Native American literature act to benefit the larger community by bringing power to the people, slaying monsters that have terrorized villages, or bringing a lasting contribution to the people, such as corn, tobacco, or salmon." Reflecting this communal identity-producing role, stories developed communally as well. The notion of a story with a single author, especially one who then has a proprietary right in the act of his or her creation, would have struck pre-Columbian Natives as absurd.[234] As Owens observes, "The privileging of the individual necessary for the conception of the modern novel . . . is a more radical departure for American Indian cultures than for the Western world as a whole, for Foucault's 'moment of individualization' represents an experience forced harshly, and rather unsuccessfully, upon Native Americans."[235]

To be a storyteller in traditional society is to be "one who participates in a traditionally sanctioned manner in *sustaining the community*."[236] Instead, contemporary writers are self-appointed. Paula Gunn Allen recalls being questioned by John Rouillard (Santee Dakota) about this status and the Western literary forms employed at a seminar on Indian literature. She remembers, "Every Indian in the room who engaged in these activities [writing] had to ask whether we were really Indian. Maybe not, if we were writers. We had to ask ourselves if we were traitors to our Indianness. Maybe we were so assimilated, so un-Indian, that we were doing white folks' work and didn't realize it!"[237] Elizabeth Cook-Lynn also discusses the dilemma for herself as poet, novelist, and scholar, saying: "The idea that poets can speak for others, the idea that we can speak for the dispossessed, the weak, the voiceless, is indeed one of the great burdens of contemporary American Indian poets today, for it is widely believed that we 'speak for our tribes.' The frank truth is that I don't know very many poets who say, 'I speak for my people.' It is not only unwise; it is probably impossible, and it is very surely arrogant, for *We Are Self-Appointed* and the self-appointedness of what we do indicates that the responsibility is ours and ours alone."[238] To be a writer is to enter a kind of privileged class, educated, separated somehow from the community. Louis Owens contends that Native writers recover authenticity by incorporation and invocation of the oral tradition in their texts.[239] Putting aside the issue of the general truth of this assertion, it nonetheless remains that to put one's authorial signature on a text is to immediately put oneself outside the oral tradition and community.

I would contend that the self-appointed status of the writer is, and must be, one of those things that makes us understand our accountability to Native community. Geary Hobson notes the "deep sense of obligation" Native writers feel toward their communities. Owens states that they write with a "consciousness of responsibility as a member of a living Native American culture" and community. Trafzer considers community "the center of the universe" for Native writers, whose work "reflects the relationship of their community with place."[240] Hobson concludes, "Literature, in all its forms, oral as well as written, is our most durable way of carrying on this continuance [of the People]. By making literature, like the singers and storytellers of earlier times, we serve the people as well as ourselves in an abiding sense of remembrance."[241] Communal, identity-producing potential exists in any contemporary Native text. Gerald Vizenor concurs, "Native American Indian authors have secured the rich memories of tribal generations on this continent; the diverse narratives of these crossblood authors would uncover the creative humor of survivance and tribal counterpoise to the literature of dominance."[242]

It is not an "immemorial . . . and static" character that has been the strength of Native culture and community but, rather, its lability—its "persistence [and] vivacity" as Natives themselves change but remain Native nevertheless.[243] As Warrior claims for Vine Deloria Jr. and John Joseph Mathews, "Both contend in their work that the success or failure of American Indian communal societies has always been predicated not upon a set of uniform, unchanging beliefs, but rather upon a commitment to the groups and the groups' futures."[244] Not to be committed to Native American community, affirming the tribes, the people, the values, is tantamount to psychic suicide. It is to lose the self in the dominant mass humanity, either ceasing to be or persisting merely as another ethnic minority, drifting with no place, no relations, no real people.[245]

I would contend that the single thing that most defines Indian literatures relates to this sense of community and commitment to it. It is what I term "communitism." Communitism, or its adjectival form "communitist," is a neologism of my own devising. Its coining, as I noted earlier, is necessary because no other word from the Latin roots *communis* or *communitas*—communitarian, communal, communist, and so on—carries the exact sense necessary. It is formed from a combination of the words "community" and "activism" or "activist."[246] Literature is communitist to the extent that it has a proactive commitment to Native community, including the wider community. In communities that have too often been fractured and rendered dysfunctional by the effects of more than 500 years of colonialism, to promote communitist values means to participate in the healing of the grief and sense of exile felt by Native communities and the pained individuals in them. It is, to borrow from Homi K. Bhabha, "community envisaged as a project—at once a vision and a construction—that takes you 'beyond' yourself in order to return, in a spirit of revision and reconstruction, to the political *conditions* of the present."[247]

Linda Hogan (Chickasaw) testifies to this healing when she titles a volume of her poetry *The Book of Medicines*.[248] Joy Harjo has declared, "To write, the act of writing, of witnessing means taking part in the healing of the people.

. . . [A] few hundred years ago, aboriginal peoples were one hundred per cent of the population of this continent. Now we're one-half of one percent of the total population! . . . [W]hy wouldn't Native writers write about disruption and disorientation? And, of course, the resolution is through reassertion of tribal self. . . . The writer has to turn to that which is nourishing, has to make sense of a senseless history."[249] Such healing is both personal and collective. Luci Tapahonso describes writing as a vehicle for reversing the diaspora begun after European invasion: "For many people in my situation, residing away from my homeland, writing is the means for returning, rejuvenation, and for restoring our spirits to the state of *'hohzo,'* or beauty, which is the basis of Navajo philosophy."[250] Discussing the responsibility of Native writers and intellectuals in the process of healing, Robert Warrior writes, "In the concrete materiality of experience, we see both the dysfunctions colonization has created for Indian communities and the ways Indian people have attempted to endure those dysfunctions." He concludes:

> The primary responsibility we face . . . is simply to speak about contemporary Indian lives and understand the ways in which, in the words of Simon Ortiz, "this America has been a burden" to us as human beings. To embrace traditions without taking seriously the path over which we trod toward that embrace is to deny our own selves. In refusing to engage in that kind of denial, we confront both the power of our traditions and the painful stories of Native people who have suffered and continue to suffer, people whose ways of survival present us with the terrible beauty of resistance that rarely finds a voice in Native political processes.[251]

As in Kanafani's resistance literature, writing becomes an essential means of struggle—in the Native case of celebrating what Warrior calls the "fragile miracle of survival."[252] In seeking to support Native people's struggle to be self-defining (for Sioui, the essence of autohistory; for McPherson, the rejection of outside view predicates), to have representational autonomy, Indian writers are engaged in an act contiguous with the struggle of Other intellectuals around the world. It is one of, in the words of Elizabeth Cook-Lynn, "defiance born of the need to survive," and, as Simon Ortiz says, "it is an act that defies oppression."[253] Gerald Vizenor declares, "The postindian warriors encounter their enemies with the same courage in literature as their ancestors once evinced on horses, and they create their stories with a new sense of survivance."[254] They are engaged in a quest for a liberative perspective in which Natives can see themselves in relationship to each other and to community.[255] What Ruppert observed with regard to modern Native fiction could be said of all Native literatures: they are "literature with a purpose."[256] Writing prepares the ground for recovery, and even re-creation, of Indian identity and culture. Native writers speak to that part of us the colonial power and the dominant culture cannot reach, cannot touch. They help Indians imagine themselves as Indians. Just as there is no practice of Native religions for personal empowerment, they write that the People might live.

In putting forward the concept of communitism, however, I am not suggesting a facile notion of authorial intent. How a given work is received, consumed, appropriated, by Native community is part of the work itself. It helps complete the process. Communitism is, as the word itself implies, communal. It is part of a shared quest for belonging, a search for community. It is the valorization of Native community and values and a commitment to them that may be, in part, politically unconscious.[257] In addition, according to Bhabha, "historical agency is transformed through the signifying process. . . . [T]he historical event is represented in a discourse that is *somehow beyond control.* This is in keeping with Hannah Arendt's suggestion that the author of social action may be the initiator of its unique meaning, but as agent he or she cannot control its outcome. It is not simply what the house of fiction contains or 'controls' *as content.*"[258]

In this shared quest, Native writers may not always agree on either the means or meaning of communitism. Community is a primary value, but today we exist in many different kinds of community—reservation, rural, urban, tribal, pan-Indian, traditional, Christian. Many move back and forth between a variety of these communities.[259] Our different locations, physical, mental, and spiritual, will inevitably lead to different conceptions of what survival, liberation, and communitism require. The following examinations of different Native writers in different eras show that this has always been the case since the arrival of Europeans.[260]

Robert Warrior, at the close of his book *Tribal Secrets,* offers his own communitist vision: "Our struggle at the moment is to continue to survive and work toward a time when we can replace the need for being preoccupied with survival with a more responsible and peaceful way of living within communities and with the ever-changing landscape that will ever be our only home."[261] In the meantime, as Deloria proclaims, our work "must certainly involve a heady willingness to struggle for both long and short term goals and at times simply for the joy of getting one's nose bloodied while blackening the other guy's eye. . . . It is the solitary acknowledgement that the question of [human] life and identity is to let the bastards know you've been there and that it is always a good day to die. We are therefore able to live."[262]

Everyone laughed at the impossibility of it,
but also the truth. Because who would believe
the fantastic and terrible story of all our survival
those who were never meant
                    to survive?
                              —Joy Harjo, *She Had Some Horses*

Chapter Two

Occom's Razor and Ridge's Masquerade (18th–19th Century)

Did Samson Occom shave? His portrait shows no hint of shadow. In his depiction, he resembles nothing so much as an ever so slightly dusky Dr. Johnson. Occom's implement of the title refers, in this case, neither to a straight-edged blade nor to the rule of logic and theology but to the precise, careful, subtle, and razorlike manner in which he employed the only tools at his disposal, a shrewd intellect and a gift with words, in order to promote communitist values by critiquing the White power structure of his day even while being a marginal figure it it.

Beth Brant is mistaken when she claims that Native writing is only about a hundred years old. Even in English, it dates at least from Occom and is thus more than two centuries old. I will argue that it is indeed much older than that. She is nonetheless correct that "[o]ur writing is, and always has been, an attempt to beat back colonization and the stereotyping of our Nations. But the writing is *not* a reaction to colonialism, it is an active and new way to tell the stories we have always been told."[1] In both its continuity and its change, it speaks to and for Native peoples.

Oral Tradition and Early Writing

LaVonne Ruoff contends, in a perhaps unconscious attempt to subsume Native literature into the national literature of the United States, that the "literature of this nation originated with the native peoples who migrated to North America over twenty-eight thousand years ago, not with the Western Europeans who began to immigrate in the late sixteenth and early seventeenth centuries."[2] More poetically, Scott Momaday argues that "American literature begins with the first human perception of the American landscape expressed and preserved in language."[3] That beginning—that first preservation in language—occurs in the orature of Native peoples.

In preliterate cultures, the oral tradition was a powerful builder and unifier of community. Much of it was didactic in nature, communicating the lessons, histories, biographies, "and rules of belief and behaviour of the diverse tribes, perpetuating their specific world views that gave the cosmos its origin, order, and meaning." According to Penny Petrone, this orature "bound 'the sacred and the profane, the individual and the tribal, the past, present, and future, and it encompasse[d] the teller, the listener, the tribe, and the land, and the universe.' By transmitting specific cultural knowledge, with its specific meanings and messages, it helped strengthen tribal identity and provided for its continuity." As Clifford Trafzer puts it, the stories of the oral tradition emphasized "that an individual was not set apart from the whole but was part of a community that required the assistance of those who could contribute most to the well-being of the family, band, or tribe." Communitism is a two-way street. Orature provided identity but also placed demands upon the individual whose identity it helped shape.[4]

Despite the framing of both Petrone's and Trafzer's discussions in the past tense, as noted in the previous chapter, tribal orature is still very much alive, giving voice to the histories and values of Native cultures.[5] Noting the coterminous nature of orature and contemporary culture, Simon Ortiz declares, "The oral tradition is not just speaking and listening, because what it means to me and to other people who have grown up in that tradition is that whole process, . . . of that society in terms of its history, its culture, its language, its values, and *subsequently*, its literature. So it's not a simple matter of speaking and listening, but living that process."[6] Yet, as Native critics like Gerald Vizenor and Amer-European scholars like Karl Kroeber both attest, the oral tradition cannot simply be reduced to a bearer of culture. It is also, and has always been, art, a creative achievement not inferior to the literature of any other people.[7]

Though pre-Columbian cultures were primarily oral, they were not completely "pre-literate." The earliest books in the Americas were produced not by European immigrants but by the Maya, whose culture extended through Guatemala, Belize, southern Mexico, and parts of Honduras and El Salvador. The most famous of these volumes was the Council Book or *Popul Vuh,* telling the Mayan creation myth and consulted by Quiché rulers as part of their decision-making process. Originally written in Mayan hieroglyphs, the book was transliterated into Spanish in the 16th century.[8] In 1562, Diego de Landa, a Catholic missionary, ordered all Mayan books destroyed as the writings of the Devil.[9]

Mayan libraries were gutted, and thousands of books were brought to the town of Mani in the Yucatan, where they were burned. Indians were tortured and forced to watch the conflagration. According to a Mayan account, "Our priests wept. How do we mourn for such a loss? Nothing could have been as cruel as the burning of our books—except the enslavement of our children. And the children, we would hide them or carry them into the forest. . . . But the books! We could not stop the fires. We could only cling desperately to our memories and weep. They took generations of our hearts and minds, the books, and they threw them into the fires. And we could not stop them."[10] Today, only four Mayan books survive.[11]

According to some accounts, the earliest known text from North America is the *Wallum Olum,* or Red Record of the Lenni Lenape (or Delaware) people—sometimes called the Hoosier Iliad or the American *Popul Vuh.* Carved and painted in pictographs on wooden tablets, the *Wallum Olum* tells the epic story of the Lenape from the creation of the world to the arrival of Europeans. The last line of the history supposedly ends in 1620 with the ironic and ominous, "Friendly people, in great ships; who are they?"

The *Wallum Olum* was reportedly given to a physician, Dr. John Russell Ward, in the summer of 1820. The tablets subsequently were turned over to Constantine Rafinesque, a professor of botany, natural history, and modern languages at Transylvania University in Kentucky, who undertook to translate the record, completing his attempt in 1833 and publishing his results in 1836. The creation, transmission, and translation of the work all are shrouded in mystery and are the subject of much uncertainty and contention. Though Rafinesque's notebooks survive, the wooden originals have been lost. Modern-day Delawares, however, consider the text an accurate account of their mythology and history, and at least some scholars take the claim seriously. Gordon Brotherston writes, "That it is an unwelcome text is clear. But that could also have to do with its political memory. Like Algonkin texts assuredly genuine, in defending the Ohio as a prime focus in ancient and modern Turtle Island it has upset yet again the official U.S. doctrine of 'American' prehistory and history, touching the particularly raw nerve of the Ohio."[12] A fragment that purportedly updated the *Wallum Olum* account was included by Rafinesque in his manuscript. According to Virgil Vogel, and quoted by Noley, this fragment reads in part, "The Wallumolum [*sic*] was made by Lekhibit (the writer) to record our glory. Shall I write another to record our fall? No! Our foes have taken care of that; but I speak what they know not or conceal."[13]

Questions about the authenticity of the *Wallum Olum* do not detract from the fact that numerous Native nations did keep tangible, material records in bark, wood, hide, or wampum. As Noley notes, "It is popular among contemporary writers of American history to say that the Indians of North America had no written records to tell their viewpoint of history. In a good many cases, records were available but in an unfamiliar medium."[14] Regardless, by the time of the "discovery" of the *Wallum Olum* in 1820, Natives had already been representing themselves in written English for more than fifty years.

Occom, Apess, and Jones

Robert Warrior, who prefers to think in terms of intellectual traditions rather than literatures, notes, "Native intellectual tradition reaches back at least to Samson Occom's . . . missionary writings in the 1700s."[15] His caution, expressed in his use of the hedge phrase "at least," is well-founded. As he has noted, America's approach-avoidance relationship with its indigenes has led to what he calls "the rhetoric of novelty." In such rhetoric, there is a constant push to identify a given Native or Native work as "the first" of a type, even when the claim is dubious or even spurious.[16]

Though Samson Occom (Mohegan) is often pointed at, justifiably, as the first Native American to write and be published in English, he was in fact only one of a number of Natives, many of them Christian missionaries, who wrote prior to the midpoint of the 19th century. LaVonne Ruoff notes the range of writings in which these Natives engaged and their purposes: "The major genre written by American Indian authors in the late eighteenth and nineteenth centuries was nonfiction prose. In addition to writing autobiographies, Indian authors wrote sermons, protest literature, tribal histories, and travel accounts. They hoped that their prose would make their white audiences recognize Indians' humanity as a people and the significance of their tribal cultures and history. Their efforts paralleled the political developments, such as the Indian Removal Bill of 1830, that threatened the sovereignty of Indian peoples."[17] Her observation encompasses the work of a diverse collection of writers that includes Occom, William Apess (Pequot), David Cusick (Tuscarora), Elias Boudinot (Cherokee), Richard Fields (Cherokee), and three notable Anishinaabe writer/historians (George Copway, Peter Jones, and George Henry). Though at the early dates at which they wrote, they could not hope to reach a wide Native audience, their work nevertheless served Native purposes and reflected communitist values as they sought not only to preserve and defend their cultures but also to assert their own and their fellow Natives' humanity. As David Murray points out, however, the specific Native purposes of a given sermon, speech, or text "becomes less important, once it is published, than its metonymic role as expression of the cultural and historical roles allotted to Indians by whites."[18] In the remainder of this chapter, we will first examine the writings of three Native Christian missionaries, Occom, Apess, and Jones. We will then explore

Boudinot, Fields, and John Rollin Ridge (Cherokee) in the context of Cherokee Removal and the debates surrounding it. Finally, we will discuss Pauline Johnson, one of the earliest prominent Native female writers.

Samson Occom was born in 1723 at Mohegan (near the present-day site of New London, Connecticut), a fragment of the Pequot nation that had been virtually destroyed ninety years earlier. Though he began to learn to speak and read English from Christian ministers as early as 1733, he knew little or nothing of Christianity until the summer of 1739, when missionaries began to proselytize more systematically among his people. He "Continued under Trouble of Mind" for about six months, but within a year he had "a Discovery of the way of Salvation through Jesus Christ, and was enabl'd to put my trust in him alone for Life and Salvation. From this Time the Distress and Burden of my mind was removed, and I found Serenity and Pleasure of Soul, in Serving God." [19] He began to read the Christian scriptures and developed a desire to gain further education in order to teach his fellow Native youths how to read. In 1743, when he was nineteen, at his own request, his mother sent him to Eleazar Wheelock, who operated Moor's Charity School for indigent young men in Lebanon, Connecticut. The arrival of Occom convinced the Congregationalist minister that his preparatory school might serve a missionary purpose. Occom expected to stay two to three weeks, but he remained four years, until his impaired eyesight made further studies impossible.

Occom's remarkable ability "inspired his teacher with a vision of educating many Indians and sending them to spread salvation among their respective tribes." [20] His dream, however, never materialized. He continued for twenty-five years, but in 1769 reorganized Moor's as Dartmouth College and moved to Hanover, New Hampshire, where he once again began training non-Natives. Indians made up only a small percentage of the student body, and these rapidly dwindled. This shift was to cause a final rupture between Wheelock and his former pupil.

Occom was licensed to preach shortly after leaving Moor's. For ten years, however, he remained unordained. He had significant success teaching and evangelizing among the Montauk and Shinnecock of Long Island and eventually made missionary visits to the Oneida. In 1766, he traveled to England to raise funds for Moor's. Like his efforts among American Natives, the trip was fruitful, lasting two years and raising more than £12,000.

Upon his return in 1768, Occom was angered that he had collected money for an enterprise that was being largely abandoned in favor of education of Whites. His correspondence with Wheelock reveals his disillusionment, his commitment to Native peoples, and his skill with English letters. He complains, "Hoping that it may be a lasting Benefet to my poor Tawnee Brethren, With this View I went [to Europe] a volunteer—and I was willing to to become a Gazing Stocke, Yea Even a Laughing Stocke, in Strange Countries to Promote your Cause," but he has been betrayed. Wheelock has turned his back on the community to whom Occom is committed. In a wicked and incisive pun, Occom writes, "I am very jealous that instead of your Semenary Becoming alma Mater, she will be too *alba mater* to Suckle the Tawnees.—I think your College has too much Worked by Grandeur for the Poor Indians, they'll never have much benefit of it." He goes on to accuse his mentor of sending him to England as part of an elaborate fraud.[21]

The same year, Occom writes an autobiographical essay to correct "several Representations . . . made by Some gentlemen in America Concerning me."[22] Though Krupat is inclined to dismiss Occom's writings, including his autobiography, as nothing more than Christian "salvationism," the subtle critical nature of them reveals an underlying communitist theme.[23] Occom had already proved himself quite capable of self-representation on the page. When a White neighbor accused him of alcoholism, he wrote back, "You represent me to be the vilest Creature in Mohegan. I own I am bad enough and too bad, Yet I am Heartily glad I am not that old Robert Clelland [the author of the accusation], his sins won't be charged to me and my Sins won't be charged to him, he must answere for his own works before his Maker and I must answere for mine. You signify, as if it was in your Power to do me harm. You have been trying all you Can and you may your worst, I am not concerned." As Murray notes, Occom's closing is both a permission to Clelland "to 'represent' him *and* a way of totally rejecting it: 'I am, Sir, Just what you Please, S. Occom.' "[24] Likewise, while in London, he found a way of expressing Native powerlessness in the face of colonial encroachment and affirming Natives' inate superiority, declaring, "I am afraid the poor Indians will never stand a good chance with the English in their land controversies, because they are very poor, they have no money. Money is almighty now-a-days, and the Indians have no learning, no wit, no cunning; the English have all."[25]

The motif of the "poor Indian" as a reference to Native peoples is common to all Occom's works and, as will be seen, to works by many other Native authors of the period. At first glance, this self-abasing appellation would seem to run counter to communitism. As Murray observes, however, "[W]hen this [formulaic] humility is accompanied by a sense of grievance, as it quite often is in the case of Samson Occom, the same gesture of abasement can carry a sting in the tail." Murray illustrates his point with a letter in which Occom complains bitterly of his own inadequate funding for a missionary endeavor but nonetheless vows to go "tho no White Missionary would go in such Circumstances." Occom closes, "In a word I leave my poor Wife and Children at your feet and if they hunger, Starve and die let them Die there. Sir, I shall endeavor to follow your Directions in all things. This in utmost hast and with Sincere obedience is from . . . Your Good for Nothing Indian Sarvant."[26]

In his autobiography, Occom delineates the difficulty he has had making ends meet in his undertakings and the shabby treatment he has received at the hands of Whites. Whereas a White missionary is paid £100 a year, plus £50 for an interpreter and £30 for an "introducer," Occom, who needs no such extraneous personnel, has received only a total of £180 over a dozen years. He writes:

> [W]hat can be the Reason that they used me after this manner? I can't think of any thing, but this as a Poor Indian Boy Said, Who was Bound out to an English Family, and he used to Drive Plow for a young man, and he whipt and Beat him allmost every Day, and the young man found fault with him, and Complained of him to his master and the poor Boy was Called to answer for himself before his master, and he was asked, what it was he did, that he was So Complained of and beat almost every Day. He Said, he did not know, but he Supposed it was because he could not drive any better, but says he, I Drive as well as I know how; and at other Times he Beats me, because he is of a mind to beat me; but says he believes he Beats me for the most of the Time "because I am an Indian." So I am *ready* to Say, they have used me thus, because I Can't Influence the Indians so well as other missionaries; but I can assure them I have endeavoured to teach them as well as I know how;—but I *must Say,* "I believe it is because I am a poor Indian." I Can't help that God made me So; I did not make myself so.[27]

With that, he breaks off his account entirely. The parable, and the work that contains it, is more than simple self-vindication. Like other works by Occom, it is a communitist vindication of Natives in general.

Occom is best-known for his "Sermon Preached at the Execution of Moses Paul, an Indian." First published in 1772, it became an early best-seller, running through several editions in both America and Great Britain.[28] As Murray recounts the circumstances, "Moses Paul had earlier been converted to Christianity but had slipped into drinking while serving in the army and then in the navy. While drunk, he had pointlessly killed a respectable member of the community and his execution was therefore an opportunity to contemplate not just one Indian's downfall but to make him symbolize the particular weaknesses and susceptibilities of Indians. By having the sermon actually preached by a virtuous Indian (though one who also had shown his weakness for alcohol . . .), it was possible to stage a sort of moral tableau which encapsulated the oral capacities and disabilities of the Indians."[29] Occom was asked to deliver the sermon, supposedly by Paul himself, and the resulting oration demonstrates that he was more than "just a pawn in a white game."[30]

In a preface to the published version of the talk, Occom writes that he hopes that it will benefit his people and, indeed, other people of color, saying, "I think they [common people] can't help understanding my talk: little children may understand me. And poor Negroes may plainly and fully understand my meaning; and it may be of service to them. Again, it may in a particular manner be of service to my poor kindred the Indians. Further, as it comes from an uncommon quarter it may induce people to read it because it is from an Indian."[31] In the sermon itself, the preacher alternately addresses both Indians and Whites, making the White audience "overhearers" of a "pre-arranged conversation between Indians." He tells Paul, and presumably his White listeners as well, that he (and the Whites) have had the advantage of education and the Christian gospel and "therefore your sins are so much more aggravated." Calling Paul "bone of my bone, and flesh of my flesh," he argues, "You are an Indian, a despised creature; but you have despised yourself." As Murray accurately avers, Occom thereby implies that because they are despised, Indians have "an obligation not to live up, or rather down" to others' expectations. Then, in a complicated rhetorical maneuver and with an only slightly veiled manner, Occom blames Whites for Indian alcoholism. He cries, "And here I cannot but observe, we find it in sacred writ, a woe denounced against men, who put their bottles to their neighbors mouth to make them drunk, and that they may see their weakness; and no doubt there are such devilish men now in our day, as there were in the days of old." Murray does not go far enough when he states, "I am certainly not claiming an overall subversive purpose here, but when we link the possible ironies shown here with those found in his letters and the letters of some of Wheelock's other pupils an impression emerges of self-expression both *within* the conventions of Christian piety they had been taught and also *beyond* them."[32] I would argue that the intent is clearly subversive. Occom uses the occasion to affirm Native personhood, and the overall message is meant to be more accusatory of Whites who created the situation by introducing alcohol and by hating Indians than it is of the condemned and unfortunate Paul. The sermon, coupled with his other writings, demonstrates the truth of Warrior's statement that "writers going back as least as far as Samson Occom have grappled with many of the same issues that remain with us today."[33]

Unfortunately, Occom met with a fate not that different from the condemned Indian he admonished and eulogized. For the next decade, he acted as local minister and tribal consultant to the Mohegans and to other Indians in the area. He "also succumbed to occasional bouts of self-pity and heavy drinking—behavior that further identified him as an Indian in the eyes of both red and white observers."[34] He died in 1792.

Murray argues that whereas Occom's "criticism of whites is at best guarded, even disguised," that of William Apess is direct.[35] The issue is not so simple, however. As I have already argued, Occom's critique is often more pointed than Murray and other scholars acknowledge. By the same token, though Apess is more often more blatantly critical, he also shows himself capable of employing Occom's same guileful rhetorical razor. Though largely forgotten until a few years ago, Apess recently has emerged as the topic of a growing scholarly disputation. At issue are matters central to communitism: namely, to what degree

Apess asserted his own Indianness and wrote from a position that was determined by that Native identity.

Warrior argues that one can find in his work "not only resources for self-determined Native engagement but also political commitments and intellectual praxes" that are the essence of Warrior's intellectual sovereignty.[36] Krupat disagrees. In Apess's writings, he detects no unique individual voice. Rather, he hears only "a voice to be heard commonly in the early nineteenth century"—salvationism. According to Krupat, although Apess is proud to acknowledge "his Indian ancestry," "even his understanding of what it means to be a 'Native' is filtered through Christian perspective." Apess's identity as a Native derives not from any indigenous, Pequot understanding but from a purely Western, Christian one. He defines himself "exclusively in relation to salvationist discourse," without any Pequot dimension whatsoever. This reflects the writer's "wish to be the licensed speaker of a dominant voice that desires no supplementation by other voices"—the "mouthpiece of the Lord." The only voice that he wants to be heard is "the only voice that came to count for him," that of the Christian God.[37] Drawing conclusions similar to Krupat's, Brumble and Hertha Wong give scant attention to Apess in their respective works on Native American autobiography, seeing his work solely in terms of Christian confessional literature. Krupat himself ignores Apess entirely in his own *For Those Who Come After: A Study of Native American Autobiography.*[38]

Other scholars have joined in the debate over Apess's self-identity and commitment toward Indians. Ruoff labels Apess "[o]ne of the most forceful Indian protest writers of the early nineteenth century." Murray takes issue directly with Krupat. Rather than seeing Apess's Indianness as submerged or obliterated by a Christian consciousness, Murray discerns in his writings "the complex relation between on the one side the Christian civilised Indian, affirmer of white values, and on the other the Indian proud of his heritage and bitterly critical of white actions." Far from "a sense of self, if we may call it that, deriving entirely from Christian culture" that Krupat would assert, one sees the subtle and difficult maneuvering between two worlds that would have been necessary for Apess to be effective as a defender of Indian rights in the era in which he lived. Admitting that Apess, a mixed-blood, rules out "a natural or unmediated Indianness as a resource to fall back on" does not necessarily make him a "white mouthpiece."[39]

Barry O'Connell, who has undoubtedly given Apess the fullest treatment, publishing the only complete collection of his works, takes a view akin to Murray's. Apess sought to forge a bond within himself of "Pequot spiritual traditions with evangelical Methodism" more than a century after the Pequot were virtually destroyed as a coherent community.[40] He was a person of mixed descent who saw in Christianity not "the community of the colorblind saved"[41] but a potentially potent weapon to be used against Whites on behalf of non-

Whites. Rather than using his Christianity as a tool of assimilation, he employed it as a means to assert his own Native identity and nationalism. He may not have believed in a "pure" or "unmediated" Indianness, but he did anticipate modern pan-Indianism to a striking degree. He also presaged the political sensibility signified by the term "people of color" in his recognition that all non-White groups, including Jews, suffered from common problems at the hands of the dominant culture.[42]

The principal sources of information about Apess's life are the two autobiographical texts that he produced: the book-length *A Son of the Forest: The Experience of William Apess, a Native of the Forest, Written by Himself,* published in 1829, and the shorter "The Experience of the Missionary" contained in his volume *The Experiences of Five Christian Indians of the Pequot Tribe,* published in 1833. In many ways, these texts are as political and polemical as his explicitly reformist writings. They thus contribute to many of the mysteries about his life, obscuring details that might be important in determining the precise extent of his communitist commitment.

William Apess was born on January 31, 1798, in Colrain, Massachusetts. Both of his parents were Pequot. He states that his father was half White but that his mother was a full-blood, descended from King Philip, the noted Indian leader who in 1675 led Natives in a war against English settlers. Apess, however, rejects any claim to "royal" lineage, stating that all humanity is descended from Adam and Eve and that he considers himself "nothing more than a worm of the earth."[43] In reality, his mother was almost certainly of mixed ancestry as well, having probably been a slave and considered a "Negro" until her emancipation.

In this first paragraph of the first chapter of his autobiography, however, Apess through clever rhetorical moves is able to accomplish a number of important things. He links himself with King Philip, a great defender of Native sovereignty whom he sets side by side with George Washington as a patriot in his most militant address, "Eulogy on King Philip," delivered twice in Boston in 1836.[44] His disguising of his mother's African descent avoided contemporary attitudes against "race mixing" between Indians and Blacks. His contention that all persons are descended from Adam establishes Indians' common humanity with his White readers. Finally, the use of the language of evangelical Christianity subverts his readers' expectations about how Indians should talk and violates romanticized stereotypes that were prevalent even in Apess's time.[45]

The rest of Apess's work must be viewed as resistance literature, affirming Indian cultural and political identity over against the dominant culture. It thus exhibits communitism. Although the term "son of the forest" seems to be playing into romanticized Amer-European expectations for "noble savages," the work also avoids any use of the word "Indian," a term that Apess rejects.[46] In *Son of the Forest,* he states that he considers it a disgrace to be called by the nickname "Indian." Looking to the Bible, he finds no reference to "indians" "and therefore deduces that it was a word imported for the special purpose of degrading us." At other times, however, he thought it derived from some form of "in-genuity." He concludes, "But the proper term which ought to be applied to our nation, to distinguish it from the rest of the human family, is that of 'Natives'—and I humbly conceive that the natives of this country are the only people under heaven who have a just title to the name, inasmuch as we are the only people who retain the original complexion of our father Adam." [47] As Murray notes, "[W]hat is notable here is the way he has rejected a name from hostile outsiders (and one which calls Indians after someone else, making them secondary, and second best), via a bit of word-play which sees them positively (ingenuity) to a claim for their primacy, not just in America but in [all] God's creation." [48]

Once again, it is easy to see Apess's subversion through rhetoric at work. He invokes the language of evangelical Christianity, with its appeal to the Bible. In all his writings, in fact, he is constantly throwing up the norms, language, and tools of Christianity into the face of Amer-Europeans in order to expose their racism and subvert their use of the same material for racist ends. He once again announces the humanity of Natives ("to distinguish it from the rest of the human family") as he simultaneously asserts their sovereignty—by demanding their own name and by calling them a "nation." Finally, he claims added authenticity for Natives because they, not the Anglo-Saxon invaders of North America, are of the same skin color as Adam, the progenitor of all humanity.

O'Connell suggests that this is the key to understanding Apess's writing. He declares:

> One could read Apess as engaged in a Native American version of what Henry Louis Gates, Jr., calls "signifyin[g]" in the African American tradition, an act of doubling and redoubling the assumed meanings of words and concepts in a dominant discourse. The term, and the language acts it indicates, speaks of the wiliness necessary to members of any group who are despised and subjugated. For such persons, to speak and to write involve always a consciousness of two audiences, one of which shares one's own experience in substantial part, the other of which belongs to a culture of domination. Straightforwardness is impossible for it risks retaliation from the powerful but to echo faithfully their language and understandings is to participate in one's own suppression. Mimicry, parody, the pretense of stupidity, exaggerated irony, all become essential devices for the inescapable duplicity required to speak "truly" in such situations. [49]

To write in such a situation one must employ Occom's razor. It is this aspect of Apess that is overlooked by Krupat, Brumble, and Wong. Apess was familiar with David Walker's *Appeal to the Coloured Citizens of the World*, written contemporaneously with *Son of the Forest*.[50] Whereas Walker writes explicitly to persons of African descent, however, Apess appears to be writing to an Amer-European audience, thus the need for signifying becomes acute. Apess uses the model of the Christian confession, or conversion narrative, or the evangelical sermon, or the proselytizing tract, but he subverts their normative language even as he uses it. This can be seen by both his writings and his praxis.

In his autobiographical works, Apess describes his conversion and his constant backsliding. All his lapses into sin and drunkenness, however, occur when he is in the company of Amer-European Christians, not Indians. He never encounters problems when in the community of Natives, where he seems to be an integrated whole.[51] A pivotal incident in Apess's life was his involvement in the Mashpee Revolt of 1833, of which he was one of the leaders. In the petition he drafted for the tribe to the Massachusetts legislature, he asks how New Englanders could so wring their hands at the plight of the Cherokee in the South while ignoring Indians in their own state that "sigh in bondage." Echoing (but reversing) Walker's language, he titles the petition "An Indian's Appeal to the White Men of Massachusetts." In his history of the revolt, he uses the arguments of the states' rights/nullification debate currently raging to assert Indian rights to political sovereignty, claiming that Indians, like states, can simply nullify unconstitutional laws passed with regard to them.[52]

A key example of Apess's use of signification can be found in his use of the claim that America's indigenes are the Ten Lost Tribes of Israel. As previously noted, Apess states that Indians are the only people with Adam's original complexion, an assertion he repeats, a reference to his belief that Indians were the Lost Tribes.[53] As such, they, like the Jews, whom he considered people of color, would be Semites and thus closer in complexion to Adam than the Gentile Amer-Europeans.[54] He includes a lengthy appendix to *Son of the Forest* in which he outlines all the various arguments in favor of this thesis.[55] He returns to the theme in a sermon titled "The Indians: The Ten Lost Tribes."[56] Far from using this myth of dominance to slur his own people, however, Apess uses it to claim their common humanity. If Indians are the Ten Lost Tribes, they are every bit as human as the Amer-European invaders. If they are human, they are entitled to equal treatment. Beyond this, if they share a common ancestry with Euro-Americans, how is there any basis for racism and discrimination against them? Finally, if it is true, then they are entitled to sovereignty because "[a]ll nations are equally free. One nation has no right to infringe on the freedom of another."[57] They have more rights to North America than their "visitors," the Amer-Europeans.[58] This Apess is clearly closer to the one limned by Murray and O'Connell (the intelligent, crafty defender of Indian rights) than to the one denigrated by Krupat (the deracinated Christian "mouthpiece").

In similar fashion, Krupat misunderstands the role Christianity plays for Apess. In Apess's conversion to the religion of the dominant culture and his use of the language of evangelical revivalism, Krupat sees an assimilationist stance. There is little doubt that Apess sought acceptance for himself and other Natives within Christianity. Much of his autobiographical writing is taken up with the subject of his difficulties in being ordained by the Methodists, difficulties he attributes to the simple fact that he is Indian.[59] Before we proceed, however, it must be noted that Apess saw very little choice.

In 1637, more than 160 years before Apess's birth, the Pequots had been attacked and massacred at their principal village near present-day Mystic, Connecticut. The tribe was virtually wiped out. Those who survived were either scattered or sold into slavery. Though O'Connell may detect in Apess's Christianity traces of Pequot spirituality, that is virtually all there could be—traces. The Pequot culture and religion were effectively destroyed. Christianity is thus, for Apess, the only way forward. Throughout the autobiographical accounts, he expresses a sense of alienation from fellow Natives as a result of this fractured history. Before Apess could achieve full personhood, he had to break out of his isolation from other Indians and be in community with them. He must therefore break the power of Amer-Europeans over Natives that justified subordination. Paradoxically, he used evangelical Christianity as the means.[60] This does not mean, however, that Apess's Christianity was merely a Red mimesis of White religion.

For Apess, as for Anne Wampy (one of the Indians whose story he chronicles in *The Experiences of Five Christian Indians*), conversion to Christianity was not a rejection of Indian ways but a breaking through of personal isolation felt by individual Natives whose traditional lifeways were being eradicated. It was "an overcoming of the oppression of white people" that the Natives themselves had internalized.[61]

Apess explicitly rejects the assimilationist message preached by the missionaries. While admitting that there have been some pious missionaries who have performed good service in Indian Country, he makes clear that Whites have actually hindered conversion of Indians by sending among them preachers whose words and personal lifestyle are contrary to the gospel. He laments that Amer-Europeans have not treated Indians right. If this were done, both Indians and Whites would be blessed threefold, but sadly this has not been the case.[62] Instead, Apess looks forward to the day "not too far distant" when justice will be dispensed and the "white man, who has most cruelly oppressed his red brother, under the influence of that Gospel which he professes to believe" will receive what he deserves.[63] He refers to racism against Indians as the "national sin" of America and states that such a transgression "will be a terrible one to balance in the chancery of heaven."[64] Envisioning such a tribunal and returning explicitly to the question of race, he states:

> Now let me ask you, white man, if it is a disgrace for to eat, drink, and sleep with the image of God, or sit, or walk and talk with them. Or have you the folly to

think that the white man, being one in fifteen or sixteen, are the only beloved images of God? Assemble all nations together in your imagination, and let the whites be seated among them. . . . Now suppose these skins were put together, and each had its national crimes written upon it—which skin do you think would have the greatest? I will ask one more question. Can you charge the Indians with robbing a nation almost of their whole continent, and murdering their women and children, and then depriving the remainder of their lawful rights, that nature and God require them to have? And to cap the climax, rob another nation to till their grounds and welter out their days under the lash with hunger and fatigue. . . . I should look at all the skins, and I know when I cast my eye upon that white skin, and if I saw those crimes written upon it, I should enter my protest and cleave to that which is more honorable.[65]

This is hardly an assimilated Christian "mouthpiece." Instead the Pequot, unlike many of his contemporaries, uses Christianity to break through his alienation. He employs it to claim the full humanity of Indians and his own Indianness in particular. In his writings he increasingly reaches for an Indian Christian nationalism that aims at separatism.[66] O'Connell offers the best summary of Apess's communitist position when he writes, "He was an inventive survivor, a man who refused to be extinguished and who understood that he could not live on unless his people also did."[67] Unfortunately, Apess's survival skills ultimately failed him. His periodic lapses into drunkenness took their toll, and he died as a result of alcoholism in the spring of 1839.[68]

Just as William Apess has until recently received little scholarly attention, Peter Jones, another Native Christian, also has been virtually ignored.[69] Despite a beginning at recovery from a Native point of view made by Noley in *First White Frost* in 1991, the Anishinaabe clergyman is still widely regarded as a fully assimilated Christian Indian, thoroughly absorbed into dominant cultural structures—the same sort of "mouthpiece" that Apess has been accused of being. A review of his life and work, however, discloses a different picture. Jones and his family were deeply involved in Native community and passionate defenders of Native rights.

Jones's half-brother, George Henry, was a Methodist clergyman who became disenchanted with Christianity because of denominational factionalism and left the Church. He went on to become a translator, form a traveling Indian dance troupe, and author works about North American Natives.[70] Jones's niece, Catherine Soneegoh Sutton, was a tireless advocate in lectures, petitions, and letters and "was one of the few Indian women of her time [1823–1865] to work [within the dominant culture] for the rights of her people." She enjoyed some notable success.[71] Jones himself produced a dictionary and hymnal in Ojibway and translated Genesis, St. Matthew, St. John, and a portion of the Methodist *Discipline* into the language. He also rendered St. Luke into Mohawk. He is best known for his *Life and Journals* and the *History of the Ojebway Indians*, both published posthumously.

In her oral history of Peruvian Indian women, Kristin Herzog quotes Nancy Scheper-Hughes: "In the act of 'writing culture,' what emerges is always a highly subjective, partial, and fragmentary—but also deeply felt and personal—record of human lives based on eyewitness and testimony. The act of witnessing is what lends our work its moral (at times its almost theological) character. So-called participant observation has a way of drawing the ethnographer into spaces of human life where she or he might really prefer not to go at all and once there doesn't know how to go about getting out except through writing, which draws others there as well, making them party to the act of witnessing."[72] The problem is complicated in the case of Natives who are both emic and etic of the cultures about which they write. Carol Hampton (Caddo) writes:

> As tribal historians, American Indian scholars must maintain some degree of aloofness from their people. As academic historians, they have a commitment to remain objective in their search for the truth. Non-Indian historians of the Native American past frequently charge that American Indian scholars are in search of a "usable" past and that they are not disinterested observers. Objectivity, they assert, remains the sole domain of the non-Indian intellect. Little do they realize that the responsibility to Indian people requires a commitment to scholarly objectivity, not the reverse. Anything less would be a disservice to other Indians and the faith and trust they have placed in their own scholars. And yet, non-Indian historians correctly assess the situation, in that American Indian scholars have a further responsibility to aid Indian people in their struggle to survive in an alien society, a society which denigrates Indians and their traditions, a society which defames Indian heroes and degrades the original inhabitants of this land.[73]

Such historiographic problematics would have struck Jones and other 19th-century Native writers who produced tribal histories as bizarre and irrelevant. They had a need to communicate and record the ways of their people, "to set the record straight in telling non-natives the true details of their past and present," to "unfold . . . a moving theme of survival" and in so doing to participate in ensuring that survival.[74] No less than the writings of other Native authors, this was "literature with a purpose."

Peter Jones was born on January 1, 1802, "at the heights of Burlington Bay, Canada West" (present-day Hamilton, Ontario).[75] His father was an American surveyor of Welsh descent, who had come to Canada for work, and Tuhbenah-neequay, the daughter of Wahbanosay, a chief of the Mississauga Ojibway. In the autobiographical sketch that precedes his published journals, a volume compiled by his widow, Jones states that he had four brothers and five sisters. However, initially he names only his older sibling, Tyenteneged ("but better known as John Jones") and notes that this name was given to the brother by "the famous Captain Joseph Brant."[76] In these few opening paragraphs, in a similar manner to Apess, Jones rhetorically accomplishes a number of things. He establishes himself as both American and Canadian—but above all as Indian, of a "royal" family. By introducing his elder brother first by his less familiar Indian name, he stresses his own (as well as his brother's) Indianness. The effect is heightened by the reference to his family's connections to Joseph Brant (Mohawk), one of the most prominent Native chiefs and diplomats of the era. Years later, on a trip to England, Jones was stung by an article that appeared in the *York Courier* which claimed that he was duping the British "by pretending that I was an Indian Chief, when I was not an Indian Chief, nor even an Indian at all."[77]

Jones's early care was left largely to his mother, who, preferring traditional Anishinaabe religious practice, raised her children that way. Though it commonly said that Jones rejected Native religious traditions after his conversion to Christianity, his relationship to his people's traditions, and indeed to Christianity, is more complexed and nuanced. Brought up among the Anishinaabe until he was fourteen, he lived completely the life of a traditional Indian. At an appropriate age, his grandfather held a feast for him, dedicating him to the guardian care of the *animekeek,* or thunder *manitouk.* He was given the name Kahkewaquonaby, or Sacred Waving Feathers. At the ceremony, he was given a war club and bundle of eagle feathers, representing the power and flight, respectively, of the thunder god. In his autobiography, it is significant that Jones notes, "I have long since lost both, and consequently became powerless and wingless."[78] He in some sense lost not only his religion but part of his identity.

When he was fourteen, his father reasserted himself and sent him to an English school, where he read the Church of England catechism and the New Testament, "but the words had no effect upon my heart."[79] In 1820, his father induced him to receive baptism from an Anglican clergyman among the Mohawks. In an unpublished autobiographical manuscript, Jones notes his reason for agreeing, stating, "The principal motives which induced me to acquiesce with this wish, were, that I might be entitled to all the privileges of the white inhabitants."[80] Baptism was thus a way of grasping at equality with Amer-Europeans and perhaps of filling in some of the gaps in his own identity. As Noley states, however, he "was very sensitive to the commitments he was 'induced' to fall into. He was dissatisfied with his baptism experience and began to doubt that it would help him, since it didn't seem to help or change the whites for the better." Jones writes, "Sometimes whilst reading the Word of God, or hearing it preached, I would be almost persuaded to become a Christian; but when I looked at the conduct of the whites who were called Christians, and saw them drunk, quarreling, and fighting, cheating the poor Indians and acting as if there were no God, I was led to think there was no truth in the white man's religion, and felt inclined to fall back again to my old superstitions. My being baptized had no effect upon my life."[81]

Significantly, it was not Whites but Indians, particularly family, that led to his ultimate conversion. In 1823, he attended a prayer meeting at the home of Mohawk chief Thomas Davis, where the Bible was read and prayers were offered in Mohawk. He writes, "It is quite evident that the Spirit of the Lord has already began to move upon the hearts of this people."[82] A short while later, he accompanied his sister Mary to a Methodist camp meeting: "I was prompted by curiosity to go and see how the Methodists worshipped the Great Spirit in the wilderness."[83] While there, "[s]ome strange feeling came over my mind, and I was led to believe that the Supreme Being was in the midst of his people who were now engaged in worshipping him."[84] He began to believe that the preachers were addressing him directly. When his brother John arrived and ridiculed the enthusiasts, Peter argued that what was happening was of the Great Spirit.

Near the end of the encampment, Jones withdrew by himself into the forest. He described the incident: "Towards evening I retired into the solitary wilderness to try to pray to the Great Spirit. I knelt down by the side of a fallen tree. The rattling of the leaves over my head with the wind, made me uneasy. I retired further into the woods, and then wrestled with God in prayer, who helped me resolve that I would go back to the camp and get the people to pray for me."[85] A voice came to him, saying, "Do you wish to obtain religion and serve the Lord?" It was the voice not of the Christian god but of a non-Native preacher named Reynolds. Though Jones replied in the affirmative, upon his return to camp, his heart hardened against the imported religion once more. Later that night, after he had gone to bed, a number of the preachers awakened him, crying, "Arise, Peter, and go with us to the prayer meeting, and get your soul converted. Your sister Mary has already obtained the Spirit of adoption, and you must seek the same blessing."[86] Determined to have the same experience, he went to his sister, and it was her exhorting that finally converted him.[87]

Though he went on to become a highly successful Christian worker in both the United States and Canada, it is clear from both his writings and his praxis that his conversion did not conform entirely to traditional Western norms. He undoubtedly wanted Christianity and "civilization" for Natives. He occasionally uses terms like "superstition" and "pagan" to refer traditional religious practice. At the same time, however, he also speaks of it in positive terms. In his autobiographical material, he mentions the "pleasure" he experienced in participating in a sacred bear-oil feast at the present site of Rochester, where he nonetheless had to "drink about a gill of what was not any more palatable than castor oil."[88] In all his writings, he employs the terms "Great Spirit," "Good Spirit," or "Supreme Being" interchangeably with the Christian name "God." He notes that Natives believe that the same Great Spirit created all nations of humanity and placed the Indians in America, giving them their own distinct languages, complexion, and religions and telling them that it "would be wrong and give great offense to their Creator, to forsake the old ways of their forefathers."[89]

His use of pejorative terms for Native religion in his writings, like his use of the "poor Indian" theme, must be viewed as part of his address to a White audience, whom he hoped to influence. His conversion, however, conforms to Joseph Epes Brown's description of Native adaptation to Christianity generally. As Brown puts it, "The historical phenomenon is thus not conversion as understood in exclusivistic manner by the bearers of Christianity, but rather a continuation of the people's ancient and traditional facility for what may be termed nonexclusive cumulative adhesion."[90]

In his written works, he is a vociferous critic of Whites both for their failure to conform to the dictates of their religion and for their treatment of Natives in general.[91] In his *History,* he writes, "Before the treacherous Spaniard made his appearance in our country the Indian could sleep peacefully in his wigwam without fear of being hunted by bloodhounds; as if the owners of its soil were beasts of prey rather than men of like passions with themselves; or as if the rich mines of Mexico were of greater value than the lives and souls of the poor aborigines, whom the Good Spirit had made lords of the land where His providence had seen fit to place them. The real man is gone, and a strange people occupy his place."[92] Like Apess, he thus asserts not only inherent Native sovereignty over North America but a primacy in the order of Creation.

Europeans were at first welcomed, he notes, but they wanted more and more. Finally, Natives were forced to defend what was theirs. "Goaded to despair, they clutched the deadly tomahawk, and sought to wield it against the encroaching whites; but, instead of conquering, the act only afforded to the calculating, remorseless foe, a pretext for a more general slaughter of the defenseless natives. Then, as if disease and the musket—both imported by whites—could not mow down the Indian fast enough, the fire-waters crept in and began to gnaw their very vitals, debasing their morals, lowering their dignity, spreading contentions, confusion and death."[93]

Alcohol, as a European import, comes in for special attack by Jones, as it did for Occom and Apess before him. Repeatedly he condemns Europeans for introduction of liquor. He declares, "Since my conversion to God, one thing has made my heart very glad, and which is, that amidst all the temptations and examples of drunkenness to which I was exposed, I never fell into that vice, although most of my young companions did. I always viewed drunkenness as beneath the character of an Indian. If at any time I was persuaded to take a little of the fire-water, I always felt sorry for it afterwards, especially when I reflected how much evil it had done to my poor countrymen, many thousands of whom have had their days shortened by it, and been hurried to destruction. Oh the miseries of drunkenness! Would to God that Indians had never tasted the fire-water!"[94]

Jones concludes that Whites have more to atone for in their treatment of Indians than they ever will be able. In language reminiscent of Apess, he looks to the ultimate judgment, writing, "Oh, what an awful account at the day of

judgment must the unprincipled white man give, who has been an agent of
Satan in the extermination of the original proprietors of the American soil!
Will not the blood of the red man be required at *his* hands, who, for paltry
gain, has impaired the minds, corrupted the morals, and ruined the constitu-
tions of a once hardy and numerous race?"[95] Such judgment, however, extends
to crimes far more numerous than simply spiritous drink. Jones declares sarcastically, "When I think of the long catalogue of evils entailed on my poor unhappy countrymen, my heart bleeds, not only on their account, but also for
their destroyers, who, coming from a land of light and knowledge, are without
excuse. Poor deluded beings! Whatever their pretensions to Christianity may
have been, it is evident the love of God was not in their hearts; for that love
extends to all mankind, and constrains to acts of mercy, but never impels to
deeds of death."[96]

Jones also takes up the issue that so interested William Apess—the debate
over the origins of Natives in the Americas. In 1831, he had discussed the
matter with Richard Watson, a notable English divine.[97] In his *History of the
Ojebway Indians,* he states that after reading Elias Boudinot's *The Star in the
West*[98] and "Smith's View of the Hebrews" he was inclined to believe that Natives were descended from the Lost Tribes of Israel. He notes that there are
many things to recommend the opinion, but there are also many against it. In
the end, dissimilarities outweigh similarities. He decides that the Bering Strait
theory is probably the more correct view. He bases this on the fact that many
Native nations look back to the West as either the home of the dead or a place
of paradise. Just as the Jews of the Exodus remembered the "leeks and onions
in Egypt," this looking toward the West is, he believes, some racial memory of
a migration. He advocates sending Indians to Asia nearest the Strait to examine
the language, customs, and manners of the inhabitants there. This "would not
only be satisfactory to know the origin of my countrymen, but might be the
means of introducing pure Christianity among the Tartars by sending native
missions from America to the other side of the great waters." However, he
leaves "the subject for the consideration of all who feel any interest in this
puzzling question."[99]

In his praxis as well as his writing, Jones championed Native community. In
the *History,* he defended Natives against the prevalent charge of cannibalism,
pointing out that Whites have made such assertions based on misinformation
and the confusion of the mythological cannibals, like the *windigo* of the Anishinaabe, with reality. He steadfastly maintained to Amer-European audiences the
capacity of Natives to progress through instruction.[100] He also authored much
protest literature. In June 1830, he wrote to Sir John Colborne of the Canadian
governmental authorities on behalf of the St. Clair Indians, voicing their request that they be allowed to remain on their ancestral lands "in as much, as
the graves of their fathers were placed here and that it was their wish to lay

down by the side of them." In the same letter, he advised of the St. Clair rejection of European ways and stated his agreement with their objections to conversion to Christianity.[101] The following year, he assisted the Anishinaabe chiefs of Lake Huron in drafting a petition to King William IV of Great Britain. The document listed a long series of grievances against Whites and commissioned Jones to act as the chiefs' ambassador to take up the matter with the monarch.[102] When he met with Queen Victoria on a later trip to England, he took the opportunity to lay before her (after presenting it to her minister Lord Glenelg) a petition from his people at River Credit in Upper Canada relating to "title-deeds" requested for her "red children." In his journal, he wrote that after presenting it, "I then proceeded to give her the meaning of the wampum [that was attached]; and told her that the white wampum signified the loyal and good feeling which prevails amongst the Indians towards Her Majesty and Her Government; but that the black wampum was designed to tell Her Majesty that their hearts were troubled on account of their having no title-deeds for their lands; and that they sent their petition and wampum that Her Majesty might be pleased to take out all the black wampum, so that the string might be all white." [103]

Jones was plagued by recurring bouts of ill health for many years, but that did not stop his activities on behalf of his community. In 1847, he attempted to resign his chieftainship, but his people refused to accept his resignation. He died on May 28, 1856. His wife, Eliza, completed publication of his autobiography, journals, and history.

Fields, Boudinot, and Ridge

The policy of the United States under George Washington was one of assimilation of Indians in situ by re-creating them as yeoman farmers. After the Louisiana Purchase in 1803, however, President Thomas Jefferson suggested that the Native nations exchange their lands in the East for territory west of the Mississippi River, which would then become the permanent line of White settlement. The Virginian even went so far as to suggest a constitutional amendment guaranteeing Native rights to land in the West. Though Jefferson quickly dropped the idea, removal remained a topic of public debate and became an increasing inevitability as Amer-Europeans in the new Republic hungered for Indian lands.[104] In 1825, James Barbour, President John Quincy Adams's secretary of war, advanced a scheme for voluntary "colonization" of individual Indians, rather than entire groups, in a new vast Indian Territory west of the Mississippi, where they would receive individual parcels of land, thus breaking up the "tribal mass." The plan paralleled proposals to colonize persons of African descent in Africa. It reflected an Amer-European approach to all social problems, involving solution through physical removal of "undesirables" from White presence.[105]

The election of Andrew Jackson as president in 1828 ensured that relocation would shortly become federal policy. The narrow passage of the Removal Act of 1830 and presidential signature on May 24 of that year sealed it. The removal crises of the 1820s and 1830s tore the Cherokee Nation apart and culminated in the forced march of the Trail of Tears in 1838. One-fourth of the Cherokee would die en route to Oklahoma.[106] In varying ways, these events form the backdrop of the work of Richard Fields, Elias Boudinot, and John Rollin Ridge.

Though Cherokee Removal was not completed until 1839, the first Cherokee moved beyond the Mississippi in 1794.[107] That year, fleeing retaliation for the so-called Mussel Shoals Massacre, Diwa'li (The Bowl, or John Bowles) and his band moved first to Missouri and later to Arkansas. In the winter of 1819–1820, the group relocated again, this time into Texas. Soon thereafter they were joined by Richard Fields.

Much about Fields's life is shrouded in mystery. No reliable portraits of him exist. He was the great-grandson of Ludovic Grant, a Scottish trader who married a Cherokee woman in the early 18th century. He is described variously as one-half, one-fourth, and one-eighth Cherokee. He fought the British in the War of 1812 and rose to prominence as a diplomat and warrior in the East. Though he filed a claim on land in Missouri in 1804, his activities are documented in the East as late as 1814. He apparently went directly to Texas around 1820. Most often, he is described by non-Native historians as an arrogant and misled dupe of White designs in Texas. Native assessments, however, sharply differ. Emmet Starr (Cherokee) writes that he was "a man of striking personality, of considerable intelligence and although he spoke the English language fluently and preferably, he was not able to sign his name. From the time that he joined [the Texas Cherokee] until his death, he was untiring in his efforts to obtain a title for the Cherokees, to the land on which they resided."[108] Despite his handicap with written English, his letters and oratory on behalf of his people open an interesting window on the Removal period and form a communitist legacy for the Cherokee.

It is not known whether Chief Bowles and his group had the permission of the Spanish government to enter Texas. Immediately upon his arrival, however, Fields undertook a diplomatic initiative to secure good title to the land they occupied so that they might remain there unmolested. On February 1, 1822, following the Mexican revolution, he wrote to James Dill, the alcalde of Nacogdoches: "Dieor Sur I wish to fall at your feet and omblay ask you what must be Dun with us pur Indians [. W]e have som Grants that was give to us when we live under the Spanish government and we wish you to send us nuws by the Next mal whether that will be Reverd or Not."[109] According to Starr, the letter continued, "And if we were permitted, we will come as soon as possible to present ourselves before you in a manner agreeable to our talents. If we present ourselves in a rough manner, we pray you to right us. Our intentions are good toward the government."[110] The missive is fascinating in several ways. Because of Fields's difficulty with writing, and his probable employ therefore of an amanuensis, it is impossible to know whether the word at the end of the last sentence means "revered" or "reversed." It is also difficult to know if "pur" is "poor" or "pure." Perhaps the ambiguity worked in Fields's favor. At any rate, though he uses the self-abasing language of the "poor Indian" throughout (apologizing in advance for presenting himself in a rude manner and praying to the alcalde for correction), one must remember the diplomatic language of subalterns and the purpose of the letter. Here the wordplay is the thing by which Fields may hope to catch the conscience of the king.

Dill ignored the Cherokee petition. Undaunted, however, Fields apparently forwarded a copy of the letter to Antonio Martínez, governor of the province of Texas. On November 8, when he still had received no satisfactory reply, Fields journeyed to Bexar (San Antonio) to see the new governor, José Felix Trespalacios. The administrator executed an agreement promising that the Cherokee could continue to "cultivate their lands and sow their crops in free and peaceful possession" until his superiors could rule on the matter.[111] Having obtained at least temporary—and highly provisional—relief, the Cherokee chief and a delegation, including Bowles, departed for Mexico City, carrying the document and a letter of introduction.

Unfortunately, the Cherokees arrived at an extremely inopportune time. Augustin de Iturbide, the military leader that secured Mexican independence from Spain and served as its ruler, had overthrown the revolutionary government in May 1822, prorogued congress, and established himself as emperor. In January 1823, his new junta promulgated an Imperial Colonization Law. Arriving late that month or in early February, the delegation never met with Iturbide, who was himself overthrown on March 19. A quick petition to the newly reestablished congress failed. Instead, the Cherokees were told in late April that they could return to Texas and that the Trespalacios-Fields agreement would remain provisionally in force, pending final determination at an unspecified later date. Further, the military commandant of the area was instructed to deny future Cherokee embassies passports to travel to the capital and to prohibit further Cherokee immigration.

Over the next year, Fields worked to consolidate the Cherokee position. He determined to unite all the Indian tribes in Texas in a single alliance. On March 6, 1824, he wrote to José Antonio Saucedo, the governor, informing him of the plan. In this letter he claimed, "The Superior Government has granted me in this province, a territory sufficient for me and that part of the tribe of Indians dependent on me to settle on, and also a commission to command all the Indian tribes and nations that are in the four eastern provinces."[112] He re-

quested that the jefe notify all the Indian nations of a Grand Council to be
held at Fields's home for the purposes of concluding a treaty. The meeting was
held on August 20, 1824, with all tribes except the Comanche and the Tonkawa
in attendance. On September 1, he wrote again to Saucedo, telling him that all
had "accepted the terms offered them" and stating that the conference purpose
was "to bring them in union one tribe with another, and all to be under true
subordination to our new republican government."[113]

Despite Fields's profession of fidelity to the government, and probably with
good reason, the prospect of a unified Native population struck fear in the
Mexicans. Minister of Relations Lúcas Alamán wrote to the Cherokee chief,
accusing him of being in league with the United States. Fields replied that his
people "have nothing to do with Anglo Americans here, and we will not submit
to their laws, or dictates, but we do, and always will, submit to the laws and
orders emanating from the Mexican nation."[114]

Two days before the Grand Council meeting, the Mexican congress passed a
National Colonization Law, and on March 25, 1825, the legislature of Coahuila
and Texas followed suit. Less than a month later, three grants were made to
settle 2,000 families on Indian territory. Particularly infuriating to Fields was a
grant to Hayden Edwards to locate 800 families on Cherokee lands. Stephen
Austin, head of a thriving colony to the west, became convinced that Fields and
the Natives were preparing for countermeasures. For over a year, tensions ran
high.

In the summer of 1826, Fields wrote to Austin and Samuel Norris, alcalde of
Nacogdoches, adding to their alarm. In a masterful example of Native indirec-
tion, he advised Austin that the Comanche planned "to attack your colony and
destroy it entirely, or compel the settlers to leave it by the beginning of the
next moon." To Norris, he asked for permission to take to the field against the
Comanche, Tonkawa, Waco, and Taovaya, adding, "[W]e consider ourselves
sons of the Mexicans, and we cheerfully offer our persons and the last drop of
our blood for the defense of the country. . . . [T]he son does no wrong when
he spills blood in defense of his down trodden father." As Dianna Everett notes,
"Fields's veiled threat was not lost on the empresario."[115] The Cherokee began
to prepare for war.

In a last effort to avoid conflict and clear title to Cherokee holdings, Fields
had dispatched John Dunn Hunter, a white adventurer, to Mexico City to plead
their cause. Hunter arrived in the capital on March 19, 1826, but when his
mission failed, he returned in September. An incensed Fields addressed his people. According to an account recorded by Ellis P. Bean, Indian agent for the
Mexican government, who was present, the speech ran:

> In my old days, I traveled two thousand miles to the City of Mexico to beg some
> lands to settle a poor orphan tribe of Red People, who looked to me for protection.

I was promised lands for them after staying one year in Mexico and spending all I had. I then came to my people and waited two years, and then sent Mr. Hunter, after selling my stock to provide him money for his expenses. When he got there, he stated his mission to the government. They said they knew nothing of this Richard Fields and treated him with contempt. I am a Red Man and a man of honor and can't be imposed on this way. We will lift up our tomahawks and fight for land with all those friendly tribes that wish land also. If I am beaten, I will resign to fate, and if not, I will hold lands by the force of my red warriors.[116]

Meanwhile, Hayden Edwards and his brother Benjamin found that their grant conflicted with earlier Spanish grants. Faced with the loss of their title, they decided to attempt to overthrow Mexican rule and establish an independent nation. At his Amer-European adviser's urging, Fields and Hunter met with the rebels in Nacogdoches on December 21. After three days of negotiations, a compact was drafted forming a "Union, League, and Confederation" and recognizing Indian land claims. The treaty was signed by Fields and Hunter on behalf of the Cherokee. An old stone fort was seized, and the Republic of Fredonia was proclaimed. Symbolizing the supposed equality of its Red and White founders, the flag of the breakaway nation consisted of one red and one white stripe, bearing the motto, "Independence, Freedom, and Justice."

The new country, however, was short-lived. Stephen Austin, who himself would revolt against Mexico ten years later, set out to quell the rebellion. He called for a mobilization. Through emissaries, he and Ellis Bean persuaded Bowles and another key chief, Big Mush, to support Mexico. The rebels, realizing that their attempt had failed, abandoned the fort.

In exchange for promises of land, Bowles ordered the assassination of Fields, who was tracked down near the Sabine River and killed. Not until February 23, 1836, did the Cherokee obtain title to their land, pursuant to a treaty with the government of the new Republic of Texas. Three years later, they were driven from their lands by the army of that same Republic and forced to immigrate to Indian Territory to the north.[117]

While Richard Fields was preparing to abandon words for warfare in the far West, Elias Boudinot was on a lecture tour. Making stops in such genteel centers of Amer-European civilization as Charleston, New York, Boston, and Philadelphia, he hoped to raise the funds to start a newspaper and a national academy on the Western model in the Cherokee Nation. In each locale he delivered essentially the same speech, outlining the progress made by his people on the road of civilization. On May 26, 1826, as Fields planned for rebellion, Boudinot was entering the First Presbyterian Church in Philadelphia. Carriages delivered the aristocracy of the City of Brotherly Love, and "[w]ith curiosity and anticipation the audience prepared to listen to an Indian direct from the wild."[118] This "copper-colored son of the southern Appalachians" was "handsome, and he looked, even in the conventional dress of the white man, every inch the

Indian." [119] Through his remarks, Boudinot hoped to address "the heart and conscience of America." [120] He knew that the church was going to publish his oration as a tract. [121]

Addressing the assembled crowd, Boudinot asked:

> What is an Indian? Is he not formed of the same materials with yourself? For "of one blood God created all the nations that dwell on the face of the earth." Though it be true that he is ignorant, that he is a heathen, that he is a savage; yet he is no more than all others have been under similar circumstances. Eighteen centuries ago what were the inhabitants of Great Britain?
>
> You here behold an *Indian*, my kindred are *Indians*, and my fathers sleeping in the wilderness grave—they too were *Indians*. But I am not as my fathers were— broader means and nobler influences have fallen upon me. Yet I was not born as thousands are, in a stately dome and amid the congratulations of the great, for on a little hill, in a lonely cabin, overspread by the forest oak, I drew my first breath; and in a language unknown to learned and polished nations, I learnt to lisp my fond mother's name. In after days, I have had greater advantages than most of my race; and I now stand before you delegated by my native country to seek her interest, to labor for her respectability, and by my public efforts to assist in raising her to an equal standing with other nations of the earth. [122]

He argued in favor of the "practicability of civilizing the Indians" and maintained that the stale phrase "Do what you will, an Indian will still be an Indian" must be banished from common speech. After outlining the steps taken by the Cherokee toward westernization, he concluded, "When before did a nation of Indians step forward and ask for the means of civilization? . . . I ask you, shall red men live, or shall they be swept from the earth? With you and this public at large, the decision chiefly rests. Must they perish? Must they all, like the unfortunate Creeks, (victims of the unchristian policy of certain persons,) go down in sorrow to their grave? . . . They hang upon your mercy as to a garment. Will you push them from you, or will you save them? Let humanity answer." [123]

Though dispatched on his journey by the Cherokee National Council, through his words Boudinot betrayed that he was distant from his people in more than geography. In his "save the savages" argument, he revealed his fervent desire to trade "savagism" for "civilization." [124] It is the tragedy of his life that though he truly wanted to defend his community, he often sought to do so by abandoning it. As Theda Perdue writes, "Throughout his life, Boudinot maintained that the preservation of his people depended solely upon abandonment of their own traditions, culture, and history." [125]

Boudinot was born Gallegina (or Kuh-le-ga-nah, or Buck) into a favored world of privilege in 1803. His mother and father, Oo-Watie (or Watie) and Susan Reese, were members of the "progressive" faction of Cherokee who, with Watie's brother The Ridge, had abandoned a traditional lifestyle in Hiwassee,

Tennessee, to move to Western-style farms in Oothcaloga, Georgia.[126] At age six, his parents sent him to school with his cousin, John Ridge, at a Moravian school at Springplace. The demands of the missionaries there on English, Western dress and customs, and Christian teachings meant that Boudinot "left behind even that remnant of Cherokee culture which existed at Oothcaloga."[127]

Young Buck remained at Springplace until 1817, when he left to enroll, along with two other Cherokee boys, at the Foreign Mission School in Cornwall, Connecticut. His cousin John would soon follow.[128] On the way to Cornwall, the Cherokees and their chaperon stopped at the home of Elias Boudinot, the head of the American Bible Society and a former member of the Continental Congress. Following the visit, Buck Watie assumed the name of the aged man and thereafter was known as Elias Boudinot.[129]

The newly christened Boudinot quickly established himself as one of the brightest students at the school. In 1820, he converted to Christianity and exhibited such talent and piety that the American Board of Commissioners for Foreign Missions (ABCFM) arranged for him to enter Andover Theological Seminary. A severe bout of illness, however, prevented him from continuing his education, and in 1822 he returned to the Cherokee Nation. The Cornwall Academy had been formative in his development, though. Perdue notes, "While he was a student in New England, Boudinot began to develop many of the ideas that would shape his career. As a convert to an evangelical Christianity, he was not content with merely his own spiritual well-being. Instead, he assumed responsibility for the welfare of his people and felt that he personally must help bring them the blessings of Christian 'civilization.' He did not believe that such an undertaking should be an individual effort but insisted that all Christians had a moral obligation to assist the transformation of 'savage' societies."[130]

Shortly after his return to Georgia, as part of his mission to Christianize his people, Boudinot published in Cherokee, using the syllabary developed by Sequoyah, *Poor Sarah, or The Indian Woman*. Shortly thereafter, he communicated a copy of the short fiction to Elisha Bates, a prominent Ohio Quaker and publisher. Through Bates, the volume was reprinted in English as *Poor Sarah, or Religion Exemplified in the Life and Death of an Indian Woman*, and like Occom's "Sermon Preached at the Execution of Moses Paul, An Indian," it became a national best-seller.[131]

Poor Sarah often is cited erroneously as the first novel by a Native American. Both Hobson and Trafzer describe it as such. Andrew Wiget notes that its brevity, only twelve pages, prevents the booklet from truly being considered a novel, but he nonetheless hails Boudinot as earning with its publication "the well-deserved title of the Father of Native American literature."[132] In reality, the production of this "first" (again demonstrating Warrior's rhetoric of novelty) Native fiction is clouded. As Wiget notes, "Exactly how the manuscript came to Bates may never be known. Neither Boudinot or [*sic*] Bates left a journal, so one simply cannot get close enough to their daily lives to establish the moment of communication."[133] The precise role of Bates is unclear, and he may merely have used Boudinot as a convenient front behind which to disseminate the tract about Indians. Boudinot simply translated a preexisting pamphlet into Cherokee, though in an era when plagiarism rules were not as well defined as they are today, he claimed authorship.[134]

The proselytizing tract is told by two narrators, Sarah herself and "Misse," an educated White woman who becomes her friend when Sarah comes to her door to beg bread. It follows the story of Sarah, who, beaten by her husband, finds great inner peace and joy when she "gives her heart to Jesus" and begins attending church regularly. She does not, however, leave her abusive spouse. Fortunately, the husband dies, and Sarah finds true happiness in the Church. Leading the devout life of a "poor Indian widow," Sarah labors virtuously and diligently until, "ripe for heavenly glories," she dies.[135]

Wiget notes, "By using two narrators, Boudinot could thus touch two audiences at once: Sarah's example could hearten struggling Indian proselytes or converts and, through Misse's response, prick the comfortable consciences of white Protestants from venerable Puritan families."[136] Published the same year that James Fenimore Cooper wrote his first great Indian romances, *Poor Sarah* reveals little in the way of communitist sentiments. Rather, it conforms closely to the Vanishing Indian myth, depicting Indians as "a disappearing people who deserved Christian compassion and humanitarian sympathy."[137]

Times were changing rapidly for the Cherokee as Amer-Europeans began to press in upon them. Boudinot developed a close relationship with Samuel Worcester, a Protestant missionary from the ABCFM, and worked with him to translate the Christian scriptures. So close were the two that when Boudinot died, the clergyman would declare, "They have cut off my right arm."[138] In 1825, the Cherokee National Council asked Boudinot to become editor of a new bilingual national newspaper. He undertook his 1826 tour, during which he delivered "An Address to the Whites," to obtain funds to purchase a printing press. He proved "a conscientious editor, thoroughly devoted to the process of acculturation and Christianization," having overcome his pain at the racism he and John Ridge experienced in Cornwall. Boudinot's biographer, Ralph Henry Gabriel, writes, "Elias Boudinot sensed the helplessness of a people who understood nothing of the world beyond their mountains. He hoped to become a leader who would guide the development of civilization among the Cherokees. Sequoyah had forged the necessary tools. Samuel Worcester had the breadth of mind necessary for the transfer of man's literature to the Cherokee. Boudinot had become partner to Worcester and successor to Sequoyah in the task of guiding the course of Cherokee thinking."[139] This mixture of ambition and patronizing care, often reminiscent of Amer-European reformers, characterized Boudinot's work for the remainder of his life. The Cherokee *Phoenix* became

Boudinot's weapon. He drew its name from "An Address to the Whites": "[U]n-der such protection, and with such assistance [from the federal government and the American people], the Indian must rise like the Phoenix, after having wallowed for ages in ignorance and barbarity."[140] As stated by Boudinot, the paper's goals included promoting the progress of "literature, Civilization, and Religion among the Cherokees."[141] More than any other individual, Boudinot sought to demonstrate that the Cherokee were deserving of inclusion among the Five *Civilized* Tribes.

During the early Removal crisis, the *Phoenix* was a powerful tool in fostering support among well-meaning Amer-Europeans and in keeping the Cherokee informed. Opposed to White encroachment and to Removal, Boudinot regu-larly wrote editorials attacking both. When the state of Georgia passed legisla-tion purporting to extend its jurisdiction over the Cherokee Nation, Boudinot declared: "We entreat you, respected reader,—we implore you, to pause after perusing the above facts, and reflect upon the effects of *civilized* legislation over poor *savages.* The laws which are the result of this legislation, are framed ex-pressly against us, and not a clause in our favor. We cannot be a party or witness in the courts where a white man is a party. Here is the secret. *Full license to our oppressors, and every avenue of justice closed against us.* Yes, this is the bitter cup prepared for us by a *republican* and *religious* Government— we shall drink it to the very dregs."[142] This is communitist language as sharp and direct as any by William Apess or Peter Jones. In 1829, he changed the name of the newspaper to *Phoenix and Indians' Advocate* in order to emphasize that it defended all Indians in the matter of Removal.[143]

The precise reasons why Boudinot gave up opposition to Removal are not certain. He continued to denounce it as late as 1831. Gabriel suggests that in the face of continual imposition by Amer-Europeans, he saw that when Red and Whites met, Indians degenerated. This theory ignores, however, his consis-tent stance in favor of assimilation and his espousal of Christianity. Theda Per-due contends that he became "dismayed" and "disillusioned" after the Cherokee victory in the U.S. Supreme Court in *Worcester v. Georgia* by the federal gov-ernment's refusal to enforce that decision.[144] In fact, it was not Boudinot but his partner and mentor, Samuel Worcester, a party in the case, who became disillusioned. As surely as John Dunn Hunter helped lead Richard Fields to disaster, Worcester now contributed to Boudinot's downfall. When it became clear that President Jackson would do nothing to carry out the Supreme Court edict, he urged Boudinot to organize a pro-Removal party. In July 1832, the editor signed a petition supporting Removal.[145] As a result of his change in position, he was forced by the Cherokee government of John Ross, which op-posed Removal, to resign as editor of the *Phoenix.*[146]

On December 29, 1835, Boudinot joined a small number of other pro-Removal Cherokees, including The Ridge and his son John and his brother

Stand Watie, in signing the Treaty of New Echota, agreeing to exchange Cherokee lands for territory in the West. The group knew that they acted against the
desires of the vast majority of Cherokees and that they violated Cherokee law
in ceding land. For their crime, they could be punished by death. As he made
his mark, The Ridge, who had been responsible for drawing up the law, reportedly said, "I have signed my death warrant." [147]

Shortly before his departure for Indian Territory in 1837, Boudinot published his final book, a pamphlet supporting the pro-Removal position, entitled
"Letters and Other Papers Relating to Cherokee Affairs: Being a Reply to Sundry Publications Authorized by John Ross." In it, again reflecting his patronizing attitude toward his own people, he defended the Treaty of New Echota,
claiming that majority rule was not always the correct one, especially in an
"Indian community." He declared, "If one hundred persons are ignorant of
their true situation, and are so completely blinded as not to see the destruction
that awaits them, we can see strong reasons to justify the action of a minority
of fifty persons—to do what the majority *would do* if they understood their
condition—to save a *nation* from political thraldom and moral degradation." [148]
As historian William McLoughlin points out, however, the signers were not 50
out of 100; they were 75 out of more than 15,000. [149] Concluding the volume,
Boudinot argued that Removal was "the only *practicable* remedy." The alternative was extinction. He wrote, "Are our people destined to such a catastrophe?
Are we to run the race of all our brethren who have gone before us, and of
whom hardly any thing is known but their name, and, perhaps, only here and
there a solitary being, walking, 'as a ghost over the ashes of his fathers,' to
remind a stranger that such a race *once* existed? May God preserve us from
such a destiny." [150] Congress reprinted the booklet at public expense as an answer to the petition of 15,000 Cherokees who sought to prevent ratification of
the treaty. [151]

After the Trail of Tears, Boudinot, The Ridge, and John Ridge were seized
and executed by forces loyal to John Ross's government. Like others, Boudinot
had realized the danger in his actions at New Echota. In signing, he spoke to
the assembly: "I know that I take my life in my hand, as our fathers have also
done. . . . Our friends can then cross the great river, but [those opposing
Removal] will put us across the dread river of death. We can die, but the great
Cherokee Nation will be saved. They will not be annihilated; they can live. Oh,
what is a man worth who will not dare to die for his people? Who is there
here that will not perish, if this great Nation may be saved?" [152] On June 22,
1839, Elias Boudinot paid that price.

Perdue defends Boudinot, writing:

Under Cherokee law, Boudinot received the punishment he deserved. He had ceded
Cherokee land without authorization and had subjected his people to a tortuous

relocation. . . . In an age of cultural pluralism, militant tribalism, and objective ethnohistory, one is tempted to condemn Elias Boudinot not only for his part in negotiating Cherokee removal but also for his narrow view of culture and society. But the issues of the twentieth century were not those of the nineteenth. . . . The survival he envisioned was not individual but involved the preservation of tribal sovereignty and ethnic identity. The Cherokees, he insisted, could achieve respect and admiration as a "civilized" Indian people from the rest of mankind. No price, even removal, was too high to pay for that recognition.[153]

Even so, in his pursuit of "civilization" for the Cherokee, it says much about his views of community that Elias Boudinot could not, over the course of his lifetime, ever envision any positive alternative other than assimilation or Removal.

The hills of Oklahoma might seemed far removed from the goldfields of California, the setting of much of the work of John Rollin Ridge, but the events of July 1839 were nonetheless to exert a powerful influence over the Cherokee poet, journalist, and novelist. Rollin Ridge was the son of John Ridge, one of the signers of the Treaty of New Echota. On July 22, as a twelve-year-old, he watched helplessly as his father was seized by a group of men loyal to the Cherokee government and executed for treason. Throughout his life, he told and retold the story of the incident, in bars, in letters, to anyone who would listen. It kindled in him a desire for revenge that never left him and shaped his thought and his writings.

John Rollin Ridge was born on March 19, 1827, in the Cherokee Nation in current-day Georgia. With his parents and other members of the pro-Removal faction, he moved to Indian Territory following the New Echota treaty. After his father's death, he and his mother, fearing for their own lives, fled to Fayetteville, Arkansas. In 1843, like his father and his cousin Elias Boudinot, he went east to school, attending the Great Barrington Academy in Great Barrington, Massachusetts. In 1845, he returned to Arkansas, where he read law.

According to David Farmer and Rennard Strickland (Cherokee/Osage), Ridge "remembered his teenage years as a time of hard riding back and forth across the Cherokee-Arkansas border, participating in the skirmishes and guerrilla warfare of the continuing Ross-Ridge vendetta."[154] Though the continued animosity and periodic raids undoubtedly affected the mind of the young Ridge and hardened his attitude against John Ross, whom he saw as responsible for his father's death, his participation is not documented and seems almost certainly the product of his desires rather than any historical reality. As early as his time at Great Barrington, Rollin wrote to his cousin Stand Watie, the brother of Elias Boudinot and the one leader of the pro-Removal party that had escaped execution, expressing his hope for vengeance, stating, "If there is no law in a Nation to [missing portion] those who take the lives of their fellow men it [is impos?]sible to have justice done . . . unless it is [missing portion] ties of kindred blood to the slain."[155] After returning to Arkansas, he again wrote to Watie, asking urgently that the latter send him "a Bowie knife."[156] His first published work, a letter to the *Arkansas Gazette* supporting the Ridge faction, appeared on August 6, 1846.[157]

The next year, Rollin Ridge married and settled back in the Cherokee Nation in Oklahoma. On January 20, 1849, his first essay was published in the Clarksville, Texas, *Northern Standard*. Entitled "The Cherokees: Their History—Present Condition and Future Prospects," the piece, according to Farmer and Strickland, demonstrated that despite his "separation from his Cherokee people, he never forgot his heritage. Indeed, he searched throughout his life for opportunities to speak on behalf of his fellow Native Americans."[158] The article deals with the current political situation in the Cherokee Nation and the state of virtual civil war that existed between the Ross and Ridge forces. Speaking of the Treaty of New Echota, Ridge writes, "The Treaty of 1835 . . . was literally forced upon them by a dire train of imperious circumstances, and those who, actuated by a generous devotion to their people, dared to sign that instrument shortly afterwards poured their pure and patriot blood on the altar of Revenge, where they were sacrificed by their own sadly mistaken race."[159] He then goes on to justify the pro-Removal leaders and demonize John Ross. He concludes with a proposal that became a life's calling for him: admission of the Cherokee into the United States as a state. He states that the internal conflict within the Nation will not abate until the federal government imposes its law. Then he writes, "I would advocate a measure therefore, which looks to the event of making the Cherokee nation an integral part of the United States, having Senators and Representatives in Congress, and possessing all the attributes, first of a territorial government, and then of a sovereign State." He proclaims, "Let her change this nominal sovereignty for a real one. Let her attach herself to the Union as one of its members, and rise with the fair sisters of the Republic to a position which is truly lofty and rationally independent."[160] Like his late father, his grandfather, and his cousin, Rollin Ridge was a "progressive" who sought for the Cherokee the benefits of "civilization."

Later the same year, an altercation occurred. He killed David Kell, a supporter of John Ross, and fled to Missouri. In April 1850, he departed for California; he arrived four months later. He took a number of odd jobs, worked in the gold mines, and eventually became a journalist. Over the remainder of his life, he owned or edited several newspapers throughout California. Always, however, he kept his eye on events in the Cherokee Nation. His greatest longing was to return and found an Indian newspaper "which would serve as an instrument of vindication for the Indian people."[161] On October 5, 1855, he wrote to Stand Watie, "I should be using my pen in behalf of our race. . . . What is the use our lying down like common men to be forgotten, when we can just as well have a trumpet of our own, that will wake the world to listen to what we say?"[162]

Besides such expressions of communitism, Ridge's journalism, like his correspondence and his poetry, often reflected a Native consideration for the wider community of nature. Though he was firmly convinced of the virtues of progress and Amer-European civilization, he recognized that there was a price to be paid for their benefits in a detachment from the natural world. He noted, "Humanity seems nobler in the mountains than in the cities," and he wrote of the "golden fetters" of living in an urban environment away from nature. He decried the propensity of "civilized ignorance . . . to destroy all that is worth anything in untutored nature."[163] As Farmer and Strickland note, he may have been writing not only about his "own 'tearful remembrances too sacred to be named' but of the experiences of his fellow Indians" when he wrote about the emotive effect of rain.[164]

In 1854, Ridge produced his most enduring contribution to Native literature, the first novel known to have been published by a Native American. Louis Owens describes *The Life and Adventures of Joaquín Murieta, the Celebrated California Bandit* as "a wild and bloody fiction." LaVonne Ruoff states that it "races at a breathless pace, filled with derring-do and punctuated by gunfire." An often quoted passage bears them out; Ridge wrote:

> He dashed along that fearful trail as if he had been mounted upon a spirit-steed, shouting as he passed:
> "I am Joaquín! Kill me if you can!" Shot after shot came clanging around his head, and bullet after bullet flattened on the wall of salt at his right. In the midst of the first firing, his hat was knocked from his head, and left his long black hair streaming behind him.[165]

Written under the pen name Yellow Bird (the translation of Ridge's Cherokee name, Cheesquatalawny), the novel tells the story of its title character, an honest and simple Mexican miner. When he is beaten, bound, forced to witness the brutal rape of his young wife, and driven from his claim by Amer-Europeans, Ridge writes, "They left him, but the soul of the young man was from that moment darkened. It was the first injury he had ever received at the hands of the Americans, whom he had always respected, and it wrung him to the soul as a deeper and deadlier wrong from that very circumstance." Despite having been "wrung . . . to the soul," Joaquín forgoes revenge and resettles with his wife on the farm. Once again, however, he is forced off his land by greedy Anglos. Still he does nothing. When he is falsely accused of stealing horses with his half-brother, Joaquín is whipped while his brother is lynched. At last, it appears, this is beyond the pale: "It was then that the character of Joaquín changed, suddenly and irrevocably. Wanton cruelty and the tyranny of prejudice had reached their climax. . . . Then it was that he declared to a friend that he would live henceforth for revenge and that his path should be marked by blood." By making Joaquín almost passive until this point, Ridge emphasizes that his hero is truly peaceful, a hardworking mestizo driven to violence by extreme and repeated injustice. Murieta goes on to become a bandit, but "not a mere outlaw, committing petty depredations and robberies, but as a *hero* who has avenged his country's wrongs and washed out her disgrace in the blood of her enemies."[166] He becomes a Mexican American Robin Hood.

Though Ridge promises in his preface that what followed would be "strictly true," and though he does take the basic outline from what was reported about an actual bandit of the period, the book is essentially a fiction. Owens overstates the case, however, when he claims that the work "marks the thinly camouflaged beginning of a long campaign by Native American writers to wrench a new genre—the novel—free from the hegemony of the dominant and . . . destructive culture of European America." He calls the novel "a disguised act of appropriation, an aggressive and subversive masquerade."[167] It *is* a masquerade, but not in the precise sense averred by Owens. Ridge is not mimicking the discourse of the *métropole* in order to write back to it to protest its treatment of Indians, whom he disguises as Hispanos to make it more indirect. Ridge is not protesting the treatment of Natives by Amer-Europeans at all. Rather he produces a thinly veiled revenge fantasy in which the Mexicans stand in for pro-Removal Cherokees and Anglos represent, not themselves, but *other Cherokees*—the Ross party. In a letter written to his cousin Stand in September 1853, about the time he was writing *Joaquín*, Ridge stated, "You recollect there is one gap in Cherokee history which needs filling up. Boudinot is dead, John Ridge and Major Ridge are dead, and they are but partially avenged."[168] Earlier, he had also told Watie of his admiration for the pro-Treaty raider Tom Starr, a figure of "wonderment" to him, saying, "He is considered a second Rinaldo Rinaldini. Robberies, house-trimmings, and all sort of romantic deeds are attributed to this fellow."[169] Ridge will evoke the romantic hero Rinaldini again in describing his Joaquín. In such a drama, Joaquín is none other than Rollin Ridge himself. The bandit dies at age twenty-two—not coincidentally, the age that Ridge was forced to flee after killing a Ross supporter. Even in giving a physical description of Murieta, he is describing himself.[170] As critic Franklin Walker puts it, "[I]n having Joaquin achieve his revenge by wiping out his degraders one by one, Ridge was vicariously blotting out each of the assassins who had driven their knives into the body of his father. He put into his book all the feeling that lay below the surface of the civilized editor."[171] He may have been motivated to write a potboiler by the forces of the literary market, but he was driven to write at all by revenge.

Owens says that in his novel, Rollin Ridge "easily embraces the nineteenth century's racist stereotypes that reduced the many Indian cultures in California to the status of 'Diggers.' "[172] This is clearly true. He adapts to the stereotypes of "Digger" Indians just as facilely as his cousin, Elias Boudinot, derisively characterized "uncivilized" Indians as "American Arabs." In his other writings, however, Ridge consistently defends Native peoples, who unquestionably were as hard-pressed in California as anywhere in the nation. In a series of articles in the *Sacramento Bee* and the *New Orleans True Delta,* he defends the "Diggers," describing many atrocities perpetrated against them and pleading for their protection, even if that meant removing them to reservations. Though he uses the racist language of the day, referring to the California Natives as "a poor, humble, degraded, and cowardly race," he does so with irony, turning Occom's razor once again against the Amer-European. It is not the Indians that he ultimately calls "soulless ignoramuses," but the Whites who perpetrate killings. In closing one article, he writes that the brutality of Amer-Europeans must be attributable to "civilized ignorance," and he says of an Indian infant torn from its mother's breast and "its brains [blown] out," "It was nothing but a d——d Digger, and what was the difference."[173]

In 1862, Ridge authored a series of three articles for *The Hesperian* meant to be a broad, more scholarly overview of Indian history, current affairs, and prospects throughout North America. He begins by taking up the question of origins that had intrigued Apess and Jones before him. Unlike either of these predecessors, however, Ridge rejects any theory that Indians derived from the outside. He notes that there are indeed similarities between Indian culture and others, but that there are also marked differences. In the end, he opts for their autochthonous character, writing in part, "Yet, nothing definite is known as to the source from which they sprung; and while there are parallelisms, social and religious, between them and Oriental nations, still the differences in other points are so wide, radical and striking as to settle the rational mind in the conclusion that this people are either indigenous to the continent, or that the period of their arrival is so remote in the past as to have effected, through climatic, geographical and other causes, a complete change in their primordial character." He goes on to point out that "the Indian cannot possibly be descended from all the branches of Old world stock at one and the same time" who evidence cultural and religious similarity.[174] He then returns to his concept of admission of Indian nations as states in the Union.

Ridge uses the series to claim the intelligence, humanity, and civilization of Native peoples. Although he does not actually endorse traditional religions, he does discuss the resistance of Indians to Christianity. Once again, his use of irony is pronounced. He writes, "We have observed . . . that the Indians have for the most part persistently rejected the tenets of the Christian faith. They find great difficulty in believing that the Great Spirit would give a book, containing his revealed will, originally to the white man and not to the Indian. They cannot see how they are to be held responsible for the conduct of Adam and Eve many years ago. In short, the logic of the gospel scheme of human salvation is beyond the grasp of their untutored reason." He then illustrates this by two examples: the famous speech of Red Jacket (Seneca), who refuses to convert until he sees how the religion affects Christians' lives, and the story of a Cherokee chief and a missionary. After the oration of Red Jacket, Ridge concludes, "Poor old Red Jacket! He desired to see faith and practice, precept and example united. He desired to see the religion of the Christians illustrated in their lives! He failed to discover it, and so remained a benighted Pagan."[175] The amusing and possibly apocryphal story of the Cherokee tells of one of the first missionaries to bring the gospel to that people. Assembling the village in the council house, he proceeded to tell the biblical story. One old chief was visibly impressed. Ridge states:

> The narration greatly moved the war-chief, and when the missionary went on to tell that, notwithstanding all the good and kind acts of Jesus, his miracles and his benefactions, he was taken up by the Jews and tried for his life, the excitement of the savage visibly increased, and he shot fiery glances around him. But, when the missionary related with painful precision the details of the cruel death upon the cross, the old warrior of a hundred fights could contain himself no longer. Springing to his feet, he brandished his tomahawk aloft and sounded the warhoop in the ears of the startled assemblage. "White Chief!" he exclaimed, "lead us on the war-path! Show us the murdering dogs of whom you speak. We will revenge the death of this good man!" It was some time before the missionary could explain to him that the killing of Christ was no recent affair, but an event very far back in the past, and that the people who did the deed were not accessible at the end of any war-path which could at that time be conveniently opened. Upon this explanation, the ardor of the chief at once abated, and he subsided into such a total indifference regarding the new religion, that he could never again be induced to pay attention to it whatever.[176]

Taken together, the two stories exemplify the characteristics of Native worldviews that do not divorce "belief" from "practice" and emphasize direct, immediate, and empirical experience.

During the American Civil War, Ridge, like most of the pro-Treaty party, supported the Confederacy. He was proslavery and became an active leader in the Knights of the Golden Circle, a Cherokee secret society along the lines of the Ku Klux Klan, meant to counteract some of the influence of John Ross.[177] Following the war, he took part in a delegation of pro-South Cherokees who went to Washington to ask for their separation from the Ross-dominated Cherokee Nation. When the embassy failed, he returned to California and died of "brain fever" within a year, continuing to feel like a "stranger in a strange land."[178] His dream of statehood for his nation remained only that. Several years earlier, he wrote to his mother, "And if I fail in all I undertake, and lie down to die with this great purpose unfulfilled, my last prayer shall be for its consummation, and the consequent happiness of the Cherokee people!" [179]

Robert Warrior has stated that Native writers as distant as Samson Occom have wrestled with the issues that still confront us today.[180] In the work of John Ridge, one can see the truth of Warrior's claim. Exile, factionalism, and the struggle for sovereignty remain current and real. Farmer and Strickland write that despite his geographic and political differences, "Ridge remained attached to his people, looking longingly toward the Cherokee Nation as later generations of urban Indians resettled by government policy in California would look homeward to the Hopi or the Navajo or the Blackfoot reservations." [181] "The error of Ridge's analysis and the tragedy of Indian experience was that the Indian could never depend upon the white man to behave in a truly civilized manner" nor, ultimately, to accept him.[182]

E. Pauline Johnson

Paula Gunn Allen writes that the publication of John Rollin Ridge's novel was followed by a "thundering silence" that lasted more than four decades.[183] A volume of Ridge's poetry was published posthumously in 1868, however, and "several men and women [had fictional work appear] in periodicals such as *Harper's Magazine* and *Atlantic Monthly* in the latter half of the nineteenth century." [184] In 1891, twenty-three-year-old Sophia Alice Callahan (Creek) published the earliest known novel by an Indian woman, *Wynema, a Child of the Forest.* The novel "describes the acculturation of a white teacher to Creek life and of Wynema to that of the southern gentry." [185] And in 1881, Emily Pauline Johnson saw the publication of her first poem. Callahan and Johnson, both writers with strong feminist views, were linked by Ruoff in her article "Justice for Indians and Women: The Protest Fiction of Alice Callahan and Pauline Johnson." [186]

E. Pauline Johnson is best remembered today for her brief appearance as a kind of Banquo's ghost in Thomas King's comic novel *Green Grass, Running Water,* a wraithlike figure who leaves copies of her books as tips in restaurants in the hope that she can induce someone to read the largely forgotten volumes. At one time, however, the Mohawk poet and writer was the best-known Indian author in the United States and Canada, lionized by the *New York Sun* as "perhaps the most unique figure in the literary world on this continent." [187]

Johnson was born March 10, 1861, in Brantford, Ontario, with a venerable heritage on both sides of her family. Her mother, Emily Howells, was the English-born cousin of the noted American author William Dean Howells, and her father, George Martin Johnson, was a chief of the Mohawk Nation. Her grandfather, John Smoke Johnson, fought alongside Joseph Brant with the British in the War of 1812 and served as speaker of the Iroquois Great Council for four decades.[188]

From an early age, Emily Johnson instilled in her daughter a love of English letters, while her grandfather and father taught her the stories and ways of the Mohawk people. Pauline published her first poem, entitled "To Jean," in the New York–based periodical *The Genius of Poetry.* Over the course of the next few years she saw several of her poems printed in journals in the United States, Canada, and Great Britain. Her breakthrough came in January 1892, when she appeared at a literary evening at the Academy of Music in Toronto. Her reading of two poems, "Cry of an Indian Wife," about the Louis Riel Rebellion, and "As Red Men Die," about a Mohawk captive who stoically endures torture and death rather than be enslaved, was a tremendous success.[189] The result was an almost nonstop series of tours in the United States and Canada that lasted over sixteen years. She produced three collections of poetry, two of prose, and an anthology of traditional Chinook myths that she had gathered.

As a performer and a writer, Johnson is often mistaken for the quintessential "White Man's Indian." Petrone sees her as a figure caught between two cultures but as one whose worldview, culture, and literary output was ultimately Western. She writes, "It is difficult enough to be a woman in one world; it is more difficult to be a woman of two worlds."[190] Daniel Francis portrays her as a complex character but one who ultimately served the myths of dominance by representing the Vanishing Indian and pandering to White tastes for stereotypical noble savages.[191] Likewise, Terry Goldie points out that while Johnson "identified herself as a Mohawk and . . . produced a number of texts in prose and verse which present a strong although ideologically undeveloped support of native people," she nonetheless is best known for lyrics that present indigenes as "fairy-like figures."[192] On the other hand, Beth Brant extols her communitist values and calls her "a spiritual grandmother" of all contemporary Native women writers.[193] As Brant states, "[A] non-Native might come away with the impression that she only wrote idyllic sonnets to the glory of nature, the 'noble savage,' or 'vanishing redman' themes that were popular at the turn of the century. It is time to take another look at Pauline Johnson."[194]

Certainly Johnson herself did much to contribute to the view that she was nothing but a "celebrity Indian" who catered to Amer-European expectations and tastes. She allowed her manager to bill her as the "Mohawk Princess." In late 1892, while touring, she adopted an Indian costume that became one of her trademarks. The buckskin, cloth, and fur dress was a pan-Indian fantasy of her own design that became increasingly elaborate as time passed, with additions such as an ermine-tail necklace. She also carried a hunting knife on her waist. Many of her poems employed stereotypical images, such as "The Happy Hunting Grounds," and she was capable of lapsing into stylized "Red English" in discussions about herself and her people.[195] Once she bitterly complained to naturalist Ernest Thompson Seton, "Oh, why have your people forced on me the name of Pauline Johnson? Was not my Indian name good enough?"[196] In actuality, her Indian name, Tekahionwake (Double Wampum), was that of her great-grandfather, which she had adopted for stage purposes.

It is hard to argue with Francis's assessment of Johnson as pandering to white expectations when one reads a piece like her "A Pagan in St. Paul's," which describes a visit she made to the London cathedral. In the article, she defends traditional religious practices. Instead of doing so, however, as the edu-cated, articulate woman she was, she writes, "So this is the place where dwells the Great White Father, ruler of many lands, lodges, and tribes. I, one of his loyal allies, have come to see his camp, known to the white man as London, his council which the whites call his Parliament, where his sachems and chiefs make the laws of his tribes, and to see his wigwam, known to the palefaces as Buckingham Palace, but to the red man as the 'Teepee of the Great White Father.' "[197] Francis sums up, "Whatever the worth of her argument about Na-tive religion, Johnson was clearing pandering to a stereotypical notion of the Indian as an artless, childlike innocent."[198]

Johnson was keenly aware of the problem. In 1894, she wrote back to a lawyer who had written to her complaining that she played too much to the White audience in her work. She answered, "More than all things I hate and despise brain debasement, literary 'potboiling' and yet I have done, will do these things, though I sneer at my own littleness in so doing. . . . The reason of my actions in this matter? Well the reason is that the public will not listen to lyrics, will not appreciate real poetry, will not in fact have me as an enter-tainer if I give them nothing but rhythm, cadence, beauty, thought."[199] In her work, Johnson sought not so much to represent the stereotypical Indian as to (re)present the Native to Amer-European and Canadian society. Duplicity was the price she had to pay in order to gain a hearing. According to Daniel Fran-cis, "What gave Johnson's work an added poignancy was the belief shared by most members of her audience that they were listening to the voice of a disap-pearing people. 'The race that is gone speaks with touching pathos through Miss Johnson,' was how the *Toronto Globe* put it. In her stage performances, she personified the Vanishing Race and people strained to hear the final whis-per before it faded away completely."[200]

Despite the necessity of catering to Amer-European tastes and expectations, Pauline Johnson fought stereotyping. Though she appeared in Indian regalia of dubious origin in her recitals, she always insisted on appearing in an evening gown for the second half of her performance. Fluent in Mohawk, she once attempted to introduce readings in her Native language into her performance but was booed from the stage. Maintaining her composure, she chastised her audience by telling them that she had had to learn their language; the least they could do was *hear* hers.[201] In an interview with a reporter for the *Boston Her-*

ald, she stated, "You're going to say I'm not like other Indians, that I'm not
representative. That's not strange. Cultivate an Indian, let him show his aptness
and you Americans say he is an exception. Let a bad quality crop out and you
stamp him an Indian immediately."[202] Like Apess before her, she rejected the
generic designation "Indian." She wrote, "The term 'Indian' signifies about as
much as the term 'European' but I cannot recall ever reading the story where
the heroine was described as 'a European.' "[203] Yet she never thought of herself
as anything other than a Native, contending that she was so "by law, by temper-
ament, by choice, and by upbringing."[204] She wrote, "There are those who
think they pay me a compliment in saying that I am just like a white woman.
My aim, my joy, my pride is to sing the glories of my own people."[205] Johnson
skillfully manipulated the "image" of the Indian to carry her message, and she
used every opportunity to "plead the cause of the Native."[206]

Johnson was capable of addressing Indian issues with great force and sophistication. Though she wrote seemingly patriotic odes to Canada, Brant points
out that they are, in actuality, hymns to the land: "She had a great love of
Canada, the Canada of oceans, pine trees, lakes, animals and birds, not the
Canada of politicians and racism that attempted to regulate her people's
lives."[207] In her poem "The Cattle Thief," she was more direct:

> How have you paid us for our game? how have you paid us for our land?
> By a *book,* to save our souls from the sins *you* brought in your other hand.
> Go back with your new religion, we have never understood
> Your robbing an Indian's *body,* and mocking his *soul* with food.
> Go back with your new religion, and find—if you can—
> The *honest* man you ever made from out of a *starving* man.
> You say your cattle are not ours, your meat is not our meat;
> When *you* pay for the land you live in, *we'll* pay for the meat we eat.[208]

Her best-known short story, "A Red Girl's Reasoning," published in 1893, presents a quick-witted, intelligent, and free-thinking Native woman as its heroine.[209] Her White husband sees her as "simpleminded" and "ignorant." When
she mentions at a party that her White father married her mother in the traditional Native way, her husband is embarrassed and outraged. She responds with
a stinging defense of Native religious traditions, which she considers more sacred than Christian ceremonies. When he persists that her father should have
had the union sanctified by a priest, she stands her ground and questions the
Immaculate Conception, asking, "Was there a *priest* at the most holy marriage
known to humanity—that stainless marriage whose offspring is the God you
white men told my pagan mother of?"[210] She leaves her husband and, despite
his entreaties, refuses to return.

Petrone contends that today Pauline Johnson's work appears "dated and shal-
low."[211] Yet pieces like "The Cattle Thief" and "A Red Girl's Reasoning" reveal

quite a contemporary sensibility. Francis writes, "But Johnson herself only went so far. She presented the plight of the Red Man, but she demanded little from her White audience beyond sentimental regret, which was easy enough to give. The land may once have belonged to her people, but she was not asking for it back."[212] Yet she clearly merits further consideration and study. She was in many ways the communitist "revolutionary" Beth Brant depicts.[213] She was the only voice her White audiences were capable of hearing.

Her health shattered by the rigors of constant touring, Pauline Johnson retired to Vancouver, where she died in 1913. Years earlier, in 1907, she read on the Chautauqua circuit in the American Midwest. She never spoke or wrote about the experience. According to her biographer, "The reaction of Midwesterners to Indians had not changed much since [the end of the Indian Wars], except that they now allowed Indians to be *either* dead or captive. They rather enjoyed seeing one now and then in a side show or a circus, because it gave them the opportunity to show their children what the enemy looked like. They treated Pauline as if she too were a circus freak, though they were a bit awed by her obvious refinement and talent."[214] From 1772 to 1900, only a few Native authors made it into print. A few, like Occom, Apess, and Johnson, became popular. For the most part, however, an Amer-European society that was still engaged in destroying the Indians was not yet prepared to listen to them.

Chapter Three

Assimilation, Apocalypticism, and Reform (1900–1967)

The last massacre of Indians in the United States occurred on February 26, 1911, at Rabbit Creek, near Winnemucca, Nevada.[1] Five months later, Ishi (Yahi), "the last wild Indian," was discovered outside an abattoir near Oroville, California, and on September 4 he took up residence at the University of California Museum of Anthropology in Berkeley.[2] Ishi expired of respiratory failure on March 25, 1916. The last survivor of the Rabbit Creek Massacre, Mary Josephine Estep, died in 1993 after being given the wrong medication at a home for the aged. Yet, for the majority of the American public, the Indian Wars were won decisively, the "Indian Problem" solved finally, and Indians ceased to exist on December 29, 1890, with the report of Hotchkiss guns at Wounded Knee on the Pine Ridge Reservation. "Waiting for the word from the West" was no longer a necessary pastime for worried easterners.

The Wounded Knee Massacre was precipitated by the spread of the Ghost Dance, a syncretic religious movement, throughout the tribes of the western United States. The new religion had begun with the Paiute Wovoka's mystical vision of the Messiah. It was an eschatological vision of Christ's parousia, a coming that would wipe Amer-Europeans off the face of the North American continent. After his righteous judgment, the buffalo would return, dead ancestors would be raised up, and all creation would be renewed. The movement had direct antecedents in the Ghost Dance of 1870 and in the Prophet Dance of Smohalla. Amer-European misunderstanding and fear of the movement as a locus of political resistance pointed the road to Wounded Knee.

As the 20th century dawned, the echoes of the shots at Pine Ridge were heard only faintly. The history of Native/Amer-European relations in this century must be viewed as a protracted struggle between those who would encourage Native identity and those who would repress it and promote assimilation. In that struggle, Natives, with differing views of what it meant to defend Indians and their interests, could be found on both sides.

In *Native Americans in the Twentieth Century,* James Olson and Raymond Wilson write, "Dependent and bewildered, thousands of Native Americans sought new ways of handling reservation life by turning to the Ghost Dance, alcohol, peyotism, the Sun Dance, and the Dream Dance. Here, in new cultural adaptations, they sought tools for interpreting their predicament." The Ghost Dance was outlawed in the aftermath of Wounded Knee. The Sun Dance similarly was forbidden. As early as 1884, in fact, the Department of the Interior promulgated the first of the so-called Religious Crimes Codes, which forbade traditional religious practices. The code was strengthened in 1904, and by the 1920s "the universal suppression of Indian religions, through the direct use of force, [was] projected by the Indian Bureau."[3] The Society of American Indians (SAI), a reform organization founded in 1911, supported the assimilationist ideology that followed Wounded Knee. Drawn, as Robert Warrior points out, "from the university-trained economic elite of eastern Native groups, mixed-blood reservation families, assimilated Native families who had lost all but nominal ties to Native culture, Christian converts who had attended seminaries, orphaned Indians who had been adopted and raised by white families, and . . . graduates of and other Natives connected with Richard Henry Pratt's Carlisle Indian Industrial School," the SAI supported a ban on peyotism as well. Among those who testified in favor of a congressional bill to suppress it were SAI leaders Gertrude Bonnin (Sioux) and Charles Eastman, the latter of whom, as a young physician, helped in the recovery of bodies and the treatment of the injured at Wounded Knee. In the end, however, Congress rejected the proposed law, and peyotism was tolerated by Amer-Europeans because, unlike the Ghost Dance, it was perceived as a quietistic response to the condition of Natives.[4]

Politically, the new era began while the Indian Wars were still being prosecuted. On January 24, 1879, Commissioner of Indian Affairs Ezra Hayt sent a letter to Carl Schurz, secretary of the interior, urging him to support legislation allotting Native lands in severalty to individual Indians. Such legislation, contended Hayt, would break up tribal relations, create a desire for private property, and prepare Natives for citizenship and final assimilation. His successor, Hiram Price, used Hayt's language virtually verbatim in a report three years later.[5] The efforts of these and other reformers culminated in 1887 with the passage of the General Allotment Act (the Dawes Act), which provided for dividing most tribal lands, except those in Indian Territory, into individual parcels. The Curtis Act, authored by Charles Curtis (Kaw), extended the provisions of the Dawes Act to the Five Civilized Tribes in 1898.[6] The Osage Allot-

ment Act completed the process in 1906. The "final promise" of the extinguish-
ment of tribes and the civilization and assimilation of the Indian seemed close
to fulfilment.[7]

This contest of assimilation—the continued conflict between Christianity
and traditional religions, allotment and attempts to break up the "tribal
mass"—and resistance to it form the backdrop for Native literature in the 20th
century. The first decades of the century produced several notable Native writers—Eastman, Bonnin, Francis La Flesche (Omaha), John Joseph Mathews,
D'Arcy McNickle, Lynn Riggs, and others. Even so, written output was thin and
sporadic, reflecting waxing and waning public interest as federal Indian policy
vacilated between assimilation and self-determination for the nation's indigenes. This chapter will examine the work of five noteworthy authors in the
period from 1900 to 1967: Alexander Posey (Creek), Lynn Riggs, Mourning
Dove, Ella Cara Deloria, and Natachee Scott Momaday, the mother of N. Scott
Momaday. In their efforts, one can see the continuing communitist struggle for
Natives as Natives that was the predominant theme during the period, in literature as in politics.

Alexander Posey and Lynn Riggs

Indices of Native identity have always been located in humor. Although it usually has been overlooked, traditional orature contains strong elements of humor.[8] Since 1492, especially, it has also become a powerful tool of survival.
Louis Owens quotes artist Sam English (Anishinaabe) as saying that, humor
has "kept us going during the bad times. A lot of people don't realize that, and
I try to show it." A fourteen-year-old Indian girl illustrates this with a mix of
self-deprecation and cutting irony, describing "the Native experience": "One
might say it is to have the 'Unity' that Natives have had since the early days of
this proud country, enabling them to sustain themselves with their simple, but
thrifty usage of such nifty trinkets as bows and arrows, woven baskets, and soft
furry blankets. Or that it is myths and fairy tales that have kept a people care-
free and happy even to this day." Gerald McMaster (Anishinaabe) calls this
"Injun-uity," the "aesthetic of tricks."[9] Native writers like Will Rogers (Cherokee), Gerald Vizenor, and Thomas King, among a multitude of others, reflect
and carry on this strong tradition.[10] Vizenor writes, "The postindian is an iro-
nist who worries about names, manners, and stories. The shadow in trickster
stories would overturn the terminal vernacular of manifest manners, and the
final vocabularies of dominance."[11] He thus points out the communitist possibility for both liberation and healing in humor, writing:

> [Terence Des Pres in *Writing into the World*] pointed out that the horrors of human
> histories have to be treated with reverence in literature; this, a "tragic seriousness,"

and the absence of humor in the experiences of real destitution and the histories of massacres are conditions that would describe the solemn responses of those who write about reservations. Too often, there is a tragic flaw in reason, and the wisdom learned by chance and adversities is lost to seriousness and the "hegemony" of histories. The tribes are reduced to the tragic in the ruins of representation; tragic wisdom endures, and is the source of trickster humor in the literature of survivance, but the wisdom has been denied to conserve the tragic as a common theme in manifest manners and dominance. The tribes have seldom been honored for their trickster stories and rich humor. The resistance to tribal humor is a tragic flaw. Laughter over that comic touch in tribal stories would not steal the breath of destitute children; rather, children would be healed with humor, and manifest manners would be undermined at the same time.[12]

As the 20th century began, one of the foremost exemplars of this tradition of Native humor was Alexander Posey. As a poet, writing in a metered and romantic style, Posey influenced generations of Indian verse, notably that of his fellow Creeks Louis Littlecoon Oliver and Joy Harjo.[13] It is, however, as a satirist that he made his most lasting contribution. Reflecting Warrior's "rhetoric of novelty," LaVonne Ruoff refers to Posey as the "first American Indian author to publish satires."[14] In fact, as Daniel Littlefield points out in his introduction to Posey's work, during the 1880s, "the decade in which Posey began reading," a number of Native writers in Indian Territory were establishing a tradition of dialect-based humor, written in Este Charte (Red English).[15] Littlefield states, "Posey was, in fact, only one of a number of Indian humorists that Indian Territory produced. From the early days of European settlement on the continent, Indians had demonstrated that they could not only laugh at themselves but also have a good laugh at the expense of the whites. In the late nineteenth century, Indians began to draw on humor in literary expression, and by the first decade of this century, a number of them in Indian Territory counted themselves as humorists."[16] Nevertheless, Posey remains the only enduring figure among such authors, the other of whose works have been forgotten.

Alexander Lawrence Posey was born on August 2, 1873, in the Taledega foothills on the Canadian River, near Eufala, Creek Nation.[17] His father was of Scots-Irish descent but a native of Indian Territory, having been born to an Amer-European interloper in the Cherokee Nation; his mother was Chickasaw and Creek. Young Alex's upbringing was dominated almost entirely by his mother, Nancy. Until he was twelve, he spoke only Creek. Around that time, however, his father determined that the boy should learn English and hired a private tutor to compel him. Two years later, he sent Alex to the Creek national boarding school in Eufala. At sixteen, the young man entered Bacone Indian University, an American Baptist-run mission school in Muskogee.

His years at Bacone, coupled with a developing friendship with a young would-be author named George Riley Hall, would set Posey on the path toward becoming a writer. At college, he wrote oratory and set down some Creek myths. He also produced four tales about Chinnubbie Harjo, who was waggish, often violent, a poet and liar. He took the moniker as a pen name for his poetry and also used it to report school news to the *Indian Journal,* a weekly newspaper in Eufala. In 1892, he published a lengthy poem entitled "The Comet's Tale," which gave a Native perspective on the arrival of the first European ships. His campus dispatches, in the persona of Chinnubbie, were humorous and followed a pattern that he would later use for his best-known literary effort, the Fus Fixico letters.

Leaving Bacone without completing his degree, Posey immediately became involved in Creek politics. In 1895, he was elected to the House of Warriors, the lower, popular chamber of the Creek National Council. In 1896, he was appointed superintendent of the Creek Orphan Asylum at Okmulgee, where he met and married his wife, Minnie Harris. He resigned his position at the orphanage in October 1897, but two months later he accepted a position as superintendent of public instruction for the Creek Nation. According to a local history by Joseph Thoburn and Muriel Wright (Choctaw), "All this time he was writing as inspiration prompted, his wife assuming the management of his business affairs in order that he might not be disturbed in his literary work." [18] Shortly thereafter, he again resigned his job in order to settle down on a farm, but he was twice more called upon to assume management of troubled schools, the Creek National High School in Eufala and a similar institution in Wetumka.

Posey's lyric poetry reflects an affinity with the wider community. Thoburn and Wright state, "He was a great lover of nature and seemed to hold communion with the birds, bees, and flowers." [19] A self-avowed skeptic and freethinker with regard to religion, he nevertheless, it appears, believed in a supreme being and the immortality of the soul. According to his friend George Riley Hall, "That soul that reveled in the beauties and spotless purity of the humble flowers of the wildwood, that soul that heard the voice of God in the wind, or listened to the pulsing throb of the world's great heart in the stillness of a summer evening, is part of eternity and can never die. Posey loved the best and purest of God's creation." [20] Feeling in his "very nerve fiber that he was being drawn by an unknown force to go back home to the earthly ones, the Common Things," Posey expressed his kinship with creation in poems, such as one he penned to the trees along his beloved Oktahutche (the Canadian River):

> Why do trees along the river
>   Lean so far out o'er the tide?
> Very wise men tell me why, but
>   I am never satisfied;
> And so I keep my fancy still,
>   That trees lean out to save
> the drowning from the clutches of
>   the cold remorseless wave. [21]

In early 1902, Posey purchased the *Indian Journal* and settled in to the life of a small-town newspaper editor. Though he continued to be active in territorial politics, journalism occupied the greatest part of his energies for the remainder of his life. As Littlefield writes, "Out of his journalism would grow his greatest literary achievement: the Fus Fixico letters," which began to appear in late 1902.[22]

In 1902 the Creek Nation was undergoing rapid changes and social dislocations. The western half of Indian Territory had already gone from common title to private ownership and was now known as Oklahoma Territory. The Curtis Act had applied allotment to the Five Civilized Tribes, including the Creek, in the eastern portion. Statehood in the United States, with the concomitant end of tribal sovereignty, seemed an inevitability. Creek society became polarized into two broad groups, the progressives and the conservatives or "pullbacks."

The Fus Fixico letters were satirical, fictional missives that reported and commented on affairs in Indian Territory. Written in the persona of Fus Fixico ("Heartless Bird"), a fullblood pullback, they are masterpieces of Este Charte, involving complicated wordplay and neologisms. Though they would be much imitated, they were seldom equaled. Posey's early rearing in the Creek language made them possible. Rudolph Flesch notes, "To write or speak 'correctly broken English' is almost impossible for anyone who isn't born to it."[23] As Littlefield points out, they derive much of their humor from their character's "lack of understanding of bureaucratic language such as 'sectionized' land, townsites, and guardianships. [The characters] are mystified, amazed, or disgusted at the whites' unceasing attempts to take their land, marry their daughters, and involve them in land grafting or politics."[24] They are perplexed at Amer-Europeans' actions, but they also recognize Native complicity in the evolving situation. Again, according to Littlefield, "Yet through it all, they show themselves coping with events while maintaining their dignity as Creeks. Always, the clear logic and common sense of the speakers who are outside the mainstream expose the weaknesses of the social and political systems they discuss."[25]

Though Posey himself was a progressive, in favor of allotment and statehood, he had great sympathy for the fullblood pullbacks of the letters. He saw the coming changes as inevitable, but he was "not blind to their impact on the Indian peoples of Indian Territory."[26] The opinions expressed by the conservative characters of the letters were largely Posey's. The letters were one way he sought to mitigate the impact of the dislocations the changes would cause.[27] Indicative of the communitist solidarity Posey felt is the poem he authored upon the arrest of Chitto Harjo, a conservative leader with whom he shared little in the way of political opinions, for his part in the Crazy Snake "uprising" of pullbacks. He writes:

> Down with him! chain him! bind him fast!
>   Slam the iron door and turn the key!
> The one true Creek, perhaps the last

To dare declare, "You have wronged me!"
Defiant, stoical, silent,
    Suffers imprisonment!

Such coarse black hair! such eagle eye!
    Such stately mien!—how arrow-straight
Such will! such courage to defy
    The powerful makers of his fate!
A traitor, outlaw,—what you will,
    He is the noble red man still.

Condemn him and his kind to shame!
    I bow to him, exalt his name![28]

Upon the death of Cheola, a fullblood who served as one of the main figures in the letters, Posey has Fus Fixico write, "Well, so I tell you bad news about my old friend Cheola. He has gone to be good Injin, like whiteman say when Injin die. It looks like all old Injins die now and make good Injin that way."[29] Through his imaginary correspondent, Posey averred that traditionals had to change in order to survive, " 'cause we was getting ready to travel a road we aint been over before."[30]

In discussing federal policy and Creek affairs, Posey reveals a consistent communitist stance. Disaffection with Amer-European material culture, Christianity, and federal government paternalism emerge as major themes. In the summer of 1906, after the passage by Congress of the legislation enabling statehood, Hotgun, the letters' principal character, says, "Well, so before statehood they was too much sentiment mixed up in the Injin problem. The missionary he tell the Injin he must lay up treasures in Heaven, but he didn't show 'im how to keep body an' soul together on earth and lay by for a rainy day; an' the school teacher he learn 'im how to read an' shade 'is letters when he write, but he didn't teach 'im how to make two blades o' grass grow out o' one; an' the philanthropist remind 'im o' the century o' dishonor instead o' the future individual responsibility; an' the government dish out beef an' annuity to 'im instead of a mule an' a plow. Everything like that make Injin no count, except give jobs to government clerks."[31] He was critical of boarding schools as deracinating: "Sometime Mr. Injin he stay in boarding school till he could touch the pen [i.e. sign his name] and then he go home and was had to let his old filly run outside all winter 'cause he don't know how to raise nubbins to feed it."[32] He opposed forced acculturation and assimilation, as evidenced by the changing of Indian names and the mandating of short haircuts for men. And he affirmed militants like Sitting Bull and Tecumseh as "real" Indians.[33]

The letters gained Posey national popularity, acclaimed as "the country's most brilliant literary Indian genius," though most people outside Indian Territory understood few of the references or issues in them.[34] Throughout his life,

Posey always resisted offers to expand the scope of the letters to take in the national scene in order to achieve a wider following. He preferred to continue to hammer away at the situation of Natives at home.

Politicians came in for special derision in the letters. With a self-deprecation often typical of Native wit, Posey poked fun at the Creek habit of dispensing political patronage—a habit from which he himself had profited.[35] He regularly lambasted the Creek government for moving too slowly in getting its citizens their allotment deeds. He criticized the Creek chief Pleasant Porter for spending too much time "in Muskogee, St. Louis, and Washington and places like that to make good chief" when he should have been attending to the needs of his constituents.[36] And he had little use for U.S. politicians who made whirlwind trips to Indian Territory without taking real time to understand the situation. Like his characters, Posey longed for the days when Indian Territory was the hunting ground of the Five Civilized Tribes " 'stead of a paradise for Illinois politicians."[37]

Posey initially had favored making a single state of Oklahoma and Indian Territories, fearing that separate statehood would retard Indian Territory. Eventually, however, he changed his mind, and his characters in the letters change theirs along with him. In August 1905, Hotgun claims that separate statehood is a way for the federal government to "keep its promise and fence us off to ourselves."[38] It becomes a way of maintaining a Native self-determination that is about to slip away. A week later, Hotgun returns to the same theme, contending in a statement of extreme communitist leanings:

[T]he Injin has spoken. Long time ago he give a war whoop and go on the warpath; this time he call a convention and go on record. Instead a making medicine he make history; instead a chasing the pioneers with the tomahawk, he preside in convention and use the tomahawk for a gavel to call the pioneers to order; and instead a swearing vengeance against the pale face, he get up and make a big talk on how to make a state. The Injin is civilized and aint extinct no more than a rabbit. He's just beginning to feel his breakfast food. . . . You could call the movement for separate statehood bosh, or fiasco, or sentiment, and names like that if you want to, but I call it a declaration a independence that was had its foundation on every hearthstone in Injin Territory. . . . The Injin was kicked out a his swaddling clothes a red tape and was ready to follow the flag and constitution without Oklahoma to give him encouragement with stimulants [i.e. alcohol]. The United States was bound by treaty and Christian duty to back the Injin up in the struggle for his rights.[39]

Separate statehood is thus made an issue not only of sovereignty but also of treaty rights and obligations. Following the achievement of separate statehood, "all Injuns be constituents instead a wards a the big man at Washington."[40] The Bureau of Indian Affairs can wind up its business and surrender power to the Natives. On that day, says Hotgun, the West will truly be won.[41]

Posey himself continued to be politically active on behalf of his people. In 1904, because of his sympathy for those in his tribe "whose interests were jeopardized in the readjustment incident to the allotment of lands in severalty," he temporarily gave up journalism to become a field agent for the Dawes Commission, "in which capacity he rendered valuable service."[42] The following year, he was selected as secretary of the constitutional convention for the state of Sequoyah, the separate state to be made of Indian Territory. According to Thoburn and Wright, "the simple, terse, clear English of the instrument framed by that convention is said to have been largely due to the writing and revising of Alexander Posey."[43] There is, however, nothing to support the contention, and according to Littlefield, there is scant evidence that he ever participated in the convention's work. During much of the time of the meeting, in fact, he was in the field for the Dawes Commission. He may, however, have had a hand in the final revision of the constitution.[44] Following his time with the commission, he returned to newspaper work.

On May 27, 1908, as he attempted to cross a flood-swollen Canadian River, he drowned. The Oktahutche he cherished and celebrated in his poetry claimed his life. His death "put a premature and greatly lamented end to what had promised to be a most useful and unusual career."[45] Louis Littlecoon Oliver praises him as "the greatest Creek Indian poet known" and speculates that had he lived, he might have done even greater things politically for his people. It is, however, as a writer that Posey remains familiar. His poetry and satire influenced not only fellow Creeks but Natives across numerous other tribal traditions as well.[46] Oliver eulogized him in verse, once again pointing out his feeling for the wider community:

Salute to Alexander Posey

As you walked your Taledega
The beauty of nature was on your mind,
You held back the welling tears.
Ahead of you Tos'kë chatters
Heralding your appearance.
All of nature bows to you
I too bend my knees.
I feel we were of one genre.
You preferred Chennube Harjo
To be a name of your choice
Your old ones were of that clan.
It may seem ridiculous
For an Indian of political stance
To give praise to a Daffodil,
But deep down you were a poet

Most worthy of a crown of Laurel,
Worthy of the Creek people—
Worthy of having an Em pona'ya
　Wotko okisce![47]

Alex Posey, in the Fus Fixico letters, covered the split between traditional and Christian Indians, the struggle for sovereignty over against paternalistic Amer-Europeans, and a tribal government accused of influence peddling, corruption, padding of tribal rolls, and conspiring with outside business interests.[48] His writings attest once again to the truth of Warrior's contention that Native intellectuals have been dealing with the same problems that face us today since they first began writing in English.

Though he wrote decades after Posey's untimely death, the issues of allotment, statehood, and changing ways that occupied the Creek journalist also run through the work of playwright and poet Lynn Riggs.[49] Born in Claremore, Cherokee Nation, on August 31, 1899, Rollie Lynn Riggs was the son of Rose Ella Riggs, one-eighth Cherokee, and William Grant Riggs, a prominent Amer-European rancher and banker who had become an adopted Cherokee citizen through marriage. Before Lynn, as the baby was known, was a year old, Rosie Riggs enrolled herself and her son on the Cherokee rolls and received an allotment of 160 acres.[50] Only a little more than a year later, however, in November 1901, Rosie died of typhoid. His father remarried seven months later to another Cherokee, Juliette Scrimsher Chambers.

By all accounts, William Riggs was a formidable presence, shrewd in business and personally domineering. Thoburn and Wright wrote of him, "He devotes all his time to buying and selling livestock, acquiring the distinction of being one of the most efficient and dependable dealers in the State."[51] Regardless of the literal truth of the historians' statements about the scope of his occupations, it is certainly true that he had little time for Lynn. Childrearing fell almost exclusively on Juliette. While she apparently did not abuse her stepchildren physically, her attitude toward them, according to Riggs biographer Phyllis Cole Braunlich, "ranged from indifference to total emotional rejection," and Lynn, the youngest, received the brunt of her wrath and rebuff.[52] Though Lynn would struggle continually to please his father and gain his approval, even dedicating his 1930 Broadway play, *Roadside,* to him, he was never able to do so.[53]

As he attended Eastern University Preparatory School in Claremore from 1912 to 1917, Riggs cultivated a growing love of drama. After graduating, he took a variety of odd jobs—cowboy, clerk, proofreader, and extra in motion picture westerns. During this period, he also began to write poetry and attempted his first screenplay. In 1920, he entered the University of Oklahoma, mortgaging his allotment to cover expenses when his father refused to pay for the education. He became poetry editor of the *University of Oklahoma Maga-*

zine and a member of the Blue Pencil literary society, in which he met another
Native who was to rise to prominence as an author in the 1930s, John Joseph
Mathews.[54] He wrote his first one-act play, *Cuckoo,* in 1923. That same year,
his health shattered by a failed romance, he left college and traveled to Santa
Fe.

At Santa Fe, he fell in with Amer-European society, socializing with prominent Anglos like Alice Corbin Henderson of the New Mexican Indian Associates
and Mabel Dodge Luhan. He also befriended actress and sculptor Ida Rauh
Eastman, who produced his second play, *Knives from Syria,* a one-act involving
the dealings of Rhodie Buster (his mother's maiden name) with an itinerate
peddler.[55] In New Mexico, Riggs finally felt accepted after his childhood trauma
and rejection. For the first time, he acknowledged his homosexuality.

The landscape and Indian cultures around Santa Fe fascinated Riggs. He
remarked, "The pueblo life must be wonderful—the real communal life. And
to think of how they are being contaminated by the damned whites and the
stinking Mexicans!"[56] Although biographer Braunlich reports the remark as a
joke, one must at least question that assessment, given a letter in which he
described his trip with some of his new friends to see a ceremony at San Felipe,
comparing the group to "silly characters" from his play *Cuckoo.* He wrote:

> It was muddy, cold—we got stuck on a hill because of a box-like Ford with all the
> family (from Lisa to Grandpa) aboard, which crawled down the hill like a snail.
> We got stuck in the mud, dismounted for lunch, and finally arrived at the village.
> Dancing was over, but there were rumors that it would start sometime in the
> afternoon. We waited.
>
> A drum began, far-off, and we decided it came from the kiva. We waited. The
> drum was intermittant. Once we drove up near the kiva and the sound stopped.
> We drove away and it began. Finally one of the party went to investigate. Behind
> the kiva two little overalled tots were playing the drum; when they got tired they
> stopped beating it![57]

On the same outing, the friends stopped at Santo Domingo. During one dance,
an Indian appeared dressed in a linen duster and carrying a suitcase and um-
brella. As Riggs describes the scene, "He scattered candy to the children and
cried in Spanish: 'How do you do? You *nice* Indians! I'm from New York and I
think you're *so* interesting!' And people are fond of believing they have no sense
of humor!"[58]

During this period, the young author began seriously to write and publish
poetry. Many of these were collected in a small anthology entitled *The Iron
Dish* in 1930. Though, as LaVonne Ruoff points out, only one of these had a
strictly Indian theme,[59] many of them express a communion with the wider
community, always placing himself secondary to place and environment. "The
Hollow" is typical; it reads:

It is quiet here. Tree shade
Is a cool place. I will rest
Easily in the shadow. I will lie
On the earth's breast,
And look at what sky I can see
Through leaves, or perhaps look
At dandelions bowing gravely
To themselves in the brook.

Not thinking of this thing or of that thing,
I will lie
And forget the road I have traveled over
To look at the sky.

Perhaps I shall forget the brown bluff
Over the brook I must climb
As high as the trees are high.
Perhaps I shall forget time
And lie here forever, forgetting
How soon it will be
Before I must leave this hollow
Reluctantly.[60]

In another, he expresses sadness at having disturbed a bumblebee during its brief rest.[61] The one piece with a Native theme is "Santo Domingo Corn Dance," in which he describes being moved to tears by the power of the ceremonial.[62]

While in Santa Fe, he also began to concentrate on drama in a more serious fashion. Theatrical publisher Samuel French published *Big Lake,* his first full-length play, in 1925. It was mounted in New York in 1927. According to Ruoff, it was a failure. Thoburn and Wright aver, however, that it "enjoyed a successful run." It did draw a mixed critical reception in New York but was nonetheless scheduled for a production in Tulsa in 1928. It has remained popular with off-Broadway theater troupes.[63] Riggs went on to write a number of plays on a wide variety of themes.[64] In 1928, he received a Guggenheim Fellowship, which he spent in Paris, writing *Roadside* and working on his two most important dramas, *Green Grow the Lilacs* and *The Cherokee Night.*

It is usually stated that *The Cherokee Night* is Riggs's only play with a Native theme.[65] His friend Paul Eliot Green states, however, that the values in his drama and poetry were both "Western and Indian."[66] Although Braunlich states that he found his Cherokee ancestry "mysterious," she also correctly notes that he "prized" it.[67] He unquestionably felt a responsibility to that part of his heritage. He staunchly opposed stereotypes of Natives. Braunlich notes that "he had no use for Hollywood-style 'movie Indians' in his works. No cowboy-vs-Indian themes are to be found in his plays."[68]

Russet Mantle, produced in New York in 1936, was one of his only attempts at a play with a contemporary setting. Set in Santa Fe at the Kincaid Ranch, the comedy can be viewed as a satire of the Amer-Europeans with whom Riggs associated while in New Mexico—those he skewered in the letter about Pueblo ritual cited earlier, living in adobe mansions decorated in the "Santa Fe style" and patronizing the local indigenous population. The play derives its humor from "the contrast between the wealthy but unrealistic older Anglo generation and the poor, earthy New Mexican Indians."[69] When Effie, the sister of Susanna Kincaid and described by Riggs in his notes as "mindless," arrives from the East, she asks if she will see any Indians during her visit. When told that she undoubtedly will, she responds, "Real live redskins?" and inquires as to where they live. Susanna tells her that they live in towns, and she is incredulous, crying, "In towns! I thought they only lived on the plains. History says that Indians are inhabitants of the Great Plains region west of the—" An amused Susanna tries to dispel the easterner's stereotyped image of Natives as 19th-century Plains Indians:

> Susanna: Effie! There aren't any plains here. These are a different kind of In-
>   dian. They're Pueblos.
> Effie: Oh, Indians are all alike! Red and bloodthirsty. I'll be scared to death
>   when I see one. Savages, they are.

Effie thus rebuffs the attempt to shake her preconceived notions. Later, when Effie finally does encounter Salvador, a family friend from San Ildefonso, she *is* terrified and gives him her scarf in the hopes that the gift of the brightly colored cloth will keep him from hurting her. When Effie's unmarried daughter reveals that she is pregnant, the mother refuses to listen to explanations, proclaiming authoritatively, "It must have been one of these natives," and demanding a "lynchin.'" Effie thus advances another stereotype, that of the lascivious savage bent on committing miscegenation with White women.[70]

In 1930, in perhaps the most ironical example of hybridity and heteroglossia, Riggs collaborated on a screenplay based on the novel *Laughing Boy.*[71] Written by Amer-European Native Americanist Oliver La Farge, the Pulitzer Prize–winning book was set among the Navajo. Although La Farge contended that his style had been influenced by a prolonged study of Indian orature, his Native biographer, D'Arcy McNickle observes, "This could well be, but the text . . . is clearly that of an outsider looking in from a defined social position upon an alien world."[72] The book was eventually filmed, starring Ramon Navarro and Lupe Velez, with "Navajos in the background," but it failed at the box office.[73]

Riggs's best-known play is *Green Grow the Lilacs,* the straight play later adapted as the musical *Oklahoma!* Geary Hobson notes that Rodgers and Hammerstein, the musical's authors, greatly modified the Cherokee's originally drama.[74] Although certain changes were made, much of the text is lifted verbatim from Riggs's original. While the turn-of-the-century Indian Territory of the play's setting was racially mixed, with Natives, African Americans, and Amer-Europeans all interacting, *Oklahoma!* contains no Blacks and no Indians. The landscape has been thoroughly ethnically cleansed until it becomes the vacant landscape of the myths of dominance. Once it is emptied out, Amer-Europeans are free to occupy it without molestation or challenge.

That one could write such a play about Oklahoma, whose very name means "land of the Red people," without any Indians is remarkable. For all the booster-ish push toward statehood in the musical, it must be remembered that by 1900 some in Indian Territory were already lobbying for separate statehood as an Indian state, leading to the Sequoyah convention, of which Posey was secretary. These people are not represented on Rodgers and Hammerstein's stage.

It is commonly assumed that *Green Grow the Lilacs,* from which *Oklahoma!* was taken, also reflects an ethnically cleansed territory. While it is easy to talk about a Cherokee crossblood like Riggs being so culturally alienated—raised in the household of a dominating Amer-European father and assimilated—that he wrote a play about the Indian Territory of his childhood without any Native characters, Riggs's life and work militates against such a conclusion. A careful and sensitive reading of his play and the historical background leads, at least tentatively, to a suggestion that something far more interesting and subtle is at work in the ethnic cleansing of *Oklahoma!*

Green Grow the Lilacs is an affectionate and romanticized depiction of the land of Riggs's youth. Set just outside Claremore, the play takes place, as the playscript states explicitly, in Indian Territory—not Oklahoma. Claremore, Riggs's birthplace, is in the heart of the Cherokee Nation. I am suggesting that it is not devoid of Indian characters at all but is, in some sense, a play *about* them. In this regard, it is significant to note that both it and *The Cherokee Night* were conceived in Rigg's mind at the same time, while he was in Paris.

It is entirely possible that Curly McClain is actually an Indian. McClain (or McLain) was a fairly prominent Native last name. The nickname "curly" could have come about because he, as a mixed-blood, had curly hair, an uncommon trait among Indians. Further, it is at least marginally more likely that Indians would have been the cattlemen and the Amer-Europeans the farmers during the period. This adds a different spin on lines like "Territory folk must stick together" and "The farmer and the cowboy must be friends." This hypothesis is bolstered by the presence of other Natives in the Riggs text. When, for instance, the posse comes to get Curly at Aunt Eller's (a character Riggs acknowledged was modeled after his Amer-European Aunt Mary and his mother, Rose Ella), she chides Territory folk for taking the side of the U.S. marshal and calls them "furriners," a perfectly sound response for any territorial citizen, either White or Native. They, defend themselves, however, in explicitly racial terms. One states, "My pappy and mammy was *both* born in Indian Territory! Why,

I'm jist plumb full of Indian blood myself." [75] To which another responds, "Me, too! And I c'n prove it!" The possibility of Curly's Indianness is not undercut by the fact that he states he was born on a farm in Kansas; such a fact is not necessarily inconsistent with Native heritage.

If this line of analysis is correct, it opens up important points, most notably traditional fears in American theater concerning interracial marriage. Laurey is clearly White. She states that she thinks Indian Territory is a "funny place to live," that she is from Missouri, and that she wishes she lived in Virginia or California. Did Rodgers and Hammerstein, not knowing the history, read Riggs's text too superficially? Or in 1943 was miscegenation more than they thought Broadway audiences would tolerate? [76] After all, Curly actually marries Laurey in both the straight play and the musical. There is no eleventh-hour revelation that he is White rather than Indian, as was the usual convention on stage in such situations. In this regard, it is interesting to note the characterization of the other man vying for Laurey's affections. In both the straight and musical versions, when Curly is told that Jeeter Fry (called "Jud" in the musical) has designs on the young woman, he explodes, "What! That bullet-colored growly man 'th bushy eyebrows that's alwys orderin' the other hands how to work the mowin' machine er sump'n!" Bushy eyebrow were considered by Cherokees to be a distinguishing mark of Amer-Europeans and "bullet-colored" (i.e., gray) would be a perfectly natural way for the browner Indian to describe a White man. Further, in the fact that Jeeter orders others around and instructs them on how to use farm implements, one can see hints of the dictatorial non-Native who assumes his technological and intellectual superiority.

Finally, it must be said that not all Indian references in *Green Grow the Lilacs* are positive. At one point, Old Man Peck entertains the crowd by singing a maudlin ditty called "Custer's Last Charge," celebrating the cavalryman's bravery. His audience roars its approval. It should be remembered, though, that the Cherokee were one of the Five Civilized Tribes. They often had scant respect for those other nations that my mother used to dismiss as "blanket Indians" or Elias Boudinot called "American Arabs." Thus the scene plausibly can be viewed as reflecting disdain for other, less "civilized," Natives. [77]

In his preface to the published text of *Green Grow the Lilacs*, Riggs stated that in the play he hoped to explore the way those who peopled the Oklahoma of his childhood "relate[d] themselves to the earth and to other people." [78] How Natives relate themselves to the earth and to each other also lies at the heart of *The Cherokee Night*, Riggs's one play widely acknowledged to possess an Indian subject. The playwright considered it his best and most important work. In late 1928, he wrote to a friend that he had long "contemplated . . . a dramatic study of the descendants of the Cherokee Indians in Oklahoma, to be called *The Cherokee Night*." In another letter three months later, he fleshed out his plan. The title was taken from a Cherokee verse that ran, "The grass is withered; Where the river was is red sand; Fire eats the timber—Night has come to our people." Riggs wrote, "The play will concern itself with that night, that darkness (with whatever flashes of light allowably splinter through) which has come to the Cherokees and their descendants. An absorbed race has its curiously irreconcilable inheritance. It seems to me the best grade of absorbed Indian might be an intellectual Hamlet, buffeted, harrassed, victimized, split, baffled—with somewhere in him great fire and some granite. And a residual lump of stranger things than the white race may fathom."[79]

Though they reflect romantic notions of essentialism and a descent from a racially pure past, such statements reflect Riggs's own inner struggle to live out his Indianness and a firm stance against assimilation and annihilation. Riggs clearly intended *The Cherokee Night* to be a communitist statement. In October 1930, he wrote to a friend about his progress on the drama: "What astonishes me and delights me now is that finally, by projection, the play has a meaning beyond the story, even beyond the theme. The last scene of all concentrates a statement about and covers the entire field of Indian-White relationships in one dramatic incident such as I could never have foreseen. And it's not a protest—but a triumphant comprehension by an old Indian, a real nobleman, which makes the whole play dignified and austere beyond my first feeble calculations. I hope it will be my best play. It can be."[80] When the play was published with *Russet Mantle* in 1936, he inscribed a copy of the volume to his friend Irwin Edman, a poet and philosopher, "For Irwin—A Cherokee really—Lynn."[81]

The play is composed of seven loosely related vignettes spanning the years from 1895 to 1931. Forgoing straight-line narrative, events skip back and forth in time. The only consistent presence is the Claremore Mound, a hill that was the site of "the last battle between the Cherokees and Osages." Riggs turns the mountain into a character that looms broodingly over the drama enacted before it, at once pointing to the Cherokee connection to the land and standing as a reminder of a time when the people were strong.

The play begins in 1915, almost eight years after statehood, at the base of the Mound, where six young Cherokees, ranging in blood quantum from one-half to one-thirty-second, picnic. Their revelry is interrupted by the arrival of Jim Talbert. Half-demented, the old man tells the youths that ten years earlier he had been given a vision on the site: he had witnessed a reenactment of that last battle. After the Cherokee victory is accomplished, a warrior approaches Talbert and says, "Now you've saw, you've been showed. Us—the Cherokees—in our full pride, our last glory! This is the way we are, the way we was meant to be." He continues:

> But this was moons ago;
> We, too, are dead.
> We have no bodies,
> We are homeless ghosts,
> We are made of air.

Who made us that way, Jim Talbert? Our children—our children's children!
They've forgot who we was, who *they* are! You too, Jim Talbert, like all the rest.

> Are you sunk already to the white man's way—with your soft
>   voice and your flabby arm?
> Have you forgotten how to use the tomahawk and the bow?

> Not only in war—in quiet times—the way we lived:
> Have you forgot the smoky fire, the well-filled bowl?
> Do you speak with the River God, the Long Person no more—
>   no more with the vast Horned-snake, the giant Terrapin,
>   with Nuta, the Sun?

> Are you a tree struck by lightnin'?
> Are you a deer with a wounded side?
> All of you—all our people—have come to the same place!

> The grass is withered.
> Where the river was is red sand.
> Fire eats the timber.
> Night—*night*—has come to our people![82]

Since his vision, Talbert states, he has returned to the location repeatedly. He declares, "And I knowed whut I had to do—I knowed how I could prove my right to be a Cherokee like my fathers before me! Even though I lived in a frame house, and paid taxes, and et my grub out of a tin can—I knowed whut I could do not to be lost. I found the way before too late." The old man's solution was to dig up arrowheads from the battle. These relics become talismans that, when touched, make Cherokees remember. He implores the children to take them. When they refuse, he lashes out, telling them that they have forgotten who and what they are: "Whut do you do to show yer birthright? Nuthin'. You're dead, you ain't no good! Night's come upon you."

The scene strikes out at assimilation and highlights the value of memory in the process of community identity. Throughout it, as through much of the play, a drum beats "like a fevered and aching disquiet at the pit of the world," both punctuating and commenting upon the drama.

In the one contemporary scene, Viney, one of the girls present in the first vignette, visits her sister, Sarah. Viney has become thoroughly acculturated and makes a good living, while Sarah, closer to her Indian heritage, is just scraping by. When Viney viciously derides a fellow Cherokee for his inability to "get hold of himself" and change with the times, her sister responds, "Everything you say shames you. You try too hard to deny what you are. It tells on you. You say [he] didn't have any *change* in him. They's nuthin' else in you *but* change. You've turned your back on what you ought to a-been proud of."[83] The "absorbed" Indian, however, stands her ground, saying, "Being a part-

Indian? What would it get me? Do you think I want to be ignorant and hungry and crazy in my head half the time like a lot of 'em around here? Do you think I want to be looked down on because I can't do anything, can't get along with other people? Do you think I want to make the kind of mess of my life *you* have—and live in a filthy hole like this the rest of my days—?"[84] The scene ends with an almost oracular pronouncement by Sarah that, because Viney has forgotten the teachings of their ancestors and turned away from her Cherokee ways, she will meet destruction: "Your cupful of ashes'll scatter on the wind!"

The final scene, of which Riggs was so proud in his correspondence, takes place in 1895. On a cold winter night, John Gray-Wolf, a full-blood, sits telling his crossblood grandson the traditional stories of the Cherokee. The scene is interrupted by the arrival of Edgar Spench. Wounded and pursued by a posse, the half-breed outlaw forces his way into the cabin and holds the pair hostage. Despite the fact that Spench has just murdered a friend of Gray-Wolf's in cold blood during a brutal robbery, the old Native has compassion for the killer and nurses his injury and encourages him to fight, to cling to life. When Spench, feeling remorse, attributes his evil ways to "[b]ad blood. Too much Indian," Gray-Wolf corrects him, contending, "Not enough Indian." The posse arrives, and the Amer-European marshal shoots Spench. When he tells the old man that they will take the body away, the latter stops him, declaring, "Leave us. It's *our* dead."[85] Spench may have been bad, but even in death, he was no less one of the community. In the concluding stage directions, Riggs writes, "A far-away look is in Gray-Wolf's eyes, a quality of magnificent dignity and despair as if he mourned for his own life, for the life of his son, for his grandson, for Spench, for the women, for a whole race gone down into darkness. The lights fade slowly. The fire flickers. Claremore Mound glitters in the night. A few stars are in the sky."

Through all seven scenes, the Cherokee characters are depicted, since statehood, as seduced by materialism, rejecting the old ways, losing their connection to the land, desiring an assimilation into Amer-European society that never truly can be accomplished. They are depicted as a divided people—divided between progressives and pullbacks, between Christians and traditionals, separated from family, friends, even themselves. Only before statehood, before the loss of political, territorial sovereignty, was there any hope for wholeness. Now the hope rests in memory, in not forgetting one's Indianness and in moving ahead along an uncertain path.

Though Lynn Riggs continued to write, none of his efforts after 1936 (the year both *Russet Mantle* and *The Cherokee Night* were staged in New York) proved as successful as those before. He died on June 29, 1954, from cancer of the stomach, resulting from an ulcer exacerbated by too much spicy food and alcohol.

Mourning Dove, Ella Cara Deloria, Natachee S. Momaday

Historian Robert Berkhofer recapitulates two distinct stereotypes of American Indians in his book *The White Man's Indian*. Both of these were bound up inextricably with White self-evaluations, describing Natives negatively in terms of what they were not or what they lacked in terms of Amer-European society. First is the Noble Savage or, for Berkhofer, the "good Indian." These Natives lived in harmony with nature in a state of "liberty, simplicity, and innocence." They were beautiful in physique and modest and regal in bearing. Brave in combat, they were tender and loyal in familial and friendship relationships. Juxtaposed with this image is that of the "bloodthirsty" or "bad Indian." Upon these Natives are heaped all the negative qualities of Amer-European society, many of them associated with sex. They are naked, lecherous debauchers. They are lazy, deceitful, and treacherous.[86] To Berkhofer's categories must be added a third, the stereotype of the half-breed. An extension of the "bad Indian" image, half-breeds have no redeeming virtues. They are neither White nor Indian. As such, they are the degenerate products of miscegenation, distrusted by both cultures and fitting in nowhere. In her writing, Mourning Dove seeks to combat these stereotypes, particularly that of the treacherous, degraded, untrustworthy crossblood.

A great deal of uncertainty surrounds the early life of the author known by the pen name Mourning Dove.[87] Even her name is not definitely known. She assumed the name Morning Dove when she began as a writer in 1912 but later changed it to Mourning Dove. Sometimes she used the Okanogan name for the bird, Hu-mi-shu-ma. She signed her Amer-European name variously as Cristal, Christina, and Catherine but was most commonly known among her people as Christine Quintasket.[88] Though she always claimed to be of mixed Amer-European and Native descent, Jay Miller, who edited her autobiography, disputes this contention. Instead, he says that evidence indicates that both her parents were Native: "Evidently Christine provided a white ancestor to appeal to her readers."[89] Louis Owens, basing his statement on Miller's scholarship, writes, "Mourning Dove shows subtle understanding of the dialogic that would come to be called heteroglossia in her insistence upon mixedblood status and in her attempt, at the same time, to establish her position within a privileged, authoritative discourse as Indian."[90] If Miller is correct, then just as Cogewea, the heroine of her novel of the same name, bridges Native and Amer-European cultures, Mourning Dove sets herself up as a culture broker, the mediator about which Ruppert writes.

Mourning Dove's writing was unquestionably "literature with a purpose." Miller notes, "Despite great hardship, both financial and emotional, she persisted in her goal of producing stories that gave Indians a sympathetic hearing."[91] Clifford Trafzer also remarks on this communitist determination, stating that "she wrote from and into and out of her own oral literary experience as an American Indian. . . . This is a technique used consciously and unconsciously by most Native American writers, and it produces literature that reflects the community of the person."[92] The author herself described her goal of representational sovereignty, stating, "It is all wrong, this saying that Indians do not feel as deeply as whites. We do feel, and by and by some of us are going to make our feelings appreciated, and then will the true Indian character be revealed."[93]

Mourning Dove was born near Bonner's Ferry, Idaho, in 1888. She had little formal schooling. During her first year at the Goodwin Catholic Mission school near Kettle Falls, she was punished for speaking only her Native language. Lonely and traumatized, she became seriously ill after only a few months. By age fourteen, she had only the equivalent of a third grade education. In 1921, when she applied to have her allotment deeded to her in fee simple, she listed eight years at various mission schools. Realizing that education was essential if she was to become a writer, she repeatedly returned to school. In the winter of 1912–1913, she entered Calgary College, a business school in Canada, where she studied English, writing, and typing until 1915. According to Lucullus McWhorter, the Amer-European who worked with her on her writing projects, she once again suffered from racism while there. He writes, "The humiliation from wanton contumely because of her Indian blood, were [*sic*] multitudinous, but, using her own phraseology, she 'stuck' through the term, not missing a class."[94] Though she worked briefly as a teacher on the Inkameep Okanogan Reserve in British Columbia, she worked most of her life as an itinerate farm laborer, writing only when her day's work was done. In a 1930 letter to McWhorter, she described the process: "I have had too much to do outside of my writing. We got work apple thinning at Brewster, Wash.; . . . and after working for ten hours in the blazing sun, and cooking my meals, I know I shall not have the time to look over very much mss. . . . [B]etween sand, grease, campfire, and real apple dirt I hope I can do the work."[95]

She also worked tirelessly as an activist for her people. Among her communitist activities, she lectured on Native issues and worked to ensure that a lumber mill on the Okanogan reservation lived up to its commitment to hire Indian workers. She successfully intervened on behalf of Indian girls "in trouble with the law, getting them released in her custody."[96] At McWhorter's urging, she recorded the orature of her people. He felt, reflecting Amer-European impulses to discover and preserve an unspoiled, "pristine" oral tradition, that she must undertake such a task "before they were hopelessly corrupted by intermarriage and the influence of white civilization."[97] The result was her volume of traditional myths, *Coyote Stories*.[98] Mourning Dove, however, found the project frustrating. She wanted to write fiction, based on the stories of the Okanogan. Her best-known work, *Cogewea, the Half Blood*, is precisely that. Though at times painfully didactic, it skillfully combines the ceremonial with Western literary forms in a manner that presages Momaday's *House Made of Dawn* and Silko's *Ceremony.*[99]

Just as the events of Mourning Dove's early life are uncertain, the production of *Cogewea* is the subject of controversy. At issue is the role of Lucullus McWhorter in the creative process. When an Indian agency employee suggested that she had not written the novel at all but had merely allowed her name to appear on McWhorter's work, Mourning Dove was incensed. She not only attempted to have the man fired but was impelled to write her autobiography in order to prove her literary ability.[100] It is true that McWhorter acted as editor, the Sho-pow-tan acknowledged on the title page, and that he added footnotes and made certain insertions in the text. Mourning Dove, however, had already completed a draft of the book, probably in 1913, while at Calgary, before she ever met the Amer-European. She apparently had been inspired by anger at reading a novel by an Amer-European set among the Flathead, *The Brand* by Theresa Broderick.[101] As Miller points out, she "provided the initial copy, discussed changes, and approved the result."[102] McWhorter's insertions consist primarily of epigrams from works like Longfellow's *Hiawatha,* several tirades against federal Indian policy and the Bureau of Indian Affairs and extraneous ethnographic data concerning the Nez Perce. As Louis Owens puts it, "[T]he reader feels throughout *Cogewea* the presence of a political disturbance permeating the text as the voices of Mourning Dove and McWhorter struggle to be heard one over the other—with Mourning Dove's easily winning out. On one level the reader feels the internal persuasiveness of Mourning Dove's depiction of a mixed blood reality, and on another level we respond to the authority of McWhorter's liberal discourse."[103]

On the surface, the novel itself appears to be little more than a western romance along the lines of Helen Hunt Jackson's *Ramona,* but according to Paula Gunn Allen, it is "[a] deeply feminist novel cast in the mode of the popular western of the day [that] draws from protest and ceremonial themes to clarify the struggle for identity that characterizes Native writing in the United States in the twentieth century."[104] Using the romance form, Mourning Dove brings in "the ancient oral stories of the Okanogan Indians to produce a novel that permitted her characters to act out the tales of Chipmunk and the lessons learned during the age of the Animal People."[105]

From the beginning, *Cogewea* is a powerful communitist statement. Mourning Dove dedicates the book to her great-grandfather, See-Whelh-Ken, a chief of the Colville, "who, in peace welcomed the coming of the pale face, only to witness the seeds of destruction scattered wide among his own once strong and contented people. To him and to the crowded death huts and burial cairns of a nation is this volume most endearingly dedicated by one who ever yearns for the uplifting of her most unhappy race." The novel is critical both of assimilation and of the ongoing colonialism practiced by Amer-Europeans. As Edward Said notes that the American settler colony was built upon the ruins of Native culture, so Mourning Dove writes, "Woe! to the Governmental structure builded on the ruins of devastated homes. For how long had any such ever survived?"

Without ever disparaging full-bloods, the novel celebrates mixed-blood identity. Cogewea and her sisters are all "half-bloods." Likewise, most of the ranch hands are crossbloods, including Jim, who eventually marries the heroine. Even the name of the spread owned by Cogewea's sister Julia's husband is the H-B, in all likelihood standing for "half-blood." As Louis Owens observes, "The ranch is a transitional world, suspended between Indian and Euramerican realities, where the owner may be white but where the cowboys are Indians, or 'breeds,' who are presented in wonderfully hybridized portraits."[106] These portraits militate against essentialism and demonstrate the role of culture in racial/ethnic identity. Cogewea and her sisters, though equal in blood quantum, represent three different possibilities. Julia is married to an Amer-European and almost fully assimilated; she even helps Densmore, the story's villain, in his designs on Cogewea because she sees Western civilization as the only way forward and wants her sibling to follow the path she has taken. Mary lives with their grandmother, the Stemteemä, and has deeply absorbed "the primitive Indian nature" from "the centuries old legends" the old woman tells. Cogewea, educated at Carlisle, is in between.

In addition to passages that speak of the "stigma" of being of mixed heritage and reject the stereotype of half-breeds as the "inferior degenerates of two races" (to use Densmore's term), there are intimations that there are even advantages to being a crossblood. Though Cogewea will later tell Densmore that her White blood is a "foreign shame," early in the novel she proudly affirms that she is both Native and Amer-European. Just as the H-B Ranch is a transitional zone, the times in which the novel is set are changing. The traditional and the modern are at variance, "[n]either comprehending or understanding the other." Cogewea *bridges* the two existences. When she encounters a snake, a creature known for its power "for doing secret evil to the people," she curses and kills it, declaring, "Your 'medicine' is strong and my grandmother would not hurt you. But I am *not* my grandmother! I am not a full-blood—only a *breed*—a *sitkum*[107] Injun and that breaks the charm of your magic with me. I do not fear you!" It is, after all, not "breeds" but Whites who are not to be trusted. Cogewea's Amer-European father deserts his daughters, leaving them to be raised by the Stemteemä, and later attempts to disinherit them. Densmore pleads his love for Cogewea, first in an attempt to get sex and later in order to cheat her out of her allotment.

Despite the affirmation of mixed-blood identity, it is clear that Mourning Dove affirms her crossblood characters *as Indians*. In a clever rhetorical move that denies Amer-Europeans indigeneity on the continent, they are referred to as "Caucasians," while Natives are called "Americans." When Densmore asks Cogewea why, despite her Amer-European ancestry, she insists on identifying herself exclusively as Native, she responds by citing the traditions of her people and kinship obligations. Densmore fails to understand. Reflecting Western universalizing tendencies, he speaks of the "imaginary barriers" that she erects in her desire to marry an Indian man. Earlier, in a devastating analogy, Cogewea tells the villain that Amer-Europeans will never understand the Native worldview, bluntly stating, "[T]hey do not understand the Indian mind; never will, it would seem. Had a tribesman gone to your European homes with the ultimatum: 'Desert your heavy houses; come into the open and adopt our mode of life,' I am sure you Caucasians would have regarded him as an unreasonably brainless arrogant. Preposterous as such an analogy may be, it adequately expresses the native conception of foreign intolerance. But I suppose that what is, was to be, and we must accept the inevitable."

Other elements of *Cogewea* also reflect a Native worldview in their attitudes toward friendship, generosity, family, death, and the natural world. In one of the Stemteemä's stories, Green-Blanket Feet says that as she left her people to follow her abusive Amer-European husband, "Every tree, every bush spoke to me; every stone called to me. . . . The birds sang in tones of sadness and the water's fret was wailing." When she at last flees to return to her kin, a wolf protects her and hunts rabbits for her to eat. Speaking for herself, the grandmother laments, "The land is now all turned over to the production of the white man's food, which we must also use. But we old people prefer our natural food; that which the earth gave us without scarring its bosom." Cogewea too offers a paean to the wider community, proclaiming, "My beautiful Eden! I love you! My valley and mountains! It is too bad that you be redeemed from the wild, once the home of my vanishing race and where the buffalo roamed at will. Where hunting was a joy to the tribesmen, who communed with the Great Spirit. I would that I had lived in those days,—that the blood of the white man had not condemned me an outcast among my own people." Later, she tells Densmore, "Isn't it grand? These are my prairies, my mountains, my Eden. I could live here always! I shall hate to leave them when the final summons comes. Wherever I go, I recall every outline of these embattled ranges, nor can the vision close at the grave. When away, I grow lonesome, as a child for its mother. I become heart-sick for a sight of those snow-shrouded peaks, so rich in legendary lore." Densmore, ever the foil, again does not understand this communitist, covenantal connection to the land. He refers to the reservation as bleak "sandy wastes" and makes reference to the positive aspects of allotment.

The novel is highly critical of both the history of Amer-European/Native relations and the contemporary situation. It decries the exploitation of Indians.

Like so many other Native writers before her, Mourning Dove attacks alcohol and the debilitating effects it has had on her people. She holds Whites accountable for its introduction, writing, "This is the heritage of the white men's civilization, forced—like the opium traffic of China—upon a weaker people by the bayonets of commercial conquest. It overshadows all the good resultant from the 'higher' life." Cogewea expresses anger at the desacralization of tobacco and the rise of cigarettes, which she calls "coffin-nails." According to her, crime and multiplicitous other ills are the result of Amer-European colonial pressure. The depredations visited upon the Native nations, however, do not stop there. When Densmore pushes Cogewea to accept the Amer-European side of her lineage, the Native woman shoots back, "When you show me a solitary treaty made with us by the Government which has not wantonly been violated; when you cite an Indian war where you have not been the flagrant agressor [*sic*]; then I will admit the *moral* superiority of the Caucasian, and in beliefs and manners become one of you." [108]

Mourning Dove criticizes the commodification of Native religion, saying, "These ceremonies, held sacred by the more primitive tribesmen, are now, shame to say, commercialized and performed for a pittance contributed by white spectators who regard all in the light of frivolity." Christianity and Native religious tradition are often contrasted in the novel, and the former is found wanting. The Stemteemä tells Cogewea and Densmore, "We have been told that it is wrong to pray to the Great Spirit as we were taught. But since we adopted prayers to the white man's God-spirit, we have died from the pestilences he brought. Even the buffalo are no more; gone to the shadowy Hunting Grounds of the hereafter, with the warriors of old. I shall soon follow, where the pale face can not dispossess us, for he will not be there. He will no longer lure our children from us with his smooth tongue and books, which here serves to make them bad by imitating the destroyers of our race." Later Densmore calls the coming of the *Mayflower* "a spiritual light bursting on a darkened New World." Cogewea reponds in a lengthy monologue, undoubtedly influenced by McWhorter but nonetheless reflecting Mourning Dove's belief. The Native heroine states, "Zealous and good Christians . . . see in the Discovery by Columbus, a guidance of Divine Providence, in that a new faith was brought to the natives. This may be, but the mistake was with the priests and teachers who did not understand that there was no fundamental difference in the attributes of the deities of the two races. . . . Viewed in its proper light the coming of the Mayflower was, to my people, the falling of the star of 'Wormwood'; tainting with death the source of our very existence." She concludes, "His teachings and example have failed to fit us for *his* heaven, while they have unfitted us for our own." [109]

Cogewea herself very nearly comes to disaster with Densmore when she forgets the old ways and ignores the Stemteemä's counsel not to marry the Amer-

European. Eventually, however, a happy ending is manufactured to conform to the requirements of the romantic genre. It is this conclusion that causes Dexter Fisher to refer to the "confusing voice" of the novel, accusing Cogewea of wanting the best of both the Native and Amer-European worlds.

Embodying the rhetoric of novelty, Lucullus McWhorter was certain that Mourning Dove was the first Native—certainly the first Native woman—to write a novel, a fact that would assure its success. However, is took fourteen years after Mourning Dove completed the first draft for the volume to be published. *Cogewea* stands as her only novel. In 1936, worn out from her many activities and years of work in the fields, Mourning Dove died of "exhaustion from manic depressive psychosis." [110] She was forty-nine years old.

Cogewea was set in a time roughly contemporaneous with its original writing. Thomas King has observed that Native writers tend to avoid historical fiction. A few authors have ventured into this territory—notably James Welch (Blackfoot/Gros Ventre) in *Fools Crow* and Joseph Marshall III (Sicangu Lakota) in *Winter of the Holy Iron.* For the most part, however, the burdens of deconstructing the history transmitted by the dominant culture have deterred Indian artists. [111] In the early 1940s, however, Ella Cara Deloria listened to the suggestions of her friends and colleagues, anthropologists Franz Boas and Ruth Benedict, "to undertake to write a novel about the life of a Sioux woman set a century in the past, before traditional culture had been significantly altered by contact with American civilization." [112]

Ella Deloria was born on the Yankton Sioux Reservation in South Dakota on January 31, 1889, the daughter of a Dakota Episcopalian priest and a mother who had been raised a traditional but later converted to Christianity. According to a biographical sketch by Agnes Picotte, Dakota was the primary language in the Deloria household during her youth, and "Sioux values mingled easily with [her parents'] devout Christian principles." [113] Graduating from boarding school, Ella enrolled at Oberlin College but later transferred to Teachers College of Columbia University in New York.

At Columbia, she studied under Franz Boas. The leading anthropologist of his day, Boas trained famous Amer-European scholars like Margaret Mead, Ruth Benedict, and Elsie Clews Parsons. He also attracted a number of Native students, including Deloria, William Jones (Fox), and Archie Phinney (Nez Perce). [114] Deloria's association with the professor, whom she referred to as Father Franz, would remain close until his death in 1942.

After receiving her bachelor's degree in 1915, Ella Deloria returned to South Dakota to teach at All Saints, the boarding school she had attended. In 1919, she took a position with the Young Women's Christian Association as health education secretary for Indian schools and reservations, but she left four years later to accept a teaching position at Haskell Institute, an Indian school in Lawrence, Kansas. In 1927, Boas, with whom she had lost contact temporarily, visited her at Haskell and asked for her help in translating and editing some Sioux texts. She consented and continued to act as a research assistant for her former teacher until his death, after which time she worked with his successor, another former student, Benedict. Following the latter's death in 1948, she kept on with research, writing, teaching, and lecturing, and became recognized as the preeminent authority on Sioux lifeways. She died in Vermillion, South Dakota, on February 12, 1971. Over the course of her association with Boas and Benedict and later, Deloria gathered and translated a large amount of traditional orature and other material, producing several manuscripts, some of which are only now beginning to be published.[115]

Throughout her career, she saw her work in communitist terms. She refused to fetishize Native culture and, according to Julian Rice, "did not insist that there was only one way to be [Sioux]."[116] She taught her students, "Our heritage is rich and good. . . . Use it, respect, and be sympathetic with those who still live entirely by it."[117] She sought to record the language and preserve it in accurate, colloquial translation, publishing *Dakota Grammar* in 1941.[118] As Rice observes, "She performed expertly in the non-Lakota [*sic*] profession of ethnological scholarship, employing her academic tools to return sustenance to the Dakota and Lakota nations in strikingly innovative ways. With subtle linguistic features, such as exclamations or compound words, that she wrote down for the first time, she supplied the emotion, humor, or irony that many folklorists have felt only oral performance could convey."[119] A progressive, she defended the humanity of her people even as she advocated for their "advancement." In 1952, she wrote to H. E. Beebe, one of her funders:

> This may sound a little naïve, Mr. Beebe, but I actually feel that I have a mission: To make the Dakota people understandable, as human beings, to the white people who have to deal with them. I feel that one of the reasons for the lagging advancement of the Dakotas has been that those who came out among them to teach and preach, went on the assumption that the Dakotas had *nothing*, no rules of life, no social organization, no ideals. And they tried to pour white culture into, as it were, a vacuum, and when that did not work out, because it was not a vacuum after all, they concluded that the Indians were impossible to change and train. What they should have done first, before daring to start their program, was to study everything possible of Dakota life, and see what made it go, in the old days, and what was still so deeply rooted that it could not be rudely displaced without some hurt. . . . I feel that I have this work cut out for me and if I do not make all I know available before I die, I will have failed by so much.[120]

Hers, however, was not the anthropology that was developed to teach colonial administrators how to control colonized populations because she saw her mission as one of promoting cultural survival as well. In his introduction to the first publication of Deloria's rendering of the traditional narrative of Iron Hawk, Rice writes, "In having Red Calf recover the grandparents in the fourth and final episode, Deloria shows that the Lakota past, its consciousness and wisdom, is never lost, although individuals like Iron Hawk, and even Red Calf very briefly in the last episode, may occasionally forget the *priority of cultural endurance.* While the individual characters are only human, the 'hero' is actually anyone who 'wears' the Lakota virtues when the people need them." [121]

The recover of familial relationship at the end of *Iron Hawk* is significant, inasmuch as the overriding theme of Deloria's work was kinship. The primary scholarly text she produced, entitled variously "Camp Circle Life" or "Dakota Family Life," dealt with filial obligation, which Deloria saw as the central feature of Sioux social life and culture. Though it was never published, she drew upon it for two other works, *Speaking of Indians* and her only novel, *Waterlily.* Discussing the latter, Raymond DeMallie writes, "[T]he exceptional adherence of the protagonists to the spirit and letter of kinship law . . . may mirror Ella Deloria's own personality rather than her reconstruction of nineteenth-century social life." [122] Whatever the truth of such a speculation, it does nothing to undercut the work's communitism: Deloria accurately depicts a society where fidelity to community is a primary responsibility.

Speaking of Indians, published by the YWCA, was Deloria's attempt to convey her knowledge of Natives to a popular audience and to inform that audience regarding contemporary problems and issues and enlist its support. Though it purports to be about Indians generally, it primarily deals with the Dakota. She rejects generalized images of America's indigenous and, in their place, asserts tribal specificity. In language reminiscent of Pauline Johnson decades earlier, she writes, "We in America must be realizing by now that too often all tribes, just because they are native Americans, are lumped together with blithe disregard of tribal differences. Do we lump together all Europeans just because they occupy the same continent? Don't we allow for the wide differences in the English, Russian, French, German temperaments? Right here in our own nation we recognize our regional differences. By what precedent, then, are all Indian tribes—speaking different languages and living different lives—expected to have the same ideas and problems? And to respond to exactly the same approach?" [123] Like McPherson and Jaimes-Guerrero, she maintains differences in Native worldviews, attributable to different geographies, but she nonetheless claims that "Indians have developed on this continent an ethos that is wellnigh universal, that makes them one in general character, though there are tribal variations." [124]

Maintaining that Native cultures are inherently like all others, Deloria contends that they would have continued to "progress" on their own course of development if the Indian's "normal life had not been suddenly disrupted, and if he had not been forced to make so drastic a change in his methods and direction." The coming of Amer-Europeans and the changes they engendered were like a "midsummer thunder storm that gathers slowly." She elaborates on the simile, writing, "For a time it appears to be only a black curtain hung clear across the west, screening out the declining sun but leaving the sky overhead an intense blue, clear and calm. In reality it is a great storm, marshaling its forces without haste as though making exact and sinister plans so that when finally it gets into action, it will be sure to make a thorough job of it—perhaps even killing many." She explains, however, that the comparison breaks down. The thunderstorm has, in reality, no evil intent, and the people can see it coming and prepare. Amer-Europeans made their preparations in secret and out of sight before launching surprise attacks on Natives—in the mass slaughter of the buffalo, the murder of Sitting Bull, and the massacre at Wounded Knee. They accomplished their work without warning until the people were brought to submission.[125]

Like many progressives, Deloria believed that conformity to Western ways was, in general, an inevitability. Natives had no other choice because many traditional ways were "no longer feasible." Addressing her White audience, she states, "Tribal life is only a phase in human development anyway. The next step, for every people, is national life. Usually that is a slow process; but in the case of the Indians it needn't be, since national life pervades the very atmosphere they breathe. The schools must help them adjust to it." Though she accepted much of the assimilationist determinism, she staunchly opposed forced acculturation because of the damage it did to Native selfhood and society. Instead she advocated a process of organic change that she thought would come about naturally.[126]

Though herself a Christian, she remained positive about traditional religious practice and meant to write about it "without any derogatory overtones." Like Bonnin and Eastman before her, however, she objected to peyotism and quotes an informant to the erroneous effect that it "keeps Indians half-doped all the time, making them all the easier prey for the crooked." Despite her respect for other Native religious traditions, she is extremely pro-Christian and favors continued mission activity among Indians. Even so, however, she critiques the Church for its racism and condescension. As Homer Noley would later from within the Church and her nephew Vine would from without, she condemns the practice of sending Amer-European missionaries into Indian Country, favoring instead the promotion of Native clergy and the growth of indigenous expressions of Christianity.[127]

Though often somewhat muddled, the volume reflects a demand for Native sovereignty and self-respect, advocating that Native tribes be allowed "to go ahead *in their own way*" on the path of development.[128] In it, Deloria deplores every form of paternalism and dependency. Though she advocates eventual acculturation, in this respect she is close to Russell Means (Oglala Lakota), who, referring to the view of some fellow Sioux concerning treaty rights, declares, "Some of our people talk about our inherent right to welfare, but that is part of the death dance of dependency. Our treaty rights do not include the right to food stamps! Our right is to have gardens again!"[129] According to Deloria, Amer-Europeans must stick to a consistent course and then give Natives time to prepare for what is expected of them. More than forty years later, Vine Deloria Jr., would touch upon the same theme, declaring:

> The real exile of the tribes occurred with . . . the failure or inability of white society to offer a sensible and cohesive alternative to the traditions which Indians remembered. . . . The new ways which they were expected to learn were in a constant state of change because they were not a cohesive view of the world but simply adjustments which whites were making to the technology they were inventing.
>
> Had whites been able to maintain a sense of stability in their own society, which Indians had been admonished to imitate, the tribes might have been able to observe the integrity of the new way of life and make a successful transition to it. But the only alternative that white society had to offer was a chaotic and extreme individualism.[130]

Published in 1944, while World War II was in progress, *Speaking of Indians* delineates in detail the outstanding service done by Natives in the armed forces in that conflict as in the Great War. When these GIs come home, says Deloria, they will want and need help. She writes, "They will come back with perspective. . . . There will be a new call to government to help them with their land and economic problems. . . . They have fought and suffered for their country. They are Americans, and they will want to be treated as such."[131] They will make a just demand, predicts Deloria, for an end to discrimination against Indians. It is ironical to her that the United States proclaims "the Four Freedoms to the world—for the liberation of all conquered people, except the one itself had conquered!"[132] Foreseeing the dislocations caused by the postwar termination and relocation policies that created large urban Indian populations, she writes:

> [W]e have to be realistic enough to admit that, in an alien setting, and increasingly as time goes on, those disciplines [of the traditional culture that sustains and strengthens the people] lose their force. This is true particularly with the younger Indians when they venture beyond their reservation boundaries. It is not bulwark enough then that they know their skill and trade so well that they can get along economically, for they still have needs that the best money-making knowledge cannot supply. Because they are few and scattered, they can be terribly lonely in their new environment, without friends to help them to find their way around and to fit into their community's life.[133]

Deprived of communitist supports, they will be, literally, Indians with "no place."

With regard to community and knowing one's place, part II of *Speaking of Indians,* which treats the Teton Dakota, is entitled "A Scheme of Life That Worked" and is taken up largely with kinship matters. Deloria writes, "Kinship was the all-important matter. Its demands and dictates for all phases of social life were relentless and exact; but, on the other hand, its privileges and honorings and rewarding prestige were not only tolerable but downright pleasant and desirable for all who conformed. . . . I can safely say that the ultimate aim of Dakota life, stripped of accessories, was quite simple: One must obey the kinship rules; one must be a good relative."[134] Kinship promoted an ethic of generosity and reciprocity and held "everybody in a fast net of interpersonal responsibility." The primary place where this stress on relationship was manifested was the *tiyospaye,* or tipi circle, denoting "a group of families, bound together by blood and marriage ties, that lived side by side in the camp-circle." The *tiyospaye* operated as a single unit for almost everything and was the basic element of corporate life. Only those within it that adhered to their filial responsibilities "were good Dakotas," trusted and included.[135] Without the aim of being a good relative and the constant struggle to attain it, writes Deloria, "the people would no longer be Dakotas in truth. They would no longer even be human. To be a good Dakota, then, was to be humanized, civilized. And to be civilized was to keep the rules imposed by kinship for achieving civility, good manners, and a sense of responsibility toward every individual dealt with. Thus only was it possible to live communally with success."[136] This responsibility to relationship was so strong among the Sioux that it even pervaded one's relationship to ultimate reality. Using her linguistic work, Deloria notes that the word for "to pray" and "to address a relative" are, in fact, the same word. Wakan Tanka must be a relative because only among relatives is one sure of what the reciprocal obligations are one to another. With a stranger, one can never know.[137]

Kinship obligations are at the core of Ella Deloria's novel as well. By the time of publication of *Speaking of Indians,* Deloria already had completed a draft of *Waterlily.*[138] In many ways, the two works are the same book. Incidents reported as true in *Speaking of Indians* recur in the fictional work.[139] In *Waterlily,* the author simply presents her ethnographic data and illustrates the workings of kinship obligations that she had discussed in her treatises and covers them with a thin veneer of fiction. Like Mourning Dove's *Cogewea,* the book is often didactic. Nevertheless, it still manages to succeed as a novel, both an explication and celebration of Dakota culture and values.

The book tells the story of Dakota social reality from a woman's perspective, tracing the life of its title character from birth. Set in the early 19th century, roughly during Deloria's great-grandparents' generation, it depicts a time when Sioux ways had already been revolutionized by the introduction of the horse but when Amer-Europeans were still a rarity around Dakota territory.[140] Despite personal tragedy and increasing threat from Amer-Europeans, Waterlily and the Dakota culture itself endure, presented by Deloria as "like the ash, resilient."

Fundamental to this survival, and to the working of the society in general, is the kinship system. Repeatedly, Deloria punctuates actions or incidents by advising the reader that the actions were performed to fulfill kinship obligations. Kinship defined one's relationships and the roles one must play. In the process of acting out these roles, one was defined as a person. Every act was, in some sense, "a kinship responsibility but also a social pleasure." As Deloria's narrator, speaking for the thoughts of Waterlily, exclaims, "How all-sufficient kinship was!" The Sun Dance figures prominently in the story. After it is performed "with punctilious care and order, and, especially, with one mind and one heart," the Dakota declare, "Surely, surely now the people will live."

Deloria discusses "the universal kinship of humans." However, she also depicts humanity's relational connection to the wider community. When the Natives uncover a winter cache of earth beans stored by fieldmice, they take them for their own food, but they dutifully return a handful of dried corn for the mice so that they too may have something on which to live.

In contrast to the Dakota, Amer-Europeans are depicted as an entirely different type of being, infinitely less civilized. In an ultimate act of horror, the Whites introduce smallpox-infected blankets among the Natives, leading to an epidemic. The kinship system facilitates the spread of the contagion. Deloria writes, "Certainly nobody dreamed of isolating the first case as a check against further spread. Had one dared suggest doing so, it would only have shocked and hurt the others. They would have thought and said, 'Our relatives are precious to us, sick or well. However loathsome might be their malady, should we separate ourselves from them, as if they were animals, just to save ourselves? It is unthinkable! It is unworthy of kinship! There is something wrong with whoever proposes such a thing.' They would have seen it as a gross repudiation of fellow human beings."

Despite this extreme emphasis on kinship values, Deloria refuses to romanticize *tiyospaye* life. There is warfare, murder, and death. There can be hunger. Near the end of the novel, the band encounters a family living off by itself. A realization dawns that the father has committed incest. This, however, like murder, is an aberration. It is a grievous offense against kinship. The perpetrator is a "degenerate character" who must suffer with his family the worst of all fates, to live "away from civilization, that is to say, the camp circle." As a result, his children are wild and uncouth, lacking "any standards of social behavior."

The novel ends with an affirmation of communitist values and kinship once more, echoing *Speaking of Indians*. Waterlily, who as a youth had often rankled at her filial responsibilities and the roles she was expected to assume, realizes the absolute worth of the system. " 'All my relatives are noble,' she thought. 'They make of their duties toward others a privilege and a delight.' It was no struggle to play one's kinship role with people like them. When everyone was up to par in this kinship interchange of loyalty and mutual dependence, life could be close to perfect."

The 1930s and 1940s were a period of increased Native literary activity. Riggs, Mathews, McNickle, and Deloria all produced important works during that time. Franklin Roosevelt's Indian New Deal, however, with its end to bans on traditional religion and its greater emphasis on tribal self-government, gave way to the era of termination and relocation. The breakup of the tribal mass and a final solution to the Indian Problem once again became official policy. Public interest in Natives quickly waned. From 1944 to 1965, only two significant works of fiction by Natives were published: McNickle's *Runner in the Sun* and Natachee Momaday's *Owl in the Cedar Tree,* both works for young adult readers.[141] *Owl in the Cedar Tree* also deals with obligations to family, reflects a keen knowledge of tribal lifeways, and possesses a wonderful sense of delight. In contrast to the world of *Waterlily,* however, where one had a clear understanding of one's obligations and belonging (though they were increasingly encroached upon), Momaday's juvenilia is of a piece with the era captured in Ella Deloria's *Speaking of Indians.* It is a time of rapid change when decisions must be made as to the path Native individuals and their communities will follow.

Mayme Natachee Scott Momaday, the woman her son said imagined herself as an Indian, was the namesake of her great-grandmother, Natachee, the Cherokee that married her French great-grandfather around 1850. When her mother wedded her father around the turn of the 20th century, her Amer-European maternal grandfather disapproved, predicting that all their children would be hanged by the time they were twenty because of "their damned Indian blood."[142] As a small child, she played in the woods "where, three generations before, her great-grandmother's people had passed on the Trail of Tears."[143] Her mother died in the great influenza epidemic of 1918, when Natachee was only five.

According to her son, Scott Momaday, it was around 1929, at age sixteen, that Natachee began to think of herself as Native. That year she left her Kentucky home to attend Haskell Institute in Kansas. She remained, however, only a short time. Restless with formal schooling, she wanted to become an author and journalist, writing about Indians. As Scott puts it, "She was a roving and unpublished correspondent, the intelligence of many Americas south of the Missouri and Ohio Rivers."[144] She married Alfred Mammedaty (who simplified the family's Kiowa name to Momaday), the cousin of her roommate at Haskell.

Al Momaday's family treated Natachee badly: "As far as they were concerned, she was an outsider who had insinuated herself into their midst, and they set out to make her life miserable." Even when she was pregnant with Scott, "[a]t every turn they reminded her that she was an interloper, that she could expect to have no place among them." [145] In 1936, Haske Norwood, a Navajo friend, invited the couple to move to the Navajo Reservation, where the Momadays hoped to find work with the Indian Service in Gallup, New Mexico.

Gallup is, even today, a tough place for Indians, the embodiment of Western individualism and racist attitudes. As Scott Momaday describes it, "Gallup is a rough-edged town of dubious character and many surfaces of rich color. It is a place of high tensions and hard distinctions. I once heard someone say that Gallup is the last frontier town in America; there is a certain truth to that, I believe. On a given day you can see in the streets of Gallup cowboys and Indians, missionaries and miscreants, tradesmen and tourists. Or you can see Billy the Kid or Huckleberry Finn or Ganado Mucho—or someone who is not impossibly all these worthies in one, Everyman realized in some desperate notion of himself." [146] Over the ensuing years, the family lived in Shiprock, Tuba City, and Chinle on the Navajo Reservation. There were also stints in Oklahoma, Kentucky, and Louisiana and on the San Carlos Apache reservation. During World War II, they moved to Hobbs, New Mexico, where Natachee took an office job at the local army airbase.

At the end of the war, Natachee took a job as a teacher at the Cañoncito Day School on the Navajo Reservation. Almost immediately, she and Al were offered the two-teacher day school at Jemez Pueblo. They took it and remained there for more than twenty-five years. Again according to Scott, "There was at Jemez a climate of the mind in which we, my parents and I, realized ourselves, understood who we were, not perfectly, it may be, but well enough. It was not our native world, but we appropriated it, as it were, to ourselves; we invested much of our lives in it, and in the end it was the remembered places of our hopes, our dreams, and our deep love." [147] Natachee Momaday, who had imagined her Indian identity as a young woman, and for whom the Navajo Reservation had been a comfortable home, reimagined herself yet again. Though her novel *Owl in the Cedar Tree* was set on the Navajo Reservation and revealed considerable knowledge of Navajo lifeways, many of the incidents recounted in the book found their antecedents in episodes of Momaday family life at Jemez. Later, Scott Momaday would locate his novel *House Made of Dawn* at Jemez Pueblo.

It is sometimes said and assumed that *Owl in the Cedar Tree* deals with the conflict between Christianity and traditional religious observance among the Navajo. [148] In actuality, the only Christians in the novel are Amer-Europeans. When Haske, the novel's young protagonist, witnesses Christmas festivities at the day school he attends, he is uncomfortable because he has never participated in the holiday before. [149] Rather, the tensions that the book highlights are between progressives and pullbacks, all of whom are, to varying degrees, traditional practitioners.

Haske's Old Grandfather (great-grandfather) is a conservative traditional. His parents, however, went to boarding school and lived away from their people: "They had learned that people must change with the changing times. They knew that much in their way of life was good, and they were proud of being Navaho. But they would not hold to the old superstitions." Old Grandfather laments to Haske, "It is a shame . . . that your father does not tell you the old truths which the Ancients taught us. How can you protect yourself if you do not know these things?" Haske begins to wonder why his father has not fulfilled this obligation. When he inquires about it, his father, Night Singer, responds with the progressive line: "That is what the Ancient Ones tell us, my son. The old people continue to believe it. But you and I need not follow their beliefs. . . . We must respect the feelings of others even though we do not agree with them. Out of respect for the Old Ones we do not kill a bear or eat his meat [because the spirits of ancestors are thought to live in bears]. But we must not let the Old Ones hold us back. We must progress with time. On the other hand, we must not push them and try to make them agree with our beliefs. But just between us, my son, do not worry. A bear is only a bear." Despite his personal disbelief in the bear taboo, the father respects it out of the communitist belief that one must not shame others.

Though Night Singer may have rejected certain "superstitions," he is not a Christian. He still sings his Sunrise Song to greet the new day and has given Haske his own song to offer to the sun. When Old Grandfather is attacked by a bear and lingers near death, Haske's parents allow minimal Western medical treatment at the hands of the local sutler, but they also summon a medicine man to perform the traditional ceremony. The fact that they are progressive is even viewed as a communitist benefit; because Navajos believe that when a person dies in their hogan the hogan must be burned, some relatives shun the old man, but Haske's family is free to take him in.

Haske, who has always been artistic, witnesses the sand painter at work in the healing ceremony and is strangely moved. He connects to the timelessness of sacred time, thinking, "It is good. It is beautiful. I am in my mother's hogan, and there is no world outside. There is no day or night or yesterday or tomorrow. It is all here and now." He decides that he must become a sand painter. Recovering, Old Grandfather supports the notion and tells him, "My grandson, you will have to give up the white man's school. You cannot follow two trails at the same time. The Indian way goes one way. The white man's goes another. You will have to decide which of the two ways you will follow." Haske is troubled by the advice. Recognizing his great-grandson's hesitancy, the old man later declares, "My grandson, you do not know what is best. You hear my words, but there is fear in your heart. The white man's teaching is making you sick. Already it has a power over you. It is a bad thing to mock the gods.

Navaho gods are powerful and will send evil to those who turn from them. When you choose the white man's trail, you offend the Navaho gods." Old Grandfather tells Haske that he must undertake a vigil to discern what he must do.[150]

When Night Singer hears of the plan, he is furious. Like Natachee and Al Momaday, Haske's parents are determined that their children will have a Western education to prepare them for participation in the dominant society. Night Singer explodes, "There will be no more such talk in our hogan! The Old One will be forbidden to speak of such things. . . . My son, you have not offended *our gods.* You are young and do not realize that Old Grandfather lives in the past. You must go to school every day and learn the new ways. The world is changing fast and we must change with it."[151] The incident causes a rift in the family that is only healed shortly before the old man's death.

Owl in the Cedar Tree affirms the Native connection to the land and the ties to the wider community. The owl of the title is understood as the traditional harbinger of bad news and impending death, as it is among many tribes. On the land, Haske is never lonely: "On the desert he played with horned toads, lizards, and prairie dogs. In the mountains he played with chipmunks and squirrels. He watched birds and listened to their songs." Even though a bear, a representative of the wider community, attacks Old Grandfather, there is general agreement among the Navajo characters of the book that something is wrong with the bear; it has been possessed by an evil spirit "making him mean and dangerous." Haske would not trade his traditional home "for any other in all the world."

When Old Grandfather dies, Night Singer comforts Haske by explaining traditional beliefs about death to him. The boy has realized that Amer-European schooling "would not make a Navaho forget the ways of his people." He recognizes the truth of what his mother had told him earlier, a lesson lying at the heart of the novel: "You have worried about which trail to follow. There is only one trail. . . . Follow it and keep the best of the old ways while learning the best of the new ways." From Alex Posey to Ella Cara Deloria, it is a vision of community central to most Native writers in the first two-thirds of the 20th century.

Chapter Four

Indian Literary Renaissance and the Continuing Search for Community (1968–)

The signal event in Native literature came in 1968 with the publication of *House Made of Dawn* by Natachee Momaday's son, N. Scott Momaday. After the novel won the Pulitzer Prize in 1969, it was as if floodgates had been opened, and through them poured a steady stream of books by Natives. As Paula Gunn Allen puts it, "As the last quarter of the century has unfolded, the tiny trickle of fiction begun by Native writers during the first seventy years has become a broad and stately river."[1] Unlike the publication boomlet of the 1930s and 1940, which quickly subsided, after Momaday's breakthrough, ever increasing numbers of writers, poets, and critics have found their way into print. The reasons for this development are manifold and complex.

Allen writes, "In the bland and blinding white cocoon of the 1950s, with its Red Scare, Cold War, and suburban fixations, a reawakened consciousness stirred in the United States. As a result, the nation returned to its former self in the 1960s, as though recovering from a profound shock. In the ferment of the sixties, via Hippies, Civil Rights, the Peace Movement, Kennedy's Manpower Act, Johnson's War on Poverty, and especially the GI Bill that educated thousands of Native vets from the Second World War and the Korean and Vietnam Wars, Native writers began to publish fiction once again."[2] By the end of the 1950s, support for termination and relocation programs was ebbing. Though the Kennedy and Johnson administrations effectively ended termination, they put in place no coherent policy to replace it. As a result of the prior policy, however, large urban populations of Natives were created, especially in those cities that had been designated as relocation centers. According to Terry Wilson

(Potawatomi): "During the 1960s, urban Indians wrestled with feelings of alienation as they attempted to make their social and economic way in the cities. Cut off from rural and reservation tribal communities, they began to seek one another out, crossing tribal lines, and gathering together in urban Indian centers. A new 'Indianness' was fostered in these local institutions and at the same time national organizations like the National Congress of American Indians and the new, more radical, National Indian Youth Council [NIYC] promoted Native unity for common political action."[3] Under the direction of the NIYC, "fish-ins" and other protests were staged between 1964 and 1966 to dramatize demands for treaty rights. In late November 1969, the same year Momaday's book was winning accolades, a group of Natives calling itself Indians of All Tribes occupied the former federal penitentiary on Alcatraz Island in San Francisco Bay, citing the 1868 Fort Laramie Treaty as legal grounds for taking over unused federal property originally belonging to Natives. Other protests followed.[4] In July 1970, in a message to Congress, President Richard Nixon renounced termination and relocation and established tribal "self-determination" as official policy.[5]

At the same time, a number of books about Indians were published by both non-Natives and Natives. Volumes like Stan Steiner's *The New Indians,* Earl Shorris's *Death of the Great Spirit,* and Dee Brown's *Bury My Heart at Wounded Knee* recast the history of White/Native relations and depicted the current state of Native America, including the growing militancy. *Custer Died for Your Sins: An Indian Manifesto,* written in 1969 by Ella Deloria's nephew, and numerous subsequent volumes established Vine Deloria Jr. as "the leading contemporary American Indian intellectual."[6]

During the fall of 1968, urban Natives in Minneapolis founded the American Indian Movement (AIM), modeled on the Black Panthers, in an effort to "police the police" and monitor civil rights abuses against Natives. The new organization used the publicity generated by the Alcatraz seizure to launch a recruiting effort and began chapters in several cities. On the eve of the 1972 presidential election, it organized a caravan called the "Trail of Broken Treaties" to Washington. Anger and confusion at the march's end led to the takeover of the Bureau of Indian Affairs building; the Natives held the building for almost a week. A few weeks later, AIM activities on the Pine Ridge Reservation, where AIM leaders had come to aid traditional Oglala Lakotas opposed to the federally supported tribal government, sparked a seventy-one-day armed confrontation at Wounded Knee, site of the 1890 massacre. According to Vine Deloria, "AIM created a feeling of solidarity among Indians which has only increased and entrenched itself during the intervening years."[7]

Suddenly, Amer-Europeans who had assumed that the Indian Problem had long since been solved and Indians assimilated became aware of continued Native presence and grievances in North America. A new "Red Scare," centered not around Soviet Communism but around America's own indigenes, descended. "Waiting for the word from the West" once more captured a breathless nation.[8] Increased Native activism and the awareness it generated, the creation of Native American studies departments in universities and greater numbers of educated Natives, the first stirrings of the New Age movement with its romantic appropriation of Native religious traditions, and the policy of self-determination all came together to ensure that Native writers would not fade away once again after the success of Momaday's first novel.

House Made of Dawn deals with its hero's attempts to achieve personal integration and healing through tribal rituals and community.[9] According to Louis Owens, "With Momaday, American Indian fiction becomes a kind of vision quest, with writing reflecting the journey of its author toward a rich self-recognition as Indian. . . . Momaday's writing illustrates a process of becoming."[10] Tying the work more closely to community and the identity engendered by that community, Gerald Vizenor quotes Amer-European critic Andrew Wiget: "Momaday is breaking new ground with his intensely personal, poetic narratives, which essay the principal dilemma of an urbanized, thoroughly acculturated Indian: how to retain continuity with one's cultural heritage though displaced from the community that sustains it. The very structures of these works express the dynamic by which the psyche internalizes the mythic, historical, and cultural components of identity."[11] The novel demonstrated that Indians survived. In a pointed reference to D'Arcy McNickle's work thirty years earlier, Paula Gunn Allen writes that it shows Natives as "[s]urrounded, engulfed, but not surrendered."[12] A similar analysis could be applied to Deloria, who deals with the question of how one becomes or remains an Indian in the twentieth century, "the deeper issues of how viable, responsible communities could emerge in Indian country."[13]

Certainly since Momaday's first book, as Paula Gunn Allen points out, much Native literature has revolved around the theme of transformation, while "the major [subthemes] ones are social change, cultural transition, and shifting modes of identity. While these subthemes may seem to result from the presence of Anglo-Europeans on Native soil, they have informed the tradition since time immemorial. White presence has, perhaps, caused writers to focus on narratives that highlight social change, cultural transition, and shifting identities, and it has also transformed structural possibilities in some fundamental ways."[14] This chapter will discuss some of the many Native writers that have emerged since Momaday, beginning with Vine Deloria Jr. Following Deloria, it will examine Leslie Marmon Silko, Gerald Vizenor, Thomas King, and Betty Louise Bell. Each offers a communitist reflection on the place of Natives in the ever changing landscape of America in the late 20th century.

Vine Deloria Jr.

Since the Red Power movement of the late 1960s, there has been, as I have noted already, a growing resurgence of traditional ways among American Natives. According to George Tinker, this widespread return to Native religious traditions has "been fueled in part by anger over generations of oppression suffered at the hands of white civilization and its institutions. The latter include the Christian churches as well as educational, economic, and political institutions. As part of this larger movement, the return to traditional religions is an exercise of self-determination and not just anger at memories or current experiences of missionary history as cultural imposition."[15] Any analysis of this neotraditionalist revival and post-Christian challenge to Christianity must begin with Vine Deloria Jr. A lawyer and activist writing out of the context of the American Indian Movement of the 1970s, he is a seminal thinker and writer of the Native resurgence.[16] He has been both prolific and protean. Because of the scope and sheer volume of his work, added to the occasional and unsystematic character of his writings, it is possible to find support for a great many divergent arguments in his texts. Yet he has remained remarkably consistent in his views on the indigenous peoples of the Americas and the place of the Christian gospel for them and in his commitment to Native community. Over twenty-five years ago, he declared that the "impotence and irrelevancy of the Christian message" was causing the revival of Native spirituality.[17]

Deloria was born in 1933 on the border of the Pine Ridge Reservation, the son and grandson of Episcopal priests. He was only a third-generation Christian, his great-grandfather having been among the first of his people to convert to the new religion. Though his father (who served eighteen chapels on the eastern half of Pine Ridge) professed throughout his life that "I only know the gospel of Jesus," in which all the answers to the questions of humankind are found, as he grew older he nonetheless became less sanguine about the possibilities for the Church among Indians.[18]

As the younger Deloria finished prep school in Connecticut, his family moved from South Dakota to Iowa. He returned to South Dakota for an extended stay only once. He attended Iowa State University and Augustana Seminary (later renamed Lutheran School of Theology) in Chicago. While he was in college, his consciousness of being Indian grew, and his antagonism toward Christianity and Amer-European culture increased while he was in seminary. What was lacking from theological systems, he felt, was any connection to day-to-day living and life's problems.[19]

In the early 1960s, he was named executive director of the National Congress of American Indians. Frustrated with the conference approach to national Indian politics, he left to go to law school at the University of Colorado. He did so because he felt that "the Indian revolution was well under way" and that someone needed a law degree in order to begin a program of defense of treaty rights. At the same time, he began fostering treaty-based activism by traditional Natives. He wrote, "The message of the traditionals is simple. They demand a return to basic Indian philosophy, establishment of ancient methods of government by open council instead of elected officials, a revival of Indian religions and the replacement of white laws with Indian customs." Thus, writes Robert Warrior, "what comes out of Deloria's writings is a portrait of a search, at once pragmatic and visionary, for answers to the problems of Native communities in the context of the world as a whole. Having experienced the educational system of mainstream culture and finding little of worth for the daily struggle of sane existence, he and others sought to affirm the values of Native traditions and hoped they would foster a moment in which communities could revive those traditions as part of a process of developing socially, economically, and spiritually." [20]

Deloria has been a professor of law, politics, and Native American studies at the University of Arizona and the University of Colorado. He emerged and remains a leading figure in Native discourse. The publication of *Custer Died for Your Sins,* his first book, in 1969, was a watershed event in Native political thinking and visibility to the dominant culture. With irony and humor tinged with biting satire, Deloria attacked the Church, the government, stereotyped images of Indians, and Amer-European culture in general. Less than two years later, Alvin Josephy could write of Deloria, "[N]o single Indian has yet emerged as a spokesman for all Indians. In his speeches and writings, however, Vine Deloria Jr., a Standing Rock Sioux, has managed to articulate, with eloquence, wit, and anger, the attitudes, frustrations, and hopes of great numbers of Indians in every part of the country." [21] An article by Deloria in the *New York Times Magazine* in 1970, as he smelled "the scent of victory in the air," accurately summarized Deloria's communitist beliefs. It was entitled "This Country Was a Lot Better Off When the Indians Were Running It." [22]

In all his writings, Deloria has been an uncompromising advocate of the personhood and humanity of Indian peoples. Throughout his lengthy career, this has been most obvious in his demands for Native sovereignty and in his claim for the superiority of Native cultures over the dominant Amer-European society.

In *Speaking of Indians,* Ella Deloria, like many Native authors before her, turned to the question of the origins of American indigenes. After setting forth the Bering Strait theory, she discusses the so-called Clovis Barrier, which for many years "established" the oldest habitation of the Americas at approximately 12,000 years. She points at evidence for earlier inhabitants, querying whether the presumed immigrants from Asia might have found a population already here when they arrived. Concluding, she writes, "Of course, every bit of this is speculative; one guess is as good as another, for we can never be sure what actually took place. . . . And it doesn't really matter, does it? All that which lies hidden in the remote past is interesting, to be sure, but not so important as the present and the future. The vital concern is not where a people came from, physically, but where they are going, spiritually."[23] Similarly, Homer Noley, in his book *First White Frost,* declares, "An interesting discussion has been going on for some time, presumably led by anthropologists and archaeologists, on the subject of the origin of Native American peoples. Unfortunately, today's public schools teach one of the theories as if it were fact, namely, the Bering Strait land bridge theory. It is a theory not supported by adequate evidence, but it is held by those who need convenient answers to their questions." The problem, for Noley, is that for centuries the discussion "has been conducted without Native American participation. The passive disinterest in the inquiry into Native Americans' origins serves to enhance the absurdity of the quest."[24]

Ella Deloria's nephew is one of those Natives who have not regarded the questions raised with the "passive disinterest" described by Noley. In a number of major works, he has set out to offer "alternative explanations to some of modern science's most cherished beliefs," "challenging the tendency of scientists and historians to interpret data in a uniformitarian manner."[25] Though he undoubtedly believes in some of the theories he explicates, it is far more important for Deloria that the questions be posed and alternatives heard than that answers be provided. The objective is to free the mind and the imagination from Western scientism. The goal is to assert the humanity of Native peoples and the value of their beliefs and systems.

In his most recent book, *Red Earth, White Lies: Native Americans and the Myth of Scientific Fact,* Deloria attacks the Bering Strait theory (in a chapter entitled "Low Bridge—Everybody Cross"), pointing out that it is little more plausible than the Ten Lost Tribes myth, except that "the Bering Strait was geographically adjacent to North America";[26] he also critiques Darwinian evolution, a theme in his 1979 volume, *The Metaphysics of Modern Existence.*[27] In both of these works, as in his well-known *God Is Red,* published in 1973, he even examines various theories of world and cosmic origins, often with reference to the work of psychoanalyst Immanuel Velikovsky, the author of *Worlds in Collision.* His aim to to demonstrate that "Western science today is akin to a world history which discusses only the Mediterranean peoples."[28]

In the 1993 revision of *God Is Red,* he addresses the humanity of Native peoples in a novel way. In a chapter newly added to that edition, entitled "Natural and Hybrid Peoples," he begins by discussing what humanity can expect in the way of a relationship with the divine, stating with typical mordant wit that he owes his entire understanding of the Christian god on this point to Oral Roberts.[29] He quickly moves on, however, to a consideration of how civilization began. Always interested in theories and phenomena on the far-outer fringe of Western scientific respectability, he now turns to the so-called ancient astronaut theory, popularized in the writings of Erik von Danniken. The theory's basic theme is that the earth was long ago visited by a superior society from space. This explains not only certain odd phenomena, such as the lines of Nazca, but also the rise of civilization in some parts of the world.

Deloria admits that the theory has been "anathema to respectable scholarship" because it has been put forward in a reckless and "irresponsible manner." One writer, however—Zecharia Sitchin, in his *Earth Chronicles* quartet—has tried, according to Deloria, to advance this ancient "invasion" in a responsible and comprehensive way. Deloria then details Sitchin's claims about a dying civilization in desperate need of gold to save its thinning atmosphere, genetic experimentation to create laborers to work mines for them in Africa, and the intermarriage between the newly created humans *(homo sapiens)* and the aliens. The rest, says Deloria, is history.[30] Once again, he acknowledges that "[s]ome of Sitchin's ideas beg credibility." His story cannot be read and accepted uncritically. Deloria believes, however, that it "has a lot to offer" and that it "ring[s] true." He notes that a great many important, and more orthodox, scholars offer support. In essence, Deloria accepts the theory as true. He then avers, however, that the proponents of ancient astronaut visitation have one crucial fact wrong: it was not to the Indians of the Americas that these extraterrestrials came but to Europeans.

The ancient astronaut theory has functioned as a slur in precisely the same fashion as the Ten Lost Tribes belief. Faced with high degrees of civilization among the American indigenes, Westerners have sought to explain it by reference to influences from the outside. In the early centuries, Israel was the source. In these postmodern times, it is outer space. Deloria, however, turns the theory on its head. In so doing, he makes essentially the same rhetorical move that William Apess made 160 year earlier. He embraces the slur and uses it as a means of the proclaiming the humanity of Native peoples. He accepts the proposition that aliens from another world visited the earth and intermarried with its inhabitants. Proponents of the theory have heretofore, however, gotten things backwards. It is not indigenous peoples, but Westerners, who were influenced by these intergalactic intruders. Europeans were the product of this miscegenation; they are, in essence, aliens themselves—the hybrid people of the chapter heading. Tribal peoples around the globe are the "natural" ones, who were "only peripherally affected" by the interstellar invasion.[31] Deloria contends that he deliberately omitted discussion of these issues when he began *God Is Red* in 1972, clearly implying that he believed it even then. He states that acceptance of the theory explains important aspects of *Western* thought and culture.[32] Only Westerners, a decided minority in the world population, have rigid, hierarchical concepts of society and order. Only they have linear concepts of time. Only they have made extreme dualisms critical to their worldview.[33] These, then, must be the result of the introduction of alien influences.

Deloria claims the personhood of Natives by his assertive valorizing of Native culture as opposed to Western culture. He states that Indians fundamentally possess and value community (based wholly on kinship) in ways Amer-Europeans (who base community primarily on affiliation) do not.[34] In his essay "Circling the Same Old Rock," he declares:

> American Indians and other tribal peoples stand today as the sole example of true humanism because they willingly recognize the attributes that serve to compose and define the human being. They revere age and recognize the growing process. They establish with some degree of clarity the difference which gender creates in human perspectives. They admit that family considerations play a critical role in the distribution of goods and the application of justice. They recognize law but they also see the fullness of the moment and ask legal and political solutions be just as well as lawful. They reject a universal concept of brotherhood in favor of respectful treatment of human beings with whom they have contact. It is not necessary, they argue, that crows should be eagles.[35]

There is obviously not a great gap between such statements in 1984 and Deloria's natural-versus-hybrid-peoples discussion a decade later. He valorizes Native culture in his strong position in favor of traditional religion over Christianity and the worldview it engenders.

Deloria defends the subjectivity and personhood of Natives in his uncompromising and relentless demand for Indian sovereignty. He voices these demands consistently in his written work. This takes the form of defense both of the sovereignty of Indian tribes as nations under definitions advanced in international law and of the special status of Natives guaranteed by both treaty and the United States Constitution. He even finds an implicit acknowledgment of sovereignty in discrimination against Native Americans. In his second book, *We Talk, You Listen,* he includes a detailed discussion of the issue in a chapter entitled "Power, Sovereignty, and Freedom." He states in part:

> In order to validate the persecution of a group, the persecutors must in effect recognize the right of that group to be different. And if the group is different in a lasting sense, then it can be kept as a scapegoat for the majority. It also suffers with respect to its deviations—blacks as to color, Indians and Mexicans as to culture. The question is then posed as to how far the deviations fall short of the white norm and how far they indicate the basic solidity and validity of the group.
>
> Implicit in the sufferings of each group is the acknowledgment of the sovereignty of the group. It is this aspect—sovereignty—which has never been adequately used by minority groups to their own advantage. Perhaps not many can conceive of sovereignty outside of a territory within which they can exercise their own will. But with the present scene strewn with victims of violence, many of the victims' intruders on the turf of local communities, this cannot be the case.[36]

This would seem to be a clear articulation of what Warrior labels intellectual sovereignty. It is also an expression of communitism.[37]

Deloria's stance with regard to Christianity is more complex that it first appears. He does reject both Christianity and Christian liberation theology as embodying worldviews and strategies incompatible with Native traditions and cultures. At times, however, he appears to moderate his rejection somewhat, rooting it in power relationships as currently configured. In both editions of *God Is Red*, Deloria begins with a brief review of the current political situation in which Native Americans find themselves. He then moves to a comparison and critique of Christianity and Western culture as compared with traditional Native thought and belief. Though it deals with a variety of concepts—beliefs about death and the afterlife, the view of the individual versus the group, the doctrine of atonement, and notions of deity—the overarching theme of the work is contrasting attitudes about creation and ideas about time and space.[38] "Circling the Same Old Rock" proceeds in like manner.

Deloria contends that Christianity is rooted in a linear Western thoughtworld in which the individual is temporally oriented, situated in and related to history. Native traditions, on the other hand, are based on cyclical concepts of time. Far less individualistic than Christians, Natives think in communal terms. Further, Native peoples and traditions are spatially rather than temporally oriented. Unlike Christianity, which can be practiced anywhere, Native faiths are land-based and often depend on specific places for their performance. Recognizing this important distinction, Deloria adds a discussion of sacred sites to his revised *God Is Red*.[39]

God Is Red is essentially polemical. It reduces both Christianity and widely diverse Native religious traditions to monoliths.[40] Deloria acknowledges this in "Circling the Same Old Rock," his broad comparison of Native worldview, Marxism, and Christianity. He writes:

> Marxism, Indian traditions, and Christianity all share a common fate, in that they represent not clear channels of thought but broad deltas of emotion and insight so that attempting to articulate one in order to compare it with another involves considerable hazard. Whichever tributary of thought one might choose for comparative analysis is almost immediately disclaimed by adherents of the respective faiths in favor of the interpretation that appears most similar to the positive interpretation which they wish to give, with the result that virtually no comparison takes place. An articulation of the Indian idea of the physical world, for example, will immediately invoke Christian claims that St. Francis, not St. Thomas represents the Christian mainstream.[41]

Those who attack Deloria, variously, for generalizations, distortions, or factual inaccuracies, Warrior contends, miss the point. As previously noted, Deloria is not trying to give definite answers to any particular question in his comparisons. "What is important is that alternative methods of asking questions or of viewing the world may arise."[42] Warrior states, "Most often, the generalized statements Deloria makes come from a desire to proceed to what he sees as more important, fundamental questions that few people are asking. To read simply these comparisons of a generalized Christianity and a generalized American Indian religious perspective is to invite frustration. In each instance Christianity and the political culture that derives from it are found severely wanting and American Indian traditions are shown to be superior."[43] Once again, then, Deloria is interested in affirming the sovereignty and personhood of Natives by arguing their superiority.

Deloria contends that "liberation theology is simply the latest gimmick to keep minority groups circling the wagons with the vain hope that they can eliminate the oppression that surrounds them." "It does not," he continues, "seek to destroy the roots of oppression, but merely changes the manner in which oppression manifests itself."[44] His critique, however, extends beyond liberation theology to Christianity itself. He maintains that Christianity, as an imported religion reflecting a European worldview, fails Natives in both its theology and its social application.[45] What is needed, he claims, is a radical shift in epistemologies. He writes, "[W]e are freed and liberated once we realize the inanity and fantasy of the present manner of interpreting our experiences in the world. Liberation, in its most fundamental sense, requires a rejection of everything we have been taught and its replacement by only those things we have experienced as having values." What is needed, he maintains, is a restoration of traditional Native religion and values. For him, this restoration requires a rejection of the linear thinking and concept of creation that charactize Western thought. "An old Indian saying captures the radical difference between Indians and Western peoples quite adequately," he writes. "The white man, the Indians maintain, has ideas; Indians have visions. Ideas have a single dimension and require a chain of connected ideas to make sense. . . . The vision, on the other hand, presents a whole picture of experience and has a central meaning that stands on its own feet as an independent revelation."[46] Though he strongly advocates for a return to tribal religious traditions "wherever possible," he concedes, in an interview with Robert Warrior, that traditional ways cannot be lived out in the city. He states, "You can't have it in an urban setting. And I wouldn't delude myself that I could go back to the reservation and live any kind of a traditional life. I've been in the cities too long."[47]

Deloria is unequivocally opposed to assimilationist, missionary Christianity. That is not to say, however, that because he rejects Amer-European mission activities among Natives, he sees no place whatsoever for Christianity—that he requires throwing the baby Jesus out with the bathwater—though he doubts the religion's continued vitality. In *Custer Died for Your Sins,* he states that the best thing mainline denominations could do to revitalize Christianity among Natives would be to assist in the creation of a national Indian Christian Church. Such an institution would incorporate all existing programs into a single church body—"to be wholly in the hands of Indian people." According to Deloria, "The actual form of ministry would not be determined by obsolete theological distinctions preserved from the middle ages, but would rather incorporate the most feasible role that religion can now play in the expanding reservation societies." All existing Native clergy would be absorbed into the new denomination, which would be governed by lay boards composed of Natives. Religious functions would thus be integrated into ongoing Native life. Amer-European missionary Carl Starkloff admits, "This is Deloria's challenge to the churches, calling them back to unity and to a genuine role in the improvement of religious life without destroying native cultures." At least at the time of *Custer,* Deloria believed "an Indian version of Christianity could do much for our society." In terms similar to those of his father, he asks, "Can the white man's religion make one final effort to be real, or must it too vanish like its predecessors in the old world?" He admits that such a vision will not be accepted by non-Native Christian denominations. Practicality is not the point, though. The issue, as always, is one of power and self-determination.[48]

Throughout his work and his writings, Deloria has remained a strong proponent of communitist values. In his essay "Religion and Revolution among American Indians," he writes, "Truth is in the ever changing experiences of the community. For the traditional Indian to fail to appreciate this aspect of his [or her] own heritage is the saddest of heresies. It means the Indian has unwittingly fallen into the trap of Western religion."[49] According to Warrior, what we learn from Deloria "is not that the traditions provide a set of actions that change us through mere performance of them. If this were the case, a great number of Boy Scouts, hobbyists, and followers of New Age religions would be radically different from what they are. Speaking of tradition in such functionalist terms, Deloria argues, requires us to 'stay in a cultural ghetto and prey upon white guilt and ask [outsiders] to respect [Native] culture.' With such a point of view, he argues, 'all you are doing is preserving the exoticism of it, and every time you try to reach out you've got to use stereotypes to begin with and you crush the process of communication.' "[50] For Deloria, then, "tradition cannot and should not be a set of prescribed activities, but rather a set of processes."[51] Discussing sovereignty, he declares, "The responsibility which sovereignty creates is oriented primarily toward the existence and continuance of the group."[52] Warrior states, "Through this process-centered definition of sovereignty, Deloria is able to avoid making a declaration of what contemporary American Indian communities are or are not. Instead, Deloria recognizes that American Indians have to go through a process of building community and that that process will define the future."[53] In such a process, "tradition provides the critical constructive material upon which a community rebuilds itself."[54] As Warrior summarizes in *Tribal Secrets,* "Deloria's consistent discussion of sovereignty as an open-ended process has not often been paralleled among contemporary American Indian intellectuals. His straightforward warning against making the rhetoric of sovereignty and tradition a final rather than a beginning step remains an important reminder to those who engage in community, federal, and other American Indian work." [55]

Leslie Marmon Silko

Many of the same themes that run through the work of Vine Deloria propel the writing of Leslie Silko. Sovereignty, community, and the vitality and power of a tradition that is constantly evolving are fundamental categories for the Laguna author. Rejecting racially based essentializing, she stated in a 1980 interview, "Community is tremendously important. That's where a person's identity has to come from, not from racial blood quantum levels." [56] Applying such a criteria to herself in an autobiographical statement six years earlier, she wrote, "I grew up at Laguna Pueblo. I am of mixed-breed ancestry, but what I know is Laguna. This place I am from is everything I am as a writer and human being." [57] Like Scott Momaday, she is a writer who sees herself as a writer (and not as a "representative Indian"), "in whom a concern with memory and the past operates as a constitutive element in both writing and personal/cultural survival and growth." [58] And like Momaday (and Mourning Dove before him), she artfully weaves traditional orature and the sacred/ceremonial into Western literary forms. [59]

Born in Albuquerque on March 5, 1948, she was raised at Laguna. Describing her crossblood heritage, she states, "The white men who came to the Laguna Pueblo Reservation and married Laguna women were the beginning of the half-breed Laguna people like my family, the Marmon family. I suppose at the core of my writing is the attempt to identify what it is to be a half-breed or mixed blooded person; what it is to grow up neither white nor fully traditional Indian." [60] At Laguna she learned the Pueblo orature from her grandmothers.

While in college at the University of New Mexico, she wrote a short story, "The Man to Send Rain Clouds," based on an actual incident at Laguna, dealing with respect for the dead and religious syncretism and dimorphism. It was published in 1969, the same year she graduated from college. Five years later, it became the title piece (published with six more of her stories) in an early anthology of Native fiction edited by Kenneth Rosen. [61] She published her first book, a collection of poetry titled *Laguna Woman*, in 1974. [62] She taught at Navajo Community College in Tsaile, Arizona, and then moved to Ketchikan, Alaska, where she completed her first novel, *Ceremony*, but returned to Laguna. She has taught at the University of New Mexico and the University of Arizona and currently resides in Tucson.

She attended the University of New Mexico's American Indian Law Program for three semesters but turned away from a legal career in favor of writing, believing that the "most effective political statement I could make is in my art work."[63] Though she began writing during the most active years of AIM protests, and though she undertands the tactics the group employed, she rejects its politics of confrontation. In a 1985 interview, she stated, "I believe in subversion rather than straight-out confrontation. I believe in the sands of time, so to speak. Especially in America, when you confront the so-called mainstream, it's very inefficient, and in every way possible destroys you and disarms you. I'm still a believer in subversion. I don't think we're numerous enough, whoever 'we' are, to take them by storm."[64] She sees her writing as an act of subversion, dealing with difficult issues like injustice, land expropriation, racism, and discrimination, in subtle and often humorous ways in order to gain a hearing among the dominant culture while still addressing a Native audience.[65]

Central to Silko's poetry and fiction is the role of orature, of the power of the story itself to heal the people. In a poetic epigram to *Ceremony*, she writes of the power of story to combat evil, its importance to the People, and its role in the ceremonial.[66]

Describing this claim to power for story in the novel, Richard Sax writes:

> The problems that have obsessed Tayo [the novel's protagonist] were real events, but the means of coping are linguistically and ritualistically centered. Kenneth Lincoln suggests, "Silko's novel is a word ceremony. It tells Tayo's story as a curative act." Just as the (re)telling of the tale begins again the cycle of the story, so the solutions to Tayo's dilemmas reside somewhere in the verbal, oral traditions of Laguna culture. When Tayo has grasped or recovered enough of the word to understand that he shares responsibility, though not necessarily guilt, in the deaths of Rocky, Josiah, and the nameless Japanese, then he is ready to make the physical, plaintive effort to recover the spotted cattle which is at once an acknowledgement to the memory and dreams of Josiah at the same time it is a reaffirmation of American property law.[67]

When the medicine man, Ku'oosh, is summoned to heal Tayo, the power and importance of language and story is reinforced. Speaking of Ku'oosh's talk with Tayo, Silko writes:

> The word he chose to express "fragile" was filled with the intricacies of a continuing process, and with it a strength inherent in spider webs woven across paths through sand hills where early in the morning the sun becomes entangled in each filament of web. It took a long time to explain the fragility and intricacy because no word exists alone, and the reason for choosing each word had to be explained with a story about why it must be said this certain way. That was the responsibility that went with being human, old Ku'oosh said, the story behind each word must be told so there could be no mistake in the meaning of what had been said; and this demanded great patience and love.

Such is the centrality of story to Silko that she entitles her autobiographical meditation *Storyteller*.

Tayo at the beginning of *Ceremony* is undefined as a person. The narrative skips back and forth in time and place, reflecting the confused state of Tayo's mind. Only after Tayo meets Betonie and begins his process of reintegration both psychologically and as a member of the community does the novel take on something resembling a straight-line narrative structure. David Murray sees *Ceremony* and James Welch's *Death of Jim Loney* as "representing alternative attitudes to modern Indian identity—the one *[Death of Jim Loney]* pessimistic and emphasizing rootlessness, the other *[Ceremony]* optimistic and emphasizing a continuity and tradition which can be salvaged and retrieved."[68] This dichotomy, however, is a false one. Both works speak to the necessity of community. Jim Loney dies because he cannot reconnect to community, whereas Tayo survives because he does. In contrast to Tayo, Rocky is thoroughly deracinated and does not care what the village people think and is thus destroyed. Tayo is almost seduced by the same impulses. The Amer-European doctors at the VA hospital "had yelled at him—that he had to think only of himself, and not about the others, that he would never get well as long he used words like 'we' and 'us,' " but Tayo knows all along that his "sickness was only part of something larger, and his cure would be found only in something great and inclusive of everything." Ultimately, Tayo is able to achieve wholeness only by re-membering himself in the collective.

This power of community and story is underlined in highly material terms in Silko's latest novel, *Almanac of the Dead*. The ancient notebooks of the title, modeled on Mayan codices, are both a symbol and a tool of Native survivance. Their potency as a weapon of resistance is underscored by the fact that their Native custodian keeps them in a wooden ammunition box. When the southern tribe that composed the almanac is dying out from the impact of the European invasion, tribal members argue among themselves as to what should be done with the book: "Because they were the very last of their tribe, strong cases were made for their dying together and allowing the almanac to die with them. After all, the almanac was what told them who they were and where they had come from in the stories. Since their kind would no longer be, they argued the manuscript should rightly die with them." Finally, however, it is decided to divide the text into parts and send it north with four children, knowing that in that way at least a part of the story would survive. "The people knew that if even a part of their almanac survived, they as a people would return someday." The power of the almanac stories to sustain the people is attested to when the children are forced to eat pages of the notebook as food. They not only survive but thrive. Otherwise they would have starved. The pages of the book have many properties, both physical and spiritual, to feed the people and make them strong.

This emphasis on tradition does not mean, however, that Silko sees that tradition as static. She notes the rapid change she has seen in her own culture during her lifetime, and, like Vine Deloria, she sees tradition as a process. She believes that if a story has relevance for the People, they will remember it and retell it. If it does not feed the People or ceases to have that relevance, however, it will disappear and die.[69] In her autobiographical *Storyteller,* she recalls having her aunts tell her stories, but always with changes in detail and description. Such change was part of the story. In the process, new stories were created—"a new story with an integrity of its own, an offspring, a part of the continuing which storytelling must be."[70] In *Ceremony,* there is an acknowledgment that the old ceremonies cannot cleanse those who fought in World War II. Instead, Tayo's grief is healed by the new ceremony devised by Betonie, whose tools include telephone books, coke bottles, and Santa Fe Railroad calendars. In *Almanac,* an old woman uses a spell to make the "white man's gadgets"—airplanes—crash. Even the ancient almanac itself changes. Pages have been lost and must be reconstructed. The current lives of the people become part of the story. Though the past determines the present, and though past wrongs must be redressed, one must not get stuck in it. Grief is that depression brought on by dwelling on the injustices of the past.

Almanac is a wildly improbable, tragicomic tale involving arms merchants, strippers, drug mules, and television psychics. Its often elliptical structure demonstrates Silko's storytelling method, borrowed from the oral tradition. There are numerous complicated digressions and narratives within narratives. Almost 800 pages in print, the manuscript was reportedly cut by half prior to publication.[71] Author and critic Thomas King states, "By the time you get to the judge who abuses bassett hounds, you're saying to yourself, 'Wait a minute! What's Indian about this?' But it's a *very* Indian piece" in its storytelling style. Comparing it to the craft of the traditional storyteller, King continues, "This story is going down the highway at 150 miles an hour. You're following close behind. Then suddenly the storyteller makes a right angle turn at full speed. If you're not careful, you just run right off the road."[72] As Silko herself describes the traditional storytelling process itself in *Almanac,* "The story they told did not run in a line from the horizon but circled and spiraled instead like the red-tailed hawk."

Silko's work reveals a Native worldview in which chronological time means little: "Sacred time is always in the Present." An incident that took place seventy years before *Almanac of the Dead* begins still has ramifications because "seventy years was nothing—a mere heartbeat at Laguna." Amer-Europeans assumed that because the Ghost Dance had not produced immediate, tangible events, it lacked efficacy. In reality, avers Silko, it began a process that still continues and will achieve its goal at the appointed time. Eventually, as the ancient prophecies foretell and as Wovoka predicted, all things European will disappear from the Americas.

Community is central to her vision. Tayo must reconnect to community in order to survive. Sterling, in *Almanac of the Dead,* is banished and suffers that greatest of losses, the loss of community and family. Yet this community includes not simply human beings, or even the wider community, but the earth itself.[73] The original English definition of the word "landscape" designated a painting—something looked upon from the outside, excluding the viewer. For Silko, however, this sense of objectivity makes the term misleading. To Silko, "viewers are as much a part of the landscape as the boulders they stand on. There is no high mesa edge or mountain peak where one can stand and not immediately be part of all that surrounds. Human identity is linked with all the elements of creation through the clan."[74] According to Lucy Jones:

> "Ancient Pueblos took the modest view that the thing itself [the landscape] could not be improved upon," Silko writes, "The ancients did not presume to tamper with what had already been created." The created thing, the squash blossom, grasshopper, or rabbit was understood as the thing it was. It could not be created by human hand. Because of this, realism in art was eschewed. Relatedness in life continues into death as the dust of the once-living is taken in and recycled by the earth and by other living creatures. "The dead become dust, and in this becoming they are once more joined with the Mother. The ancient Pueblo people called the earth the Mother Creator of all things in this world. Her sister, the Corn Mother, occasionally merges with her because all succulent green life rises out of the depths of the earth." In this [attitude], all life cycles are linked together in a chain that always includes the earth.[75]

In *Almanac,* a geologist is stricken for violating Mother Earth. Her short fiction "Storyteller," in the book of the same name, "demonstrates that nature's patience is wearing thin and humankind is threatened"; "[t]he prophetic tone of the story is ominous, [suggesting] that mankind will not be able to rescue itself from its own rapaciousness." The essays in *Yellow Woman and a Beauty of the Spirit* "emphasize the inextricable links between human identity, imagination and Mother Earth," links forged and mediated in story.[76]

In this view of the earth, nuclear power holds a special place in Silko's work. The author grew up at Laguna, "not far from the Los Alamos uranium mines and the Trinity Site, where on July 16, 1945, the first atomic bomb was detonated."[77] Men from Laguna worked those mines and died as a result.[78] The final denouement of *Ceremony* takes place near these sites, and there is a sense in which the atomic bomb has made all creation one again: "There was no end to it; it knew no boundaries; and he had arrived at the point of convergence where the fate of all living things, and even the earth had been laid." In *Almanac,* the old ones warned against uranium mining because "all the people would pay, and pay terribly, for this desecration, this crime against all living things." In *Sacred Water,* her paen to the sacrality of water for all life, Silko relates the effects of fallout from the Chernobyl disaster on her home in Ketchican. It decreased the toad population and caused a strange red algae to grow in a rain pool behind her house. Rather than destroy the pond, she transplanted water hyacinths into it. She writes:

> The water in the pool began to clear and smell cleaner because water hyacinths digest the worst sorts of wastes and contamination: decomposing rodents and dead toads—nothing is too vile for the water hyacinth. Water hyacinths even remove lead and cadmium from contaminated water. I write in appreciation of the lowly water hyacinth, purifyer of defiled water.
>
> Only the night-blooming datura, jimson weed, sacred plant of the Pueblo priests, mighty hallucinogen and deadly poison, only the datura has the power to purify plutonium contamination. Datura not only thrives in soil contaminated by plutonium, the datura actually removes the plutonium from the soil so that the soil is purified and only the datura plant itself is radioactive. The datura metabolizes "heavy water," contaminated with plutonium, because, for the datura, all water is sacred.
>
> Across the West, uranium mine wastes and contamination from underground nuclear tests in Nevada ruin the dwindling supplies of fresh water. Chemical pollutants and heavy metals from abandoned mines leak mercury and lead into aquifers and rivers. But human beings desecrate only themselves; the Mother Earth is invioable [*sic*]. Whatever may become of us human beings, the Earth will bloom with hyacinth purple and the white blossoms of the datura.[79]

In all her writings, Silko uses her skills of subversion to defend Native peoples and community, decrying "hundreds of years of exploitation of the Native American people here."[80] Her characters are not merely surviving but resisting. Even the crimes, such as drug dealing and bank robbery, in which the characters engage in *Almanac* are viewed as resistance. The war for Native lands and sovereignty has never ended. As she writes in that volume, "There were hundreds of years of blame that needed to be taken by somebody."

Gerald Vizenor

In his introduction to *Shadow Distance: A Gerald Vizenor Reader,* A. Robert Lee writes, "One of Native America's leading writer-contemporaries who considers 'Indians' to be inventions? An enrolled member of White Earth Reservation, Minnesota, whose own crossblood Anishinaabe (or Chippewa/Ojibway) descent could not more have drawn him to past legacies of Native-white encounter yet whose best-known writing displays a wholly postmodern virtuosity? A Professor of Ethnic Studies at Berkeley while at the same time an adept in the oral and improvisatory, and so anything but academic, story-telling of the trickster?"[81] Obviously, for anyone desiring to believe that Natives are stoic and unchanging, the work of Gerald Vizenor, with its "bravura unpredictability," like the visual art of artists like Richard Glazer Danay (Mohawk) or Norman

Akers (Osage/Pawnee), is unnerving.[82] Such discomfiture is strictly intentional. As Vizenor himself often has said, "[S]ome upsetting is necessary."[83]

Gerald Vizenor was born on October 22, 1934, in Minneapolis, where his father worked as a housepainter. A year and a half later, Clement William Vizenor, at twenty-six, was beaten in an alley and his throat cut. The murder was never solved "because no one paid much attention to the murder of an Indian in those days."[84] The son was deposited with relatives. As Robert Lee writes, "It was a passed-around young life and anything but well-served."[85]

On his eighteenth birthday, Gerald Vizenor enlisted in the United States Army. He was shipped out for Korea, but the war came to an end before he could complete training in Japan. Transferring from a tank battalion to special services, he studied dance, music, and theater. In his autobiography, *Interior Landscapes,* he writes, "Japan was my liberation, and the literature, the haiku poems, are closer to me now in imagination, closer to a tribal consciousness, than were the promises of missionaries and academic careers." He remains widely recognized as among the foremost writers of haiku in America. Discharged from the army in 1955, he returned to the United States and began college at New York University, eventually graduating from the University of Minnesota. Like Leslie Silko, he began law school—at William Mitchell College of Law—but quit after one semester. He also completed two years of graduate school in library science and Asian studies. He worked as a journalist and a social worker in the Minnesota State Reformatory. He has held numerous teaching posts, beginning in 1970 at Lake Forest College in Illinois and culminating with his present position as professor of ethnic studies at the University of California, Berkeley.

He published his first work, *Born in the Wind,* "ten pages of privately printed, intimate and celebratory, lyrics" in March 1960 to commemorate the birth of his son, Robert.[86] He followed it in 1962 with *Two Wings the Butterfly: Haiku Poems in English.* These were the first works of a prolific writing career that includes six novels; an autobiography; several works of criticism, tribal history, orature, and myth; numerous volumes of poetry and short stories; and a produced screenplay.

Between 1964 and 1968, he also worked as a community organizer. Owens writes, "Always active in Native American concerns, Vizenor headed the American Indian Employment and Guidance Center in Minneapolis, organized protests, and wrote troubling articles and essays about injustices directed at Native Americans."[87] His work as director at the center was formative. In a 1985 interview, he stated that because of the magnitude and immediacy of the problems he encountered there, he "internalized a lot of pain and suffering." He continued, "I've had people just walk into an office I opened on Franklin Avenue with nothing left in their psychic energy but that last effort to open the door. And often all you can say is, 'Too bad.' You can't solve people's lives; you can only work with humor and material." [88] In *Interior Landscapes*, he concludes the chapter about his experience there with the story of one particular couple that came in one particular day near closing time. The man, a mixed-blood, "had a primal sense of personal and cultural doom." The woman wore a shirt stained with vomit. "She was drunk, ancient from abuse, and when she moved her lips to speak the dark creases on her face sagged under an awesome cultural burden." Spurred by the presence in the room of a traditional ceremonial staff, she sang. She may have been inebriated, but when she sang her tribal songs, she was sober. [89] Counterposed with that nameless woman is Dennis Banks. In a story that he relishes repeating, Vizenor describes how he organized the first urban Indian protest movement against the BIA in Minneapolis. Banks, the future AIM founder, came into his office wearing a suit and tie and announced without a shred of irony, "Demonstrations are not the Indian way." [90]

Consistent with his views of communitism and his belief in community-based organizing, Vizenor has always been critical of many AIM activists. Covering the 1973 siege at Wounded Knee for the *Minneapolis Tribune*, he saw them as urban radicals who sought to reinvent themselves as Indians from the sepia-tone photographs of Edward Curtis without any real connection to the reservation people they sought to help. In a piece entitled "Confrontation Heroes," he wrote, "Since then [Dennis Banks's appearance in Vizenor's office], Banks and hundreds of young adventurers have trouped across the country from Plymouth Rock to Alcatraz, dressed in century-old tribal vestments, demanding recognition of treaty rights, equal justice and sovereignty. The occupation of Wounded Knee may be the last symbolic act for the aging militant leaders. . . . The American Indian Movement is an urban revolutionary movement whose members have in recent years tried to return to the reservations as the warrior heroes of tribal people. To some, they are the heroes of contemporary history—but to others they are the freebooters of racism." [91] He was equally critical of the self-appointed activists in "Urban Radicals on Reservations" and other pieces. [92] Characteristically, he also made them the point of stinging satire in his fiction. In his novel *The Trickster of Liberty*, as Owens notes, "Vizenor launches another of his many attacks upon those he sees as hypocritical activists pandering to whites' conception of invented Indians." [93] In *Trickster*, he introduces Coke de Fountain, "an urban pantribal radical and dealer in cocaine," a convicted felon whose "tribal career unfolded in prison, where he studied tribal philosophies and blossomed when he was paroled in braids and a bone choker. He bore a dark cultural frown, posed as a new colonial victim, and learned his racial diatribes in church basements."

Like Leslie Silko, Vizenor honors and celebrates the role of story for Native identity, community, and culture. Of the intoxicated woman who sang in his office, he writes, "That tribal woman in the shirt stained with vomit imagined the stories she told; she sang in a good time, a visual time of wonder and memories, about her experiences in the new urban world, and her collective memories from the tribal past. She moved me in her stories, and we remember her creation on the urban reservation."[94] He told interviewer Laura Coltelli, "You can't understand the world without telling a story. There isn't any center to the world but a story."[95] When we lose our stories, he says, we lose ourselves. The telling of stories is both spiritual and essential: spiritual because of their ability to form identity and community, and essential as a means of claiming representational sovereignty against the forces in the dominant culture that suppress them and collapse the diversity and richness of Native lives into homogenized banality.

This is not to say that the stories themselves, any more than Native cultures in general, are static and unchanging. Louis Owens writes, "In the oral tradition a people define themselves and their place in an imagined order, a definition necessarily dynamic and requiring constantly changing stories. The listeners are coparticipants in the 'behavioral utterance' of the story; as Vizenor himself has written elsewhere, 'Creation myths are not time bound, the creation takes place in the telling, in present-tense metaphors.' Predetermined values represent stasis and cultural suicide."[96] Condemning the uniformity of orature in print, Vizenor speaks of the tragedy of lifeless stories that become a "standardized liturgy, as if [they] were scripture."[97] This dynamic view of stories and community is a potent force in Vizenor's fiction.

Describing Vizenor's first novel, *Darkness in Saint Louis Bearheart* (reissued in 1990 as *Bearheart: The Heirship Chronicles*), Owens writes, "Unarguably the most radical and startling of American Indian novels, *Darkness in Saint Louis Bearheart* is paradoxically also among the most traditional of novels by Indian authors, a narrative deeply in the trickster tradition, insisting upon the values of community versus individuality, upon syncretic and dynamic values versus the cultural suicide inherent in stasis, upon the most delicate of harmonies between humanity and the world we inhabit, and upon our ultimate responsibility for that world."[98] Like most of Vizenor's other writings, it reflects a strong postmodernist idiom. In writing thus, Vizenor, like many other contemporary Native writers, achieves a remarkable synthesis of form and content that places unusual demands on readers, especially non-Native readers, to recognize patterns, structures, motifs, and themes.[99]

At first glance, the use of postmodernism would seem an odd choice for a Native author. Two great sciences rose to prominence in the 19th century. Sociology studied that which was deemed normative, the dominant culture. Anthropology, a favorite object of Vizenor's scorn, studied the Others. Attacking the false outside view predicates of anthropology, Vizenor writes, "Science, translation, and the discoveries of otherness in tribal cultures are the histories of racialism and the metanarratives of dominance."[100] Similarly, in the late 20th century two major movements have emerged as people seek to understand their changing world: postcolonialism and postmodernism. It is no coincidence that just as postcolonial peoples find the power to assert their own autonomy and personhood, the postmodern theorists of continental Europe and their Amer-European disciples proclaim an end to subjectivity. It serves once again to preserve the myths of conquest and the literature of dominance.

For Vizenor, however, the postmodern is startlingly akin to the premodern, to the tribal, to the dynamism of traditional orature. It thus becomes for him a powerful revolutionary tool for breaking down dominant structures. As Ashcroft, Griffiths, and Tiffin point out, "[Postmodern] theories, seen as disruptive, subversive, and innovative, were instantly recognized by critics in both settler colonies and colonies of intervention . . . as expressive of much of their situation, and quite consistent with the direction of most of their existing literature and criticism. It is perhaps an indication of the persisting hegemony of Europe that theories such as poststructuralism are adopted more readily than similar views derived from the conditions of post-colonial experience."[101] Vizenor, however, declares, "The simulations of survivance are heard and read stories that mediate and undermine the literature of dominance."[102] Postmodernism thus becomes an expression of communitism. Quoting Jean-François Lyotard, Vizenor states that the postmodern is the breakdown of and "incredulity toward metanarratives."[103] He uses the postmodern to deconstruct outside view predicates of what constitutes "Indians" and, in so doing, to create new potential for cultural identity and coherence. In 1987, he told Joseph Bruchac (Abenaki):

Philosophically, I think we should break out of all the routes, all the boxes, break down the sides. A comic spirit demands that we break from formula, break out of program, and there are some familiar ways to do it and then there are some radical or unknown ways. I suppose I am preoccupied with this theme because the characters I admire in my own imagination and the characters I would like to make myself to be break out of things. They break out of all restrictions. They even break out of their blood. They break out of the mixture in their blood. They break out of invented cultures and repression. I think it's a spiritual quest in a way. I don't feel that it's transcendence—or escape as transcendence. That's not the theme I'm after, but I'm after an idea of the comic, that the adventures of living and the strategies of survival are chances. They're mysteries because they're left to chance. Life is a chance, all life is a chance. And that's the comic spirit. A tragic spirit is to trudge down the same trail, try to build a better path, make another fortune, build another monument and contribute it to another museum and establish more institutions to disguise our mortality. I consider all of that a formula to control and oppress—not evil, not evil in manner, but it does control. So I feel a need to break out of the measures that people make.[104]

Central to Vizenor's work is that "comic spirit" and the figure of the trickster, which he writes about with tremendous sophistication. Fellow writer Thomas

King, who has himself employed tricksters in his fiction, states, "Probably more than any other Native writer, Vizenor understands the trickster figure. And he writes about that trickster figure over and over and over again in a very complex and, I think, very savvy way." [105] Emphasizing the communitist character of the trickster, Vizenor contends, "[Y]ou could characterize Western patriarchal monotheistic manifest-destiny civilizations as tragic. It doesn't mean they're bad, but they're tragic because of acts of isolation, their heroic acts of conquering something, always overcoming adversity, doing *better than* whatever, proving something, being rewarded for it, facing the risks of doing this and usually doing it alone and almost always at odds with nature. Part of that, of course, is the idea of the human being's divine creation as superior. The comic spirit is not an opposite, but it might as well be. You can't act in a comic way in isolation. You have to be included. There has to be a collective of some kind." [106] The trickster's business is to disrupt and subvert social and cultural values while puncturing every pomposity and pretension. Through the very process of disruption, the world is imaginatively kept in balance. By trickster's actions, the world is defined and re-created. This, however, is always accomplished by Vizenor's trickster with humor and compassion, characteristics of trickster, avers Vizenor, that are often overlooked by anthropologists. Rob Niewenhuys points out that satire is often a means of distantiation: "Humorists are always relativists who keep their distance and express themselves indirectly." [107] Louis Owens, however, disagrees in the case of Vizenor, writing, "Harsh laughter is the matrix out of which Vizenor's fiction arises, the kind of laughter Mikhail Bakhtin finds at the roots of the modern novel. 'As a distanced image a subject cannot be comical,' Bakhtin writes; 'to be made comical, it must be brought close.'" [108]

Just as Vizenor's trickster breaks conventions, his characters even "break out of the mixture in their blood." As Mourning Dove does in *Cogewea*, without ever denigrating full-bloods, Vizenor unswervingly champions the identity of mixed-blood Indians, those he calls "crossbloods." [109] Such individuals "[loosen] the seams in the coarse shrouds of imposed identities." [110]

Frantz Fanon argued that the Third World created Europe. Such a "preposterous reordering of things" is the starting point of Vizenor's novel *The Heirs of Columbus*, his contribution to the Columbus Quincentenary melee. [111] It is history turned inside out and then dumped on its head, exposing the fragility and subjectivity of "historical truth" for all to see. A group of crossbloods is shown to be descended from the fabled explorer, a consquence of the latter's coupling with a Native woman during his first voyage. Columbus himself, however, was a crossblood as well, the result of a Mayan "discovery" of Europe long before Europeans could even contemplate returning the favor. The Admiral of the Ocean Sea was thus merely bringing his genes back to the land of his ancestors. On October 12, 1992, his crossblood heirs, a new breed of shamans who use computers and biogenetics to substantiate their claims, declare a new nation where "humor rules and tricksters heal." They even threaten to annex the United States in satisfaction of the unpaid tithe on all the wealth of the continent promised to Columbus by his royal patrons Ferdinand and Isabella.

Dead Voices is a much-needed antidote to "plastic medicine men," those spiritual hucksters like Sun Bear and Wallace Black Elk, who peddle a mixture of real and fraudulent spiritual tradition to unsuspecting non-Natives.[112] The "dead voices" of the title are those heard by non-Natives. Divorced from nature, they have lost the stories that liberate the mind and hold the world together. Now they are only "wordies," hearing the dead voices of the printed page and the university lecture. The results are disastrous for their personal lives and for the environment.

On the other hand, Bagese, the shaman heroine of the tale, hears great voices. She and the book's unnamed crossblood narrator (a university lecturer in "tribal philosophies") play the wanaki chance, a meditation game in which (stressing the connection to the wider community) the participants actually become animals by entering into their images on tarotlike cards. Through the wanaki, the pair become bears, fleas, mantises, crows, and beavers. Unlike the urban-dwelling Natives, these animals live tribally. Yet, hunted, exterminated, and captured for study by scientists, their experiences mirror those of America's indigenous peoples. As the shape-shifting duo goes from one transformation to the next, Bagese's pupil learns to hear the voices, understanding finally that crossbloods (and Natives in general) must survive, simply "go on" in a world where the tribes are gone and the voices dead.

In *Landfill Meditation*, a collection of short stories, the characters are once again crossbloods.[113] Many of them are city dwellers seeking to recover an identity. In San Francisco, urban Sun Dancers must raise their own artificial sun because of unrelenting cloud cover. "Urban reservations" are shown to be no better than their traditional, colonial counterparts. In one story, Vizenor quotes Anaïs Nin, who describes city Indians as being on a "slow walk like a somnambulist emeshed in the past and unable to walk into the present." He employs the same quotation as an epigram at the beginning of *Bearheart*. The sad reality for such persons, as Fanon and Memmi remind us, is that the dominant culture, not satisfied with controlling the Native's present and future, has rewritten that past as well.

To read Vizenor's work is to enter a self-referential, satiric world. Characters recur from book to book, and their stories are retold, becoming in the process new tribal myths. Repetition serves as a mnemonic shorthand. Thus, in *Dead Voices*, the story of Martin Bear Charme, who establishes a meditation center on landfill in San Francisco Bay, is retold from *Landfill Meditation*. The story of a hunter who watches a squirrel he has shot struggle valiantly but futilely to survive is repeated in *Dead Voices* from *Interior Landscapes* and an autobiographical essay in Brian Swann and Arnold Krupat's *I Tell You Now*.[114] The creation myth of the Anishinaabe recurs again and again, reshaped to fit each new circumstance. Satire serves as a magical connection with oral tradition. His works may be labeled as novels or as collections of stories, but as characters flow from one piece to the next, either form can be read alternatively as the other. In his postmodern vision, conventional narrative matters little. He regularly employs novels-within-novels and stories-within-stories. Time and place flow mythically together. His words tumble over each other with a poetic ferocity. Neologisms abound—"sollutionation" (both sollution and hallucination), "terrocious" (a combination of terrific and ferocious), "socioacupuncture" (applying the right pressure to the right place at the right time).

Vizenor's is also an intensely Native world where the wider community is celebrated and brought near. In one of the most discussed aspects of his novel *Bearheart,* a woman has sex with two boxer dogs. The author contends, however, that anyone who is offended has misread the story, pointing out its clear connection to tribal orature. In such stories, animals are not lower in the economy of creation than humans, and humans often mix freely with them as equals. He declares:

> I've told you stories before, other characters have told you stories in the novel about creation possibilities that all life has some relationship—it's a worldview. There have been marriages between animals and humans. And you can accept that on a kind of folk level, mythic level, but here it is, now what do you do? Is it too real? Has it lost its mythic power or is myth just make-believe? Is myth just for fairy-tale movies or is myth a powerful reality, a truth that can be experienced? I believe it can be experienced and I did it on the page. My second statement . . . is you'd better reread it and tell me what's wrong with a human being loving an animal. What's wrong with that is Judeo-Christian, not tribal. That doesn't mean that. tribal people are sleeping with animals, I don't mean that, but in the story there isn't anything wrong with it.[115]

In his 1987 interview with Joseph Bruchac, he states succinctly, "What I am doing is simply saying—though there is nothing simple about it—that there isn't anything wrong, is there, with a human being expressing some love of a physical and emotional kind for animals."[116] It is an expression of connection and emotive bond with the wider community, considered no less than humans in creation. This affinity for the wider community and the earth runs throughout Vizenor's work. In *Landfill Meditation,* for example, the landfill where Martin Bear Charme establishes his meditation center is itself an attempt to make something human, something humane, from the detritus of "civilization." In his latest book, *Hotline Healers: An Almost Browne Novel,* he returns to his familiar theme of "panic holes." These are openings dug into the ground and into which people scream as therapy, as if the earth itself were absorbing their grief.

In a 1992 review of *Dead Voices,* the reviewer called Vizenor "the literary equivalent of a drive-by shooting."[117] Anything can become a target of his satiric sensibilities, and being "on his side" is no guarantee of safe conduct through his mythic territory. In *Dead Voices,* for instance, anthropologists are revealed to have been made out of excrement. An urban shaman makes money by using her powers on weekends to clean up a chemical company's toxic wastes. With equally sharp gaze, Vizenor skewers tribal officials, Indian activists, identity politics, reservation gambling, and fellow Native academics. He condemns the arrogance of "last lectures" or "terminal creeds," the dogmatic absolutism that people use to define and control the world without ever really engaging it. To take oneself too seriously is a cardinal sin. The problem, in almost every case, is those who seek to define who is an Indian and then proclaim that anyone not fitting the invented definition cannot be one.

In "Four Skin Documents," a story in *Landfill Meditation,* the first-person narrator is a crossblood trickster-author with a computer. His editor rejects his material, declaring that "satire is not truth." The writer responds that satire is a legitimate expression of what Natives have become in the world. It is a world of pan-tribal urban emptiness where "people are severed like dandelions on suburban lawns, separated from living places on the earth." In cities, Natives are forced to become the invented Indians of popular imagination, wearing long hair, beads, plastic ornaments, and imported leather. And not to play the invention game is to become utterly invisible. Yet even in such a place, Vizenor sees possibilities. In *Dead Voices,* he articulates the choice as being between the chance offered by his urban tricksters and the "drone of cultural pride on reservations." His narrator declares, "I would rather be lost at war in the cities than at peace in a tame wilderness."

It may be that in "Four Skin Documents" and in the penultimate chapter of *Dead Voices* one comes closest to catching a glimpse of the "real" Gerald Vizenor. It is best, however, not to think that one understands him too easily. He is a contrarian, closely identifying with the crossblood trickster he celebrates. His stories are comic, communitist acts of survival, helping crossbloods imagine themselves and negotiate their world the same way their ancestors imaginatively found their way through their own via story. Throughout his work one confronts the shared experience of having to use personal symbology to make sense of daily schisms between the old and new, Western and Native, the personal and the communal.[118] His work contains truth, but it is truth that transcends mere fact. And as a character in one of his stories states, "In a world of lies, the best deception is the truth."

Thomas King

Many of the same themes that pervade the writing of Gerald Vizenor—identity, cultural alienation, the role of trickster, the meaning of historical reality—are played out as well in the work of Thomas King. Once again, the tools for that exploration are humor and subversion. Acknowledging the affinity, King states, "I would love to think of myself as subversive. I would like to be half as subversive as Gerry Vizenor is."[119] King, in fact, has led a life as variegated and unlikely as one of Vizenor's crossblood tricksters, testimony to the diversity of Native experience in America.

Thomas King was born on April 24, 1943, in Sacramento, California, location of the hospital closest to his mother's home in Roseville. Even at an early age, King was raised in a woman's world. His father, a Cherokee, was in the army and "never around." When King was five, his father deserted the family for good. Four years later, he sought a reconciliation, but though King's mother agreed, the alcoholic father never returned and was presumed dead. The absence of a male parent is dramatized in King's first novel, *Medicine River*, in which Will, the book's lead figure, reflects on childhood memories of a similar life and eventually gets the opportunity to meet and confront the missing man. In a case of life imitating art, in 1995, King was contacted by a private detective and learned that his father had not perished but had gone on to raise two more families before recently passing away. Though King missed his character's chance for a reunion, he discovered a raft of relations he never knew he had.[120]

In his father's absence, King's mother raised two sons, supporting herself as a hairdresser. Her beauty shop was in the front of a warehouse, in which the family also lived. The back portion of the building was still used for storage. Their home had no windows; the only light came from whatever electric lights they turned on. King, a photographer, remembers it as like living in a darkroom. During these years, it was his mother, a non-Native, who kept alive her sons' sense of being Cherokee, even taking them to back to Oklahoma to see relatives. When King was fourteen, his mother sent him to a Catholic boarding school in Sacramento.

After finishing high school in public school in Roseville, King went to Sacramento State. He spent his time there playing hearts in the cafeteria and acting in student dramas. He flunked out after one year with a .9 grade-point average. Stints as an actor in summer stock, a dealer and croupier at a casino in Tahoe, and in the U.S. Navy (which he left after only a month because of a blown knee) followed. He returned to Sierra Junior College in Rockland, California, where he earned his A.A. in business administration. More odd jobs—ambulance driver and bank teller—followed.

In 1964, he signed on to work his way one way to New Guinea on a tramp steamer. Only when the ship was under way did he realize that he had made a mistake and that it was actually bound for New Zealand. Though he was only in New Zealand on a thirty-day tourist visa, he remained nine months before immigration authorities discovered him and forced his departure for Australia. His jobs in the Southern Hemisphere were as diverse as they had been before. He worked at a freezing plant and as a deer culler (a job he got simply because he had a rifle and was Native American), a bouncer in a strip joint, a beer bottle sorter, and a gold assayer (because the regular assayer injured himself falling off a barstool and King was the only other person who could read in the outback mining camp).

Finally, he got a job as a photojournalist for the Sunday supplement magazine *Everybody's*. His assignments usually consisted of offbeat, fish-out-of-water pieces, such as describing what it was like to be an American Indian on a surfboat. During this period, he also wrote a novel, a "penny dreadful" about American astronauts hiding from Russian spies in a college dormitory. According to King, even his grandmother, who normally showered unstinting praise on any of his endeavors, didn't like it. It was never published.

In 1967, he returned to the United States, first hanging around Haight Ashbury in San Francisco and then working as a draftsman for Boeing in Seattle, where he took courses at the Seattle Free University. Between 1968 and 1971, he completed a bachelor's in English at Chico State, where he founded the first Indian organization with Rick Glazer Danay. His years at Chico State were followed by stays at the University of Utah, where he eventually earned a master's and Ph.D. and served as coordinator of American Indian studies and the History of the Americas program, and in Eureka, California, where he headed the association for special support programs (which included programs for Native students).

In 1980, a friend, Leroy Littlebear, asked him to come to the University of Lethbridge in Alberta to teach Native studies. He remained for nine years, then left to take a similar position at the University of Minnesota. He currently teaches at the University of Guelph in Ontario. While in Lethbridge, his experiences with the Blood Reserve community and playing on an all-Native basketball team gave him the material for short stories that evolved into his first published novel, *Medicine River*. He has gone on to write two more novels, *Green Grass, Running Water,* and *Truth and Bright Water* (the latter yet to appear in print); publish a collection of his short fiction, *One Good Story, That One;* and edit an anthology of Canadian Native literature, *All My Relations*.[121]

King acknowledges influences in his writing from sources as divergent as Natives Vizenor, Momaday, Silko, Welch, and Louise Erdrich (Anishinaabe) and non-Natives Herman Melville, Alice Munro, and Margaret Atwood. Of special significance for him was the comic orature of Harry Robinson, whose Okanagan stories were compiled by Wendy Wickwire.[122]

In King's fiction as in Vizenor's, the figure of the trickster plays an important role. Discussing the trickster's liberative and communitist role, Vizenor writes: "The trickster is reason and mediation in stories, the original translator of tribal encounters; the name is an intimation of transformation, men to women, animals to birds, and more than mere causal representation in names. Tricksters are the translation of creation; the trickster creates the tribe in stories, and pronounces the remembrance as the trace of liberation. The animals laughed, birds cried, and there were worried hearts over the everlasting humor that would liberate the human mind in trickster stories. Trickster stories are the translation of liberation, and the shimmer of imagination is the liberation of the last trickster stories."[123] In *Medicine River,* and *Truth and Bright Water,* King's tricksters are human in form. In *Truth and Bright Water,* Monroe Swimmer, "famous Indian artist," buys an old mission church on the reserve and moves in. He paints the outside of the building in trompe d'oeil sky and clouds until it becomes virtually invisible, and then he places sculptures of buffalo around it. In effect, he erases the alien, Christian presence and restores the land to its natural, Native state—at least to the unwitting eye. In *Medicine River,* Maydean Joe, a retarded girl who breaks into play whenever she feels like it, and Harlen Bigbear, who lures Will back to the reserve, both function as tricksters. No one knows what Harlen does for a living or where he comes from. He simply appears magically everywhere. Just as he cajoled Will back home, he gives people what they need whether they realize it or not. In the film version of *Medicine River,* for which King wrote the screenplay, Harlen is flattened out and appears less as a trickster than a reservation hustler, a used car salesman. Most often, in short stories and in *Green Grass,* King's trickster figure takes the form of Coyote, the best-known western Native trickster. King recognizes, however, that despite Coyote's importance in many Native cultures it runs the risk of becoming a cliché in Native written literature. He hopes Native authors will consider a moratorium on Coyote tales and explore, as Vizenor has, the possibilities of other traditional tricksters, such as mink or raven. He himself is thinking of writing about one of the Cherokee tricksters, *Jisdu,* the rabbit. In a 1993 interview, King stated, "I suppose if there's any weakness in *Green Grass* it's that I didn't follow Vizenor's example and make Coyote more complex."[124] Coyote in *Green Grass* serves mainly as a foil for the Creator. It is this lack of complexity that leads Vizenor to criticize King's treatment as "trickster silhouettes."[125]

A theme in King's work closely related to his work with the trickster is the Native value of harmony and balance. In his introduction to *All My Relations,* he writes, "The trickster is an important figure for Native writers for it allows us to create a particular kind of world in which the Judeo-Christian concern with good and evil and order and disorder is replaced with the more Native concern for balance and harmony." His short story "The One about Coyote Going West" is "part of a long tradition of stories that speak to the nature of the world and the relatedness of all living things."[126] Elucidating the concept, King states, "I think there is within Native communities, the ones I've worked in, a great desire to maintain a balance, to make things right if they're wrong—not to make everything good but to maintain a balance. There's a big difference. For Harlen that's certainly true; he wants to see that bubble in the level stay right where it is. And the old Indians recognize that they didn't take all that good care of the world. Things went wrong—as things will—and they understand that too. But they're trying to maintain some kind of a balance." [127] The "old Indians" referred to by King are the four ancient Natives who escape from a mental hospital at the beginning of *Green Grass* in the hope of "fixing things." Their repeated breakouts—thirty-seven to date—have coincided with, and perhaps *caused,* disasters: the eruptions of Krakatoa and Mount Saint Helens, the 1929 stock market crash, Richard Nixon's inauguration. According to King, "I wanted to make sure when I worked with the old Indians that the sense of control that is there in the universe was marginal at best. Within Native cosmology there isn't that sort of omniscience, omnipresence, and omnipotence that you have in a Judeo-Christian world." [128]

Just as it was important for King in *Green Grass* to dispel the popular image of old Indians as "reservation shamans" from whose mouths great truths pour, struggling against stereotypes has been a consistent part of King's life and writing. His short story "A Seat in the Garden" is a parody of Thomas Kinsella's novel *Shoeless Joe,* which became the film "Field of Dreams." The unspoken joke is that Kinsella has also written numerous stereotyped "Native" stories featuring Silas Ermineskin and Frank Fencepost. According to Terry Goldie, "Kinsella's fiction remains circumscribed. The few Indians who deviate from the established semiotic field are given very limited roles. Any who are successful in the white world are immediately rejected as central subjects, unless they are perceived as buffoons. The obvious problem for such characters in overtly 'Indian' texts is that an Indian who does not fit within the semiotic field loses the shape identifiable as an Indian, an important element of the 'exotic' in Kinsella's fiction." [129] It is precisely this exoticism and stereotyped representation that King lampoons.

King has always been intentional in identifying himself as of "Cherokee, Greek and German descent" so that the dominant culture will not misunderstand that in him they are not getting their romanticized image of an "authentic Indian." He believes that his eclectic career and his urban, mixed-blood upbringing allows him a freedom to address these issues that some other Native writers may not have, that they allow him to ask some of the "really nasty questions that need to be asked." He declares:

> I'm in a position where I don't have anything to lose—or anything to gain—by asking some of the questions I ask. You know, in some ways, I'm this Native writer who's out in the middle—not of nowhere, but I don't have strong tribal affiliations. I wasn't raised on Cherokee land. . . . That's a hard thing for me because I'd

rather be accepted across the board by Native communities and Native people. I really don't care about the White audience . . . because they really don't have an understanding of the intricacies of Native life, and I don't think they are much interested in it, quite frankly. They're interested in aspects of it but not in the intricacies. So I think there are questions that are important to ask: "Who is an Indian?" How do we develop this idea of Indianness? I like to show Indians in different positions, different blood quantums if you will, but a mix. So that there are Indian people out there who see that and say, "Oh, OK, I don't feel so bad now that I'm not a fullblood Indian on the back of a pinto pony, living in the 19th century." I even get letters from Indians around the country. . . . If I were Pueblo, very much tied to the culture, part of a kiva society, I think I would have a hard time asking some serious questions because I'd be so close to it and the responsibilities would be much larger.[130]

The questions King asks are not so much specific to any given tribal culture as they are pan-Indian.

Non-native scholars like Åke Hultkrantz and William Starna disparage pan-Indianism as, to use Hultkrantz's description, "a late idea, formed under the pressure of white domination."[131] Behind such a condemnatory tone is a view of Native cultures as unchanging and any move away from 19th-century stereotypes as a descent from a culturally and racially pure past. King takes issue with this belief, which for him is a tragic view of Natives, stating:

> I think a lot of people think of pan-Indianness as a diminution of "Indian," but I think of it as simply a reality of contemporary life. Native culture has never been static even though Western literature would like to picture it that way. In Louis l'Amour and Frank Waters, for instance, and others who write about Indians, there is that sense that if Indian culture moves *one inch* further away from what it really used to be that it's going to be dead. And there are Indians upon Indians in novels who go off the reservation into the city and are destroyed, who come back to the reserve and can't make it. I think that's bullshit myself. In reality there are a lot of Indians who go off the reserve, who come back to the reserve, who work, who go off the reserve again, who keep going back and forth, and they manage. Unfortunately, there are a lot of Indian people who buy into that concept that if they leave the reserve they'll never get back, and that just isn't true.[132]

Behind such attitudes, King believes, is a continuing position that Natives who do not conform to expected stereotypes are "phonies," as Henry Luce said. In *Green Grass* an exchange between Eli Stands Alone, a university professor who has moved away from the reserve, and Cliff Sifton, a representative of the hydro-electric company that wants to flood Eli's homestead but is blocked by Eli, captures King's stance well, affirming the dynamic nature of Native culture while at the same time asserting Native sovereignty and survival:

> Sifton stayed in the chair. "You know what the problem is? This country doesn't have an Indian policy. . . ."

"Got the treaties."

"Hell, Eli, those treaties aren't worth a damn. Government only made them for convenience. Who'd of guessed that there would still be Indians kicking around in the twentieth century."

"One of life's little embarrassments."

"Besides, you guys aren't real Indians anyway. I mean, you drive cars, watch television, go to hockey games. Look at you. You're a university professor."

"That's my profession. Being Indian isn't a profession."

"And you speak as good English as me."

"Better," said Eli. "And I speak Blackfoot too. My sister Norma speaks Blackfoot. So do my niece and nephew."

"That's what I mean. Latisha runs a restaurant and Lionel sells televisions. Not exactly traditionals, are they?"

"It's not exactly the nineteenth century, either."

King, a Cherokee, set his first two novels on the Blood Reserve in Alberta. Though the main characters in *Truth and Bright Water* are again Blackfoot, the matter is seldom discussed. It is King's attempt to "move away from a culturally specific area completely. The Indians in that piece really aren't identified by tribe, and they're not even identified by geographic area much. So I really am trying to move toward a more pan-Indian novel and to try to figure out ways to do that." According to King, some fellow Native authors to whom he has mentioned the idea of a "pan-Indian novel" reject it as "a bad idea—that you ought to write about particular tribes because it's important for people to hear those names. I grant that, but I'll let other writers do that. I'll concentrate on what I know, and that's more of a pan-Indian existence and more urban and rural existence than a reservation one." [133]

King sees his accountability as being to that pan-Indian community and to those whose lives his work reflects. He contends, "My responsibilities are to the story. My responsibilities are to the people from whom I get some of the stories or who share stories with me or about whom I'm going to write." He states that he used to apologize when he was younger for his lack of strong tribal ties but that he stopped because he recognizes that there are "a number of other Native people who are in somewhat the same situation." Echoing the location of many urban Natives, he continues, "What we do primarily is we do what we can." He approaches his Native material with a sense of responsibility—"things I can do, things I can't do." For instance, though the Sun Dance on the Blood Reserve provides the backdrop for a critical scene in *Green Grass,* the event is not described to give the reader a picture. There are no descriptions of the ceremony itself. Instead, what the reader sees are people interacting on the periphery but never inside the lodge.

Despite his pan-Indian view of community, the theme of cultural alienation is also strong throughout King's work. In *Medicine River,* Will moves back home but cannot live on the Blood Reserve because he's not a full-blood. Eli is removed from the reserve. Both wonder if they can truly go home again. Sometimes they do not want to. Behind such characters is a desire to combat the "romantic notion that every Indian in the world longs to go back to the reserve."[134] For King, such an image is simply part of the gymnastics of authenticity, a reflection of an Amer-European belief that the only true Native experience is that of the reservation. It is part of what Vizenor calls a "simulation of tribal identity"; he writes, "The reservation simulations are the notion that reservation experiences determine obvious tribal identities. Thousands of tribal people have moved from reservations to cities in the past century to avoid poverty, sexual abuse, and the absence of services, education, and employment."[135] King refuses to romanticize Native life and make it "all roses and clover."[136]

King's fiction reflects a strong commitment to Native community, even if the shape of that community is not one that would be recognized by Amer-Europeans. In *All My Relations*—itself a communitist reflection as it acknowledges the interrelatedness of all life—he writes, "A most important relationship in Native cultures is the relationship which humans share with each other, a relationship that is embodied within the idea of community. Community, in a Native sense, is not simply a place or group of people, rather it is, as novelist Louise Erdrich describes it, a place that has been 'inhabited for generations,' where 'the landscape becomes enlivened by a sense of group and family history.' "[137] This sense of group—the idea of community—suffuses King's writing. In his short story "Bingo Bigbear and the Tie-and-Choker Bone Game," for instance, a dispute between two characters is resolved because "being related was more important than some difference of opinion or a little name calling."[138] As King writes, "All [the many different kinds of Native] communities exist as intricate webs of kinship that radiate from a Native sense of family." He concludes, "This idea of community and family is not an idea that is often pursued by non-Native writers who prefer to imagine their Indians as solitary figures poised on the brink of extinction. For Native writers, community—a continuous community—is one of the primary ideas from which our literature proceeds."[139]

Nor is the wider community excluded from King's vision. His writing often bows to the interrelatedness of all the creatures of creation. In *Green Grass*, the Grande Baleine dam that threatens Eli's home is an obvious parody of the James Bay Great Whale Project, which threatened to destroy not only a vital living ecosystem but also the resident Crees' way of life. In an interview, King related a story formative to his understanding of the wider community. While in New Zealand, he was hired to cull the deer that had been introduced into the area and were, according to the government, becoming a problem. Though he had never hunted anything before, he dutifully hiked into the bush with his rifle. Coming upon a deer, he took aim and fired, hitting the animal. When he approached, he saw that his shot had broken the doe's back but had not killed her. In that moment he wished he could recall his bullet. He had not killed for food. He had shot a defenseless fellow creature that had never done anything to him. Though it was against policy to use a second bullet to dispatch wounded animals (hunters were supposed to cut their throats), he shot the animal again to put her out of her agony. Nauseated, he walked straight back to the coast, quit his job, and sold his gun.[140] The incident is reminiscent of Gerald Vizenor's account of the anguished communion he shared with the dying red squirrel he had shot while hunting.[141]

In his introduction to *All My Relations,* King notes that Native writers have, for the most part, "assiduously avoid[ed]" writing historical fiction. He elaborates:

> Some of the reasons for this avoidance are obvious. The literary stereotypes and clichés for which the period [the 19th century] is famous have been, I think, a deterrent to many of us. Feathered warriors on Pinto ponies, laconic chiefs in full regalia, dusky, raven-haired maidens, demonic shamans with eagle-claw rattles and scalping knives are all picturesque and exciting images, but they are, more properly, servants of a non-Native imagination. Rather than try to unravel the complex relationship between the nineteenth-century Indian and the white mind, or to craft a new set of images that still reflects the time, but avoids the flat, static depiction of the Native and the two-dimensional quality of the culture, most of us have consciously set our literature in the present, a period that is reasonably free of literary monoliths and which allows for greater latitude in the creation of characters and situations, and, more important, allows us the opportunity to create for ourselves and our respective cultures both a present and a future.[142]

He goes on to speculate that perhaps Native writers will begin to produce historical fiction "once we discover ways to make history our own."[143]

Despite the inherent difficulties he cites, King's commitment to Native community and to helping ensure both "a present and a future" for that community has led King to confront and assail the myths of conquest and dominance by going back into the history of White/Native relations on the continent. In "A Coyote Columbus Story," a short story included in *One Good Story, That One* and published separately in Canada as a children's book, King imagines the great culture-hero of the myths of conquest, Christopher Columbus, as having been created by accident by a very apologetic Coyote, his ubiquitous trickster. Another short story, "Joe the Painter and the Deer Island Massacre," recounts a group of Natives entering a contest to produce a pageant to commemorate the founding of San Francisco. Their effort, a re-creation of a massacre of Indians by early settlers, though accurate, infuriates the city fathers, who deem it not "appppproooopriate" to the self-congratulatory mood of the competition. As the title character remarks, "Most people can't manage honesty."[144]

In *Green Grass, Running Water*, King makes his most ambitious attempt to "make history our own" by reimagining that history in a bold way similar to the expansive revisioning Silko undertakes in *Almanac of the Dead*.[145] The four old Indians may be the last survivors of the Natives interned as prisoners of war at Fort Marion, Florida, in the late 19th century. Or, alternatively, perhaps they are the first human beings as described in tribal protologies. Mixing satire, myth, and magic, King's complicated story line "moves smartly from Canada to Wounded Knee to Hollywood, and to a place beyond time" where Coyote converses with ultimate reality.[146] Fictional characters mingle casually with historical personages like John Collier, Mary Rowlandson, Henry Schoolcraft, and George Custer. The Fort Marion internment, the Sand Creek Massacre, and the occupation of Wounded Knee are all reinvented. According to King, "I wanted to create this sort of world in which all of these things come together in a particular space and time, where they could all co-exist as they do in our brains, as they do in what Perry Miller calls the American Mind. . . . It is a crazy world, but for me it also has an awful sense of reality to it. These people are not dead. They are very much alive, and they are in positions of power. If we lose track of that we are in a lot of danger."[147]

This concern for power relationships leads King in *Green Grass* to delve into the complex relationship of Christianity to Natives. Jewish-Christian protologies are juxtaposed and conflated with traditional Native creation myths, drawn from King's doctoral dissertation at the University of Utah. Recalling the syncretic religious movements of the 18th and 19th centuries, Jesus is depicted as an Indian youth. In one of the most devastating satiric moments, King imagines Mary's ability to refuse the Annunciation. He views Christianity as "an imposition on Indian cultures," one that has had devastating effects for those cultures and for Natives themselves.[148]

A brief episode in King's film of *Medicine River* (drawn from one of his poems and absent in the novel) encapsulates King's view of White/Native relations. As a group of Natives walks along, an elder shares a Coyote story. The trickster is summoned to Ottawa by the government. The Prime Minister thanks him for coming and asks his assistance in solving their Indian Problem. Coyote, always eager to help, replies, "Sure, what's the problem?"

Betty Louise Bell

"It takes a long time to remember, it takes generations, sometimes nations, to make a story," states Lucie, the first-person narrator of Betty Bell's *Faces in the Moon*, a novel about a woman's coming to terms with her estranged mother's life and her Cherokee heritage. Like other Native writers, Bell finds the source of her narrative in the events of her own biography.

Betty Louise Bell was born on November 23, 1949, at Davis, Oklahoma.[149] Growing up in the Oklahoma of the 1950s, she knew poverty. Her mother worked as a domestic, babysitting and cleaning houses, to support her family. Beginning at age two, she was sent periodically to stay with her Aunt Lizzie, who lived nearby. At ten, her family moved to the Bay Area. She attended the State University of New York and earned her Ph.D. in English at Ohio State University in 1985. In 1993, she taught Native literature at Harvard. She is currently an assistant professor of English, American culture, and women's studies at the University of Michigan in Ann Arbor, where she teaches Native literature and directs the Native American Studies Program.

In an autobiographical essay, published in Joseph Bruchac's *Aniyunwiya/Real Human Beings,* Bell relates that a Creek medicine man once told her that all human traits are already present at birth. She writes, "For him, the matter was simple: people are born with the seed of their being. The lucky few who trust and nurture that seed, without the need for evidence or explanation, live happy lives. His words, for me, are wise and true. The whys of our desires, ambitions, the way we do or do not love are mysteries that can be unraveled only so far before we begin to speak of dreams and hopes and other insubstantial but life-consuming passions."[150] She recounts the incident to explain why she became a writer.

Books were "as rare as money to buy food at the end of the month" during her upbringing—"books, even imagination, were unthinkable luxuries in our makeshift survival." Bell, however, "learned the agency of literacy" from the pride her mother vicariously felt at the achievements of the children for whom whe cared in her work. Her mother also told stories, predominantly about Bell's grandmother. Bell writes, "She talked about being Indian, not because she knew anything about being an Indian, but because her mother was Indian. Her nostalgia for her Indian past was not the imperialistic nostalgia of colonial America but personal and dear. Her memories of her mother were all she ever really owned and from that small space in her life, she created stories of hardship, suffering, courage and love."[151] It is from those stories, woven with her own life, that Bell wrote *Faces in the Moon,* with its themes of assimilation, identity, and cultural persistence.

The Oklahoma of *Faces* is a land of plastic seat covers, crushed velvet, blond furniture, and cheap ceramic figurines. Bell writes of growing up in that place and time with an eye for authenticity of detail that might escape the unknowl-edgeable or the inattentive. Gracie Evers, Lucie's mother, is a largely deracinated Cherokee, who bleaches and perms her hair and wouldn't know her Native language if she heard it. She considers her mother's sister, Lizzie, who resists such a loss, to be an "uppity" Indian. She bounces from husband to husband in search of security and acceptance. Like Bell's own mother, she often broods and guards a dark secret of sexual abuse at the hands of a stepfather. In the novel, this malevolent figure is named Jeeter, the name of Lynn Riggs's violent villain in *Green Grow the Lilacs*. Despite her attempts to disappear into the dominant culture, there is in Gracie and her sister, Rozella, at least a generalized sense of Indian identity. They remember their mother's oft-spoken admonition to Whites, which they gleefully repeat in a spirited exchange:

> "Don't mess with Indian women."
> "Less you're a fool."
> "Even a fool got more sense 'n that."

Lucie is ashamed of her mother. From the books she is able to procure, she invents a new identity: "The short fat woman, working in the cafeteria, was not my real mother, my real mother lived in New York, the daughter of an industrialist, forced to give up her only child because of a teenage pregnancy." At her first opportunity, she "gave up Oklahoma without so much as a glance. . . . I learned to draw my words together, to speak rapidly and convincingly, to learn the good manners of middle-class ambition."

In contrast to the assimilated Gracie stands Lizzie Sixkiller, Lucie's great-aunt, to whom she is sent to live during one of her mother's more tempestuous marriages. Lizzie is the personification of Indianness. She is taciturn and possessed of a haughty pride. When gravely ill with tuberculosis, she refuses to go to the hospital. From her and her husband, Uncle Jerry, Lucie learns what it is to be Cherokee.

The issue of identity is central to *Faces*. Uncle Jerry asks Lucie if her mother told her the stories of the Cherokee: "Your momma tell ya 'bout your people? She teach ya to know who ya are?" The girl replies, "She says we's Indian." The old man retorts, "Well, now, there's Indians and there's Indians." Lizzie knows the stories and the family histories because "a body's gotta know family." [152] After her mother's death, Lucie goes to the historical society to research her family in the Dawes Rolls. When a bemused clerk asks, "Who do you think you are?" and looks skeptical at her claim to be Cherokee, an assertion he has heard from countless Amer-European wannabes, Lucie explodes:

> I watch myself reach down and take hold of his collar. My hands curl around the cotton and the top button flies. I pull him across the desk into my face. I speak slowly deliberately, beyond the rush of anger, blood talking low and clear.
> "I ain't asking you to tell me who I *think* I am. I am the great-granddaughter of Robert Henry Evers, I am the granddaughter of Hellen Evers Jeeter, I am the daughter of Gracie Evers, the niece of Rozella Evers, and the grandniece of Lizzie Sixkiller Evers."
> My hands almost relax, but I catch a grin forming at the corners of his pale thin mouth.

"Let me put it this way. I am a follower of stories, a negotiator of histories, a wild dog of many lives. I am Quanah Parker swooping down from the hills into your bedroom in the middle of the night. And I am centuries of Indian women who lost their husbands, their children, their minds so you could sit there and grin your shit-eating grin."

I eased him back against his chair and took a pen from my pocket.

I said, waving the pen, "I am your worst nightmare: I am an Indian with a pen."[153]

She repeats to him the familiar "Don't mess with Indian women" injunction that she had learned from her mother and auntie. She is one of them. She is no longer ashamed of who she is. The women of her family are with her. The message is that the all-important bonds of kinship may sometimes be strained, but they can never be broken. It speaks to that universal moment when a child realizes, for good or ill, that in some way he or she has become his or her parent. And as Lucie ages, she admits, "Every year I become more Indian. . . . Every year the blood grows stronger."

A sense of powerlessness against the dominant Amer-European culture pervades the novel. When Lucie visits her dying mother in the hospital, she feels the palpable racism of that culture and responds with Native humor. Lucie states, "The Oklahoma State Indian Hospital was the newest and biggest Indian hospital in the state. It was tucked in the corner of the mammoth health complex, miles and miles of hospitals and clinics and research laboratories quarantined in the northwest corner with the state capitol and government offices. What, I wondered, came first, the government men or the sickness? I couldn't imagine a better Indian joke, placing the contagions together and hoping they would kill each other off." Her crazy Uncle Jerry talks constantly and futilely back to the radio, providing a running commentary from a Native viewpoint. When Lucie asks him about it, he replies, "I git tired all these white voices talking, and I try to give 'em the Indian point of view. Like my daddy woulda done. Just the other day, this man in the radio talkin 'bout how this here Eisenhower's a great chief. Shoot! I put 'im straight right away. 'Ain't ya never heard a Quanah Parker?' I asks. He didn't know what to say."

Though dispossessed and disempowered, Natives are not beaten. They still have their connection to the land and to the wider community. Uncle Jerry tells her that Oklahoma isn't Indian Territory but rather an Indian cemetery. The earth lives for Indian blood. The red soil has absorbed "so much blood it can't git back to its natural color." Jerry is never lonely: "He was a fellow who found company in every earthly thing." At Gracie's interment, that wider community comes to mourn and pay its respects. Bell writes:

Then I saw her. A doe came out of the trees on the hill. She fixed on me with her eyes and waited. . . . We stood, the two of us, each watching the other. A stillness surrounded her, no leaf fluttered and no bird sang, the earth paused, waiting as I waited, giving up this moment to her peace. She came a little closer, stared at me and spoke, some untranslatable language known only to the spirit and her stillness entered my blood.

From behind the trees another doe appeared and another, a dark-eyed beauty with her small fawn. They came to the side of the doe and stood, unafraid and watchful, interested observers, protected in her stillness. Only the fawn skittered and leaped behind the trees. The other three remained.

The relationship of Natives to Christianity in *Faces* is complex, reflecting modern realities. Lucie states, "The women in my family raised me with a proud faith in the Cherokee and God." Lizzie, though wholly unassimilated, is a Christian. There are numerous hints of religious dimorphism, and when Lucie falls ill, she summons a traditional healer to treat her. This is not out of the ordinary, however. Jack and Anna Kilpatrick (Cherokee) highlight "the amazing ability of the Cherokees to maintain an equilibrium between two opposing worlds of thought. Even today the Cherokee businessman, on his way to the country club, can be wrapped in deep speculation as to the exact height of the slant-eyed giant, Tsuhl'gûl', or the correct dosage of a decoction of *dalôn'ust'* for a recalcitrant kidney. Behind the television set in the cabin of his fellow tribesman lurk the Little People, and the Bible and Thunder share Cherokee reverence."[154]

The Cherokees of *Faces in the Moon* maintain their identity and their culture no matter how assimilated they appear to their Amer-European neighbors. Throughout the novel, Whites continually express misconceptions of Natives, saying things like "I never met a real Indian before." Gracie's White landlady says she has heard that "a lot of Injuns can't trust their own families." It is a level of racism with which Natives must live constantly. Lucie states:

> "What's it like being Indian?" friends ask. I want to respond, "What's it like being alive?" But they demand difference, want to believe in Indian transcendence and spirituality, as if their own survival depended on the Indian. I wish I had Indian stories, crazy and romantic vignettes of a life lived apart from them. Anything to make myself equal to their romance. Instead I can offer only a picture of Momma's rented house, a tiny flat two-bedroom shack in a run-down part of town.
>
> "It means living like this," I would say, knowing I've told them nothing, sure I've kept my secrets.

In one of his discussions with the radio, Uncle Jerry snorts at the Lone Ranger, "Now whoever heard a Indian named Tonto?"[155] Bell resists stereotyping. As Lizzie describes Cherokees, "This here's a story 'bout plain folks just trying to get through this here life 'out more'n their share of trouble." Gracie later echoes the sentiment in her autobiography that she leaves for Lucie, saying, "Its a good storie plain working people jest gitting by in this wurld out

much to be proud cep a loving and a helping one another in a hard times."
Lucie writes:

> I have tried to circumvent the storyteller and know my life with an easy Indian
> memory, but I knew no Indian princesses, no buckskin, no feathers, no tomahawks.
> My mother and aunt chose high heels over moccasins; they would have chosen
> blue eyes over black eyes. I have tried to know Momma, Auney, and Lizzie as
> Indian women, but all that surfaces is tired worn-out women, stooped from picking
> cotton and the hard work of tenant farming. I know women burnt by the hot
> Oklahoma sun and wasted by their men, women scared into secrets, women of a
> solid and steady patience. But mostly I know them by their hunger to talk.

In *Faces in the Moon,* in an act of communitism, Betty Bell lets their voices be
heard.[156]

Conclusion: Anger Times Imagination

Kwanlin, 1986

A cheap motel in Whitehorse.
On a hot August afternoon, there is no air-conditioning.
Room doors and windows are all open,
   Hoping to generate a breeze.
Indian families are sprawled on beds and floors.
The hall smells of sweat and broken promises.
The air is heavy and hard to breathe for lack of hope.

5 a.m.
An insistent knock on the door.
When I open it,
   A young woman with lobotomy eyes enters.
Stoned or drunk, she sees nothing and no one.
My hands on her shoulders pivot and turn her,
And she exits as quickly as she came,
Somnambulistic in gait.
It's morning in Kwanlin.

                                    —Jace Weaver

Survival = Anger × Imagination. Imagination is the only weapon on the reservation.
     —Sherman Alexie, *The Lone Ranger and Tonto Fistfight in Heaven*

Is survival enough?
     —Muriel Borst (Kuna/Rappahannock), "More Than Feathers and Beads"

In the communitist parable "The Night George Wolfe Died," Robert Conley (Cherokee) relates the story of a prosperous full-blood Cherokee at the turn of the century who had sought to model his life on the *yoneg*, the White, speaking in English and wearing Western suits. Arrested after an altercation with a drunken White man who accosts him, George Wolfe spends the night in jail simply because he is an Indian. Conley writes, "When the deputy marshal opened the cell door the next day and said, 'All right, Indian, get on out of here, and watch your step from here on,' George said, '*Ge ga, yoneg*,' and it was not George Wolfe who walked out of the jail, for that name stayed behind him

160

in the cell, and he never spoke another word of English." [1] Similarly, Conley's Ned Christie, when pushed to the breaking point and declared an outlaw for his patriotic commitment to the Cherokee Nation, states, "Hla Gilisi yijiwonis-gesdi" (I will never speak English again).[2]

Even in this image-dominated age, language—the word, written and spoken—retains a special power to move and affect. As Gerald Vizenor notes in *Manifest Manners*, "Native American Indians have endured the lies and wicked burdens of discoveries, the puritanical destinies of monotheism, manifest manners, and the simulated realities of dominance, with silence, traces of natural reason, trickster hermeneutics, the interpretation of tribal figurations, and the solace of heard stories." [3] Stories can heal. I have already noted that Paula Gunn Allen points out that what she calls the Native Narrative Tradition has, as a central theme, transformation. Both Momaday and Silko speak of the transformative power of language and story. James Ruppert highlights this potentiality when he writes, "In short, texts aspire to change readers. The more complete the fusion between the implied reader and the real reader, the more complete the change." [4] Native writers, in their commitment to Native communities, write to and for Native peoples. They take cultural endurance as a priority and provide an "abiding sense of remembrance." They write that the People might live.

Louis Owens, borrowing a phrase from James Clifford, calls American Indian novels "local narratives of cultural continuity and recovery." [5] For Owens such novels are concerned with a search for identity, the recovery of a personal identity by the books' protagonists. I have contended that Native literatures are, ultimately, quests for community. Such readings, however, are not mutually exclusive. Native peoples find their individual identities in the collectivity of community. Clifford himself captures this sense with the prescient question, "[W]hat if identity is conceived not as a boundary to be maintained but as a nexus of relations and transactions actively engaging a subject?" [6] Even autobiographies, that seemingly most individuated form of monological discourse, can serve communitist ends by affirming Native personhood and subjectivity and asserting Native representational sovereignty. Elizabeth Cook-Lynn powerfully challenges such a view in her essay "Some Thoughts about Biography," writing:

> The biography . . . does not exist in the Oral Traditions of the Tribes, nor does it exist in any Traditional Native American Literary offspring—not even in "Oratory." It is written by people who are no longer attached to their native national origins, people who want to exploit them*selves,* usually giving in to their deficit lives and pimping the stereotypes, with the main purpose to appeal to white audiences. Those who think it doesn't matter, that these people are just "getting published" and "giving readings," and "doing workshops" (attended mostly by non-Indians) are simply wrong. It does matter if First Nations are to continue into the twenty-

first century and beyond. Without a useful *communal* literature, a People has no meaning.[7]

She goes on to state that traditionally storytellers tell *tribal stories* and "deliberately omit . . . the stories about the Self."[8] Brian Swann and Arnold Krupat support Cook-Lynn in their collection of Native literary autobiography, *I Tell You Now*, when they point out that "the notion of telling the whole of any one individual's life or taking merely personal experience as of particular significance was, in the most literal way, foreign to them, if not also repugnant."[9] Vizenor, however, disagrees, maintaining, "Nothing . . . is foreign or repugnant in personal names and the stories of nicknames. The risks, natural reasons, and praise of visions are sources of personal power in tribal consciousness; personal stories are coherent and name individual identities within communities, and are not an obvious opposition to communal values."[10]

Communitism means more than merely "community." It involves a particular way of attempting to live in community as Natives. This is not to say that there is only one type of community. Today Natives live their lives participating—as Natives—in many different kinds of communities. Nor does it mean that they always agree about what communitism entails. The visions of community of Richard Fields, Elias Boudinot, Pauline Johnson, Gerald Vizenor, or Thomas King are as different one from another as are the times in which they write and the communities in which they lived (or live) their lives. Even so, there is a consistent commitment to Native community and to persons within that community. They seek creative ways in which to survive and persist as Natives in the midst of an alien culture that continues to dominate Native existence.

In such a counterdiscursive search, these writers have most often adopted the genres of the dominant culture. Their work remains, however, identifiably and defiantly Native. As Ruppert observes, "Their works may grow out of Western literary forms, but they are forms being used for Native purposes that may vary from negating stereotypes to emphasizing cultural survival."[11] Any writing by a Native can serve these communitist ends. For this reason, I have maintained that Native literature must be broadly conceived as the total written output of the People. With LaVonne Ruoff, I find utility in the definition of literature offered by William Bright as "that body of discourses or texts which, within any society, is considered worthy of dissemination, transmission, and preservation in essentially constant form."[12] Though such a definition could possibly be seen as excluding traditional orature, which, as Silko and Vizenor have illustrated, is not the static form Amer-European ethnographers and anthropologists would depict, I believe it is useful nevertheless in bringing under a single rubric a wide variety of literary production, including, finally, orature as well.[13]

Because most Amer-European analysis of Native texts has focused on those texts' relation to orature, in this study, I have deliberately dealt with literatures primarily on the level of content and commitment. I have attempted to situate the literary moment in historical and political context in terms of the writer's communitism. It is clear that Native literatures differ from dominant discourse in their commitment to community. This includes a shared sense of story, the orature that first served to define and shape tribal realities. The play of language becomes a common bond. In some fashion, works by Native writers, though often highly Western in form, may mimic, perhaps even unconsciously, the tribal stories their authors heard as children. It is equally self-evident that these oral traditions vary widely among tribal groupings. Thus Gerald Vizenor, who heard rich Anishinaabe trickster stories from his grandmother and uncles, reflects a worldview in which chance is critical. Ella Deloria or Leslie Silko, coming from traditions that are more ritually grounded, stress the importance of the ceremonial in novels like *Waterlily* and *Ceremony.* Betty Bell's *Faces in the Moon* is permeated with an aching sense of exile, evoking memories of removal and the Trail of Tears. This too reflects the influence of community.

As I have argued, the communitism of these writers extends beyond simple human community to the entire created order, what I have labeled the wider community, presenting what David Murray calls an "invocation of unity."[14] Nature, an understanding of which was essential to Native survival, is viewed and characterized in kinship terms.[15] More than simply a sense of place, though it is often that as well, this view of "creation as kin" imbues the work of Native writers, in different ways, with a potent sense of interrelatedness.[16] Such a view stands in stark contrast to the myths of conquest and dominance that turn the land, which was once community, into mere property and the other-than-human persons and Mother Earth herself into simple commodities to be exploited.

Though, of necessity, Native writers, in their communitist commitments, are often subversive, this is not meant to imply that such artists are somehow communitist commandos, employing the stylus rather than Sten guns or word processors instead of plasticage. It does mean, however, that they refuse to be colonialist minstrels in Redface on the dominant culture's showboat. They resist the often nearly irresistable pull to remake Native peoples in the image of White America.

In the act of writing, they are affirming Native subjectivity and "redefining American Indian identity . . . in the face of often stunning ignorance of American Indian cultures on the part of the rest of the world."[17] It is, to use Cook-Lynn's expression, "an act of defiance born of the need to survive."[18] By (re)presenting the Indian, they are asserting Native representational sovereignty. It is a declaration that the Native is self-defining, producing an "autovision" and "autohistory" in the face of Amer-European heterohistory, "establishing a new history [a new story] to match the image of themselves that people have always had, or should have."[19] Georges Sioui claims that the aim is to "repair the damage . . . caused to the integrity of Amerindian cultures."[20] It reverses assimilation and dispels the myths of conquest and dominance.[21] It aspires to participate in the healing of grief and sense of exile. In the process, new constellations of Native community are made possible. As Joy Harjo stated in a recent interview, the questions as we approach the 21st century are the same questions that have motivated us since the advent of Europeans on the continent: "Who are we? How are we? Who are our children? And what are we all becoming together?"[22] Vizenor states, "[P]ostindian warriors of postmodern simulations would undermine and surmount, with imagination and the performance of new stories, the manifest manners of scriptural simulations and 'authentic' representations of the tribes in the literature of dominance."[23]

By writing out of and into Native community, for and to Native peoples, these writers engage in a continuing search for community. Georges Erasmus, a president of the Dene Nation in Canada, states, "Our old people, when they talk about how the [traditional] ways should be kept by young people, they are not looking back, they are looking forward. They are looking as far ahead into the future as they possibly can."[24] Like those elders, Native writers are not gazing ethnostalgically on pre-Contact society. Their work attests to the lability of Native cultures while affirming Native values. They are looking back and looking forward for new myths, creating in the process new, praxis-oriented views of identity and community. In counterpoint to these writers stand anti-communitist "plastic medicine men" who peddle Native traditions—real and fictive—for material gain and recognition, those who write revenge fantasies about their lack of acceptance by tribal peoples, who must distort the chronology of Native history to fit their genealogies, who essentialize Natives and blame their Indian blood for their own alcoholism, those who write "autobiographies" in which it is impossible to tell from what tribal tradition they come. They are White lies and Redskin reveries. As Gerald Vizenor would state, such simulations "would bear minimal honor in tribal memories."[25]

Penny Petrone notes, "The 'purist' attitudes of literary critics in North America have hampered serious critical study of native literatures. Indeed, the history of native literatures has been plagued by this cultural chauvinism."[26] Until recently, the critical arrogance of Amer-European scholars and the relative written silence of Natives allowed the persistence of Amer-European "critical and theoretical domination" of the study of American indigenes, their cultures, their religious traditions, and their literatures.[27] In the case of literatures, as previously noted, this criticism most often has been merely form or source criticism, scrutinizing texts for elements taken from orature or ceremony and for indices of Indianness as defined by the dominant culture. More recently, with the emergence of postmodernist forms of literary criticism, there has been what African American critic Barbara Christian calls a "race for theory," in which criticism tends to respond only to the critical theory of other critics and the literatures themselves are largely ignored.[28] As a result of this limited perspective, observes Ruppert, "Community, continuity, myth, ritual, and identity can easily be overlooked as the goals of the dominant discourse take over."[29]

The race for theory, though, resembles nothing so much as Lewis Carroll's caucus race in *Alice in Wonderland,* in which, at the sound of the starter's pistol, participants run in whatever direction they choose with no particular goal line in mind. In the colonialist enterprise of literary criticism, Amer-European critics seek to separate out and bracket the writer, seeking Foucault's moment of "individualization," supposed necessary for literary creation.[30] As Robert Warrior states with regard to religion, "If we learn anything from living in a culture dominated by the dictates of Christianity, then, it is that going through the motions of a religious tradition is often nothing more than going through the motions of a religious tradition. We say little or nothing about what possibilities traditions open up for finding a way to relate to the world of which we are a part. . . . Most important, the focus of discussion remains on individuals and their consciousness rather than on communities and environments."[31] Amer-European critics separate Native authors from their communitist values and, in the process, say nothing about or to Native communities and less and less about the literatures themselves.

Only when we relate Native literatures to, and situate them in, Native history and the changes in Native cultures can we begin to understand them. As Rob Nieuwenhuys reminds us, without an understanding of the writer's social location and her or his place in Native community, criticism "will be little more than a paraphrase or a commentary, and any treatment of its writers merely biographical."[32] Moreover, every act of criticism contains, as does every myth, a pragmatic element. And as Christian notes, criticism not rooted in practice becomes prescriptive.[33] Criticism not focused on and rooted in Native community only serves the myths of conquest and dominance that seek to subdue and conquer, render tame, our stories. Once again, Vizenor points this up forcefully when he writes, "The postindian simulations are the core of survivance, the new stories of tribal courage. The simulations of manifest manners are the continuance of surveillance and domination of the tribes in literature. Simulations are the absence of the tribal real; the postindian conversions are in the new stories of survivance over dominance. The natural reason of the tribes anteceded by thousands of generations the invention of the Indian. The postindian outs the inventions with humor, new stories, and the simulations of survivance."[34] Native internal criticism or theorizing must strive for literary emancipation of Natives and Native communities.

As I suggested in chapter 1, there is a natural and altogether healthy distrust of critical theorizing among many contemporary Natives. This is a reality shared with much of the postcolonial world. Homi K. Bhabha writes, "There is a damaging and self-defeating assumption that theory is necessarily the elite language of the socially and culturally privileged. It is said that the place of the academic critic is inevitably within the Eurocentric archives of an imperialist or neo-colonial West. The Olympian realms of what is mistakenly labeled 'pure theory' are assumed to be eternally insulated from the historical exigencies and tragedies of the wretched of the earth. Must we always polarize in order to polemicize?" The critic concludes, however, that what "does demand further discussion" is "whether the 'new' languages of theoretical critique" simply reinforce the dominant culture's hegemony. "Is the language of theory merely another power ploy of the culturally privileged Western elite to produce a discourse of the Other that reinforces its own power-knowledge equation?" [35]

In a recent exchange, Robert Warrior asked Joy Harjo how Native intellectuals could make their work part of their communities. She replied that the Native writer should always be responsible to community. In her own work, she said, she constantly asks herself, "How does this make sense on the stomp grounds? How does it matter when I go home, when I'm there?" She went on to inquire, "What is there in a story or a poem that makes it matter to the community?" [36] These are questions, as this book demonstrates, that have been asked and continue to be asked, with variations, by Native authors at least since Samson Occom first represented himself in English. Barbara Christian asks for people of color generally (and for women of color particularly) a question of fundamental importance for Native intellectuals, those whom Elizabeth Cook-Lynn reminds us are "the self-appointed," "[F]or whom are we doing what we are doing?" [37] When we write about Native religious traditions, when we produce criticism—whenever we create literature—it is a threshold inquiry we must use to interrogate ourselves. Among Natives, every part of the community has a responsibility to every other part of that community, be it the tribal or the larger pan-Indian community that has emerged strongly in recent decades.

Religious scholarship and literary criticism have an aspect of advocacy as well as study. What Christian avers of her own project, I would also contend, more modestly, for my own:

> My readings do presuppose a need, a desire among folk who like me also want to save their own lives. My concern, then, is a passionate one, for the literature of people who are not in power has always been in danger of extinction of co-optation, not because we do not theorize, but because what we can even imagine, far less who we can reach, is constantly limited by societal structures. For me, literary criticism is promotion as well as understanding, a response to the writer to whom there is no response, to folk who need the writing as much as they need anything. I know, from literary history, that writing disappears unless there is a

response to it. Because I write about writers who are now writing, I hope to ensure that their tradition has continuity and survives.[38]

In dominant Amer-European discourse, the same small group of writers is almost always that analyzed, to the exclusion of all others. Momaday (almost always *House Made of Dawn*), Silko (almost exclusively *Ceremony*), Louise Erdrich *(Love Medicine)*, and James Welch form the informal canon of Native writers. In addition, two others, Vizenor and McNickle, sometimes are included.

In this work, I have attempted to begin the recovery for Native intellectual history and literature of persons like Richard Fields and Peter Jones. I have also tried to give critical attention to writers and works that are seldom discussed. Some of these writers have been largely ignored because their works have somehow been deemed "unworthy" (Pauline Johnson, Lynn Riggs, Natachee Scott Momaday). Some have been excluded from discussion by definitions that fragment Native literary output and fail to recognize much of their work as "literature" (Elias Boudinot, Alex Posey, Vine Deloria Jr.). Still others have emerged too recently to gain much serious critical notice (Thomas King, Betty Louise Bell). As Nieuwenhuys said of those whom he attempted to recover for the colonial literature of the Dutch Indies, they are those "about whom I have been able to write with a different and better kind of pen, I would like to think."[39]

Time and space considerations have caused me to limit my discussions, and there are several figures that I have been forced to exclude that could usefully have been brought to the table to share the discussion. Charles Eastman, Joy Harjo, D'Arcy McNickle, John Joseph Mathews, and James Welch are all important Native literary figures who are only discussed in passing, their participation in the dialogue limited to the setting of context and the occasional remark that I allow them. New writers continue to find their way, albeit often with difficulty, into print. A. A. Carr (Navajo/Laguna) stretches the bounds of Native literature with an erotic thriller that brings together Native traditions with European vampire legends.[40] Greg Sarris depicts a polyglot neighborhood of Natives, Chicanos, African Americans, and Portuguese in his novel *Grand Avenue*.[41] Beth Brant and Chrystos (Menominee) speak out of their experiences as Native women and as lesbians.[42] Sherman Alexie and Jim Northrup (Anishinaabe) continue the Native tradition of humor with an edge.[43] In both those who have been included herein and those who have not can be discerned the same commitment to Native personhood, representational sovereignty, and other elements that make up communitism.

Long ago, there lived a man who was not very skilled at the daily work of survival. He was not a very good hunter or planter. He was not a fine craftsman. He did, however, have a gift for storytelling. At night, as members of the tribe gathered around the campfire, he would tell stories about the day's events and about the great leaders of the past. His stories were so vivid that his words would actually come alive and dance around the fire. Some of the other men became jealous, and they worried about the power this man had with his words. They feared that he might tell lies about them, which would take on life because of his eloquence. So they killed him. But his stories continued to live in the hearts of the people.

Words cannot be killed. Thoughts cannot be silenced. Identity, ultimately, cannot be suppressed. Native writers, as they have for over 200 years, reflect and shape Native identity and community in a reciprocal relationship with their communities. They are finding their voices in ever increasing numbers, and as they write they help "create a new tribal presence in stories."[44] They help "push things on to another place."[45] As Leslie Silko has said, they are making English speak for them.[46] Like the boys in Jim McKinney's dorm room, they are discovering new languages and lifting them up in a polyphony of songs and stories. In contrast to the students at Isabelle Knockwood's Mi'kmaw residential school, now, as the bruises begin to fade, they are just starting to talk.

> Don't fret.
> Warriors will keep alive in the blood.
> —Simon Ortiz,
> *From Sand Creek*

Notes

Preface

1. William Baldridge, "Toward a Native American Theology," *American Baptist Quarterly,* December 1989, p. 228.

2. Jack D. Forbes, *Columbus and Other Cannibals* (Brooklyn: Autonomedia, 1992), p. 138.

3. Tom F. Driver, *The Magic of Ritual* (San Francisco: HarperCollins, 1991), p. 38.

4. Forbes, *Columbus,* p. 138.

5. Charles Eastman, *The Soul of an Indian: An Interpretation* (Boston: Houghton Mifflin, 1911), p. 47.

6. Georges Sioui, *For an Amerindian Autohistory* (Montreal: McGill-Queen's University Press, 1992), p. 68.

7. Forbes, *Columbus,* p. 26.

8. Baldridge, "Toward a Native American Theology," p. 228.

9. Achiel Peelman, *Christ Is a Native American* (Maryknoll: Orbis Books, 1995), p. 41.

10. Dennis McPherson and J. Douglas Rabb, *Indian from the Inside: A Study in Ethno-Metaphysics* (Thunder Bay, Ont.: Lakehead University, Centre for Northern Studies, 1993), p. 1.

11. Rob Nieuwenhuys, *Mirror of the Indies: A History of Dutch Colonial Literature* (Amherst: University of Massachusetts Press, 1982), pp. 189–193; A. LaVonne Brown Ruoff, *American Indian Literatures: An Introduction, Bibliographic Review, and Selected Bibliography* (New York: Modern Language Association, 1990); Paula Gunn Allen, ed., *Voice of the Turtle: American Indian Literature, 1900–1970* (New York: Ballantine, 1994), p. 6; Penny Petrone, *Native Literature in Canada* (Toronto: Oxford University Press, 1990).

12. Petrone, *Native Literature,* p. 1.

13. Robert Allen Warrior, *Tribal Secrets: Recovering American Indian Intellectual Traditions* (Minneapolis: University of Minnesota Press, 1995), p. xxii. In suggesting an analytical tool and illustrating its use, I am also following, I hope, Reinhold Niebuhr, whose concept of irony has, I believe, continued utility and vitality. See Jace Weaver, "Original Simplicities and Present Complexities: Reinhold Niebuhr, Ethnocentrism, and the Myth of American Exceptionalism," *Journal of the American Academy of Religion* 63, no. 2 (Summer 1995); Reinhold Niebuhr, *The Irony of American History* (New York: Charles Scribner's Sons, 1952).

14. Ibid., pp. 97–98.

15. Jack D. Forbes, "Colonialism and Native American Literature: Analysis," *Wicazo Sa Review* 3 (1987): p. 18; Ruoff, *American Indian Literatures,* p. vi; Geary Hobson, ed., *The Remembered Earth* (Albuquerque: University of New Mexico Press, 1979), p. 8.

16. See, e.g., Noel Dyck, ed., *Indigenous Peoples and the Nation-State: Fourth World Politics in Canada, Australia, and Norway* (St. John's: Institute of Social and Economic Research, Memorial University of Newfoundland, 1985); M. A. Jaimes, "Native American Identity and Survival: Indigenism and Environmental Ethics," in Michael K. Green, ed., *Issues in Native American Cultural Identity, Critic of Institutions* 2 (1995), p. 273. "Fourth World" was coined to distinguish indigenous peoples around the planet from the Third World. "Third World" was first employed by Alfred Sauvy in *France Observateur* in 1952. The appellation "Fourth World" was coined in Canada in the 1970s. George Manuel and M. Posluns, *The Fourth World: An Indian Reality* (Toronto: Collier-Macmillan, 1974). "Indigenism" was created by Ward Churchill (Creek/Cherokee Métis) and is illustrated in his essay "I Am Indigenist." Ward Churchill, *Struggle for the Land* (Monroe, Me.: Common Courage Press, 1993), p. 403.

17. See, e.g., Tomson Highway, *The Rez Sisters* (Saskatoon: Fifth House, 1988); Tomson Highway, *Dry Lips Oughta Move to Kapuskasing* (Saskatoon: Fifth House, 1989); Ruby Slipperjack, *Honour the Sun* (Winnipeg: Pemmican Publications, 1987); Jordan Wheeler, *Brothers in Arms* (Winnipeg: Pemmican Publications, 1989); Howard Adams, *Prison of Grass: Canada from a Native Point of View,* rev. ed. (Saskatoon: Fifth House, 1989); Rudolfo A. Anaya, *Bless Me, Ultima* (Berkeley: TQS Publications, 1972); Miguel Mèndez, *Pilgrims in Aztlán* (Tempe: Bilingual Press, 1992).

18. Hobson, *Remembered Earth,* p. 8.

19. Warrior, *Tribal Secrets,* p. xvi.

20. Ibid., p. 113.

21. See Ngugi wa Thiong'o, *Decolonising the Mind: The Politics of Language in African Literature* (London: James Currey, 1986), p. 95.

22. Gerald Vizenor, *Manifest Manners: Postindian Warriors of Survivance* (Hanover, N.H.: Wesleyan University Press, 1994), p. 75.

23. Both "metropolis" and *métropole* come from the Greek *metropolis,* meaning the mother city or state of a colony, as in ancient Greece. In English, however, the metropolis more commonly designates a large or important city. The French term will, I hope, allow the reader more distantiation and allow her or him to recognize the colonial implications of the term. In the case of France, of course, there was a colonial myth that the *métropole* included not simply the *hexagone*—France itself—but also its princi-

pal colony, Algeria. See Homi K. Bhabha, *The Location of Culture* (London: Routledge, 1994), p. 6.

24. See, e.g., John Joseph Mathews, *Talking to the Moon* (Norman: University of Oklahoma Press, 1945), p. 227.

25. For a further discussion of this point, see Jace Weaver, ed., *Defending Mother Earth: Native American Perspectives on Environmental Justice* (Maryknoll: Orbis Books, 1996), p. 30.

26. McPherson and Rabb, *Indian from the Inside*, p. 1.

Chapter One

1. Leslie Marmon Silko, "Foreword," in Leslie Marmon Silko, ed., *Dancing with the Wind* 4 (1992/93): pp. 6–7 (emph. original).

2. N. Scott Momaday, "Foreword," in N. Scott Momaday, ed., *Dancing with the Wind* 3 (1991): p. 6.

3. Louis Owens, *Other Destinies: Understanding the American Indian Novel* (Norman: University of Oklahoma Press, 1992), p. 3.

4. Gregory Gagnon, "American Indian Intellectuals: Are They Above Reproach, or Easy Targets?" *Tribal College* (Summer 1995): p. 43.

5. Sherman Alexie, *Old Shirts and New Skins* (Los Angeles: American Indian Studies Center, University of California, Los Angeles, 1993), p. 4.

6. See Ashis Nandy, *The Intimate Enemy: Loss and Recovery of Self under Colonialism* (Delhi: Oxford University Press, 1983), p. 102.

7. Wub-e-ke-niew [Francis Blake Jr.], *We Have the Right to Exist* (New York: Black Thistle Press, 1995), pp. xiv–xv, xxvi, xliii, xlvii. Blake also calls his volume, on Anishinaabe history and thought, the "first book ever published from an *Ahnishinahbœó ± jibway* Perspective" despite numerous volumes by Gerald Vizenor and others.

8. Thomas King, ed., *All My Relations* (Toronto: McClelland & Stewart, 1990), p. xi.

9. Hobson, *Remembered Earth*, p. 8.

10. A. T. Anderson, *Nations within a Nation: The American Indian and the Government of the United States* (Chappaqua, N.Y.: Privately printed, 1976), pp. 75–77.

11. McPherson and Rabb, *Indian from the Inside*, pp. 21–22.

12. N. Scott Momaday, *The Names: A Memoir* (New York: Harper & Row, 1976), pp. 23–25.

13. Hobson, *Remembered Earth*, pp. 8–9.

14. Ibid., p. 9.

15. See Richard Drinnon, *White Savage: The Case of John Dunn Hunter* (New York: Schocken Books, 1972), p. 183; Jace Weaver, "Poetry," *Native Journal*, January 1993, p. 23; Jace Weaver, "Dreaming Fredonia," in Caroline Sullivan and Cynthia Stevens, eds., *Distinguished Poets of America* (Owings Mills, Md.: National Library of Poetry, 1993), p. 402.

16. Leslie Silko declares, "The community is tremendously important. That's where a person's identity has to come from, not from racial blood quantum levels." Leslie Silko, "Stories and Their Tellers: A Conversation with Leslie Marmon Silko," in Dexter Fisher,

ed., *The Third Woman: Minority Women Writers of the United States* (New York: Houghton Mifflin, 1980), p. 19. For a discussion of this point in another colonial context, see Nieuwenhuys, *Mirror of the Indies,* p. 196.

17. Hobson, *Remembered Earth,* p. 9.

18. King, *All My Relations,* pp. x–xi.

19. Arnold Krupat, *The Voice in the Margin: Native American Literature and the Canon* (Berkeley: University of California Press, 1989), pp. 13–14; H. David Brumble III, *American Indian Autobiography* (Berkeley: University of California Press, 1988), p. 174; Paula Gunn Allen, ed., *Spider Woman's Granddaughters* (New York: Fawcett Columbine, 1989), p. 168; Ngugi, *Decolonising the Mind,* p. 17.

20. David Murray, *Forked Tongues: Speech, Writing and Representation in North American Indian Texts* (Bloomington: Indiana University Press, 1991), p. 81.

21. King, *All My Relations,* p. x.

22. Edward W. Said, *The World, the Text, and the Critic* (Cambridge: Harvard University Press, 1983), pp. 19–20.

23. See Roger Welsch, *Touching the Fire: Buffalo Dancers, the Sky Bundle, and Other Tales* (New York: Villard Books, 1992).

24. Peelman, *Christ Is a Native American,* p. 33. Emphasis mine.

25. Owens, *Other Destinies,* p. 12.

26. Viine Deloria Jr., *We Talk, You Listen: New Tribes, New Turf* (New York: Macmillan, 1970).

27. Hobson, *Remembered Earth,* p. 10.

28. Lester Standiford writes, "Of course, a shortsighted view of the application of minorities literature would exclude even those members of a group whose place might be validated by blood heritage, but whose life experience lies largely outside the normal experience of the group: i.e., should the Anglo farmer be permitted to read *Moby Dick?*" Lester A. Standiford, "Worlds Made of Dawn: Characteristic Image and Incident in Native American Imaginative Literature," in Wolodymyr T. Zyla and Wendell M. Aycock, eds., *Ethnic Literatures since 1776: The Many Voices of America* (Lubbock: Texas Tech Press, 1978), p. 331. But should the Anglo farmer who knows nothing about whaling and who has never even seen the sea *write Moby Dick?*

29. D'Arcy McNickle, *Indian Man: A Life of Oliver La Farge* (Bloomington: Indiana University Press, 1971); John Joseph Mathews, *Life and Death of an Oilman: The Career of E. W. Marland* (Norman: University of Oklahoma Press, 1951); Jace Weaver, *Then to the Rock Let Me Fly: Luther Bohanon and Judicial Activism* (Norman: University of Oklahoma Press, 1993).

30. King, *All My Relations,* p. xi. Scott Momaday concurs: "The phrase 'American Indian Writer' I understand to indicate an American Indian who writes. It does not indicate anything more than that to me." Standiford, "Worlds," p. 332.

31. Martin William Smith [Martin Cruz Smith], *The Indians Won* (New York: Belmont, 1970); Robbie Robertson and the Red Road Ensemble, "Music for 'Native Americans'" (Hollywood, Calif.: Capital Records, 1994; Canadian Broadcasting Corporation, "Interview with Robbie Robertson," October 14, 1994.

32. Forbes, "Colonialism," pp. 19–20.

33. Krupat, *Voice in the Margin,* p. 207.

34. Ruoff, *American Indian Literatures*, p. vi.

35. Brian Swann, "Introduction: Only the Beginning," in Duane Niatum, ed., *Harper's Anthology of 20th Century Native American Poetry* (San Francisco: HarperSanFrancisco, 1988), p. xx.

36. King, *All My Relations*, p. x.

37. Bill Ashcroft, Gareth Griffiths, and Helen Tiffin, *The Empire Writes Back: Theory and Practice in Post-Colonial Literatures* (London: Routledge, 1989), p. 2.

38. In fairness to Ashcroft and his coauthors, they do define postcolonial as that period commencing with the moment of colonization and continuing to the present day, a time frame and definition that would encompass American Indians. Nevertheless, by their own admission, the only literatures they discuss are those of peoples who have already achieved political independence. Ibid., pp. 2, 6. If we accept, rather, E. M. Beekman's definition of colonialism, in the preface to the English edition of Nieuwenhuys's *Mirror of the Indies*, as "the subjugation of an *entire* area, and [dating] from the time when the last independent domain was conquered," we would be forced to ask when colonialism took final hold in the area now called the United States. Nieuwenhuys, *Mirror of the Indies*, p. x; emphasis original.

39. See Michael Hector, *The Celtic Fringe in British National Development, 1536–1966* (Berkeley: University of California Press, 1975); Robert K. Thomas, "Colonialism: Classic and Internal," *New University Thought* 4, no. 4 (Winter 1966–1967); Churchill, *Struggle for the Land*, pp. 23–24, 31.

40. Of course, even in classic colonialism, a class of colonizer is created that is born in the colony, and while largely continuing to possess and identify with the values and worldview of the *métropole*, these people identify the geographic area of the colony as their homeland. The French called such persons *pieds-noirs*. Nieuwenhuys describes the situation of such persons when Dutch rule of Indonesia ended. He writes, "The massive repatriation of people from Indonesia to the Netherlands, timely or not, forced a lot of those people to regard their past in the Indies as nothing but a memory. But memory is not quite the same thing as nostalgia or 'a longing for that which has been lost.' This nostalgia exists, naturally, among broad segments of the Indies community in the Netherlands, part of which—particularly its older members—considers itself to be in some kind of exile. This feeling of being cut off creates the nostalgia, which in turn colors people's memories. These memories can extend so far and so deep that they cause pain, even a great deal of pain." According to Nieuwenhuys, it creates a distorted remembrance that is a familiar theme in romantic literature. Nieuwenhuys, *Mirror of the Indies*, p. 298. Such a "remembrance" may go partway toward explaining, since the reassertion of Native tribal identity and sovereignty in the late 1960s and early 1970s, the increasing fascination of Amer-Europeans with idealized, romanticized, and fictive images of Indians and their spiritualities.

41. Ashcroft, Griffiths, and Tiffin, *Empire Writes Back*, p. 25.

42. Edward W. Said, *Culture and Imperialism* (New York: Alfred A. Knopf, 1993), p. xxv.

43. Vizenor, *Manifest Manners*, p. 69.

44. Tony Bennett and Valda Blundell, "First Peoples," *Cultural Studies* 9 (January 1995): p. 2.

45. Barbara Harlow, *Resistance Literature* (New York: Methuen, 1987).

46. Menno Boldt, *Surviving as Indians* (Toronto: University of Toronto Press, 1993), p. 176.

47. Ibid., p. 175.

48. Ibid.

49. Edward W. Said, *The Pen and the Sword: Conversations with David Barsamian* (Monroe, Me.: Common Courage Press, 1994), p. 105.

50. Ashcroft, Griffiths, and Tiffin, *Empire Writes Back,* p. 25.

51. Ibid., pp. 29–30; Nieuwenhuys, *Mirror of the Indies,* p. 307.

52. Ashcroft, Griffiths, and Tiffin, *Empire Writes Back,* p. 30.

53. Bhabha, *Location of Culture,* p. 4.

54. Nandy, *Intimate Enemy,* pp. xii, xix.

55. Ngugi, *Decolonising the Mind,* pp. 14–16.

56. Dana Milbank, "What's in a Name?: For the Lumbees, Pride and Money," *Wall Street Journal,* November 13, 1995, p. 1.

57. Owens, *Other Destinies,* p. 7.

58. Ngugi, *Decolonising the Mind,* p. 9.

59. Isabelle Knockwood, *Out of the Depths* (Lockport, N.S.: Roseway Publishing, 1992), p. 98.

60. Linda Cavanaugh and Tony Stizza, prods., "Strangers in Their Own Land" (Oklahoma City: Strangers in Their Own Land, Inc., 1993); Jim McKinney, interview with author, June 10, 1994; Quanah Tonemah, interview with author, June 10, 1994; Knockwood, *Out of the Depths,* p. 98. Knockwood also notes that Native languages also were routinely labeled "gibberish" and "mumbo jumbo" to denigrate them. This process continues to the present even in unlikely places. For a recent re-release of the ethnographic/colonialist film "In the Land of the Headhunters" (discreetly retitled "In the Land of the War Canoes" [New York: Milestone Film & Video, 1992]) by Edward S. Curtis, the University of Washington and the Field Museum in Chicago provided a new soundtrack for the silent film, recorded by Kwakiutl Indians. Though the track consists largely of spoken dialogue, no subtitles are provided for the viewer. What is being said is unimportant, merely colorful background noise, simply gibberish.

61. Joseph Bruchac, ed., *Survival This Way: Interviews with American Indian Poets* (Tucson: University of Arizona Press, 1987), pp. 284–285; Luci Tapahonso, *Sáanii Dahataal, The Women Are Singing* (Tucson: University of Arizona Press, 1993), pp. x–xi. Beth Brant (Mohawk) observes, "There are women who are writing bilingually. Salli Benedick, Lenore Keeshig-Tobias, Rita Joe, Beatrice Medicine, Anna Lee Walters, Luci Tapahonso, Mary TallMountain, Nia Francisco, Ofelia Zepeda, Donna Goodleaf are just some of the Native women who are choosing to use their own Nation's languages when English won't suffice or convey the integrity of the meaning. I find this an exciting movement. And an exciting consequence would be the development of *our own* critics, and publishing houses that do bilingual work. Our languages are rich, full of metaphor, nuance, and life. Our languages are not dead or conquered—like women's hearts, they are soaring and spreading the culture to our youth and our unborn." Beth Brant, *Writing as Witness* (Toronto: Women's Press, 1994). While Brant is correct that the movement is exciting and that bilingual publishing would be equally so, such a development is, at best, temporally remote and, at worst, highly unlikely.

62. Murray, *Forked Tongues*, p. 92.

63. Owens, *Other Destinies*, p. 6; Ashcroft, Griffiths, and Tiffin, *Empire Writes Back*, p. 11.

64. Bruchac, *Survival This Way*, p. 94; "The Spectrum of Other Languages: An Interview with Joy Harjo," *Tamaqua* 3, no. 1 (Spring 1992): pp. 11–13.

65. Vizenor, *Manifest Manners*, pp. 105–106.

66. McPherson and Rabb, *Indian from the Inside*, pp. 14–15. Emphasis original.

67. Ngugi, *Decolonising the Mind*, p. 29.

68. Nieuwenhuys, *Mirror of the Indies*, p. 177.

69. George Tinker, "An American Indian Theological Response to Ecojustice," in Weaver, *Defending Mother Earth*, p. 166; see also George Tinker, "Columbus and Coyote: A Comparison of Culture Heroes in Paradox," *Apuntes* (1992): pp. 78–88. Elucidating the Columbus myth, Jack Forbes writes, "[T]he so-called 'discovery' of Columbus is a preposterous myth, and has long been known as such. It is true, of course, that Columbus' voyage was an important undertaking, much the same as Marco Polo's land journey to China two centuries earlier. But no one pretends that Marco Polo 'discovered' China! Why? Perhaps because there are no European colonial settlers in China who need to evoke Marco Polo as a symbol for a successful but still contested conquest." *Columbus*, pp. 37–38.

70. Tinker, "Response," pp. 166–167.

71. Peelman, *Christ Is a Native American*, p. 59.

72. Ngugi, *Decolonising the Mind*, p. 3.

73. Enrique Dussel, *The Invention of the Americas: Eclipse of "the Other" and the Myth of Modernity* (New York: Continuum, 1995), p. 12.

74. Owens, *Other Destinies*, p. 7.

75. Homer Noley, *First White Frost* (Nashville: Abingdon Press, 1991), p. 18, citing Barry Fell, *America B.C.: Ancient Settlers in the New World* (New York: Quadrangle/New York Times, 1976), pp. 15–16; John Ehle, *Trail of Tears: The Rise and Fall of the Cherokee Nation* (New York: Doubleday, 1988), p. 1; George Sanderlin, ed., *Witness: Writings of Bartolomé de Las Casas* (Maryknoll: Orbis Books, 1992), p. xvii; see generally Ronald Sanders, *Lost Tribes and Promised Lands: The Origins of American Racism* (New York: Harper, 1978). The slur persists in Mormonism, with its teachings about American Indians as Lamanites, and continues to revive in both popular and scholarly discourse. See Gordon Bronitsky, "Jews and Indians: Old Myths and New Realities," *Jewish Spectator* (Winter 1991–1992): p. 39.

76. Francis Jennings, *The Invasion of America: Indians, Colonialism, and the Cant of Conquest* (New York: W. W. Norton, 1976), pp. 10–11 (emphasis original); Djelal Kadir, *Columbus and the Ends of the Earth: Europe's Prophetic Rhetoric as Conquering Ideology* (Berkeley: University of California Press, 1992); Niebuhr, *Irony of American History*, p. 24. Even Niebuhr, however, who spent much effort attempting to dispel the myth of American exceptionalism, was ultimately seduced by the myths of conquest. He writes that Europeans found here a "vast virgin continent, populated sparsely by Indians in a primitive state of culture." Reinhold Niebuhr and Alan Heimert, *A Nation So Conceived* (London: Faber & Faber, 1964), p. 7; Weaver, "Original Simplicities," pp. 206–207. As for the myths' codification in law, see James Kent, *Commentaries on American Law*, vol. 1 (New York: O. Halsted, 1826), p. 243; vol. 3 (New York: O. Halsted, 1828), p. 312.

77. Terry Goldie, *Fear and Temptation: The Image of the Indigene in Canadian, Australian, and New Zealand Literatures* (Kingston, Ont.: McGill-Queen's University Press, 1989), p. 100. See James O. Gump, *The Dust Rose Like Smoke: The Subjugation of the Zulu and the Sioux* (Lincoln: University of Nebraska Press, 1994).

78. Goldie, *Fear and Temptation*, pp. 158, 149.

79. D. P. Kidder, "Missions," in John McClintock and James Strong, eds., *Cyclopedia of Biblical, Theological, and Ecclesiastical Literature*, vol. 6 (New York: Harper Brothers, c. 1877; reprint, Grand Rapids: Baker Book House, 1981), p. 375; see Jace Weaver, "Missions and Missionaries," in Mary B. Davis, ed., *Native America in the Twentieth Century* (New York: Garland Publishing, 1994), p. 346. For general discussions of the "Vanishing Indian" or "doomed culture" and other stereotypes of Native Americans, see Brian W. Dippie, *The Vanishing American: White Attitudes and U.S. Indian Policy* (Lawrence: University Press of Kansas, 1982); Robert F. Berkhofer Jr., *The White Man's Indian: Images of the American Indian from Columbus to the Present* (New York: Vintage Books, 1978); Daniel Francis, *The Imaginary Indian: The Image of the Indian in Canadian Culture* (Vancouver: Arsenal Pulp Press, 1992).

80. Elsie Clews Parsons, ed., *American Indian Life*, 2d Bison Book ed. (Lincoln: University of Nebraska Press, 1991), pp. ix–x. It is interesting to note that even in Mark's modern discussion one can see the imperialist impulse of anthropology at work. Changes in Native society are seen as akin to *biological species* becoming extinct! Bruce Trigger writes that early anthropologists "were also convinced that native cultures were disintegrating as a result of European contact; hence the primary aim of ethnologists was to record these cultures as thoroughly as possible before they disappeared completely." Bruce G. Trigger, "Ethnohistory: The Unfinished Edifice," *Ethnohistory* 33 (Summer 1986): p. 256, quoted in Margaret Connell Szasz, *Between Indian and White Worlds: The Cultural Broker* (Norman: University of Oklahoma Press, 1994), p. 7. In 1995, Achiel Peelman can still write, "Fifty years ago, many anthropologists, missionaries, medical doctors and politicians *rightly* described the Indians as 'vanishing peoples.' They did not hesitate to conclude that the only survival open to them was through total assimilation or individual integration into . . . North American society." Peelman also endorses the myth of the Vanishing Indian when he referred to "indigenous beliefs and values (the past)." *Christ Is a Native American*, pp. 21, 27.

81. Goldie, *Fear and Temptation*, pp. 158, 155.

82. Alvin Josephy, "New England Indians: Then and Now," in Laurence M. Hauptman and James D. Wherry, eds., *The Pequots in Southern New England: The Fall and Rise of an American Indian Nation* (Norman: University of Oklahoma Press, 1990), p. 7. Georges Sioui also speaks of non-Natives' "crystallized perception" of Indians. *Amerindian Autohistory*, p. 32.

83. See generally, Dussel, *Invention of the Americas;* Edward W. Said, *Orientalism* (New York: Random House, 1978); and Christopher Frayling, *Spaghetti Westerns: Cowboys and Europeans from Karl May to Sergio Leone* (London: Routledge & Kegan Paul, 1981), pp. 103–104. Ngugi writes of the inferiority inculcated when Blacks read H. Rider Haggard. How much equally so the Indian child who reads pulp westerns, Cooper, or May?

84. Vine Deloria Jr., "Foreword: American Fantasy," in Gretchen M. Bataille and Charles L. P. Silet, eds., *The Pretend Indians: Images of Native Americans in the Movies*

(Ames: Iowa State University Press, 1980), p. xvi; see also Jace Weaver, "Ethnic Cleansing, Homestyle," *Wicazo Sa Review* 10, no. 1 (Spring 1994): pp. 27–39.

85. Albert Memmi, *The Colonizer and the Colonized,* exp. ed. (Boston: Beacon Press, 1967), p. 52; Said, *Culture,* p. 237; Frantz Fanon, *The Wretched of the Earth* (1961; reprint, New York: Grove, 1968), p. 210.

86. Howard Adams, *Prison of Grass,* p. 43; Jace Weaver, "American Indians and Native Americans: Reinhold Niebuhr, Historiography, and Indigenous Peoples," in Sylvia O'Meara and Douglas A. West, eds., *From Our Eyes: Learning from Indigenous Peoples* (Toronto: Garamond Press, 1996), p. 29.

87. Johannes Fabian, *Time and the Other: How Anthropology Makes Its Object* (New York: Columbia University Press, 1983), p. 17.

88. Said, *Culture,* p. 152; Sioui, *Amerindian Autohistory,* p. 101; Vizenor, *Manifest Manners,* pp. 68–69; Ngugi, *Decolonising the Mind,* p. 16; George Tinker, *Missionary Conquest* (Minneapolis: Fortress Press, 1993), pp. 118, 2; Sioui, *Amerindian Autohistory,* p. 32, 100; Jace Weaver, "Notes from a Miner's Canary," in Weaver, *Defending Mother Earth,* p. 16.

89. Leslie Marmon Silko, *Storyteller* (New York: Arcade Publishing, 1981), back cover.

90. Denise Lardner Carmody and John Tully Carmody, *Native American Religions: An Introduction* (New York: Paulist Press, 1993), pp. 225, 67.

91. Karl Kroeber, ed., *Traditional Literatures of the American Indian* (Lincoln: University of Nebraska Press, 1981), pp. 1, 2. Emphasis mine.

92. Petrone, *Native Literature,* pp. 17, 9–34.

93. Vizenor, *Manifest Manners,* p. 72.

94. John Bierhorst, ed., *Four Masterworks of American Indian Literature* (New York: Farrar, Straus, and Giroux, 1974), p. xii.

95. Karl Kroeber, *Traditional Literatures,* p. 2.

96. Gerald Vizenor, ed., *Narrative Chance: Postmodern Discourse on Native American Indian Literatures* (Albuquerque: University of New Mexico Press, 1989), p. 4.

97. Bill Ashcroft, Gareth Griffiths, and Helen Tiffin, eds., *The Post-Colonial Studies Reader* (London: Routledge, 1995), pp. 2–3; Vizenor, *Manifest Manners,* pp. 77, 80; Owens, *Other Destinies,* p. 21.

98. Warrior, *Tribal Secrets,* pp. xviii–xix.

99. See Harlow, *Resistance Literature,* p. xvi. It should be noted that as internal Native criticism grows, some Amer-European critics accuse Natives, who merely are struggling to make their voices heard, of attempting to establish hegemony over Native studies. Arnold Krupat notes that Hertha Wong, for instance, was forced to assert tenuous claims to Native heritage in order to gain a hearing for her work on Native autobiography, calling the move "coy and potentially opportunistic." Elizabeth Cook-Lynn writes of the volume that the "wannabee sentiment . . . clutters an otherwise tolerable piece of redundant scholarship" and that the "unnecessary claim . . . to be 'part Native American' is so absurd as to cast ridicule on the work itself." Gerald Vizenor notes that the "racialism of [Wong's] romantic notions [of identity] would bear minimal honor in tribal memories." Robert Warrior, "A Marginal Voice," *Native Nations* (March/August 1991), pp. 29–30; Daniel Littlefield Jr., "American Indians, American Scholars and the American Literary Canon," *American Studies* 33 (1992), pp. 96–108; Arnold Krupat, "Scholar-

ship and Native American Studies: A Response to Daniel Littlefield, Jr.," *American Studies* 34 (1993), pp. 91–92; Vizenor, *Manifest Manners*, pp. 61, 88; see Hertha Dawn Wong, *Sending My Heart Back across the Years: Tradition and Innovation in Native American Autobiography* (New York: Oxford University Press, 1992), pp. v–vi. Krupat reprints a revised version of his essay under the title "Criticism and Native American Literature" in his recent book, *The Turn to the Native: Studies in Criticism and Culture* (Lincoln: University of Nebraska Press, 1996), pp. 1–29.

100. Bierhorst, *Four Masterworks*, p. xi.

101. Krupat, *Voice*, p. 209.

102. Gauri Viswanathan, *Masks of Conquest: Literary Study and British Rule in India* (New York: Columbia University Press, 1989), pp. 166–167.

103. Goldie, *Fear and Temptation*, p. 108; Walter J. Ong, *Orality and Literacy: The Technologizing of the Word* (London: Methuen, 1982), p. 32.

104. Krupat, *Voice*, p. 232.

105. See ibid., p. 17.

106. Ashcroft, Griffiths, and Tiffin, *Empire Writes Back*, p. 145.

107. Harlow, *Resistance Literature*, p. xvi; Owens, *Other Destinies*, p. 16.

108. Further, many Indian writers have written in a rather pan-Indian fashion stories set in tribal traditions other than their own. Thus, Momaday and Ron Querry (Choctaw) have written about the Navajo and Pueblos, and Thomas King has written about the Blood. See e.g., Ron Querry, *The Death of Bernadette Lefthand* (Santa Fe: Red Crane Books, 1993).

109. Hector St. John de Crèvecoeur, *Letters from an American Farmer* (reprint, New York: Penguin, 1981), pp. 60–70, 120–124; Ashcroft, Griffiths, and Tiffin, *Empire Writes Back*, 136; Niebuhr and Heimert, *Nation So Conceived*, p. 11. In writing as he does, Niebuhr gives a perfect definition, not of indigeneity, but of Amer-Europeans.

110. Ashcroft, Griffiths, and Tiffin, *Empire Writes Back*, p. 143. Such indigenizing strategies are reminiscent of the Jindyworobak movement in the 1930s and 1940s in Australia, whose name is taken from an Aboriginal word meaning "to annex." Concerning the indigenous response to such efforts, Goldie writes, "Many Aborigines have questioned the hubris of the Jindyworobak group in their attempts to transmute bourgeois white experience through the simple evocation of Aboriginal signifiers." *Fear and Temptation*, p. 144.

111. Krupat, *Voice*, pp. 213–214. Emphasis original.

112. Vizenor, *Manifest Manners*, p. 59.

113. James Ruppert, *Mediation in Contemporary Native American Fiction* (Norman: University of Oklahoma Press, 1995), pp. 6–7. Emphasis mine.

114. Murray, *Forked Tongues*, pp. 3, 80.

115. Goldie, *Fear and Temptation*, p. 217.

116. Simon Ortiz, "Toward a National Indian Literature: Cultural Authenticity in Nationalism," *MELUS* 8, no. 2 (1981): pp. 9–10. Geary Hobson also maintains that it is Indian despite its written form. Hobson, *Remembered Earth*, p. 4.

117. Paula Gunn Allen, *The Sacred Hoop: Recovering the Feminine in American Indian Traditions*, 2d ed. (Boston: Beacon Press, 1992), p. 79; Ortiz, "National Indian Literature," p. 8.

118. Ngugi, *Decolonising the Mind*, pp. 67–69, 64–65, 85–86.

119. King, *All My Relations*, pp. ix–x.

120. Ibid., p. xi.

121. Clifford E. Trafzer, ed., *Earth Song, Sky Spirit* (New York: Doubleday, 1993), p. 7; Ruoff, *American Indian Literatures*, p. 114; Petrone, *Native Literature*, pp. 183–184. African postcolonial critic Abdul JanMohamed, who adapts Fanonian thought to literary criticism, writes, "The Third World's literary dialogue with Western cultures is marked by two broad characteristics: its attempts to negate the prior European negation of colonized cultures and its adoption and creative modification of Western languages and artistic forms in conjunction with indigenous languages and forms." Abdul R. JanMohamed, "The Economy of Manichean Allegory: The Function of Racial Difference in Colonialist Literature," *Critical Inquiry* 12, no. 1 (1985), quoted in Ashcroft, Griffiths, and Tiffin, *Post-Colonial*, p. 23.

122. Murray, *Forked Tongues*, pp. 87–88.

123. Allen, *Voice*, p. 7.

124. King, *All My Relations*, p. xii.

125. Warrior, *Tribal Secrets*, p. 117.

126. This is akin to what JanMohamed terms "Manichean aesthetics" and Ngugi calls the "aesthetic of oppression" versus that of "liberation." See Abdul R. JanMohamed, *Manichean Aesthetics: The Politics of Literature in Colonial Africa* (Amherst: University of Massachusetts Press, 1983); Ngugi wa Thiong'o, "Literature in Schools," in his *Writers in Politics* (London: Heinemann, 1981), p. 38.

127. Owens, *Other Destinies*, p. 20.

128. Ruoff, *American Indian Literatures*, p. 2.

129. Calvin Martin, ed., *The American Indian and the Problem of History* (New York: Oxford University Press, 1987), pp. 3–34, passim.

130. Rosemary McCombs Maxey, "Who Can Sit at the Lord's Table?: The Experience of Indigenous Peoples," in Daniel L. Johnson and Charles Hambrick-Stowe, eds., *Theology and Identity: Traditions, Movements, and Polity in the United Church of Canada* (New York: Pilgrim Press, 1990), p. 54.

131. Johannes Olivier states, "There is as it were a veil between the natives and their European masters on account of which the essential character of the former remains almost entirely unknown to the latter." Nieuwenhuys, *Mirror of the Indies*, p. 53. Eduardo and Bonnie Duran have attempted to redress this imbalance in a psychotherapeutic context. See Eduardo Duran and Bonnie Duran, *Native American Postcolonial Psychology* (Albany: State University of New York Press, 1995), pp. 13–21.

132. Peelman, *Christ Is a Native American*, p. 44.

133. Owens, *Other Destinies*, p. 8.

134. Sioui, *Amerindian Autohistory*, p. 31.

135. James Treat, ed., *Native and Christian: Indigenous Voices on Religious Identity in the United States and Canada* (New York: Routledge, 1996), p. 20.

136. Ruoff, *American Indian Literatures*, p. 2.

137. Åke Hultkrantz, *Native Religions of North America* (New York: Harper & Row, 1987), p. 20.

138. Carmody and Carmody, *Native American Religions*, pp. 106–107.

139. David A. Rausch and Blair Schlepp, *Native American Voices* (Grand Rapids: Baker Books, 1994), pp. 52, 51–53.

140. McPherson and Rabb, *Indian from the Inside*, pp. 83–107.

141. Ngugi also notes that a people's culture is an essential component in defining and revealing their worldview. Ngugi, *Decolonising the Mind*, p. 100.

142. Peelman, *Christ Is a Native American*, p. 202; Carmody and Carmody, *Native American Religions*, pp. 191–193.

143. A. Jaimes-Guerrero, "Native Womanism: The Organic Female Archetype—Kinship and Gender Identity within Sacred Indigenous Traditions" (paper read at American Academy of Religion meeting, Philadelphia, November 20, 1995). Guerrero goes on to state, however, that Indians are "universal people" and that "cultural diversity derived from the environment is very different from saying that Indians were different cultures." She notes that indigenous peoples worldwide have a "universal connection with each other." As Robert Warrior notes, "Fourth World" and "indigenist" discourse, of which Jaimes-Guerrero is a leading exponent, has adhered to "idealism . . . and essentialism." *Tribal Secrets*, pp. xvii, xviii.

144. McPherson and Rabb, *Indian from the Inside*, p. i.

145. Ibid., p. 3.

146. Ibid.

147. Sioui, *Amerindian Autohistory*, p. 69.

148. JanMohamed, "Economy," pp. 21–22. See also Ronald Takaki, *A Different Mirror: A History of Multicultural America* (Boston: Little, Brown, 1993), pp. 25–50. Takaki writes, "*The Tempest* can be approached as a fascinating tale that served as a masquerade for the creation of a new society in America. Seen in this light, the play invites us to view English expansion not only as imperialism, but also as a defining moment in the making of an English-American identity based on race" (pp. 25–26).

149. Tinker, *Missionary Conquest*, p. 2.

150. William Baldridge, "Christianity after Colonialism" (unpublished paper, 1992), p. 4, published as "Reclaiming Our Histories," in David Batstone, ed., *New Visions for the Americas: Religious Engagement and Social Transformation* (Minneapolis: Fortress Press, 1993), pp. 23–32.

151. Vine Deloria Jr., *Custer Died for Your Sins* (New York: Macmillan, 1969), p. 112.

152. Carl K. Starkloff, "American Indian Religion and Christianity: Confrontation and Dialogue," in Martin E. Marty and Dean G. Peerman, eds., *New Theology No. 9* (New York: Macmillan, 1972), p. 122.

153. Carl K. Starkloff, "Religious Renewal in Native North America: The Contemporary Call to Mission," *Missiology* 13, no. 1 (January 1985): p. 83. George Sioui notes that the myth of the Vanishing Indian, not unlike the argument articulated by Starkloff, is the "main reason for a certain reluctance . . . to incorporate an ethical dimension into their discourse pertaining to Native peoples." *Amerindian Autohistory*, p. 99.

154. James A. Treat, "Native Americans, Theology, and Liberation: Christianity and Traditionalism in the Struggle for Survival" (master's thesis, Pacific School of Religion, 1989), p. 77. Emphasis original.

155. Peelman, *Christ Is a Native American*, pp. 95–96; Carmody and Carmody, *Native American Religions*, p. 170. Carmody and Carmody are not immune, however, from falling into the imperialistic trap of fulfillment theology. In approvingly discussing cur-

rent missiological theory, they write, "Nowadays, much missionary theology embraces virtually the opposite position: leave native peoples alone, look for expressions of grace in their traditional ways, and offer them Christian ways completely freely, emphasizing how Christian faith is consonant with their best native traditions and may fulfill them. This newer missionary theology seems quite wise, as long as it does not mean that one becomes completely uncritical about native ways. Ideally, natives and outsiders would discuss their beliefs as equals, full of mutual respect. Ideally, only when natives were truly persuaded that the religion of outsiders offered them a depth and beauty, a salvation and divinization, that they wanted to embrace because of their own best traditional instincts would one speak of conversion. The sun dance might serve as a concrete focus for such a discussion" (pp. 70–71). The two authors do not discuss how such a discursive equality can occur, given differences in power between colonizer and colonized, nor do they reflect upon just how much "mutual respect" there can be when the agenda of the "outsiders" remains one of "conversion." Native traditions, unlike Christianity, are not proselytizing faiths. Catholics, in particular, have been active in advancing fulfillment theology. See e.g., William Stolzman, *The Pipe and Christ*, 4th ed. (Chamberlain, S.D.: Tipi Press, 1992); Sister Charles Palm, *Stories That Jesus Told: Dakota Way of Life* (Sioux Falls: American Indian Culture Research Center of Blue Cloud Abbey, 1985).

156. Peelman, *Christ Is a Native American*, p. 13. In fairness, Peelman would probably maintain that his *Christ Is a Native American* (in the original French, *Le Christ est amérindien*) is written for a non-Native Christian audience. The issue still remains, however, why Natives need to be so represented by an outsider. As for contemporary Native Christian theology, James Treat gathers a few of these expressions together in an anthology. Treat, *Native and Christian*.

157. Tinker, *Missionary Conquest*, p. 3. I have termed this self-hating theological stance "Apply Piety." Apple is one of the Indian equivalents for an "Oreo"—Red on the outside, White on the inside.

158. Noley, *First White Frost*, pp. 140, 85.

159. Treat, *Native and Christian*, p. 9.

160. Jace Weaver, "Native Reformation in Indian Country?," *Christianity and Crisis*, February 15, 1993, p. 40.

161. Peelman, *Christ Is a Native American*, p. 23.

162. Ibid. Emphasis original.

163. Ibid.; Robert Allen Warrior, "Tribal Secrets" (Ph.D. diss., Union Theological Seminary, 1991), p. 8.

164. Peelman, *Christ Is a Native American*, p. 23.

165. Vine Deloria Jr., *God is Red*, 2d ed. (Golden, Colo.: Fulcrum, 1992), p. 79.

166. Peelman, *Christ Is a Native American*, p. 46; Allen, *Spider Woman's*: "Right relationship, or right kinship is fundamental to Native aesthetics" (p. 9).

167. Moises Colop, interview with author, September 22, 1995.

168. Goldie, *Fear and Temptation*, p. 127.

169. McPherson and Rabb, *Indian from the Inside*, p. 10.

170. William Wantland, interview with author, December 21, 1992.

171. See Steve Charleston, "The Old Testament of Native America," in Susan Brooks Thistlethwaite and Mary Potter Engel, eds., *Lift Every Voice: Constructing Christian Theologies from the Underside* (San Francisco: Harper & Row, 1990), p. 49.

172. As an added example, I do not believe that Native communities, assaulted and deeply damaged by more than 500 years of colonialism, can believe that God in any way wanted or needed the death of Jesus on the cross to be "reconciled" with humanity. Rather, many Natives aver that the crucifixion was the work of humanity and that when it occurred God wept. Then, however, as Psalm 2 states, God laughs with derision at the folly of humanity. God asks, "Is that all there is? Is that the best you can do?" Then came, in response, the Resurrection. It is true that the most familiar Cherokee Christian hymn is the atonement-oriented "One Drop of Blood," but culturally this hymn takes on a this-worldly character as it recalls the Trail of Tears upon which it was sung, becoming a plaint and a metaphor for that event. Jennie Lee Fife's (Cherokee) paraphrase captures this: "Our heavenly Father, what do I have to do for you to save me? It only takes one drop of blood to wash away our sins. You are King of Kings, the Creator of all things." Marilyn M. Hofstra, ed., *Voices: Native American Hymns and Worship Resources* (Nashville: Discipleship Resources, 1992), pp. 45–48. In like fashion, Native religions have no concept of salvation beyond the continuance of the People and no concept of sin beyond, perhaps, failure to live up to one's responsibilities to the community.

173. McPherson and Rabb, *Indian from the Inside,* p. 10.

174. Richard Rorty, "Cosmopolitanism without Emancipation: A Response to Jean-François Lyotard," in his *Objectivity, Relativism, and Truth: Philosophical Papers, Volume 1* (Cambridge: Cambridge University Press, 1991), p. 213.

175. Tinker, "Response," p. 173.

176. Goldie, *Fear and Temptation,* p. 221; Kim Benterrak, Stephen Muecke, and Paddy Roe, *Reading the Country: Introduction to Nomadology* (Fremantle, Australia: Fremantle Arts Centre, 1984), p. 126.

177. Aloysius Pieris, *An Asian Theology of Liberation* (Maryknoll: Orbis Books, 1988), pp. xi–xii.

178. See, e.g., Ashcroft, Griffiths and Tiffin, *Empire Writes Back,* pp. 8–9.

179. *Han* is a kind of existential angst that is a defining element of the Korean character. See Andrew Sung Park, *The Wounded Heart of God: The Asian Concept of Han and the Christian Doctrine of Sin* (Nashville: Abingdon, 1993); Chung Hyun-Kyung, *Struggle to Be the Sun Again* (Maryknoll: Orbis Books, 1990), pp. 23, 44, 66, 99.

180. Philip P. Arnold, "Wampum, the Land, and the Abolition of Grief" (paper read at American Academy of Religion meeting, Philadelphia, November 20, 1995).

181. Noley, *First White Frost,* p. 79; Mary Churchill, "Native Struggles for Freedom in the Land" (response at American Academy of Religion meeting, Philadelphia, November 20, 1995). The title of Noley's book, *First White Frost,* is a marvelous work of signification, possessing a double meaning. In an epigram at the book's opening, Noley explains, "Nitakechi, leader of the Choctaw Southern District, one of the most traditional of the Choctaw leaders, had the sad task of leading the people of his district on the forced march from Mississippi to Indian Territory. He said that three thousand Choctaw men, women, and and children 'would be ready to start "the first white frost of October" ' " (p. 9). At the same time it expresses the "covering" of Native spirituality with the "white frost" of the religion of the colonizer, Christianity.

182. Treat, *Native and Christian,* p. 12.

183. Greg Sarris, *Keeping Slug Woman Alive: A Holistic Approach to American Indian Texts* (Berkeley: University of California Press, 1993), p. 121.

184. Szasz, *Between Indian and White Worlds;* Dorothy R. Parker, "D'Arcy McNickle: Living a Broker's Life," in ibid.; Ruppert, *Mediation;* Murray, *Forked Tongues,* p. 1.

185. Ruppert, *Mediation,* pp. 3, 20.

186. Ibid. pp. 19–20, quoting Gerald Vizenor, *Earthdivers: Tribal Narratives on Mixed Descent* (Minneapolis: University of Minnesota Press, 1981), p. xvii.

187. Nieuwenhuys, *Mirror of the Indies,* pp. 273, 324, 186.

188. Treat, *Native and Christian,* p. 18.

189. Mourning Dove, *Cogewea, the Half-Blood* (Boston: Four Seas, 1927), p. 41. Emphasis original. The work was actually completed in 1916 but remained unpublished for eleven years.

190. Owens, *Other Destinies,* p. 19.

191. Ibid.

192. Murray, *Forked Tongues,* pp. 88–89.

193. Ruppert, *Mediation,* p. 19.

194. Ibid., p. 29.

195. Ibid., pp. 32–33; see Paula Gunn Allen, *The Woman Who Owned the Shadows* (1983; reprint, San Francisco: Aunt Lute Books, 1994).

196. Jace Weaver, "PW Interviews: Thomas King," *Publishers Weekly,* March 8, 1993, quoted in Vizenor, *Manifest Manners,* p. 174.

197. See Owens, *Other Destinies,* pp. 14–15.

198. Petrone, *Native Literature,* p. 182.

199. Petrone here reveals a Eurocentric bias as she writes patronizingly, "Already many [Native writers] are able to deal with the culture clash and their own identity not only with perception but with some detachment and control, moving beyond the worst excesses of emotion and diction that marred much earlier protest writing" (ibid.). In this regard, it is worth noting that one of my female students stated that to characterize what has occurred in this hemisphere as a "clash of cultures" is akin to calling rape a "clash of genders."

200. Vine Deloria Jr., "Sacred Lands and Religious Freedom," *American Indian Religions* 1, no. 1 (Winter 1994): pp. 75–76. Once again, in Deloria's statement one can recognize Said's distinction between filiation and affiliation.

201. William G. McLoughlin, *After the Trail of Tears: The Cherokees' Struggle for Sovereignty, 1839–1880* (Chapel Hill: University of North Carolina Press, 1993), p. xv.

202. In discussing whether the decolonizing world had the wherewithal for democracy, Niebuhr and his coauthor, Allen Heimert, raise doubts about whether indigenous or traditional societies "possess the elementary preconditions of community, the cohesions of a common language and race, for instance, which European nations possessed at least two centuries before the rise of free institutions." *Nation So Conceived,* p. 149. For a critique of this wildly Eurocentric and ethnocentric query, see Weaver, "Original Simplicities," pp. 211–212.

203. Carmody and Carmody, *Native American Religions,* p. 70.

204. King, *All My Relations,* pp. xiii–xiv.

205. Warrior, *Tribal Secrets,* pp. xxii–xxiii.

206. Hobson, *Remembered Earth*, p. 14.

207. Pieris makes a distinction between what he calls "cosmic" religions, such as Native traditions, which have been pejoratively labeled "animism," and "metacosmic" religions, which possess an otherworldly soteriology. *Asian Theology,* pp. 71–74; Peelman, *Christ Is a Native American,* p. 44.

208. Goldie, *Fear and Temptation,* p. 120; David Thompson, *David Thompson's Narrative of His Explorations in Western America, 1784–1812,* ed. J. B. Tyrell (Toronto: Champlain Society, 1916), p. 362.

209. Allen, *Sacred Hoop,* 2d ed., p. 55. This relation of traditional religious practice to community is acknowledged even by many fundamentalist Native Christians otherwise opposed to traditional religion. Peelman notes that even the pentecostal Native denomination of the Body of Christ Independent church, which is radically opposed to traditional Lakota religion and "rejects all traditional religious symbols as a means of true Lakota identity," nonetheless recognizes the importance of community in traditional cultural features like the *tiyospaye. Christ Is a Native American,* p. 77.

210. Carmody and Carmody, *Native American Religions,* p. 51; Rausch and Schlepp, *Native American Voices,* pp. 141–146.

211. Clifford Geertz, "From the Native's Point of View: On the Nature of Anthropological Understanding," in Richard Shweder and Robert LeVine, eds., *Culture Theory: Essays on Mind, Self and Emotion* (Cambridge: Cambridge University Press, 1984), p. 126.

212. Arnold Krupat, ed., *Native American Autobiography: An Anthology* (Madison: University of Wisconsin Press, 1994), p. 4; Donald Fixico, *The Invasion of Indian Country in the Twentieth Century: American Capitalism and Tribal Natural Resources* (Boulder: University of Colorado Press, forthcoming). Fixico writes, "Traditional Native Americans believe that they are part of a whole. Indian people are not solitary. They historically have preferred a culture stressing community as more important than a single member of the group. The tendency is to see the whole or the group and want to be part of it. The group is seen as happiness of relatives and friends talking and laughing, the content of socialization among members, the security found among community and kinfolk. To want to be part of the whole and to see onself as a small part of the 'one' refocuses the emphasis on group-ego rather than self-ego. In order to belong to the group and to be accepted by others, one places the needs of the group before the needs of the individual." "The Struggle for Our Homes: Indian and White Values and Tribal Lands," in Weaver, *Defending Mother Earth,* pp. 37–38.

213. Allen, *Sacred Hoop,* p. 55; McPherson and Rabb, *Indian from the Inside,* p. 100.

214. Fixico, "Struggle," p. 38.

215. McPherson and Rabb, *Indian from the Inside,* p. 6; King, *All My Relations,* p. ix. See also Trafzer, *Earth Song,* p. 7.

216. Carmody and Carmody, *Native American Religions,* pp. 100–101; Peelman, *Christ Is a Native American,* p. 198. This split, of course, has been analyzed and critiqued by a number of Christian theologians. See e.g., Paul Tillich, *Systematic Theology* (Welwyn: J. Nisbet, 1960), parts I and II; Karl Rahner, *Foundations of Christian Faith* (New York: Seabury Press, 1978), pp. 44–89.

217. Peelman, *Christ Is a Native American,* p. 54.

218. Christopher Ronwanièn:te Jocks, "Combing Out Snakes: Violence in the Longhouse Tradition" (paper read at American Academy of Religion meeting, Chicago, November 21, 1994). For a discussion of knowledge and power, see generally, Gayatri Chakravorty Spivak, *Outside in the Teaching Machine* (New York: Routledge, 1993).

219. Leslie Marmon Silko, quoted in Trafzer, *Earth Song,* p. 21; see also Silko, "Foreword," pp. 7–8.

220. Vizenor, *Manifest Manners,* p. 56.

221. Vizenor, *Narrative Chance,* p. 3.

222. Alister McGrath, *Evangelicalism and the Future of Christianity* (Downers Grove, Ill.: InterVarsity Press, 1995), p. 18. For more information about the Kiowa Apache, see Edward H. Spicer, *The American Indians* (Cambridge: Harvard University Press, 1980), pp. 92–95.

223. Kroeber, *Traditional Literatures,* pp. 21–22. See also Krupat, *Voice,* p. 220. Ngugi discusses the importance of story at Ngugi, *Decolonising the Mind,* pp. 10–11.

224. Trafzer, *Earth Song,* p. 21. Vizenor writes, "Postindian simulations arise from the silence of heard stories, or the imagination of oral literature in translation, not the absence of the real in simulated realities; the critical distinction is that postindian warriors create a new tribal presence in stories." Vizenor, *Manifest Manners,* p. 12. He also contends, "This is a continuous turn in tribal narratives, the oral stories are dominated by those narratives that are translated, published, and read at unnamed distances" (ibid.). Thus, once again the printed story is considered normative. The myth of conquest, of literacy over orature, must once again prove itself by conquering other stories.

225. Petrone, *Native Literature,* p. 5. Emphasis mine.

226. See Ruppert, *Mediation,* p. 12.

227. Trafzer, *Earth Song,* p. 8. This is especially true for often displaced urban Indians. Thomas King is not alone among Native authors in receiving letters from Native readers thanking him for helping him make sense of contemporary Native experience. Thomas King, interview with author, January 27, 1993. For a discussion of contemporary urban Natives, see Lynda Shorten, *Without Reserve: Stories from Urban Natives* (Edmonton: NeWest Press, 1991).

228. Allen, *Spider Woman's,* p. 5.

229. King interview. King dedicates his anthology of contemporary Native fiction to Robinson. King, *All My Relations,* p. v.

230. Allen, *Voice,* p. 6.

231. See Ruppert, *Mediation,* p. 25. Sioui states: "Through their music and poetry and their arts in general, the . . . nations also express a keen awareness of their Amerindianness." *Amerindian Autohistory,* p. 33. Owens notes that the "recovering or rearticulation of an identity, a process dependent upon a rediscovered sense of place as well as community," lies at the heart of contemporary Indian fiction. *Other Destinies,* p. 5. Similarly, Ruppert observes that Native protagonists in current fiction are continually examining where they fit in and how they are seen by others. Their actions are judged by a "communal standard and definition of identity." *Mediation,* p. 28.

232. Vizenor, *Manifest Manners,* p. 8.

233. Said, *Culture,* pp. xii–xiii.

234. Owens, *Other Destinies,* p. 9; Trafzer, *Earth Song,* p. 4.

235. Owens, *Other Destinies,* p. 10.

236. Krupat, *Voice,* pp. 162–163. Emphasis mine.

237. Allen, *Spider Woman's,* p. 4. Of course, Allen resolves this existential dilemma by deciding that Indian writers *are* Indian.

238. Elizabeth Cook-Lynn, "You May Consider Speaking About Your Art . . . ," in Brian Swann and Arnold Krupat, eds., *I Tell You Now: Autobiographical Essays by Native Americans* (Lincoln: University of Nebraska Press, 1987), p. 58. Emphasis original.

239. Ashcroft, Griffiths, and Tiffin, *Empire Writes Back,* p. 5; Owens, *Other Destinies,* p. 11; see Robert Allen Warrior, "An Interview with Vine Deloria, Jr.," *The Progressive,* April 1990.

240. Hobson, *Remembered Earth,* pp. 9, 10; Owens, *Other Destinies,* p. 11; Trafzer, *Earth Song,* p. 7. It may be that the discourse of other Others, of other oppositional literatures, carries this same sense of responsibility to community. It is not, however, generally true of writers from the dominant culture, who, pursuing the writer's craft, follow Polonius's injunction to Laertes, "To thine own self be true."

241. Ibid., p. 11. Thomas King notes that they may portray Indians outside of "traditional" contexts but "maintain their literary connection to Native culture." *All My Relations,* p. xv.

242. Vizenor, *Manifest Manners,* p. 95; see also Ruppert, *Mediation,* p. 30.

243. Ruppert, *Mediation,* pp. 28–29; Sioui, *Amerindian Autohistory,* p. 22.

244. Warrior, *Tribal Secrets,* p. xx.

245. For a discussion of mass humanity, see Romano Guardini, *The End of the Modern World,* trans. Joseph Theman and Herbert Burke (New York: Sheed & Ward, 1956).

246. Although Natives, as noted throughout, speak of Native community a lot, "communitist" is a word created by me. In coining such a term, I am not alone. Nieuwenhuys, to characterize a certain aspect of the Dutch Indies character, employs "d'artagnanism," a certain "bravura and posturing" in the manner of Dumas's musketeer, when other terms are "unworkable." *Mirror of the Indies,* p. 198. In like manner, Alice Walker coined "womanist," and the term has since been picked up by the community itself. See Delores S. Williams, *Sisters in the Wilderness: The Challenge of Womanist God-Talk* (Maryknoll: Orbis Books, 1993), p. 243.

247. Bhabha, *Location of Culture,* p. 3. Emphasis original.

248. Linda Hogan, *The Book of Medicines* (Minneapolis: Coffee House Press, 1993). Robert Warrior also notes that poet Wendy Rose (Hopi/Miwok), in breaking her own silence, brings to the conversation "a stark reminder of the need for healing in Indian communities and presents a challenge for American Indian intellectuals to be more honest, more inclusive, and to recognize the profound challenges we face." *Tribal Secrets,* p. 121. See also Bruchac, *Survival This Way,* pp. 254–258.

249. "Spectrum," p. 21; see also Joy Harjo, *The Woman Who Fell from the Sky* (New York: W. W. Norton, 1994), p. 19.

250. Tapahonso, *Sáanii Dahataal,* p. xii. Echoing this reversal of exile, Dennis Lee states that the "first necessity for the colonial writer" is for the imagination to "come home." Ngugi writes that the biggest problem for him as a writer is finding the appropriate fictional language to communicate with "the people I left behind." Ashcroft, Griffiths, and Tiffin, *Empire Writes Back,* p. 142; Ngugi, *Decolonising the Mind,* p. 75.

251. Warrior, *Tribal Secrets*, pp. 118, 112–113.

252. Ibid., p. 125.

253. Vizenor, *Manifest Manners*, pp. 93–94. Said declares that "criticism must think of itself as life-enhancing and constitutively opposed to every form of tyranny, domination, and abuse: its social goals are noncoercive knowledge produced in the interest of human freedom." *World*, p. 29. Louis Owens contends, "The noble savage's refusal to perish throws a monkey wrench into the drama. . . . With few exceptions, American Indian novelists . . . are in their fiction rejecting the American gothic with its haunted, guilt-burdened wilderness and doomed Native and emphatically making the Indian the hero of other destinies, other plots," *Other Destinies*, p. 18.

254. Vizenor, *Manifest Manners*, p. 4.

255. Ngugi, *Decolonising the Mind*, p. 87. It is this that Ngugi calls the "quest for relevance."

256. Ruppert, *Mediation*, p. xii.

257. See Owens, *Other Destinies*, p. 20; Ngugi, *Decolonising the Mind*, pp. 82–83.

258. Bhabha, *Location of Culture*, p. 13. Emphasis original.

259. See King, *All My Relations*, pp. xiii–xiv. As an example of disagreement over means, one could note that Deloria decries Western education as making overeducated, deracinated Indians, whereas Warrior advocates it as a potential tool in the struggle for liberation in the dominant culture, a tool that does not *necessarily* lead to assimilation but can aid cultural survival. See Vine Deloria Jr., *Red Earth, White Lies* (New York: Scribner's, 1995); Warrior, *Tribal Secrets*, p. 123.

260. In speaking so, it is not my intent to fetishize or romanticize pre-Contact society. There were conflicts and problems as in any other cultures. America was not some Edenic paradise. It was simply *ours*. Besides, as Trafzer notes, "Native Americans act as a community [to survive] even when individual members of the community refuse to cooperate in the maintenance of the people." *Earth Song*, p. 20. See also Donald A. Grinde and Bruce E. Johansen, *Ecocide of Native America* (Santa Fe: Clear Light, 1995); Sioui, *Amerindian Autohistory*, p. 26.

261. Warrior, *Tribal Secrets*, p. 126. Penny Petrone touches upon the same theme and relates it to healing but reflects a more decidedly Eurocentric bias that too often sees subaltern groups as whining. She writes, "Native writers will create their own forms, in responding to the fast-changing society they live in. Once the outrage has been exorcised, the self-pity and self-indulgence worked out, and the frictional heat of catharsis has subsided, new subjects and themes will take their place. In drawing upon traditional values to heal their scars, they will become liberated, and the victim syndrome will disappear." *Native Literature*, p. 183. Despite her tone, by bringing together survival, healing, and liberation, she points at communitism and brings literature together with the religious enterprise. On this subject of whining and anger, see Standiford, "Worlds," p. 336 ("Often, a native writer is overcome with the urgency of his message and forsakes all concerns of craft in the effort to make his point"); and G. W. Haslam, *Forgotten Pages of American Literature* (Boston: Houghton Mifflin, 1970), p. 24. (Haslam looks forward to "when Indian writers as a group forsake blatant protest and employ more imaginative—and probably more persuasive—forms; the pressure of their plight has tended to force Indian writers into desperate excoriations of conditions. Like Afro-

Americans who have found that subtlety is often a more effective social weapon than shrill anger, native American artists are beginning to discover their own most moving modes of expression.")

262. Vine Deloria Jr., "It is a Good Day to Die," *Katallagete* 4, nos. 2–3 (Fall–Winter 1972); p. 65.

Chapter Two

1. Brant, *Writing as Witness*, pp. 39–40. Emphasis original.

2. Ruoff, *American Indian Literatures*, p. 1.

3. Ibid. In this quotation, cited by Ruoff, it is arguable that Momaday also urges the inclusion of Native work in the national literature.

4. Brant, *Writing as Witness*, p. 40; Petrone, *Native Literature*, pp. 3–4; Trafzer, *Earth Song*, p. 4.

5. It is also, of course, as also noted, carried on by contemporary writers who, in Paula Gunn Allen's phrase, are "furthering and nourishing it and being furthered and nourished by it." *Sacred Hoop*, 2d ed., p. 79. For but two illustrations of the continued vitality and evolution of the oral tradition, see Joseph Bruchac, ed., *New Voices from the Longhouse* (Greenfield Center, N.Y.: Greenfield Review Press, 1989), and Herbert T. Schwarz, ed., *Tales from the Smokehouse* (Edmonton: Hurtig Publishers, 1974).

6. Simon Ortiz, quoted in Ruoff, *American Indian Literatures*, p. 5. Emphasis mine.

7. Vizenor, *Manifest Manners*, p. 75; Karl Kroeber, *Traditional Literatures*, p. 17. Kroeber advises, "One should begin by assuming that an Indian oral narrative may be a first-rate work of art. One must abandon the misconception that this literature is 'primitive.' It is not" (pp. 2–3). Today a great deal of the oral tradition, much of it recorded by 19th-century ethnographers, has found its way into print. I will not deal with the problems that orthography and translation present, but they are manifold. Petrone asks a pertinent question: "Can the translator ever accurately reproduce on the printed page an oral literature that depends so much on performance?" Her conclusion is "probably not." *Native Literature*, p. 7.

8. See Dennis Tedlock, trans., *Popul Vuh* (New York: Simon & Schuster, 1985).

9. For more on the opinion of de Landa and other Spaniards, see Fernando Cervantes, *The Devil in the New World: The Impact of Diabolism in New Spain* (New Haven: Yale University Press, 1994), pp. 16, 51.

10. Quoted in White Deer of Autumn [Gabriel Horn], *The Native American Book of Knowledge* (Hillsboro, Ore.: Beyond Words Publishing, 1992), p. 33.

11. Similar hieroglyphic codices exist for other Mesoamerican tribes, including the Mixtec.

12. Gordon Brotherston, *Book of the Fourth World: Reading the Native Americas through Their Literature* (Cambridge: Cambridge University Press, 1992), p. 191. Brotherston continues, "By expropriating this region and flouting its own notions of legality, the United States converted itself from a coastal to a continental power; and its defense was a main objective of the campaign orchestrated by the Ottawa Pontiac in 1762–3, in which the Lenape were much involved, and of the last-ditch and truly international

crusade of the Shawnee Tecumseh in 1812, which also embraced the Muskogee Mound Builder heirs of the south" (pp. 191–192). For discussions of the *Wallum Olum* and its uncertain provenance and history, as well as a translation, see ibid., pp. 191–192, 387; Noley, *First White Frost,* p. 17; David McCutchen, *The Red Record: The Wallum Olum* (Garden City, N.Y.: Avery Publishing Group, 1993).

13. Noley, *First White Frost,* p. 16; Virgil J. Vogel, *This Country Was Ours: A Documentary History of the American Indian* (New York: Harper & Row, 1974), p. 94. Vogel also provides valuable information about the publication history of the document.

14. Noley, *First White Frost,* p. 16.

15. Warrior, *Tribal Secrets,* p. 3.

16. Robert Warrior, "William Apess: Recovering a Christian Native Nationalist Past" (paper read at Native American Religion Forum, School of Theology at Claremont, Claremont, Calif., August 11, 1995).

17. Ruoff, *American Indian Literatures,* p. 62.

18. Murray, *Forked Tongues,* p. 44.

19. Samson Occom, "A Short Narrative of My Life," reprinted in Krupat, *Native American Autobiography,* p. 107.

20. Henry Warner Bowden, *American Indians and Christian Missions* (Chicago: University of Chicago Press, 1981), p. 139.

21. Murray, *Forked Tongues,* p. 55. Emphasis mine.

22. Ibid., p. 54. The autobiography remained in the Dartmouth archives, unpublished, until Bernd C. Peyer, ed., *The Elders Wrote: An Anthology of Early Prose by North American Indians, 1768–1931* (Berlin: Dietrich Reimer Verlag, 1982).

23. Krupat, *Voice,* p. 146. Murray's work on Occom in *Forked Tongues* is described by Krupat as "useful for further study" and causes perhaps a reevaluation of at least the autobiography. Krupat writes, "The document is, in David Brumble's sense, one of self-vindication, and so, for all Occom's Christian acculturation, it perhaps also exhibits elements of traditional Mohegan narrative modes." *Native American Autobiography,* pp. 105–106.

24. Murray, *Forked Tongues,* pp. 53–54. Emphasis original.

25. Ibid.; Bernd Peyer, "Samson Occom: Mohegan Missionary and Writer of the 18th Century," *American Indian Quarterly* 6, nos. 3–4 (1982): p. 211.

26. Murray, *Forked Tongues,* p. 53.

27. Occom, "Short Narrative," p. 113. Emphasis original.

28. Lavonne Ruoff reprinted the sermon with an introduction in *Studies in American Indian Literatures* 4 (1992): pp. 75–105. See also Ruoff, *American Indian Literatures,* p. 62.

29. Murray, *Forked Tongues,* p. 45.

30. Ibid., p. 46.

31. Occom, quoted in ibid.

32. Ibid., pp. 46–47. Emphasis original.

33. Warrior, *Tribal Secrets,* p. 44.

34. Bowden, *American Indians,* p. 144.

35. Murray, *Forked Tongues,* p. 63.

36. Warrior, *Tribal Secrets,* pp. 3, 44, 98. I could also add, of communitism.

37. Krupat, *Voice,* pp. 144, 145, 145–149.

38. Brumble, *American Indian Autobiography,* p. 122; Wong, *Sending My Heart Back,* p. 108.

39. Ruoff, *American Indian Literatures,* pp. 62–63; Murray, *Forked Tongues,* p. 57; Krupat, *Voice,* p. 148; Murray, *Forked Tongues,* pp. 58–64; see Kim McQuaid, "William Apes, Pequot, an Indian Reformer in the Jackson Era," *New England Quarterly* 50 (1977): pp. 605–625.

40. Barry O'Connell, ed., *On Our Own Ground: The Complete Writings of William Apess, a Pequot* (Amherst: University of Massachusetts Press, 1992), p. lxi.

41. Krupat, *Native American Autobiography,* p. 121.

42. O'Connell, *On Our Own Ground,* pp. xiv–xv.

43. William Apess, *A Son of the Forest,* in ibid., pp. 3–4.

44. William Apess, "Eulogy on King Philip," in ibid., pp. 305–306.

45. Even his title, *A Son of the Forest,* plays with expectations and stereotypes. Petrone writes, "During the nineteenth century the Indian was seen as the simple child of nature just a little above the anthropoids, whom the blessings of civilization and Christianity could raise to a respectable level. When these 'blessings' did not prove too successful, the Indians were seen as a social nuisance, blocking progress and impossible to civilize. More recently the stereotypes have settled either on the welfare bum or on the tragic victim debased by alcohol, disease, and treatment of the whites." *Native Literature,* p. 2.

46. Though he makes this statement in *Son of the Forest,* it is not precisely correct. He does prefer the term "Native." He will, however, use the term "Indian" in some of his other works, especially "An Indian's Looking-Glass for the White Man," in O'Connell, *On Our Own Ground,* pp. 155–161; *Indian Nullification of the Unconstitutional Laws of Massachusetts Relative to the Marshpee Tribe: Or, the Pretended Riot Explained,* in ibid., pp. 166–274; and "Eulogy on King Philip," pp. 277–310.

47. Apess, *Son,* p. 10. Emphasis original.

48. Murray, *Forked Tongues,* p. 58. Gerald Vizenor writes, "The Indian became the homogenous name for thousands of distinct tribal cultures. The Anishinaabe were named the Chippewa. The Dakota were named the Sioux. Other tribal names are colonial inventions sustained in the literature of dominance. That some postindians renounce the inventions and final vocabularies of manifest manners is the advance of survivance hermeneutics." *Manifest Manners,* p. 167.

49. O'Connell, *On Our Own Ground,* p. xxi.

50. David Walker, *Appeal to the Coloured Citizens of the World* (1829; reprint, New York: Hill and Wang, 1965).

51. See, e.g., Apess, *Son,* pp. 31–33.

52. Apess, *Indian Nullification,* pp. 205, 169ff.

53. Apess, *Son,* p. 34. More than 150 years later, Vine Deloria will employ rhetorical moves similar to Apess's use of the Ten Lost Tribes myth to assert Native humanity.

54. Apess, "The Experiences of Five Christian Indians" in O'Connell, *On Our Own Ground,* p. 160. Elsewhere, in a "scathing pun," Apess looks at Amer-Europeans' complexion and their treatment of Indians, concluding that their Christian values must be only "skin-deep." See, Murray, *Forked Tongues,* p. 61.

55. Apess, *Son,* pp. 52–97.

56. William Apess, "The Indians: The Ten Lost Tribes," in O'Connell, *On Our Own Ground,* pp. 113–115.

57. Apess, *Son,* p. 54. Apess is quoting Bartolomé de Las Casas at this point.

58. Apess, "The Indians," p. 115.

59. Apess, *Son,* pp. 45–46. It is interesting to note the similarity in conclusion reached by Apess with that of Occom in his autobiography, regarding the reasons for his own mistreatment.

60. See O'Connell, *On Our Own Ground,* p. lv.

61. Apess, *Experience,* pp. 151–152.

62. Apess, *Son,* p. 33.

63. William Apess, "The Increase of the Kingdom of Christ," in O'Connell, *On Our Own Ground,* pp. 101–112.

64. Ibid., pp. 106–107.

65. Apess, quoted in O'Connell, *On Our Own Ground,* p. xiii.

66. Ibid., p. lxxiv.

67. Ibid., p. lxxvii.

68. Krupat, *Native American Autobiography,* p. 121. Apess disappeared from public life suddenly around 1838, and there has been much speculation as to his fate, including the possibilities of alcohol-related death and even murder. Recently, however, his obituaries have been discovered in the *New York Sun* and *New York Observer.* Ibid.

69. Vizenor uses some of the material set down by Jones about his people in Gerald Vizenor, *The People Named the Chippewa: Narrative Histories* (Minneapolis: University of Minnesota Press, 1984). Petrone provides some useful discussion of him. See, e.g., Petrone, *Native Literature,* pp. 36ff. Ruoff devotes less than a paragraph to him in her bibliographic study. Ruoff, *American Indian Literatures,* pp. 64, 141; see also A. LaVonne Brown Ruoff, *Literatures of the American Indian* (New York: Chelsea House, 1991). One modern biography of Jones exists. Donald Smith, *Sacred Feathers: The Reverend Peter Jones (Kahkewaquonoby) and the Mississauga Indians* (Toronto: University of Toronto Press, 1987).

70. George Henry [Maungwudaus], *Remarks Concerning the Ojibway Indians, by One of Themselves Called Maungwudaus, Who Has Been Traveling in England, France, Belgium, Ireland, and Scotland* (Leeds: C. A. Wilson, 1847); *An Account of the Chippewa Indians, Who Have Been Traveling in the United States, England, Ireland, Scotland, France and Belgium; with Very Interesting Incidents in Relation to the General Characteristics of the English, Irish, Scotch, French, and Americans, with Regard to Their Hospitality, Peculiarities, etc.* (Boston: Privately printed, 1848); *An Account of the North American Indians, Written for Maungwudaus, a Chief of the Ojibway Indians Who Has Been Travelling in England, France, Belgium, Ireland, and Scotland* (Leicester: T. Cook, 1848). Henry is often described as Jones's cousin, but he was his half-brother, sharing a common mother, Tuhbenahneequay. See, e.g., Penny Petrone, ed., *First People, First Voices* (Toronto: University of Toronto Press, 1983), p. 94.

71. Petrone, *Native Literature,* pp. 65–66.

72. Kristin Herzog, *Finding Their Voice: Peruvian Women's Testimonies of War* (Valley Forge: Trinity Press International, 1993), p. vi.

73. Carol Hampton, "Tribal Esteem and the American Indian Historian," in Clifford E. Trafzer, ed., *American Indian Identity: Today's Changing Perspectives* (Sacramento: Sierra Oaks Publishing, 1989), p. 86.

74. Petrone, *Native Literature,* p. 183.

75. Peter Jones, *Life and Journals of Kah-ke-wa-quo-na-by (Rev. Peter Jones). Wesleyan Minister* (Toronto: Anson Green, 1860), p. 1.

76. Ibid., pp. 1–2.

77. Ibid., p. 314.

78. Ibid., p. 2. For a discussion of the thunder gods of the Anishinaabe, see Theresa S. Smith, *The Island of the Anishinaabeg: Thunderers and Water Monsters in the Traditional Ojibwe Life-World* (Moscow: University of Idaho Press, 1995), pp. 68–69.

79. Ibid., p. 6.

80. Peter Jones, "Autobiography of Peter Jones" (microfilm, General Commission on Archives and History, The United Methodist Church, Drew University, Madison, N.J., n.d.), p. 7. This manuscript is substantially similar, though not identical, to that published by his wife in the *Life and Journals.*

81. Ibid.

82. Peter Jones, *Life,* pp. 8–9.

83. Peter Jones, "Autobiography," p. 9.

84. Ibid., pp. 9–10.

85. Peter Jones, *Life,* p. 11.

86. Ibid., p. 12.

87. This typically Native stress on family can be seen throughout Jones's life. Late in his career, he would write that he never felt "really happy, but when surrounded by my own precious family." Ibid., p. 411.

88. Peter Jones, *History of the Ojebway Indians: With Especial Reference to Their Conversion to Christianity* (London: A. W. Bennett, 1861), pp. 92–93; Peter Jones, *Life,* p. 3.

89. Jones, *History,* p. 31. He also notes that the Great Spirit "understands all languages." *Life,* p. 15. "Great Spirit" is, of course, itself a Christianized term for the Native high gods, in the case of the Anishinaabe for "Kitchi Manitou."

90. Joseph Epes Brown, *The Spiritual Legacy of the American Indian* (New York: Crossroad, 1989), p. 27.

91. Perhaps thinking of his brother George Henry, he also notes denominational factionalism as an inhibitor to Christianity among Natives. Peter Jones, *Life,* p. 362.

92. Peter Jones, *History,* p. 25.

93. Ibid., pp. 27–28.

94. Peter Jones, *Life,* pp. 7–8.

95. Peter Jones, *History,* p. 29. Emphasis original.

96. Ibid., pp. 29–30.

97. Peter Jones, *Life,* p. 312.

98. Elias Boudinot, *A Star in the West; or, A Humble Attempt to Discover the Long Lost Ten Tribes of Israel, Preparatory to Their Return to Their Beloved City, Jerusalem* (Trenton, N.J.: D. Fenton, S. Hutchinson, and J. Dunham, 1816). The author of this work is not the Native discussed later but the Amer-European head of the American Bible Society whose name he took.

99. Peter Jones, *History,* pp. 36–38.

100. Ibid., pp. 221–222, 189–206.

101. Letter, Peter Jones Collection, Victoria University Library, University of Toronto, quoted in Petrone, *Native Literature*, p. 61.

102. Ibid., quoted at pp. 62–63.

103. Peter Jones, *Life*, p. 407. The journal also records the humorous incident of a discussion with her ministers as to whether Jones should present himself to the queen in Western garb or, as was his preference, in Indian dress, which provided a "perfect covering." In the end, Jones wins and goes before her in traditional costume.

104. See Reginald Horsman, *Expansion and American Indian Policy, 1783–1812* (East Lansing: Michigan State University Press, 1967), p. 113.

105. Anthony F. C. Wallace, *The Long, Bitter Trail: Andrew Jackson and the Indians* (New York: Hill and Wang, 1993), p. 38.

106. During this period, all of the so-called Five Civilized Tribes (Cherokee, Choctaw, Chickasaw, Creek, and Seminole) were removed from their traditional homes in the Southeast to Indian Territory at terrible costs. Recent work by demographer Russell Thornton (Cherokee) suggest that the commonly cited figure of Cherokee population losses at one-fourth (or roughly 4,000 persons) may be remarkably low. He suggests that a figure twice this is not unreasonable. Russell Thornton, "The Demography of the Trail of Tears: A New Estimate of Cherokee Population Losses," in William L. Anderson, ed., *Cherokee Removal: Before and After* (Athens: University of Georgia Press, 1991), p. 93.

107. Cherokee memory preserves a story of a band of Cherokee who crossed the river long ago and were never heard from again, wandering eternally in the western land of the dead.

108. Drinnon, *White Savage*, p. 183; Dianna Everett, *The Texas Cherokees: A People between Two Fires, 1819–1940* (Norman: University of Oklahoma Press, 1990), p. 132; Emmet Starr, *History of the Cherokee Indians* (1921; reprint, Muskogee: Hoffman Printing, 1984), p. 40.

109. Weaver, "Poetry," p. 23; Drinnon, *White Savage*, p. 178. The letters and other documents concerning Fields continue to exist in archives in Texas. His letters and his well-known speech appear in a number of printed sources, sometimes with spelling corrected and sometimes not. For the sake of reading ease, hereafter the corrected texts will be used where available.

110. Starr, *History*, p. 188.

111. Ibid., p. 191. In addition to Starr, Drinnon, and Everett, Mary Whatley Clarke, *Chief Bowles and the Texas Cherokees* (Norman: University of Oklahoma Press, 1971), also contains a retelling of the events of Fields's life and writings.

112. Starr, *History*, p. 191.

113. Everett, *Texas Cherokees*, p. 32.

114. Ibid., p. 36.

115. Ibid., p. 43.

116. Starr, *History*, pp. 192–193.

117. Ibid., p. 40.

118. Ralph Henry Gabriel, *Elias Boudinot, Cherokee, and His America* (Norman: University of Oklahoma Press, 1941; edited and recorded by Willena Robinson, Tulsa: Cherokee Language and Culture Series, 1991).

119. Ibid.

120. Ibid.

121. Elias Boudinot, *An Address to the Whites* (Philadelphia: William F. Geddes, 1826).

122. Ibid. Emphasis original.

123. Ibid. The Creeks, of course, were not dead. Like the Cherokee, they would be removed West to Indian Territory.

124. See Roy Harvey Pearce, *Savagism and Civilization* (Berkeley: University of California Press, 1988; originally published as *The Savages of America* [Baltimore: Johns Hopkins University Press, 1953]).

125. Theda Perdue, ed., *Cherokee Editor: The Writings of Elias Boudinot* (Knoxville: University of Tennessee Press, 1982), p. 3.

126. Ehle, *Trail of Tears,* p. 69.

127. Perdue, *Cherokee Editor,* p. 6.

128. Thurman Wilkins, *Cherokee Tragedy: The Ridge Family and the Decimation of a People,* 2d rev. ed. (Norman: University of Oklahoma Press, 1986), p. 115. For a brief, highly readable account of Boudinot's and Ridge's stay at Cornwall in novelistic form, see Everett O. Campbell, *The Eagle Flies at Dawn: A Saga of the Cherokee People* (New York: Vantage Press, 1989).

129. Though the elder Boudinot pronounced his name in the French with a terminal long "o" sound, the Cherokee became known by a name that ended in the syllable "not," pronouncing the "t." Andrew Wiget contends that Buck Watie received his new name at Springplace, where other students received the names of leading Amer-European religious figures such as Lyman Beecher and James Coe. Andrew Wiget, "Elias Boudinot, Elisha Bates and *Poor Sarah:* Frontier Protestantism and the Emergence of the First Native American Fiction," *Journal of Cherokee Studies* 8, no. 1 (Spring 1983): p. 6.

130. Perdue, *Cherokee Editor,* p. 9.

131. Elias Boudinot, *Poor Sarah, or Religion Exemplified in the Life and Death of an Indian Woman* (Mount Pleasant, Ohio.: Elisha Bates, 1823); Geary Hobson, "From 'Literature of Indian Oklahoma: A Brief History,' " in Joseph Bruchac, ed., *Aniyunwiya/Real Human Beings: An Anthology of Contemporary Cherokee Prose* (Greenfield Center, N.Y.: Greenfield Review Press, 1995), p. 174; Wiget, "Elias Boudinot," p. 12.

132. Hobson, *Remembered Earth,* p. 5; Trafzer, *Earth Song,* p. 4; Wiget, "Elias Boudinot," p. 17. Hobson and Owens also give the date of publication as 1833. In a later essay, Hobson writes, *"Poor Sarah"* has been called by several scholars the first American Indian novel, but due to the work's length (less than twenty pages) and its propagandizing element, it is by all accounts a religious tract set in an extremely artificial fictional mode." "Literature," p. 174.

133. Wiget, "Elias Boudinot," p. 12.

134. Perdue, *Cherokee Editor,* p. 15. Boudinot also translated and published other religious material, including the New Testament and a hymnal (ibid.). With regard to plagiarism, it is useful to note that a number of works attributed to John Wesley were in fact copied and/or condensed from other sources. See, e.g., Albert Outler, ed., *John Wesley* (New York: Oxford University Press, 1964), pp. 121–123.

135. Boudinot, *Poor Sarah;* see, generally, Wiget, "Elias Boudinot," pp. 10–11.

136. Wiget, "Elias Boudinot," p. 9.

137. William McLoughlin, *Cherokee Renascence in the New Republic* (Princeton: Princeton University Press, 1986), p. 371.

138. Gabriel, *Elias Boudinot,* ed. Willena Robinson.

139. Ibid.; McLoughlin, *Cherokee Renascence,* p. 403.

140. Boudinot, "Address."

141. Elias Boudinot, "Prospectus for Publishing at New Echota, in the Cherokee Nation, a Weekly Newspaper to be called the Cherokee *Phoenix*" (October 1827).

142. *Phoenix,* May 29, 1830. Emphasis original.

143. Perdue, *Cherokee Editor,* p. 18. This is not to say that Boudinot's journal was supportive of all Indians. He denounced "attrocities" committed by Plains Indians, whom he described as "American Arabs."

144. After John Marshall's decision in the Cherokee case, President Andrew Jackson reportedly remarked, "The Chief Justice has made the law; now let him try to enforce it." Weaver, *Then to the Rock,* p. 174. See, generally, Bernard W. Sheehan, *Seeds of Extinction: Jeffersonian Philanthropy and the American Indian* (Chapel Hill: University of North Carolina Press, 1973).

145. William McLoughlin, *The Cherokees and Christianity, 1794–1870: Essays on Acculturation and Cultural Persistence,* ed. Walter H. Conser Jr. (Athens: University of Georgia Press, 1994), p. 72; Perdue, *Cherokee Editor,* p. 25.

146. John Ross's writings have been collected in Ross Moulton, ed., *The Papers of Chief John Ross,* 2 vols. (Norman: University of Oklahoma Press, 1985).

147. Wilkins, *Cherokee Tragedy,* p. 289. John Ridge is said to have made a similar statement. He signed the treaty when his father brought it to Washington for ratification. Ehle, *Trail of Tears,* p. 296.

148. Elias Boudinot, *Letters and Other Papers Relating to Cherokee Affairs: Being a Reply to Sundry Publications Authorized by John Ross* (Athens, Ga., 1837). Emphasis original.

149. McLoughlin, *Cherokee Renascence,* p. 450.

150. Boudinot, *Letters.* Emphasis original.

151. Perdue, *Cherokee Editor,* pp. 29–30.

152. Ibid., p. 27.

153. Ibid., p. 31.

154. David Farmer and Rennard Strickland, eds., *A Trumpet of Our Own: Yellow Bird's Essays on the North American Indian* (San Francisco: Book Club of California, 1981), p. 19. A full-length treatment of Ridge's life is provided by James W. Parins, *John Rollin Ridge: His Life and Works* (Lincoln: University of Nebraska Press, 1991).

155. Parins, *John Rollin Ridge,* p. 37. John Rollin Ridge's letters, along with those of other members of his family, have been collected in Edward Everett Dale and Gaston Litton, eds., *Cherokee Cavaliers: Forty Years of Cherokee History as Told in the Correspondence of the Ridge-Watie-Boudinot Family* (Norman: University of Oklahoma Press, 1939).

156. Dale and Litton, *Cherokee Cavaliers,* pp. 38–39.

157. Parins, *John Rollin Ridge,* pp. 50–51.

158. Farmer and Strickland, *Trumpet of Our Own,* p. 48.

159. Ibid., p. 50.

160. Ibid., pp. 52–53.

161. Ibid., p. 28.

162. Dale and Litton, *Cherokee Cavaliers*, pp. 85–87.

163. Farmer and Strickland, *Trumpet of Our Own*, pp. 32, 24, 13.

164. Ibid., p. 33. Ridge wrote, "What hopes have we not all buried, and what dreams have we not all mourned, that come to us again with the soft music of the rhythmic rain? Have we trusted and been deceived? Have we lost what we loved? Have we seen joy after joy fade in the sky of our fate! All comes to us again in sad and mournful memory as we listen to the patter of the rain."

165. Owens, *Other Destinies*, p. 32; Ruoff, *American Indian Literatures*, p. 76; John Rollin Ridge, [Yellow Bird], *The Life and Adventures of Joaquín Murieta, the Celebrated California Bandit* (1854; reprint, Norman: University of Oklahoma Press, 1977), p. 87; quoted in, e.g., Ruoff, *American Indian Literatures*, p. 65; Ruoff, *Literatures of the American Indian*, p. 76.

166. Emphasis original.

167. Owens, *Other Destinies*, p. 33.

168. Farmer and Strickland, *Trumpet of Our Own*, pp. 23–24.

169. McLoughlin, *After the Trail of Tears*, p. 50.

170. Parins, *John Rollin Ridge*, p. 111.

171. Franklin Walker, *San Francisco's Literary Frontier* (Seattle: University of Washington Press, 1969), p. 53.

172. Owens, *Other Destinies*, p. 39.

173. Farmer and Strickland, *Trumpet of Our Own*, pp. 55–65.

174. Ibid., pp. 67–69.

175. Ibid., pp. 100–102.

176. Ibid., pp. 102–103.

177. William G. McLoughlin, *Champions of the Cherokees: Evan and John B. Jones* (Princeton: Princeton University Press, 1990), pp. 364–365; McLoughlin, *After the Trail of Tears*, p. 155; Parins, *John Rollin Ridge*, pp. 180–183. Ridge's cousin Stand Watie served as a Confederate general.

178. John Rollin Ridge, *Poems* (San Francisco: Payot, 1868), p. 50.

179. Dale and Litton, *Cherokee Cavaliers*, p. 87.

180. Warrior, *Tribal Secrets*, p. 44.

181. Farmer and Strickland, *Trumpet of Our Own*, p. 33.

182. Ibid.

183. Allen, *Voice*, p. 8.

184. Warrior, *Tribal Secrets*, p. 4. For examples of Native literary production during this supposedly interstitial period, see Daniel F. Littlefield Jr. and James W. Parins, eds., *Native American Writing in the Southeast: An Anthology, 1875–1935* (Jackson: University Press of Mississippi, 1995).

185. A. LaVonne Brown Ruoff, "Literature," in Davis, *Native America*, p. 317.

186. A. LaVonne Brown Ruoff, "Justice for Indians and Women: The Protest Fiction of Alice Callahan and Pauline Johnson," *World Literature Today* 66, no. 2 (Spring 1992): pp. 249–255.

187. Francis, *Imaginary Indian*, p. 113. Petrone takes the rhetoric of novelty to new heights when she proclaims Johnson "the first Canadian woman, the first Canadian

Indian, and the first Canadian writer to be honoured by a commemorative Canadian stamp in 1961 on the 100th anniversary of her birth." *Native Literature,* p. 78.

188. For full treatments of Pauline Johnson's life, see Anne Foster, *The Mohawk Princess: Being Some Account of the Life of Tek-hion-wake (E. Pauline Johnson)* (Vancouver: Lion's Gate, 1931); Betty Keller, *Pauline: A Biography of Pauline Johnson* (Vancouver: Douglas, 1981). Arguably, Johnson might be excluded from any work that deals only with *American* Indians. She, however, had familial ties in the United States and performed there. She was also published in the United States and became an important American literary figure. Ruoff includes her in her bibliographic work on American Indian literatures.

189. For a recent history of Louis Riel's rebellions, see Maggie Siggins, *Riel: A Life of Revolution* (Toronto: HarperCollins, 1994).

190. Petrone, *Native Literature,* p. 84.

191. Francis, *Imaginary Indian,* pp. 111–123.

192. Goldie, *Fear and Temptation,* pp. 61–62.

193. Brant, *Writing as Witness,* p. 7.

194. Ibid., p. 6.

195. Keller, *Pauline,* p. 272, 267.

196. Francis, *Imaginary Indian,* p. 115.

197. E. Pauline Johnson, *The Moccasin Maker* (Toronto: Ryerson, 1913), p. 139.

198. Francis, *Imaginary Indian,* p. 120.

199. Petrone, *Native Literature,* p. 82.

200. Francis, *Imaginary Indian,* pp. 118–119.

201. Brant, *Writing as Witness,* p. 14.

202. Keller, *Pauline,* pp. 234–235.

203. Francis, *Imaginary Indian,* p. 119.

204. Petrone, *Native Literature,* p. 84.

205. E. Pauline Johnson, *The Shaganappi* (Toronto: William Briggs, 1913), p. 5.

206. Francis, *Imaginary Indian,* p. 119.

207. Brant, *Writing as Witness,* p. 7.

208. E. Pauline Johnson, *Flint and Feather* (Toronto: Musson, 1912). Emphasis original.

209. Paula Gunn Allen gives the date of this story as 1906. *Voice,* p. 20. In fact, however, it won a prize in *Dominion Illustrated's* short story contest in 1892 and was published there in February 1893.

210. Emphasis original.

211. Petrone, *Native Literature,* p. 84.

212. Francis, *Imaginary Indian,* p. 122.

213. Brant, *Writing as Witness,* p. 6.

214. Keller, *Pauline,* p. 234. Emphasis mine.

Chapter Three

1. On that date "Shoshone Mike" and his band, which had been pursued over a 200-mile trail for murders that were never proven, were attacked and killed. Steven J. Crum,

Po'i Pentun Tammen Kimmappeh—The Road on Which We Came: A History of the West-ern Shoshone (Salt Lake City: University of Utah Press, 1994), p. 70. For a fictional account of the incident by a non-Native, see Frank Bergon, *Shoshone Mike* (New York: Viking Penguin, 1987).

2. Theodora Kroeber, *Ishi in Two Worlds: A Biography of the Last Wild Indian in North America* (Berkeley: University of California Press, 1961), pp. 3, 9.

3. John Collier, *The Indians of the Americas* (New York: W. W. Norton, 1947), pp. 233–234. According to comparative religionist W. Y. Evans-Wentz, "Unconstitution-ally, religious freedom was thus prohibited to [Natives] in the United States. . . . Prot-estant Christianity made it a fixed policy to destroy the native American culture. Stu-dents in its mission schools were forbidden to attend Navaho religious ceremonials and even to converse in Navaho [for example]. In addition, they were subject to uncalled-for brutality if they failed to be amenable to Christianization." W. Y. Evans-Wentz, *Cuchama and Sacred Mountains,* ed. Frank Waters and Charles L. Adams (Athens: Swal-low Press/Ohio University Press, 1981), p. 94. Though the code remained in effect until 1933 and did tremendous damage, it proved impossible, finally, to destroy Native reli-gious traditions. The gods of Native North America never left themselves without wit-nesses.

4. James S. Olson and Raymond Wilson, *Native Americans in the Twentieth Century* (Urbana: University of Illinois Press, 1986), p. 51; Warrior, *Tribal Secrets,* pp. 5–6. Bon-nin and Eastman were both noted Native writers in the first decades of the century. Space prevents full treatment in this current volume of these complex figures. Bonnin wrote fiction and recorded Native stories (writing under the name Zitkala-Ša). Eastman strongly defended Natives and yet also advocated assimilation. Among his oddest writing is a volume produced for the scouting movement, which, in addition to other things, tells romanticizing youths how to select an "Indian" name. Zitkala-Ša [Gertrude Bon-nin], *American Indian Stories* (Washington, D.C.: Hayworth Publishing House, 1921); Zitkala-Ša [Gertrude Bonnin], *Old Indian Legends* (Boston: Ginn, 1901); Charles A. Eastman, *Indian Scout Talks: A Guide for Boy Scouts and Camp Fire Girls* (Boston: Little, Brown, 1914).

5. Francis Paul Prucha, ed., *Americanizing the American Indians* (Cambridge: Harvard University Press, 1973), pp. 82, 89.

6. See Weaver, *Then to the Rock,* p. 17. Curtis, a Kaw, later served as vice president of the United States under Calvin Coolidge.

7. See, generally, Frederick E. Hoxie, *A Final Promise: The Campaign to Assimilate the Indians, 1880–1920* (Lincoln: University of Nebraska Press, 1984).

8. See, e.g., Schwarz, *Tales from the Smokehouse.*

9. Owens, *Other Destinies,* pp. 5–6; Columpa Bobb, "The Native Experience," *Gather-ings* 2 (1991): p. 45; Gerald R. McMaster, "Border Zones: The 'Injun-uity' of Aesthetic Tricks," *Cultural Studies* 9 (January 1995): p. 85.

10. The homespun, commonsensical populism of Rogers may seem remote from a Native worldview, but it nevertheless has clear roots there. Rogers's father was prominent in the political affairs of Indian Territory, and Rogers never thought of himself as any-thing other than that oxymoron to Amer-European ears, an "Indian cowboy," a "half-breed" Cherokee ropesmith. He delighted in tracing his lineage, stating, "My ancestors

didn't come over on the *Mayflower*, but they met the boat." See Will Rogers, *There's Not a Bathing Suit in Russia* (New York: Albert & Charles Boni, 1927); Weaver, "Ethnic Cleansing," pp. 36–37; Jim Rogers, "Introduction," in Joseph H. Carter, *Never Met a Man I Didn't Like: The Life and Writings of Will Rogers* (New York: Avon Books, 1991), pp. viii–ix; Carter, *Never Met a Man*, p. 5; James M. Smallwood, ed., *Will Rogers' Weekly Articles* (Stillwater: Oklahoma State University Press, 1980); Richard M. Ketcham, *Will Rogers: The Man and Times* (New York: McGraw-Hill, 1973).

11. Vizenor, *Manifest Manners*, p. 68.

12. Ibid., p. 83.

13. "Spectrum," pp. 19–20; Louis Littlecoon Oliver, *Chasers of the Sun: Creek Indian Thoughts* (Greenfield Center, N.Y.: Greenfield Review Press, 1990), pp. 88–91.

14. Ruoff, *American Indian Literatures*, p. 67.

15. Alexander Posey, *The Fus Fixico Letters*, ed. Daniel F. Littlefield Jr. and Carol A. Petty Hunter (Lincoln: University of Nebraska Press, 1993), pp. 23–24.

16. Ibid., p. 1. Littlefield, however, yields to the temptations of the rhetoric of novelty when he declares that Posey's writings "represent the first major excursion into literary humor by an Indian" (p. 9).

17. The best source of information about Posey's life and career is Daniel F. Littlefield Jr., *Alex Posey: Creek Poet, Journalist, and Humorist* (Lincoln: University of Nebraska Press, 1992).

18. Joseph B. Thoburn and Muriel H. Wright, *Oklahoma: A History of the State and Its People*, 4 vols. (New York: Lewis Historical Publishing, 1929), vol. 2, pp. 628–629. Wright was the granddaughter of Allen Wright, Choctaw chief and a graduate of Union Theological Seminary, who first suggested the name "Oklahoma." In 1855 the older Wright became the first Native to receive a master's degree in the United States.

19. Ibid., vol. 2, p. 629. Affirming the statement, and engaging in the sort of hyperbole that is the building block of legend, Louis Littlecoon Oliver writes, "As he walked his Taledega, his favorite wooded area, the flowers bowed in obesance, hawks and eagles swooped down to greet him, the meadowlark sang its best aria and the deer were not afraid of him. He understood the language of the babbling brook, the bees brought ambrosia to his lips and his pen recorded the joys of them. Oh my soul—I would that I could walk in his moccasins—just for one day." *Chasers of the Sun*, p. 88.

20. Littlefield, *Alex Posey*, p. 252.

21. Alexander Posey, quoted in Oliver, *Chasers of the Sun*, p. 89.

22. Littlefield, *Ales Posey*, p. 137.

23. Posey, *Fus Fixico Letters*, p. 36.

24. Ibid., p. 29.

25. Ibid., p. 39.

26. Ibid., p. 48.

27. See ibid.

28. Alexander Posey, quoted in Thoburn and Wright, *Oklahoma*, vol. 2, p. 618.

29. Posey, *Fus Fixico Letters*, p. 76.

30. Ibid., p. 117.

31. Ibid., p. 248. The phrase "century o' dishonor" alludes to an exposé published in 1881 that gave impetus to the reform movement that led to the Dawes Act. See Helen

Hunt Jackson, *A Century of Dishonor: A Sketch of the United States Government's Dealings with Some of the Indian Tribes* (New York: Harper & Brothers, 1881).

32. Posey, *Fus Fixico Letters*, p. 81. The Indian in question could write but had to let his horse forage all winter because the owner didn't know how to raise food for it.

33. Ibid., p. 87. With regard to changed names in boarding schools, Joseph Dudley notes that his grandfather entered school as David Iron Eye and emerged as David Dudley. Joseph Iron Eye Dudley, *Choteau Creek* (Lincoln: University of Nebraska Press, 1992), p. 73; interview with author, June 10, 1994. The name "David Iron Eye" was, of course, already a sign of forced assimilation, as the once descriptive name of an ancestor, Iron Eye, became a familial surname to which Amer-European names were appended.

34. Posey, *Fus Fixico Letters*, p. 21.

35. Ibid., p. 66.

36. Ibid., p. 70.

37. Ibid., p. 235.

38. Ibid., p. 214.

39. Ibid., pp. 217–218.

40. Ibid., p. 227.

41. Ibid.

42. Thoburn and Wright, *Oklahoma*, vol. 2, p. 629.

43. Ibid.

44. Posey, *Fus Fixico Letters*, 217; Littlefield, *Alex Posey*, pp. 213–215.

45. Thoburn and Wright, *Oklahoma*, vol. 2, p. 768.

46. Littlefield, *Alex Posey*, p. 259.

47. Oliver, *Chasers of the Sun*, p. 91. *Tos'ke* means "speckled sapsucker"; *Em pona'ya*, "one who speaks for another"; *Wotko okisce!*, "I of the Raccoon clan have spoken."

48. See, e.g., Posey, *Fus Fixico Letters*, p. 119.

49. The best biography of Riggs is Phyllis Cole Braunlich, *Haunted by Home: The Life and Letters of Lynn Riggs* (Norman: University of Oklahoma Press, 1988). An older but still useful treatment can be found in Thomas Erhard, *Lynn Riggs, Southwest Playwright* (Austin: Steck-Vaughn, 1970). Erhard also provides a helpful, brief sketch of Riggs's life in Andrew Wiget, ed., *Handbook of Native American Literature* (New York: Garland Publishing, 1996), pp. 289–293. Shortly after Riggs's death, Charles Aughtry completed a doctoral essay on the playwright. Charles E. Aughtry, "Lynn Riggs, Dramatist: A Critical Biography" (Ph.D. diss., Brown University, 1959).

50. Braunlich, *Haunted by Home*, pp. 22–23.

51. Thoburn and Wright, *Oklahoma*, vol. 3, p. 207.

52. Braunlich, *Haunted by Home*, p. 24.

53. See Lynn Riggs, *Roadside* (New York: Samuel French, 1930).

54. Braunlich, *Haunted by Home*, pp. 35–42.

55. Ibid., p. 16. Braunlich notes that the Syrian peddler was a familiar figure in Indian Territory when Riggs was growing up. The character would return in Riggs's *Green Grow the Lilacs*.

56. Ibid., pp. 8–9.

57. Ibid., p. 10.

58. Ibid. Emphasis original.

59. See Ruoff, *American Indian Literatures*, p. 74.

60. Lynn Riggs, *The Iron Dish* (Garden City, N.Y.: Doubleday, Doran, 1930), p. 18.

61. Ibid., p. 19.

62. Ibid., p. 10.

63. Lynn Riggs, *Big Lake* (New York: Samuel French, 1925); Ruoff, *American Indian Literatures*, p. 74; Thoburn and Wright, *Oklahoma*, vol. 3, p. 207; Braunlich, *Haunted by Home*, p. 46.

64. See, e.g., Lynn Riggs, *"Sump'n Like Wings" and "A Lantern to See By"* (New York: Samuel French, 1928); Lynn Riggs, *Toward the Western Sky* (Cleveland: Press of Western Reserve University, 1951).

65. See, e.g., Ruoff, *American Indian Literatures*, p. 75; Braunlich, *Haunted by Home*, p. xii.

66. Braunlich, *Haunted by Home*, p. 157.

67. Ibid., pp. xii, 23.

68. Ibid., p. xii.

69. Ibid., p. 140.

70. It is a mark of patriarchy that miscegenation fears run only to White women. It is perfect acceptable, and indeed historically common, for White men to have sex with and/or marry Indian women. Weaver, "Ethnic Cleansing," p. 30; see also Andy Smith, "Christian Conquest and the Sexual Colonization of Native Women," in Carol J. Adams and Marie M. Fortune, eds., *Violence against Women and Children: A Christian Theological Sourcebook* (New York: Continuum, 1995), pp. 377–403.

71. Braunlich, *Haunted by Home*, pp. 127, 207.

72. McNickle, *Indian Man*, pp. 56–57.

73. Ibid., p. 96.

74. Hobson, *Remembered Earth*, p. 7. Robert Benchley, in reviewing *Oklahoma!*, noted, "After rereading Mr. Riggs's drama . . . I can't see that the version . . . has omitted anything of consequence." Braunlich, *Haunted by Home*, p. 183.

75. Emphasis original.

76. Though Riggs publically stated that he was pleased with *Oklahoma!*, in private he expressed his displeasure to friends. Braunlich, *Haunted by Home*, p. 182. With regard to the question of "race mixing," it is interesting to note that Hammerstein had dealt with the issue before. In the 1920s he wrote *Show Boat* with Jerome Kern. The musical treats miscegenation in one of its subplots. Perhaps it was this very aspect that attracted Hammerstein to the Riggs text.

77. For an earlier discussion of *Green Grow the Lilacs* and its possible Native themes, see Weaver "Ethnic Cleansing," pp. 32–33.

78. He also stated that, in writing, he liked to let his characters take control and that a playwright should not interfere. He writes, "And sometime, his characters may do stirring things he could never have calculated. And sometime, if he is fortunate, he may hear from the people he has set in motion (as Shakespeare and Chekhov often heard) things to astonish him and things to make him wise."

79. Braunlich, *Haunted by Home*, pp. 77, 80.

80. Ibid., p. 95.

81. Copy of *"Russet Mantle" and "The Cherokee Night,"* Butler Library, Columbia University, New York, N.Y.

82. Emphasis original.

83. Emphasis original.

84. Emphasis original.

85. Emphasis original.

86. Berkhofer, *White Man's Indian,* pp. 26–28. See also Weaver, "Ethnic Cleansing," pp. 27, 30.

87. Though it does not resolve many lingering questions, the best source of information about her life is her own autobiographical material, edited with an informative introduction by Jay Miller, formerly of the D'Arcy McNickle Center for the History of the American Indian at the Newberry Library in Chicago. Mourning Dove, *Mourning Dove: A Salishan Autobiography,* ed. Jay Miller (Lincoln: University of Nebraska Press, 1990).

88. Ibid., pp. xvii, xx; Allen, *Voice,* p. 10.

89. Mourning Dove, *Mourning Dove,* p. xvi.

90. Owens, *Other Destinies,* p. 42.

91. Mourning Dove, *Mourning Dove,* p. xi.

92. Trafzer, *Earth Song,* p. 6.

93. Mourning Dove, *Mourning Dove,* p. xxi.

94. Ibid., p. xiii; Mourning Dove, *Cogewea,* p. 12.

95. Mourning Dove, *Cogewea,* p. vii.

96. Mourning Dove, *Mourning Dove,* p. xxv.

97. Mourning Dove, *Cogewea,* p. viii.

98. Mourning Dove, *Coyote Stories* (Caldwell, Idaho: Caxton Printers, 1933).

99. See Allen, *Voice,* p. 11.

100. Mourning Dove, *Mourning Dove,* pp. xi, xxv–xxvi.

101. Ibid., xvii. Cogewea reads the same book and is equally enraged, stating that it "was not suited to her ideals" and calling it "bosh."

102. Ibid., p. xii.

103. Owens, *Other Destinies,* p. 44.

104. Allen, *Voice,* p. 11.

105. Trafzer, *Earth Song,* p. 6.

106. Owens, *Other Destinies,* p. 44.

107. I.e., half. Emphasis original.

108. Emphasis original.

109. Emphasis original.

110. Mourning Dove, *Mourning Dove,* p. xxvi.

111. King, *All My Relations,* p. xi; James Welch, *Fools Crow* (New York: Viking, 1986); Joseph Marshall III, *Winter of the Holy Iron* (Santa Fe: Red Crane Books, 1994).

112. Raymond J. DeMallie, "Afterword," in Ella Cara Deloria, *Waterlily* (Lincoln: University of Nebraska Press, 1988), p. 239.

113. Agnes Picotte, "Biographical Sketch of the Author," in Ella Cara Deloria, *Waterlily,* p. 230.

114. Ruoff, *American Indian Literatures,* p. 121.

115. Deloria did publish one volume of orature, containing sixty-four stories, prior to her death. Ella Cara Deloria, *Dakota Texts* (1932; reprint, New York: AMS Press, 1974).

116. Julian Rice, ed., *Ella Deloria's Iron Hawk* (Albuquerque: University of New Mexico Press, 1993), p. 14.

117. Ibid.

118. Ella Cara Deloria, *Dakota Grammar* (1941; reprint, Vermillion, S.D.: Dakota Press, 1982).

119. Rice, *Ella Deloria's Iron Hawk*, p. 14.

120. DeMallie, "Afterword," pp. 237–238. Emphasis original.

121. Rice, *Ella Deloria's Iron Hawk*, p. 17. Emphasis mine.

122. DeMallie, "Afterword," p. 242.

123. Ella Cara Deloria, *Speaking of Indians* (New York: Friendship Press, 1944), p. 21.

124. Ibid., pp. 18, 129.

125. Ibid., pp. 8, 77–79.

126. Ibid., pp. 77, 148, 160–161.

127. Ibid., pp. 50, 83, 20, 98ff., 158–159.

128. Ibid., p. 152. Emphasis original.

129. Russell Means, "Foreword," in Weaver, *Defending Mother Earth*, p. xii; see, generally, Russell Means, *Where White Men Fear to Tread: The Autobiography of Russell Means* (New York: St. Martin's Press, 1995).

130. Vine Deloria Jr., "Out of Chaos," *Parabola* 10, no. 2 (May 1985): p. 20.

131. Ella Cara Deloria, *Speaking of Indians*, p. 148.

132. Ibid., p. 162.

133. Ibid., p. 149.

134. Ibid., pp. 24–25.

135. Ibid., pp. 31–32, 41.

136. Ibid., p. 25.

137. Ibid., p. 28–29. In her novel *Waterlily*, Deloria also depicts the transcendent god as the god who draws near. When Waterlily's mother, Blue Bird, finishes praying to Wakan Tanka for the life of her struggling infant, she hears an audible "Hao!," the Dakota word for assent or approval, in her ear. The baby lives.

138. Though written around 1942, the novel remained unpublished until 1988. In the editing process, certain changes, not always felicitous, were made. For instance, while "sinful" has been changed to "evil" and "superstition" to "common belief," "routine" has been revised as "ritual actions." "Publisher's Preface," in Ella Cara Deloria, *Waterlily*, p. xi.

139. For example, a murder after which the murderer assumed the kinship obligations of the deceased is reported as having been told to her by Simon Antelope (Yankton). Ella Cara Deloria, *Speaking of Indians*, pp. 34–36.

140. The horse reached the Teton Dakota in the early 18th century. By 1800, they were thoroughgoing horse people. In the main, except for traders, the Teton remained undisturbed by Amer-Europeans until around 1849. See Clark Wissler, *Indians of the United States*, rev. ed. (Garden City, N.Y.: Doubleday, 1966), p. 190; see, generally, Robert Moorman Denhardt, *The Horse of the Americas* (Norman: University of Oklahoma Press, 1947).

141. See Donald Fixico, *Termination and Relocation: Federal Indian Policy, 1945–1960* (Albuquerque: University of New Mexico Press, 1986); D'Arcy McNickle, *Runner in the*

Sun: A Story of Maize (New York: Holt, Rinehart and Winston, 1954); Natachee Scott Momaday, *Owl in the Cedar Tree* (Boston: Ginn, 1965).

142. Though sketchy, impressionistic, and highly personal, the best source about the life of Natachee Momaday remains N. Scott Momaday, *The Names* (p. 19).

143. Ibid., p. 22.

144. Ibid., p. 38.

145. Ibid., pp. 38–39.

146. Ibid., p. 70.

147. Ibid., p. 152.

148. Jace Weaver, "Natives and Community: Native American Literature as a Resource for Doing Theology" (lecture delivered at Union Theological Seminary, New York, September 1995).

149. The character of Haske is a composite of family friends, especially Haske Norwood and Quincy Tahoma (Navajo) and Natachee's son Scott.

150. Commonly called a "vision quest," the phenomenon is found in many Native religious traditions. The term "vision quest" is, however, a generic phenomenological description. See McPherson and Rabb, *Indian from the Inside*, pp. 59–82.

151. Emphasis mine.

Chapter Four

1. Allen, *Voice*, p. 5.

2. Ibid.

3. Terry P. Wilson, "Alcatraz Occupation," in Davis, *Native America*, p. 21.

4. For an excellent retelling of the militant events of the 1960s and 1970s, see Paul Chaat Smith and Robert Allen Warrior, *Like a Hurricane* (New York: New Press, 1996).

5. See Jack D. Forbes, *Native Americans and Nixon: Presidential Politics and Minority Self-Determination, 1969–1972* (Los Angeles: American Indian Studies Center, University of California, Los Angeles, 1981).

6. Warrior, *Tribal Secrets*, p. xiv.

7. Vine Deloria Jr., *Custer Died for Your Sins*, 2d ed. (Norman: University of Oklahoma Press, 1988), p. x.

8. A concomitant awakening was occurring in Canada during this period. Harold Cardinal's *The Unjust Society* and, later, *The Rebirth of Canada's Indians* were that country's equivalent of *Custer Died for Your Sins*. See Harold Cardinal, *The Unjust Society* (Edmonton, Alb.: Hurtig, 1969); and *The Rebirth of Canada's Indians* (Edmonton, Alb.: Hurtig, 1977); James Burke, *Paper Tomahawks: From Red Tape to Red Power* (Winnipeg: Queenston House, 1976).

9. For more on Momaday and his works, see Matthias Schubnell, *N. Scott Momaday: The Cultural and Literary Background* (Norman: University of Oklahoma Press, 1985); Charles L. Woodard, *Ancestral Voices: Conversations with N. Scott Momaday* (Lincoln: University of Nebraska Press, 1989).

10. Owens, *Other Destinies*, p. 25.

11. Vizenor, *Manifest Manners*, p. 78.

12. Allen, *Voice,* p. 17.

13. Warrior, *Tribal Secrets,* p. 93.

14. Allen, *Voice,* p. 8.

15. Tinker, *Missionary Conquest,* p. 3.

16. Despite the voluminous nature of his work (over a dozen books and innumerable short pieces) and his importance in Native American studies, Deloria has generated remarkably little in the way of secondary literature about himself. This may be a mark of his contemporary nature; he is, after all, still very much active. Alternatively, it may reflect the position of power and respect that he has held for many years in the Indian community. He is without question the most quoted Native author by both Indians and Amer-Europeans, but very little has been written *about* him. The only significant serious treatment of his thought is Robert Warrior's *Tribal Secrets.*

17. Vine Deloria Jr., *Custer Died,* p. 122.

18. Vinc Deloria Sr., "The Establishment of Christianity among the Sioux," in Raymond J. DeMallie and Douglas R. Parks, eds., *Sioux Indian Religion* (Norman: University of Oklahoma Press, 1987), p. 111. He wrote, "We Christians need to shape up and think about where we're going if we want Indian people to remain in the church." As will be seen, this echoes the words of his son in *Custer Died for Your Sins.* It must remain a point of conjecture as to whether father influenced son or vice versa.

19. Warrior, *Tribal Secrets,* p. 32.

20. Ibid., pp. 33–34.

21. Alvin M. Josephy Jr., *Red Power: The American Indian's Fight for Freedom* (New York: McGraw-Hill, 1971), p. 235. Josephy denies his own evidence that the tremendous diversity of Indian peoples makes it *impossible* that any one Indian could speak for *all* Indians. See also, generally, Jay David, ed., *The American Indian: The First Victim* (New York: William Morrow, 1972).

22. Vine Deloria Jr., "This Country Was a Lot Better Off When the Indians Were Running It," *New York Times Magazine,* March 8, 1970, quoted in Josephy, *Red Power,* pp. 235–247.

23. Ella Cara Deloria, *Speaking of Indians,* pp. 1–2.

24. Noley, *First White Frost,* pp. 17–18. For an alternative theory, see Jeffrey Goodman, *American Genesis* (New York: Summit Books, 1981).

25. Vine Deloria Jr., *The Metaphysics of Modern Existence* (San Francisco: Harper & Row, 1979), p. 214.

26. Vine Deloria Jr., *Red Earth,* pp. 61–107.

27. Vine Deloria Jr., *Metaphysics,* pp. 46ff., 214–215.

28. Vine Deloria Jr., *Red Earth,* p. 231.

29. Vine Deloria Jr., *God Is Red,* 2d ed., pp. 150–151.

30. Ibid., pp. 158–159.

31. Ibid., pp. 158–163.

32. Ibid., pp. 150, 158.

33. Vine Deloria Jr., *Metaphysics,* p. 152.

34. Vine Deloria Jr., "Sacred Lands," pp. 75–76.

35. Vine Deloria Jr., "Circling the Same Old Rock," in Ward Churchill, ed., *Marxism and Native Americans* (Boston: South End Press, 1984), p. 136.

36. Vine Deloria Jr., *We Talk*, pp. 117–118.

37. Besides those already cited, Deloria's principal texts dealing with the sovereignty question are Vine Deloria Jr. and Clifford Lytle, *The Nations Within* (New York: Random House, 1984); Vine Deloria Jr. and Clifford Lytle, *American Indians, American Justice* (Austin: University of Texas Press, 1983); Vine Deloria Jr., *Behind the Trail of Broken Treaties: An Indian Declaration of Independence* (New York: Delacorte, 1974); Vine Deloria Jr., ed., *American Indian Policy in the Twentieth Century* (Norman: University of Oklahoma Press, 1985). These works remain enormously influential. In 1992, Augie Fleras and and John Leonard Elliott took *The Nations Within* and its discussion of sovereignty as a starting point of their own study, *The Nations Within: Aboriginal-State Relations in Canada, the United States, and New Zealand* (Toronto: Oxford University Press, 1992). See also John R. Wunder, *"Retained by the People": A History of American Indians and the Bill of Rights* (New York: Oxford University Press, 1994).

38. Deloria returns to conceptualizations of deity in *The Metaphysics of Modern Existence*, in which he identifies the most common feature of tribal belief as "the feeling or belief that the universe is energized by a pervading power" (p. 152).

39. Deloria, *God Is Red*, 2d ed., pp. 267–282.

40. Warrior, *Tribal Secrets*, p. 71.

41. Vine Deloria Jr., "Circling," pp. 113–114.

42. Vine Deloria Jr., *God Is Red*, p. 89.

43. Warrior, *Tribal Secrets*, pp. 70–71.

44. Vine Deloria Jr., "A Native Perspective on Liberation," *Mission Trends No. 4* (offprint), p. 262.

45. Vine Deloria Jr., *God Is Red*, pp. 57–74.

46. Vine Deloria Jr., "Native American Perspective," pp. 263–270.

47. Vine Deloria Jr., *Custer Died*, p. 124; Warrior, "Interview," p. 26.

48. Vine Deloria Jr., *Custer Died*, pp. 112, 123–124; Starkloff, "American Indian Religion," p. 124.

49. Vine Deloria Jr., "Religion and Revolution among American Indians," *Worldview*, 17, no. 1 (January 1974): p. 14.

50. Warrior, *Tribal Secrets*, pp. 105–106.

51. Ibid., p. 98.

52. Vine Deloria Jr., *We Talk*, p. 123.

53. Warrior, *Tribal Secrets*, p. 91.

54. Ibid., p. 95.

55. Ibid., p. 97.

56. Fisher, *Third Woman*, p. 19.

57. Kenneth Rosen, ed., *The Man to Send Rain Clouds* (New York: Random House, 1975), p. 176.

58. Murray, *Forked Tongues*, p. 80.

59. Arnold Krupat may be correct when he writes in 1989, "Momaday is not only the best known and celebrated contemporary Native American writer, recipient of a Pulitzer Prize for fiction (1969), but for Silko's work to date, the presumptive groundbreaker or forefather." He goes too far, however, when he declares, "Her *Ceremony* (1977), it is said (with some justice), is heavily dependent upon his *House Made of Dawn* (1968);

her *Storyteller* (1981) perhaps no more than a rerun of his *The Names* (1976)." *Voice,* p. 177.

60. Joseph Bruchac, ed., *The Next World: Poems by Third World Americans* (Trumansburg, N.Y.: Crossing Press, 1978), p. 1730, quoted in Owens, *Other Destinies,* p. 167.

61. Laura Coltelli, *Winged Words: American Indian Writers Speak* (Lincoln: University of Nebraska Press, 1990), *Man to Send Rain Clouds,* pp. 135; Rosen, p. 3–8.

62. Leslie Marmon Silko, *Laguna Woman* (Greenfield Center, N.Y.: Greenfield Review, 1974).

63. Coltelli, *Winged Words,* p. 147.

64. Ibid., pp. 147–148.

65. Ibid., p. 147.

66. Leslie Marmon Silko, *Ceremony* (New York: Viking, 1977). Non-Native writer Barry Lopez captures some of this flavor in his children's book *Crow and Weasel,* written in a supposed Native idiom. In it, Badger tells the protagonists, "The stories people tell have a way of taking care of them. If stories come to you, care for them. And learn to give them away where they are needed. Sometimes a person needs a story more than food to stay alive. That is why we put these stories in each other's memory. This is how people care for themselves. One day you will be good storytellers. Never forget these obligations." Barry Lopez, *Crow and Weasel* (San Francisco: North Point Press, 1990), p. 48. Similarly, Lester Standiford writes, "Properly cared for, preserved intact, a story has the power to sustain an entire culture." "Worlds," p. 341.

67. Richard Sax, "Laguna Values in Anglo Classrooms: The Delicacy and Strength of the Writings of Leslie Silko," in Thomas E. Shirer and Susan M. Branster, eds., *Native American Values: Survival and Renewal* (Sault Ste. Marie, Mich: Lake Superior State University Press, 1993), p. 139. The story is, as Lincoln observes, itself a ceremony, in which the reader becomes a participant through the reading, reenacting it anew each time.

68. Murray, *Forked Tongues,* p. 87.

69. See Coltelli, *Winged Words,* pp. 143, 149.

70. Silko, *Storyteller,* p. 227.

71. Leslie Marmon Silko, *Almanac of the Dead* (New York: Simon & Schuster, 1991).

72. Thomas King, interview with author, January 27, 1992.

73. I am indebted in many of these remarks to the insights of one of my students, Lucy Jones, who prior to returning for graduate education had a background in botanical work. Lucy Jones, "The Land and the Spirit" (unpublished paper, Union Theological Seminary, January 22, 1996). See also Richard F. Fleck, "Sacred Land in the Writings of Momaday, Welch, and Silko," in Thomas E. Shirer, ed., *Entering the 90s: The North American Experience* (Sault Ste. Marie, Mich.: Lake Superior State University Press, 1991), pp. 125–133.

74. Lucy Jones, "The Land," p. 8; Leslie Marmon Silko, "Landscape, History and the Pueblo Imagination," in John Elder and Hertha D. Wong, eds., *Family of Earth and Sky* (Boston: Beacon Press, 1994), p. 249.

75. Lucy Jones, "The Land," p. 19; Silko, "Landscape," pp. 247–249.

76. Herb Barrett, "The 'Storyteller' of Leslie Marmon Silko: A Commentary" (unpublished paper, Yale University, December 18, 1996), pp. 17–18; Leslie Marmon Silko, *Yel-*

low Woman and a Beauty of the Spirit (New York: Simon & Schuster, 1996); "*Yellow Woman and a Beauty of the Spirit,*" *Publishers Weekly,* January 22, 1996, p. 54.

77. Coltelli, *Winged Words,* p. 135.

78. See Peter H. Eichstaedt, *If You Poison Us: Uranium and Native Americans* (Santa Fe: Red Crane Books, 1994).

79. Leslie Marmon Silko, *Sacred Water* (Tucson: Flood Plain Press, 1993), pp. 72–76.

80. Coltelli, *Winged Words,* p. 152.

81. Gerald Vizenor, *Shadow Distance: A Gerald Vizenor Reader* (Hanover, N.H.: Wesleyan University Press, 1994), p. xi.

82. Ibid.; Edwin L. Wade and Rennard Strickland, *Magic Images* (Norman: University of Oklahoma Press, 1981), p. 96.

83. Owens, *Other Destinies,* p. 15. Louis Owens offers an excellent reading of Vizenor and his work in *Other Destinies,* pp. 225–254. Jonathan Boyarin provides a similarly sophisticated analysis in "Europe's Indian, America's Jew: Modiano and Vizenor," in his *Storm from Paradise: The Politics of Jewish Memory* (Minneapolis: University of Minnesota Press, 1992), reprinted in Karl Kroeber, ed., *American Indian Persistence and Resurgence* (Durham, N.C.: Duke University Press, 1994), pp. 198–223. Kimberly Blaeser (Anishinaabe) has written a study of her fellow White Earth author, *Gerald Vizenor: Writing in the Oral Tradition* (Norman: University of Oklahoma Press, 1996). Vizenor also has produced an autobiography: *Interior Landscapes: Autobiographical Myths and Metaphors* (Minneapolis: University of Minnesota Press, 1990).

84. Owens, *Other Destinies,* p. 227.

85. Vizenor, *Shadow Distance,* p. xv.

86. Ibid., p. xvi.

87. Owens, *Other Destinies,* p. 228.

88. Coltelli, *Winged Words,* p. 167.

89. Vizenor, *Interior Landscapes,* p. 197–198.

90. Ibid., p. 191.

91. Gerald Vizenor, *Crossbloods: Bone Courts, Bingo, and Other Reports* (Minneapolis: University of Minnesota Press, 1990), p. 159.

92. Ibid., pp. 183–187.

93. Owens, *Other Destinies,* p. 254.

94. Vizenor, *Interior Landscapes,* p. 198.

95. Coltelli, *Winged Words,* p. 156.

96. Owens, *Other Destinies,* p. 238.

97. Bruchac, *Survival This Way,* p. 301.

98. Owens, *Other Destinies,* p. 230. Gerald Vizenor, *Darkness in Saint Louis Bearheart* (St. Paul: Truck, 1978); *Bearheart: The Heirship Chronicles* (Minneapolis: University of Minnesota Press, 1990).

99. See Nieuwenhuys, *Mirror of the Indies,* pp. 187, 314.

100. Vizenor, *Manifest Manners,* p. 67.

101. Ashcroft, Griffiths, and Tiffin, *Empire Writes Back,* p. 164.

102. Vizenor, *Manifest Manners,* p. 12.

103. Ibid., pp. 66–67.

104. Bruchac, *Survival This Way,* p. 290.

105. King, interview with author, January 27, 1993.

106. Ibid., p. 295. Emphasis original.

107. Nieuwenhuys, *Mirror of the Indies*, p. 284.

108. Owens, *Other Destinies*, pp. 225–226.

109. Much of what follows is adapted from Jace Weaver, "Trickster among the Word-ies," *Christianity and Crisis*, August 17, 1992, pp. 285–286. It should be pointed out that Vizenor, like many Native authors for generations, rejects the term "Indian" as an outside view predicate. In *Manifest Manners*, he employs the term "postindian." He told Bruchac, "The word 'indian,' for example: I try to avoid it in almost all my writing. Where I've used *indian*, I've identified it as a problem word in some writing or italicized it in others. I think it ought to be lower-case italicized everywhere. It is one of those troublesome words. It doesn't mean anything, it is a historical blunder, and has negative associations." *Survival This Way*, p. 292.

110. Vizenor, *Interior Landscapes*, p. 262.

111. Said, *Culture*, p. 197; Gerald Vizenor, *The Heirs of Columbus* (Hanover, N.H.: Wesleyan University Press, 1991).

112. The theme of "invented Indians" runs through Vizenor's other works as well. For instance, in *The Trickster of Liberty*, illustrates Owens, "[p]ointedly calling to mind published doubts concerning the authenticity of author Jamake Highwater's claim to an Indian identity, Homer Yellow Snow's confession lays bare the essence of the controversy when he says to his tribal audience: 'If you knew who you were, why did you find it so easy to believe in me? . . . because you want to be white, and no matter what you say in public, you trust whites more than you trust Indians, which is to say, you trust pretend Indians more than real ones.' " Owens, *Other Destinies*, p. 254.

113. Gerald Vizenor, *Landfill Meditation* (Hanover, N.H.: Wesleyan University Press, 1991).

114. Vizenor, *Interior Landscapes*, pp. 167–170; Swann and Krupat, *I Tell You Now*, pp. 105–108.

115. Coltelli, *Winged Words*, pp. 175–176. According to Goldie, "Scatological and sexual language simply represents one more way in which orality transmits natural truth." *Fear and Temptation*, p. . For a further example of stories in which such an interplay takes place, see Adrian C. Louis, *Wild Indians and Other Creatures* (Reno: University of Nevada Press, 1996).

116. Bruchac, *Survival This Way*, pp. 296–297.

117. Weaver, "Trickster," p. 286.

118. See Norman Akers, notes to exhibition, Heard Museum, Phoenix, Ariz. (January 1995).

119. King, interview with author, January 27, 1993.

120. Thomas King, interview with author, February 2, 1996.

121. Thomas King, *Medicine River* (New York: Viking, 1990); Thomas King, *Green Grass, Running Water* (Boston: Houghton Mifflin, 1993).

122. Harry Robinson, *Write It on Your Heart: The Epic World of an Okanagan Story-teller*, comp. and ed. Wendy Wickwire (Vancouver: Talon Books, 1989). King includes a piece by Robinson in *All My Relations* (pp. 1–26).

123. Vizenor, *Manifest Manners*, p. 15.

124. King, interview with author, January 27, 1993.

125. Vizenor, *Manifest Manners,* pp. 91, 173.

126. King, *All My Relations,* p. xiii.

127. King, interview with author, January 27, 1993.

128. [Jace Weaver], *"Green Grass, Running Water,"* *Publishers Weekly,* January 25, 1993, p. 78; King, interview with author, January 27, 1993.

129. Goldie, *Fear and Temptation,* p. 52.

130. King, interview with author, January 27, 1993.

131. Hultkrantz, *Native Religions,* p. 27; Grinde and Johansen, *Ecocide,* p. 30. McPherson and Rabb challenge both the historicity of Hultkrantz's description and his tone. See McPherson and Rabb, *Indian from the Inside,* pp. 1–2.

132. King, interview with author, January 27, 1993.

133. Ibid.

134. Ibid.

135. Vizenor, *Manifest Manners,* p. 60.

136. King, interview with author, January 27, 1993.

137. King, *All My Relations,* pp. xiii–xiv.

138. Quoted in Petrone, *Native Literature,* pp. 146–147.

139. King, *All My Relations,* pp. xiv–xv.

140. King, interview with author, February 2, 1996.

141. Vizenor, *Interior Landscapes,* pp. 167–170.

142. King, *All My Relations,* pp. xi–xii.

143. Ibid., p. xii.

144. Quoted in Petrone, *Native Literature,* p. 147.

145. King states, "I said to myself, if we had to write an historical novel, or if I had to write an historical novel, what is the first thing I have to do. The first thing is I have to make history my own. I have to in some way, *in some way,* not just take history and revise it, I have to recreate it. Which, of course, gave me the idea of recreating the world while I was at it. I mean, why stop with history." Interview with author, January 27, 1993.

146. [Weaver], *"Green Grass,"* p. 78.

147. King, interview with author, January 27, 1993.

148. Ibid.

149. Details of Bell's life are from an interview with the author on February 18, 1996, and from a brief autobiographical sketch. Betty Louise Bell, "Coming to *Faces in the Moon,*" in Bruchac, *Aniyunwiya,* pp. 43–45; Betty Louise Bell, *Faces in the Moon* (Norman: University of Oklahoma Press, 1994).

150. Bruchac, *Aniyunwiya,* p. 43.

151. Ibid., pp. 43–44.

152. In the arguments over allotment, Lizzie's father had been a pullback, who "didn't hold with breaking up Cherokee land," seeing it as the fastest way of destroying sovereignty. Lizzie acknowledges that he was right.

153. Emphasis original. Though Lucie is Cherokee, she feels a special affinity for the great Comanche leader Quanah Parker. In a dream, she encounters Parker, who ques-

tions her as to her Indianness. When she replies that her mother told her so, the warrior replies that "Indian is a favored lie."

154. Jack F. Kilpatrick and Anna G. Kilpatrick, *Friends of Thunder: Folktales of the Oklahoma Cherokees* (Dallas: Southern Methodist University Press, 1964), p. v.

155. The name Tonto is, of course, a racial slur, meaning in Spanish "silly" or "stupid."

156. In her autobiographical essay, Bell notes, "When I wrote *Faces in the Moon*, I knew I had to let my mother and auntie speak for themselves. Certainly, the stories of my grandmother belonged to them and could only be told through them. But more, their voices, holding lives and humor, *was* the story." "Coming to *Faces in the Moon*," p. 45; emphasis original.

Conclusion

1. Robert J. Conley, *The Witch of Goingsnake and Other Stories* (Norman: University of Oklahoma Press, 1988), pp. 68–70.

2. Robert J. Conley, *Ned Christie's War* (New York: M. Evans, 1990), p. 78. Christie was a historical personage (1852–1892) whose story Conley recounts in fictionalized form.

3. Vizenor, *Manifest Manners*, pp. 16–17.

4. Ruppert, *Mediation*, p. 11.

5. Owens, *Other Destinies*, p. 22.

6. James Clifford, *The Predicament of Culture: Twentieth-Century Ethnography, Literature, and Art* (Cambridge: Harvard University Press, 1988), p. 344.

7. Elizabeth Cook-Lynn, "Some Thoughts about Biography," *Wicazo Sa Review* 10, no. 1 (Spring 1994): p. 73. Emphasis original.

8. Ibid., p. 74.

9. Swann and Krupat, *I Tell You Now*, p. ix.

10. Vizenor, *Manifest Manners*, p. 57.

11. Ruppert, *Mediation*, p. x.

12. Ruoff, *American Indian Literatures*, p. vii.

13. As Marxist literary critic Terry Eagleton has observed, even a subway sign can be given a literary reading. Krupat, *Voice*, p. 236.

14. Murray, *Forked Tongues*, p. 88.

15. See Peelman, *Christ Is a Native American*, p. 48.

16. See George Tinker, "Creation as Kin: An American Indian View," in Dieter Hessel, ed., *After Nature's Revolt: Eco-Justice and Theology* (Minneapolis: Fortress Press, 1992), pp. 144–153.

17. Owens, *Other Destinies*, p. 7.

18. Cook-Lynn, "You May Consider," p. 55.

19. Sioui, *Amerindian Autohistory*, p. 37.

20. Ibid.

21. See ibid., pp. xxii–xxiii.

22. Joy Harjo and Robert Warrior, "Tribal Aesthetics: A Conversation" (panel held at Stanford University, Palo Alto, Calif., January 17, 1996).

23. Vizenor, *Manifest Manners*, p. 17.

24. Dene Nation, *Denedeh: A Dene Celebration* (Toronto: McClelland and Stewart, 1984), p. 65.

25. Vizenor, *Manifest Manners*, p. 61.

26. Petrone, *Native Literature*, p. 3.

27. See Ashcroft, Griffiths, and Tiffin, *Empire Writes Back*, p. 139.

28. Barbara Christian, "The Race for Theory," in Gloria Anzaldúa, ed., *Making Face, Making Soul/Haciendo Caras: Creative and Critical Perspectives by Women of Color* (San Francisco: Aunt Lute, 1990), pp. 335–345. The title of Christian's essay is itself a wonderful act of signification, "race" doubling as competition and racial origin.

29. Ruppert, *Mediation*, pp. 16–17.

30. See Owens, *Other Destinies*, p. 10.

31. Warrior, *Tribal Secrets*, p. 106.

32. Nieuwenhuys, *Mirror of the Indies*, p. xxvi.

33. Christian, "Race," p. 337.

34. Vizenor, *Manifest Manners*, pp. 4–5.

35. Bhabha, *Location of Culture*, pp. 19–21.

36. Harjo and Warrior, "Tribal Aesthetics," January 17, 1996.

37. Christian, "Race," p. 343.

38. Ibid., pp. 344.

39. Nieuwenhuys, *Mirror of the Indies*, p. 329.

40. A. A. Carr, *Eye Killers* (Norman: University of Oklahoma Press, 1995).

41. Greg Sarris, *Grand Avenue* (New York: Hyperion, 1994).

42. See, e.g., Beth Brant, *Food and Spirits* (Vancouver: Press Gang Publishers, 1991); Chrystos, *In Her I Am* (Vancouver: Press Gang Publishers, 1993).

43. See, e.g., Sherman Alexie, *First Indian on the Moon* (Brooklyn: Hanging Loose Press, 1993); Jim Northrup, *Walking the Rez Road* (Stillwater, Minn.: Voyageur Press, 1993).

44. Vizenor, *Manifest Manners*, p. 12.

45. Harjo and Warrior, "Tribal Aesthetics," January 17, 1996.

46. Coltelli, *Winged Words*, pp. 143–144. Likewise, Joy Harjo, speaking of Gloria Bird (Spokane), has cautioned against essentializing by lifting language up as the sole conduit of culture. She states that one cannot "make strict boundaries . . . because human beings aren't like that." Harjo and Warrior, "Tribal Aesthetics," January 17, 1996.

Bibliography

Books

Adams, Carol J. and Marie M. Fortune, eds. *Violence Against Women and Children: A Christian Theological Sourcebook.* New York: Continuum, 1995.

Adams, Howard. *Prison of Grass: Canada from a Native Point of View.* Rev. ed. Saskatoon: Fifth House, 1989.

Alexie, Sherman. *First Indian on the Moon.* Brooklyn: Hanging Loose Press, 1993.

———. *The Lone Ranger and Tonto Fistfight in Heaven.* New York: Atlantic Monthly Press, 1993.

———. *Old Shirts and New Skins.* Los Angeles: American Indian Studies Center, University of California, Los Angeles, 1993.

Allen, Paula Gunn. *The Sacred Hoop: Recovering the Feminine in American Indian Traditions.* Boston: Beacon Press, 1986.

———. *The Sacred Hoop: Recovering the Feminine in American Indian Traditions.* 2d ed. Boston: Beacon Press, 1992.

———. *The Woman Who Owned the Shadows.* Reprint. San Francisco: Aunt Lute Books, 1994.

———, ed. *Spider Woman's Granddaughters.* New York: Fawcett Columbine, 1989.

———, ed. *Voice of the Turtle: American Indian Literature, 1900–1970.* New York: Ballantine, 1994.

Anaya, Rudolfo A. *Bless Me, Ultima.* Berkeley: TQS Publications, 1972.

Anderson, A. T. *Nations within a Nation: The American Indian and the Government of the United States.* Chappaqua, N.Y.: Privately printed, 1976.

Anderson, William L., ed. *Cherokee Removal: Before and After.* Athens: University of Georgia Press, 1991.

Anzaldúa, Gloria, ed. *Making Face, Making Soul/Haciendo Caras: Creative and Critical Perspectives by Women of Color.* San Francisco: Aunt Lute, 1990.

Ashcroft, Bill, Gareth Griffiths, and Helen Tiffin. *The Empire Writes Back: Theory and Practice in Post-Colonial Literatures.* London: Routledge, 1989.

————, eds. *The Post-Colonial Studies Reader.* London: Routledge, 1995.

Barker, Francis, Peter Hulme, and Margaret Iversen, eds. *Colonial Discourse/Post-Colonial Theory.* Manchester: Manchester University Press, 1994.

Bataille, Gretchen M., and Charles L. P. Silet, eds. *The Pretend Indians: Images of Native Americans in the Movies.* Ames: Iowa State University Press, 1980.

Batstone, David, ed. *New Visions for the Americas: Religious Engagement and Social Transformation.* Minneapolis: Fortress Press 1993.

Bell, Betty Louise. *Faces in the Moon.* Norman: University of Oklahoma Press, 1994.

Benterrak, Krim, Stephen Muelcke, and Paddy Roe. *Reading the Country: Introduction to Nomadology.* Fremantle, Australia: Fremantle Arts Centre, 1984.

Bergon, Frank. *Shoshone Mike.* New York: Viking Penguin, 1987.

Berkhofer, Robert F., Jr. *The White Man's Indian: Images of the American Indian from Columbus to the Present.* New York: Vintage Books, 1978.

Best, Steven, and Douglas Kellner. *Postmodern Theory: Critical Interrogations.* New York: Guilford Press, 1991.

Bhabha, Homi K. *The Location of Culture.* New York: Routledge, 1994.

Bierhorst, John, ed. *Four Masterworks of American Indian Literature.* New York: Farrar, Straus, and Giroux, 1974.

Blaeser, Kimberly M. *Gerald Vizenor: Writing in the Oral Tradition.* Norman: University of Oklahoma Press, 1996.

Boldt, Menno. *Surviving as Indians.* Toronto: University of Toronto Press, 1993.

Boudinot, Elias. *A Star in the West; or, A Humble Attempt to Discover the Long Lost Ten Tribes of Israel, Preparatory to Their Return to Their Beloved City, Jerusalem.* Trenton, N.J.: D. Fenton, S. Hutchinson, and J. Dunham, 1816.

Boudinot, Elias [Buck Watie]. *An Address to the Whites.* Philadelphia: William F. Geddes, 1826.

————. *Letters and Other Papers Relating to Cherokee Affairs: Being a Reply to Sundry Publications Authorized by John Ross.* Athens, Ga., 1837.

————. *Poor Sarah, or Religion Exemplified in the Life and Death of an Indian Woman.* Mount Pleasant, Ohio: Elisha Bates, 1823.

Bowden, Henry Warner. *American Indians and Christian Missions.* Chicago: University of Chicago Press, 1981.

Boyarin, Jonathan. *Storm from Paradise: The Politics of Jewish Memory.* Minneapolis: University of Minnesota Press, 1992.

Brant, Beth. *Food and Spirits.* Vancouver: Press Gang Publishers, 1991.

————. *Writing as Witness.* Toronto: Women's Press, 1994.

Braunlich, Phyllis Cole. *Haunted by Home: The Life and Letters of Lynn Riggs.* Norman: University of Oklahoma Press, 1988.

Brotherston, Gordon. *Book of the Fourth World: Reading the Native Americas through Their Literature.* Cambridge: Cambridge University Press, 1992.

Brown, Joseph Epes. *The Spiritual Legacy of the American Indian.* New York: Crossroad, 1989.

Bruchac, Joseph, ed. *Aniyunwiya/Real Human Beings: An Anthology of Contemporary Cherokee Prose.* Greenfield Center, N.Y.: Greenfield Review Press, 1995.

———. *New Voices from the Longhouse.* Greenfield Center, N.Y.: Greenfield Review Press, 1989.

———. *The Next World: Poems by Third World Americans.* Trumansburg, N.Y.: Crossing Press, 1978.

———. *Survival This Way: Interviews with American Indian Poets.* Tucson: University of Arizona Press, 1987.

Brumble, H. David, III. *American Indian Autobiography.* Berkeley: University of California Press, 1988.

Buell, Frederick. *National Culture and the New Global System.* Baltimore: Johns Hopkins University Press, 1994.

Burke, James. *Paper Tomahawks: From Red Tape to Red Power.* Winnipeg: Queenston House, 1976.

Campbell, Everett O. *The Eagle Flies at Dawn: A Saga of the Cherokee People.* New York: Vantage Press, 1989.

Cardinal, Harold. *The Rebirth of Canada's Indians.* Edmonton, Alb.: Hurtig, 1977.

———. *The Unjust Society.* Edmonton, Alb.: Hurtig, 1969.

Carmody, Denise Lardner, and John Tully Carmody. *Native American Religions: An Introduction.* New York: Paulist Press, 1993.

Carr, A. A. *Eye Killers.* Norman: University of Oklahoma Press, 1995.

Carter, Joseph H. *Never Met a Man I Didn't Like: The Life and Writings of Will Rogers.* New York: Avon Books, 1991.

Cervantes, Fernando. *The Devil in the New World: The Impact of Diabolism in New Spain.* New Haven: Yale University Press, 1994.

Chrystos. *In Her I Am.* Vancouver: Press Gang Publishers, 1993.

Chung Hyun-Kyung. *Struggle to Be the Sun Again.* Maryknoll: Orbis Books, 1990.

Churchill, Ward, ed. *Marxism and Native Americans.* Boston: South End Press, 1984.

———. *Struggle for the Land.* Monroe, Me.: Common Courage Press, 1993.

Clarke, Mary Whatley. *Chief Bowles and the Texas Cherokees.* Norman: University of Oklahoma Press, 1971.

Clifford, James. *The Predicament of Culture: Twentieth-Century Ethnography, Literature, and Art.* Cambridge: Harvard University Press, 1988.

———, ed. *The Invented Indian: Cultural Fictions and Government Policies.* New Brunswick, N.J.: Transaction Publishers, 1990.

Collier, John. *The Indians of the Americas.* New York: W. W. Norton, 1947.

Coltelli, Laura. *Winged Words: American Indian Writers Speak.* Lincoln: University of Nebraska Press, 1990.

Cone, James H. *A Black Theology of Liberation.* 2d ed. Maryknoll: Orbis Books, 1986.

Conley, Robert J. *Ned Christie's War.* New York: M. Evans, 1990.

———. *The Witch of Goingsnake and Other Stories.* Norman: University of Oklahoma Press, 1988.

Crèvecoeur, J. Hector St. John de. *Letters from an American Farmer*. Reprint. New York: Penguin, 1981.

Crum, Steven J. *Po'i Pentun Tammen Kimmappeh = The Road on Which We Came: A History of the Western Shoshone*. Salt Lake City: University of Utah Press, 1994.

Dale, Edward Everett and Gaston Litton, eds. *Cherokee Cavaliers: Forty Years of Cherokee History as Told in the Correspondence of the Ridge-Watie-Boudinot Family*. Norman: University of Oklahoma Press, 1939.

David, Jay, ed. *The American Indian: The First Victim*. New York: William Morrow, 1972.

Davis, Mary B., ed. *Native America in the Twentieth Century*. New York: Garland Publishing, 1994.

Deloria, Ella Cara. *Dakota Grammar*. 1941. Reprint, Vermillion, S.D.: Dakota Press, 1982.

———. *Dakota Texts*. 1932. Reprint, New York: AMS Press, 1974.

———. *Speaking of Indians*. New York: Friendship Press, 1944.

———. *Waterlily*. Lincoln: University of Nebraska Press, 1988.

Deloria, Vine, Jr. *Behind the Trail of Broken Treaties: An Indian Declaration of Independence*. New York: Delacorte, 1974.

———. *Custer Died for Your Sins*. New York: Macmillan, 1969.

———. *Custer Died for Your Sins*. 2d ed. Norman: University of Oklahoma Press, 1988.

———. *God Is Red*. New York: Delta, 1973.

———. *God Is Red*. 2d ed. Golden, Colo.: Fulcrum, 1992.

———. *The Metaphysics of Modern Existence*. San Francisco: Harper & Row, 1979.

———. *Red Earth, White Lies*. New York: Scribner's, 1995.

———. *We Talk, You Listen: New Tribes, New Turf*. New York: Macmillan, 1970.

——— ed. *American Indian Policy in the Twentieth Century*. Norman: University of Oklahoma Press, 1985.

Deloria, Vine, Jr., and Clifford Lytle. *American Indians, American Justice*. Austin: University of Texas Press, 1983.

———. *The Nations Within*. New York: Random House, 1984.

DeMallie, Raymond J., and Douglas R. Parks, eds. *Sioux Indian Religion*. Norman: University of Oklahoma Press, 1987.

Dene Nation. *Denedeh: A Dene Celebration*. Toronto: McClelland and Stewart, 1984.

Denhardt, Robert Moorman. *The Horse of the Americas*. Norman: University of Oklahoma Press, 1947.

Dippie, Brian W. *The Vanishing American: White Attitudes and U.S. Indian Policy*. Lawrence: University Press of Kansas, 1982.

Drinnon, Richard. *White Savage: The Case of John Dunn Hunter*. New York: Schocken Books, 1972.

Driver, Tom F. *The Magic of Ritual*. San Francisco: HarperCollins, 1991.

Dudley, Joseph Iron Eye. *Choteau Creek*. Lincoln: University of Nebraska Press, 1992.

Duran, Eduardo, and Bonnie Duran. *Native American Postcolonial Psychology*. Albany: State University of New York Press, 1995.

Dussel, Enrique. *The Invention of the Americas: Eclipse of "the Other" and the Myth of Modernity.* New York: Continuum, 1995.

Dyck, Noel, ed. *Indigenous People and the Nation-State: Fourth World Politics in Canada, Australia, and Norway.* St. John's: Institute of Social and Economic Research, Memorial University of Newfoundland, 1985.

Eagleton, Terry. *The Illusions of Postmodernism.* Oxford: Blackwell Publishers, 1996.

Eastman, Charles A. *Indian Scout Talks: A Guide for Boy Scouts and Camp Fire Girls.* Boston: Little, Brown, 1914.

———. *The Soul of an Indian: An Interpretation.* Boston: Houghton Mifflin, 1911.

Ehle, John. *Trail of Tears: The Rise and Fall of the Cherokee Nation.* New York: Doubleday, 1988.

Eichstaedt, Peter H. *If You Poison Us: Uranium and Native Americans.* Santa Fe: Red Crane Books, 1994.

Elder, John, and Hertha D. Wong, eds. *Family of Earth and Sky.* Boston: Beacon Press, 1994.

Erdrich, Louise. *Love Medicine.* New York: Holt, 1984.

———. *Love Medicine.* Exp. ed. New York: HarperCollins, 1993.

Erhard, Thomas. *Lynn Riggs, Southwest Playwright.* Austin: Steck-Vaughn, 1970.

Evans-Wentz, W. Y. *Cuchama and Sacred Mountains.* Edited by Frank Waters and Charles L. Adams. Athens: Swallow Press/Ohio University Press, 1981.

Everett, Dianna. *The Texas Cherokees: A People between Two Fires, 1819–1940.* Norman: University of Oklahoma Press, 1990.

Fabian, Johannes. *Time and the Other: How Anthropology Makes Its Object.* New York: Columbia University Press, 1983.

Fanon, Frantz. *Black Skin, White Mask.* New York: Grove, 1967.

———. *A Dying Colonialism.* 1959. Reprint. New York: Grove, 1967.

———. *Toward the African Revolution.* 1964. Reprint, New York: Grove, 1969.

———. *The Wretched of the Earth.* 1961. Reprint, New York: Grove, 1968.

Farmer, David, and Rennard Strickland, eds. *A Trumpet of Our Own: Yellow Bird's Essays on the North American Indian.* San Francisco: Book Club of California, 1981.

Fell, Barry. *America B.C.: Ancient Settlers in the New World.* New York: Quadrangle/New York Times, 1976.

Fisher, Dexter, ed. *The Third Woman: Minority Women Writers of the United States.* New York: Houghton Mifflin, 1980.

Fixico, Donald. *The Invasion of Indian Country in the Twentieth Century: American Capitalism and Tribal Natural Resources.* Boulder: University of Colorado Press, forthcoming.

———. *Termination and Relocation: Federal Indian Policy, 1945–1960.* Albuquerque: University of New Mexico Press, 1986.

Fleras, Augie, and John Leonard Elliott. *The Nations Within: Aboriginal-State Relations in Canada, the United States, and New Zealand.* Toronto: Oxford University Press, 1992.

Forbes, Jack D. *Columbus and Other Cannibals.* Brooklyn: Autonomedia, 1992.

————. *Native Americans and Nixon: Presidential Politics and Minority Self-determination, 1969–1972.* Los Angeles: American Indian Studies Center, University of California, Los Angeles, 1981.

Foster, Anne. *The Mohawk Princess: Being Some Account of the Life of Tek-hion-wake (E. Pauline Johnson).* Vancouver: Lion's Gate, 1931.

Francis, Daniel. *The Imaginary Indian: The Image of the Indian in Canadian Culture.* Vancouver: Arsenal Pulp Press, 1992.

Frayling, Christopher. *Spaghetti Westerns: Cowboys and Europeans from Karl May to Sergio Leone.* London: Routledge & Kegan Paul, 1981.

Gabriel, Ralph Henry. *Elias Boudinot, Cherokee, and His America.* Norman: University of Oklahoma Press, 1941.

————. *Elias Boudinot, Cherokee, and His America.* 1941. Edited and recorded by Willena Robinson. Tulsa: Cherokee Language and Culture Series, 1991.

Goldie, Terry. *Fear and Temptation: The Image of the Indigene in Canadian, Australian, and New Zealand Literatures.* Kingston, Ont.: McGill-Queen's University Press, 1989.

Goodman, Jeffrey. *American Genesis.* New York: Summit Books, 1981.

Green, Michael K., ed. "Issues in Native American Cultural Identity." *Critic of Institutions* 2 (1995).

Grinde, Donald A., and Bruce E. Johansen. *Ecocide of Native America.* Santa Fe: Clear Light, 1995.

Guardini, Romano. *The End of the Modern World.* Translated by Joseph Theman and Herbert Burke. New York: Sheed & Ward, 1956.

Gump, James O. *The Dust Rose Like Smoke: The Subjugation of the Zulu and the Sioux.* Lincoln: University of Nebraska Press, 1994.

Gutiérrez, Gustavo. *We Drink from Our Own Wells: The Spiritual Journey of a People.* Maryknoll: Orbis Books, 1984.

Haig-Brown, Celia. *Resistance and Renewal: Surviving the Indian Residential School.* Vancouver: Tillacum Library, 1988.

Harjo, Joy. *She Had Some Horses.* New York: Thunder's Mouth Press, 1983.

————. *The Woman Who Fell from the Sky.* New York: W.W. Norton, 1994.

Harlow, Barbara. *Resistance Literature.* New York: Methuen, 1987.

Haslam, G. W. *Forgotten Pages of American Literature.* Boston: Houghton Mifflin, 1970.

Hauptman, Laurence M., and James D. Wherry, eds. *The Pequots in Southern New England: The Fall and Rise of an American Indian Nation.* Norman: University of Oklahoma Press, 1990.

Hector, Michael. *The Celtic Fringe in British National Development, 1536–1966.* Berkeley: University of California Press, 1975.

Henry, George [Maungwudaus]. *An Account of the Chippewa Indians, Who Have Been Traveling in the United States, England, Ireland, Scotland, France and Belgium; with Very Interesting Incidents in Relation to the General Characteristics of the English, Irish, Scotch, French, and Americans, with Regard to Their Hospitality, Peculiarities, etc.* Boston: Privately printed, 1848.

————. *An Account of the North American Indians, Written for Maungwudaus, a Chief of the Ojibway Indians Who Has Been Travelling in England, France, Belgium, Ireland, and Scotland.* Leicester: T. Cook, 1848.

————. *Remarks Concerning the Ojibway Indians, by One of Themselves Called Maungwudaus, Who Has Been Traveling in England, France, Belgium, Ireland, and Scotland.* Leeds: C. A. Wilson, 1847.

Herzog, Kristin. *Finding Their Voice: Peruvian Women's Testimonies of War.* Valley Forge: Trinity Press International, 1993.

Hessel, Dieter, ed. *After Nature's Revolt: Eco-Justice and Theology.* Minneapolis: Fortress Press, 1992.

Highway, Tomson. *Dry Lips Oughta Move to Kapuskasing.* Saskatoon: Fifth House, 1989.

————. *The Rez Sisters.* Saskatoon: Fifth House, 1988.

Hirschfelder, Anne B., and Beverly R. Singer, eds. *Rising Voices: Writings of Young Native Americans.* New York: Charles Scribner's Sons, 1992.

Hobson, Geary, ed. *The Remembered Earth.* Albuquerque: University of New Mexico Press, 1979.

Hoesterey, Ingeborg, ed. *Zeitgeist in Babel: The Post-Modernist Controversy.* Bloomington: Indiana University Press, 1991.

Hofstra, Marilyn M., ed. *Voices: Native American Hymns and Worship Resources.* Nashville: Discipleship Resources, 1992.

Hogan, Linda. *The Book of Medicines.* Minneapolis: Coffee House Press, 1993.

Horsman, Reginald. *Expansion and American Indian Policy, 1783–1812.* East Lansing: Michigan State University Press, 1967.

Hoxie, Frederick E. *A Final Promise: The Campaign to Assimilate the Indians, 1880–1920.* Lincoln: University of Nebraska Press, 1984.

Hultkrantz, Åke. *Native Religions of North America.* New York: Harper & Row, 1987.

Jackson, Helen Hunt. *A Century of Dishonor: A Sketch of the United States Government's Dealings with Some of the Indian Tribes.* New York: Harper & Brothers, 1881.

————. *Ramona.* 1884. Reprint, Boston: Little, Brown, 1912.

JanMohamed, Abdul R. *Manichean Aesthetics: The Politics of Literature in Colonial Africa.* Amherst: University of Massachusetts Press, 1983.

Jaskoski, Helen, ed. *Early Native American Writing: New Critical Essays.* Cambridge: Cambridge University Press, 1996.

Jennings, Francis. *The Invasion of America: Indians, Colonialism, and the Cant of Conquest.* New York: W. W. Norton, 1976.

Johnson, Daniel L., and Charles Hambrick-Stowe, eds. *Theology and Identity: Traditions, Movements, and Polity in the United Church of Canada.* New York: Pilgrim Press, 1990.

Johnson, E. Pauline. *Flint and Feather.* Toronto: Musson, 1912.

————. *The Moccasin Maker.* Toronto: Ryerson, 1913.

————. *The Shaganappi.* Toronto: William Briggs, 1913.

Jones, John. *The Gospel According to St. John.* Revised and corrected by Peter Jones. 1831.

Jones, Peter. *Collection of Hymns for the Use of Native Christians of the Chipeway Tongue.* New York: J. Collord, 1829.

———. *A Collection of Ojebway and English Hymns for the Use of the Native Indians.* Toronto: Methodist Missionary Society, 1877.

———. *History of the Ojebway Indians: With Especial Reference to Their Conversion to Christianity.* London: A. W. Bennett, 1861.

———. *Life and Journals of Kah-ke-wa-quo-na-by (Rev. Peter Jones), Wesleyan Minister.* Toronto: Anson Green, 1860.

Josephy, Alvin M., Jr. *Red Power: The American Indian's Fight for Freedom.* New York: McGraw-Hill, 1971.

Kadir, Djelal. *Columbus and the Ends of the Earth: Europe's Prophetic Rhetoric as Conquering Ideology.* Berkeley: University of California Press, 1992.

Kasinitz, Philip, ed. *Metropolis: Center and Symbol of Our Times.* New York: New York University Press, 1995.

Keller, Betty. *Pauline: A Biography of Pauline Johnson.* Vancouver: Douglas, 1981.

Kennedy, Gerald. *Fresh Every Morning.* New York: Harper & Row, 1966.

Kent, James. *Commentaries on American Law.* 4 vols. New York: O. Halsted, 1826–1830.

Ketcham, Richard M. *Will Rogers: The Man and Times.* New York: McGraw-Hill, 1973.

Kilpatrick, Jack F., and Anna G. Kilpatrick. *Friends of Thunder: Folktales of the Oklahoma Cherokees.* Dallas: Southern Methodist University Press, 1964.

King, Thomas. *Green Grass, Running Water.* Boston: Houghton Mifflin, 1993.

———. *Medicine River.* New York: Viking, 1990.

———. *One Good Story, That One.* Toronto: HarperCollins, 1993.

———. *Truth and Bright Water.* Forthcoming.

———, ed. *All My Relations.* Toronto: McClelland & Stewart, 1990.

Knockwood, Isabelle. *Out of the Depths.* Lockport, N.S.: Roseway Publishing, 1992.

Kroeber, Karl, ed. *American Indian Persistence and Resurgence.* Durham, N.C.: Duke University Press, 1994.

———. *Traditional Literatures of the American Indian.* Lincoln: University of Nebraska Press, 1981.

Kroeber, Theodora. *Ishi in Two Worlds: A Biography of the Last Wild Indian in North America.* Berkeley: University of California Press, 1961.

Krupat, Arnold. *For Those Who Come After: A Study of Native American Autobiography.* Berkeley: University of California Press, 1985.

———. *The Turn to the Native: Studies in Criticism and Culture.* Lincoln: University of Nebraska Press, 1996.

———. *The Voice in the Margin: Native American Literature and the Canon.* Berkeley: University of California Press, 1989.

———, ed. *Native American Autobiography: An Anthology.* Madison: University of Wisconsin Press, 1994.

Laubin, Reginald, and Gladys Laubin. *Indian Dances of North America.* Norman: University of Oklahoma Press, 1977.

Lesley, Craig, ed. *Talking Leaves: Contemporary Native American Short Stories.* New York: Dell, 1991.

Littlefield, Daniel F., Jr. *Alex Posey: Creek Poet, Journalist, and Humorist.* Lincoln: University of Nebraska Press, 1992.

Littlefield, Daniel F., Jr., and James W. Parins, eds. *Native American Writing in the Southeast: An Anthology, 1875–1935.* Jackson: University Press of Mississippi, 1995.

Llanque Chana, Domingo. *Ritos y Espiritualidad Aymara.* La Paz, Bolivia: Asett Idea CTP.

Long, Charles H. *Alpha: The Myths of Creation.* New York: G. Braziller, 1963.

———. *Significations: Signs, Symbols, and Images in the Interpretation of Religion.* Philadelphia: Fortress Press, 1986.

Lopez, Barry. *Crow and Weasel.* San Francisco: North Point Press, 1990.

Louis, Adrian C. *Wild Indians and Other Creatures.* Reno: University of Nevada Press, 1996.

McClintock, John, and James Strong, eds. *Cyclopedia of Biblical, Theological, and Ecclesiastical Literature.* 12 vols. New York: Harper Brothers, 1867–1887. Reprint, Grand Rapids: Baker Book House, 1981.

McCutchen, David. *The Red Record: The Wallum Olum.* Garden City, N.Y.: Avery Publishing Group, 1993.

McGrath, Alister. *Evangelicalism and the Future of Christianity.* Downers Grove, Ill.: InterVarsity Press, 1995.

McLoughlin, William G. *After the Trail of Tears: The Cherokees' Struggle for Sovereignty, 1839–1880.* Chapel Hill: University of North Carolina Press, 1993.

———. *Champions of the Cherokees: Evan and John B. Jones.* Princeton: Princeton University Press, 1990.

———. *Cherokee Renascence in the New Republic.* Princeton: Princeton University Press, 1986.

———. *The Cherokees and Christianity, 1794–1870: Essays on Acculturation and Cultural Persistence.* Edited by Walter H. Conser Jr. Athens: University of Georgia Press, 1994.

McNickle, D'Arcy. *Indian Man: A Life of Oliver La Farge.* Bloomington: Indiana University Press, 1971.

———. *Runner in the Sun: A Story of Maize.* New York: Holt, Rinehart and Winston, 1954.

———. *The Surrounded.* 1936. Reprint, Albuquerque: University of New Mexico Press, 1988.

———. *Wind from an Enemy Sky.* 1978. Reprint, Albuquerque: University of New Mexico Press, 1988.

McPherson, Dennis, and J. Douglas Rabb. *Indian from the Inside: A Study in Ethno-Metaphysics.* Thunder Bay, Ont.: Lakehead University, Centre for Northern Studies, 1993.

Manuel, George, and M. Posluns. *The Fourth World: An Indian Reality.* Toronto: Collier-Macmillan, 1974.

Marshall, Joseph, III. *Winter of the Holy Iron.* Santa Fe: Red Crane Books, 1994.

Martin, Calvin, ed. *The American Indian and the Problem of History.* New York: Oxford University Press, 1987.

Marty, Martin E., and Dean G. Peerman, eds. *New Theology No. 9.* New York: Macmillan, 1972.

Mathews, John Joseph. *Life and Death of an Oilman: The Career of E. W. Marland.* Norman: University of Oklahoma Press, 1951.

―――. *Talking to the Moon.* Norman: University of Oklahoma Press, 1945.

Means, Russell. *Where White Men Fear to Tread: The Autobiography of Russell Means.* New York: St. Martin's Press, 1995.

Memmi, Albert. *The Colonizer and the Colonized.* Exp. ed. Boston: Beacon Press, 1967.

Méndez, Miguel. *Pilgrims in Aztlán.* Tempe: Bilingual Press, 1992.

Momaday, Natachee Scott. *Owl in the Cedar Tree.* Boston: Ginn, 1965.

Momaday, N. Scott. *The Ancient Child.* New York: Doubleday, 1989.

―――. *House Made of Dawn.* New York: Harper & Row, 1968.

―――. *The Names: A Memoir.* New York: Harper & Row, 1976.

―――, ed. *Dancing with the Wind* 3 (1991).

Moquin, Wayne, and Charles Van Doren, eds. *Great Documents in American Indian History.* New York: Praeger Publishers, 1973.

Morris, Pam, ed. *The Bakhtin Reader.* London: Edward Arnold, 1994.

Moses, Daniel David, and Terry Goldie, eds. *An Anthology of Canadian Native Literature in English.* Toronto: Oxford University Press, 1992.

Moulton, Ross, ed. *The Papers of Chief John Ross.* 2 vols. Norman: University of Oklahoma Press, 1985.

Mourning Dove. *Cogewea, the Half-Blood.* Boston: Four Seas, 1927.

―――. *Coyote Stories.* Caldwell, Idaho: Caxton Printers, 1933.

―――. *Mourning Dove: A Salishan Autobiography.* Edited by Jay Miller. Lincoln: University of Nebraska Press, 1990.

Murray, David. *Forked Tongues: Speech, Writing and Representation in North American Indian Texts.* Bloomington: Indiana University Press, 1991.

Nandy, Ashis. *The Intimate Enemy: Loss and Recovery of Self under Colonialism.* Delhi: Oxford University Press, 1983.

Ngugi wa Thiong'o. *Decolonising the Mind: The Politics of Language in African Literature.* London: James Currey, 1986.

―――. *Writers in Politics.* London: Heinemann, 1981.

Niatum, Duane, ed. *Harper's Anthology of 20th Century Native American Poetry.* San Francisco: HarperSanFrancisco, 1988.

Niebuhr, Reinhold. *Irony of American History.* New York: Charles Scribner's Sons, 1952.

Niebuhr, Reinhold, and Alan Heimert. *A Nation So Conceived.* London: Faber & Faber, 1964.

Nieuwenhuys, Rob. *Mirror of the Indies: A History of Dutch Colonial Literature.* Amherst: University of Massachusetts Press, 1982.

Noley, Homer. *First White Frost.* Nashville: Abingdon Press, 1991.

Northrup, Jim. *Walking the Rez Road.* Stillwater, Minn.: Voyageur Press, 1993.

O'Connell, Barry, ed. *On Our Own Ground: The Complete Writings of William Apess, a Pequot.* Amherst: University of Massachusetts Press, 1992.

Oliver, Louis Littlecoon. *Chasers of the Sun: Creek Indian Thoughts.* Greenfield Center, N.Y.: Greenfield Review Press, 1990.

Olson, James S., and Raymond Wilson. *Native Americans in the Twentieth Century.* Urbana: University of Illinois Press, 1986.

O'Meara, Sylvia, and Douglas A. West, eds. *From Our Eyes: Learning from Indigenous Peoples.* Toronto: Garamond Press, 1996.

Ong, Walter J. *Orality and Literacy: The Technologizing of the Word.* London: Methuen, 1982.

Ortiz, Simon. *From Sand Creek.* Oak Park: Thunder's Mouth, 1981.

———. *The People Shall Continue.* Rev. ed. San Francisco: Children's Book Press, 1988.

Outler, Albert, ed. *John Wesley.* New York: Oxford University Press, 1964.

Owens, Louis. *Other Destinies: Understanding the American Indian Novel.* Norman: University of Oklahoma Press, 1992.

Palm, Sister Charles. *Stories That Jesus Told: Dakota Way of Life.* Sioux Falls: American Indian Culture Research Center of Blue Cloud Abbey, 1985.

Parins, James W. *John Rollin Ridge: His Life and Works.* Lincoln: University of Nebraska Press, 1991.

Park, Andrew Sung. *The Wounded Heart of God: The Asian Concept of Han and the Christian Doctrine of Sin.* Nashville: Abingdon, 1993.

Parsons, Elsie Clews, ed. *American Indian Life.* 2d Bison Book ed. Lincoln: University of Nebraska Press, 1991.

Pearce, Roy Harvey. *Savagism and Civilization.* Berkeley: University of California Press, 1988.

Peelman, Achiel. *Christ Is a Native American.* Maryknoll: Orbis Books, 1995.

Perdue, Theda, ed. *Cherokee Editor: The Writings of Elias Boudinot.* Knoxville: University of Tennesee Press, 1982.

Petrone, Penny. *Native Literature in Canada.* Toronto: Oxford University Press, 1990.

———, ed. *First People, First Voices.* Toronto: University of Toronto Press, 1983.

Peyer, Bernd C., ed. *The Elders Wrote: An Anthology of Early Prose by North American Indians, 1768–1931.* Berlin: Dietrich Reimer Verlag, 1982.

———. *Singing Spirit: Early Short Stories by North American Indians.* Tucson: University of Arizona Press, 1989.

Pieris, Aloysius. *An Asian Theology of Liberation.* Maryknoll: Orbis Books, 1988.

Posey, Alexander. *The Fus Fixico Letters.* Edited by Daniel F. Littlefield Jr. and Carol A. Petty Hunter. Lincoln: University of Nebraska Press, 1993.

Prucha, Francis Paul, ed. *Americanizing the American Indians.* Cambridge: Harvard University Press, 1973.

Querry, Ron. *The Death of Bernadette Lefthand.* Santa Fe: Red Crane Books, 1993.

Rahner, Karl. *Foundations of Christian Faith.* New York: Seabury Press, 1978.

Rausch, David A., and Blair Schlepp. *Native American Voices.* Grand Rapids: Baker Books, 1994.

Rice, Julian, ed. *Ella Deloria's Iron Hawk.* Albuquerque: University of New Mexico Press, 1993.

Ridge, John Rollin [Yellow Bird]. *The Life and Adventures of Joaquín Murieta, the Celebrated California Bandit.* 1854. Reprint, Norman: University of Oklahoma Press, 1977.

———. *Poems.* San Francisco: Payot, 1868.

Riggs, Lynn. *Big Lake.* New York: Samuel French, 1925.

———. *Green Grow the Lilacs.* New York: Samuel French, 1930.

———. *The Iron Dish.* Garden City, N.Y.: Doubleday, Doran, 1930.

———. *Knives from Syria.* New York: Samuel French, 1927.

———. *Roadside.* New York: Samuel French, 1930.

———. *"Russet Mantle" and "The Cherokee Night".* New York: Samuel French, 1936.

———. *"Sump'n Like Wings" and "A Lantern to See By."* New York: Samuel French, 1928.

———. *Toward the Western Sky.* Cleveland: Press of Western Reserve University, 1951.

Robinson, Harry. *Write It on Your Heart: The Epic World of an Okanagan Storyteller.* Compiled and edited by Wendy Wickwire. Vancouver: Talon Books, 1989.

Rogers, Will. *There's Not a Bathing Suit in Russia.* New York: Albert & Charles Boni, 1927.

Rorty, Richard. *Objectivity, Relativism, and Truth: Philosophical Papers, Volume 1.* Cambridge: Cambridge University Press, 1991.

Rosen, Kenneth, ed. *The Man to Send Rain Clouds.* New York: Random House, 1975.

Rosenblum, Mort. *Mission to Civilize.* New York: Doubleday, 1988.

Ruoff, A. LaVonne Brown. *American Indian Literatures: An Introduction, Bibliographic Review, and Selected Bibliography.* New York: Modern Language Association, 1990.

———. *Literatures of the American Indian.* New York: Chelsea House, 1991.

Ruppert, James. *Mediation in Contemporary Native American Fiction.* Norman: University of Oklahoma Press, 1995.

Said, Edward W. *Culture and Imperialism.* New York: Alfred A. Knopf, 1993.

———. *Orientalism.* New York: Random House, 1978.

———. *The Pen and the Sword: Conversations with David Barsamian.* Monroe, Me.: Common Courage Press, 1994.

———. *The World, the Text, and the Critic.* Cambridge: Harvard University Press, 1983.

Sanderlin, George, ed. *Witness: Writings of Bartolomé de Las Casas.* Maryknoll: Orbis Books, 1992.

Sanders, Ronald. *Lost Tribes and Promised Lands: The Origins of American Racism.* New York: Harper, 1978.

Sarris, Greg. *Grand Avenue.* New York: Hyperion, 1994.

———. *Keeping Slug Woman Alive: A Holistic Approach to American Indian Texts.* Berkeley: University of California Press, 1993.

Schubnell, Matthias. *N. Scott Momaday: The Cultural and Literary Background.* Norman: University of Oklahoma Press, 1985.

Schwarz, Herbert T., ed. *Tales from the Smokehouse.* Edmonton: Hurtig Publishers, 1974.

Sheehan, Bernard W. *Seeds of Extinction: Jeffersonian Philanthropy and the American Indian.* Chapel Hill: University of North Carolina Press, 1973.

Shirer, Thomas E., ed. *Entering the 90s: The North American Experience.* Sault Ste. Marie, Mich.: Lake Superior State University Press, 1991.

Shirer, Thomas E., and Susan M. Branster, eds. *Native American Values: Survival and Renewal.* Sault Ste. Marie, Mich.: Lake Superior State University Press, 1993.

Shorten, Lynda. *Without Reserve: Stories from Urban Natives.* Edmonton: NeWest Press, 1991.

Shweder, Richard, and Robert LeVine, eds. *Culture Theory: Essays on Mind, Self and Emotion.* Cambridge: Cambridge University Press, 1984.

Siggins, Maggie. *Riel: A Life of Revolution.* Toronto: HarperCollins, 1994.

Silko, Leslie Marmon. *Almanac of the Dead.* New York: Simon & Schuster, 1991.

————. *Ceremony.* New York: Viking, 1977.

————. *Laguna Woman.* Greenfield Center, N.Y.: Greenfield Review Press, 1974.

————. *Sacred Water.* Tucson: Flood Plain Press, 1993.

————. *Storyteller.* New York: Arcade Publishing, 1981.

————. *Yellow Woman and a Beauty of the Spirit.* New York: Simon & Schuster, 1996.

————, ed. *Dancing with the Wind* 4 (1992/93).

Sioui, Georges. *For an Amerindian Autohistory.* Montreal: McGill-Queen's University Press, 1992.

Slipperjack, Ruby. *Honour the Sun.* Winnipeg: Pemmican Publications, 1987.

Smallwood, James M., ed. *Will Rogers' Weekly Articles.* Stillwater: Oklahoma State University Press, 1980.

Smith, Donald. *Sacred Feathers: The Reverend Peter Jones (Kahkewaquonoby) and the Mississauga Indians.* Toronto: University of Toronto Press, 1987.

Smith, Martin William [Martin Cruz Smith]. *The Indians Won.* New York: Belmont, 1970.

Smith, Paul Chaat, and Robert Allen Warrior. *Like a Hurricane.* New York: New Press, 1996.

Smith, Theresa S. *The Island of the Anishinaabeg: Thunderers and Water Monsters in the Traditional Ojibwe Life-World.* Moscow: University of Idaho Press, 1995.

Spicer, Edward H. *The American Indians.* Cambridge: Harvard University Press, 1980.

Spivak, Gayatri Chakravorty. *In Other Worlds: Essays in Cultural Politics.* New York: Routledge, 1988.

————. *Outside in the Teaching Machine.* New York: Routledge, 1993.

————. *The Post-Colonial Critic: Interviews, Strategies, Dialogues.* Edited by Sarah Harasym. New York: Routledge, 1990.

Starr, Emmet. *History of the Cherokee Indians.* 1921. Reprint, Muskogee: Hoffman Printing, 1984.

Stolzman, William. *The Pipe and Christ.* 4th ed. Chamberlain, S.D.: Tipi Press, 1992.

Strickland, Rennard. *Fire and the Spirits: Cherokee Law from Clan to Court.* Norman: University of Oklahoma Press, 1975.

Suleri, Sara. *The Rhetoric of English India.* Chicago: University of Chicago Press, 1992.

Sullivan, Caroline, and Cynthia Stevens, eds. *Distinguished Poets of America.* Owings Mills, Md.: National Library of Poetry, 1993.

Swann, Brian, and Arnold Krupat, eds. *I Tell You Now: Autobiographical Essays by Native Americans.* Lincoln: University of Nebraska Press, 1987.

Szasz, Margaret Connell, ed. *Between Indian and White Worlds: The Cultural Broker.* Norman: University of Oklahoma Press, 1994.

Takaki, Ronald. *A Different Mirror: A History of Multicultural America*. Boston: Little, Brown, 1993.

Tapahonso, Luci. *Sáanii Dahataal, The Women Are Singing*. Tucson: University of Arizona Press, 1993.

———. *This Is How They Were Placed for Us*. Kansas City: Feuillets, 1994.

Tedlock, Dennis, trans. *Popul Vuh*. New York: Simon & Schuster, 1985.

Thistlethwaite, Susan Brooks, and Mary Potter Engel, eds. *Lift Every Voice: Constructing Christian Theologies from the Underside*. San Francisco: Harper & Row, 1990.

Thoburn, Joseph B., and Muriel H. Wright. *Oklahoma: A History of the State and Its People*. 4 vols. New York: Lewis Historical Publishing, 1929.

Thompson, David. *David Thompson's Narrative of His Explorations in Western America, 1784–1812*. Edited by J. B. Tyrell. Toronto: Champlain Society, 1916.

Tillich, Paul. *Systematic Theology*. Welwyn: J. Nisbet, 1960.

Tinker, George. *Missionary Conquest*. Minneapolis: Fortress Press, 1993.

Trafzer, Clifford E., ed. *American Indian Identity: Today's Changing Perspectives*. Sacramento: Sierra Oaks Publishing, 1989.

———. *Earth Song, Sky Spirit*. New York: Doubleday, 1993.

Treat, James, ed. *Native and Christian: Indigenous Voices on Religious Identity in the United States and Canada*. New York: Routledge, 1996.

Velie, Alan. *Four American Indian Literary Masters: N. Scott Momaday, James Welch, Leslie Marmon Silko, and Gerald Vizenor*. Norman: University of Oklahoma Press, 1982.

———. *Native American Perspectives on Literature and History*. Norman: University of Oklahoma Press, 1994.

———, ed. *American Indian Literature: An Anthology*. Norman: University of Oklahoma Press, 1979.

———, ed. *The Lightning Within: An Anthology of Contemporary American Indian Fiction*. Lincoln: University of Nebraska Press, 1991.

Viswanathan, Gauri. *Masks of Conquest: Literary Study and British Rule in India*. New York: Columbia University Press, 1989.

Vizenor, Gerald. *Crossbloods: Bone Courts, Bingo, and Other Reports*. Minneapolis: University of Minnesota Press, 1990.

———. *Darkness in Saint Louis Bearheart*. St. Paul: Truck, 1978.

———. *Earthdivers: Tribal Narratives on Mixed Descent*. Minneapolis: University of Minnesota Press, 1981.

———. *Griever: An American Money King in China*. Normal, Ill.: Illinois State University/Fiction Collective, 1987.

———. *The Heirs of Columbus*. Hanover, N.H.: Wesleyan University Press, 1991.

———. *Hotline Healers: An Almost Browne Novel*. Hanover, N.H.: Wesleyan University Press/University Press of New England, 1997.

———. *Interior Landscapes: Autobiographical Myths and Metaphors*. Minneapolis: University of Minnesota Press, 1990.

———. *Landfill Meditation*. Hanover, N.H.: Wesleyan University Press, 1991.

———. *Manifest Manners: Postindian Warriors of Survivance*. Hanover, N.H.: Wesleyan University Press, 1994.

————. *The People Named the Chippewa: Narrative Histories.* Minneapolis: University of Minnesota Press, 1984.

————. *Shadow Distance: A Gerald Vizenor Reader.* Hanover, N.H.: Wesleyan University Press, 1994.

————, ed. *Narrative Chance: Postmodern Discourse on Native American Indian Literatures.* Albuquerque: University of New Mexico Press, 1989.

Vogel, Virgil Jr. *This Country Was Ours: A Documentary History of the American Indian.* New York: Harper & Row, 1974.

Wade, Edwin L., and Rennard Strickland. *Magic Images.* Norman: University of Oklahoma Press, 1981.

Walker, David. *Appeal to the Coloured Citizens of the World.* 1829. Reprint, New York: Hill and Wang, 1965.

Walker, Franklin. *San Francisco's Literary Frontier.* Seattle: University of Washington Press, 1969.

Wallace, Anthony F. C. *The Long, Bitter Trail: Andrew Jackson and the Indians.* New York: Hill and Wang, 1993.

Warrior, Robert Allen. *Tribal Secrets: Recovering American Indian Intellectual Traditions.* Minneapolis: University of Minnesota Press, 1995.

Weaver, Jace. *Then to the Rock Let Me Fly: Luther Bohanon and Judicial Activism.* Norman: University of Oklahoma Press, 1993.

————, ed. *Defending Mother Earth: Native American Perspectives on Environmental Justice.* Maryknoll: Orbis Books, 1996.

Welch, James. *The Death of Jim Loney.* 1979. Reprint, New York: Penguin, 1987.

————. *Fools Crow.* New York: Viking, 1986.

————. *Winter in the Blood.* 1974. Reprint, New York: Penguin, 1986.

Welsch, Roger. *Touching the Fire: Buffalo Dancers, the Sky Bundle, and Other Tales.* New York: Villard Books, 1992.

Wheeler, Jordan. *Brothers in Arms.* Winnipeg: Pemmican Publications, 1989.

White Deer of Autumn [Gabriel Horn]. *The Native American Book of Knowledge.* Hillsboro, Ore.: Beyond Words Publishing, 1992.

Wiget, Andrew, ed. *Handbook of Native American Literature.* New York: Garland Publishing, 1996.

Wilkerson, Barbara, ed. *Multicultural Religious Education.* Birmingham: Religious Education Press, forthcoming.

Wilkins, Thurman. *Cherokee Tragedy: The Ridge Family and the Decimation of a People.* 2d rev. ed. Norman: University of Oklahoma Press, 1986.

Williams, Delores S. *Sisters in the Wilderness: The Challenge of Womanist God-Talk.* Maryknoll: Orbis Books, 1993.

Williams, Patrick, and Laura Chrisman, eds. *Colonial Discourse and Post-Colonial Theory.* New York: Columbia University Press, 1994.

Wise, Jennings C. *The Red Man in the New World Drama.* Rev. and ed. by Vine Deloria Jr. New York: Macmillan, 1971.

Wissler, Clark. *Indians of the United States.* Rev. ed. Garden City, N.Y.: Doubleday, 1966.

Wolf, Helen Pease. *Reaching Both Ways.* Laramie: Jelm Mountain Publications, 1989.

Wong, Hertha Dawn. *Sending My Heart Back across the Years: Tradition and Innovation in Native American Autobiography.* New York: Oxford University Press, 1992.

Woodard, Charles L. *Ancestral Voices: Conversations with N. Scott Momaday.* Lincoln: University of Nebraska Press, 1989.

Wub-e-ke-niew [Francis Blake Jr.]. *We Have the Right to Exist.* New York: Black Thistle Press, 1995.

Wunder, John R. *"Retained by the People": A History of American Indians and the Bill of Rights.* New York: Oxford University Press, 1994.

Zitkala-Ša [Gertrude Bonnin]. *American Indian Stories.* Washington, D.C.: Hayworth Publishing House, 1921.

Zyla, Wolodymyr T., and Wendell M. Aycock, eds. *Ethnic Literatures since 1776: The Many Voices of America.* Lubbock: Texas Tech Press, 1978.

Articles

Baird, W. David. "Are There 'Real' Indians in Oklahoma?: Historical Perceptions of the Five Civilized Tribes." *Chronicles of Oklahoma* 68 (Spring 1990).

Baldridge, William. "Toward a Native American Theology." *American Baptist Quarterly,* December 1989.

Bennett, Tony, and Valda Blundell. "First Peoples." *Cultural Studies* 9 (January 1995).

Blaeser, Kimberly M. "Learning 'The Language the Presidents Speak': Images and Issues of Literacy in American Indian Literature." *World Literature Today* 66 (Spring 1992).

Bobb, Columpa. "The Native Experience." *Gatherings* 2 (1991).

Bronitsky, Gordon. "Jews and Indians: Old Myths and New Realities." *Jewish Spectator* (Winter 1991–1992).

Colbert, Thomas Burnell. "Visionary or Rogue?: The Life and Legacy of Elias Cornelius Boudinot." *Chronicles of Oklahoma* 65 (Fall 1987).

Cook-Lynn, Elizabeth. "Some Thoughts about Biography." *Wicazo Sa Review* 10, no. 1 (Spring 1994).

Deloria, Vine, Jr. "It Is a Good Day to Die." *Katallagete* 4, nos. 2–3 (Fall-Winter 1972).

———. "A Native Perspective on Liberation." *Mission Trends No. 4.* Offprint.

———. "Out of Chaos." *Parabola* 10, no. 2 (May 1985).

———. "Religion and Revolution among American Indians." *Worldview* 17, no. 1 (January 1974).

———. "Sacred Lands and Religious Freedom." *American Indian Religions* 1, no. 1 (Winter 1994).

———. "This Country Was a Lot Better Off When the Indians Were Running It." *New York Times Magazine,* March 8, 1970.

Ellis, Clyde. "'Our Ill Fated Relative': John Rollin Ridge and the Cherokee People." *Chronicles of Oklahoma* 68 (Winter 1990–1991).

Forbes, Jack D. "Colonialism and Native American Literature: Analysis." *Wicazo Sa Review* 3 (1987).

Gagnon, Gregory. "American Indian Intellectuals: Are They Above Reproach, or Easy Targets?" *Tribal College* (Summer 1995).

Hochbruck, Wolfgang. "Breaking Away: The Novels of Gerald Vizenor." *World Literature Today* 66 (Spring 1992).

JanMohamed, Abdul R. "The Economy of Manichean Allegory: The Function of Racial Difference in Colonialist Literature." *Critical Inquiry* 12, no. 1 (1985).

King, Thomas. "Borders." *World Literature Today* 66 (Spring 1992).

Krupat, Arnold. "Scholarship and Native American Studies: A Response to Daniel Littlefield, Jr." *American Studies* 34 (1993).

Littlefield, Daniel, Jr. "American Indians, American Scholars, and the American Literary Canon." *American Studies* 33 (1992).

McMaster, Gerald R. "Border Zones: The 'Injun-uity' of Aesthetic Tricks." *Cultural Studies* 9 (January 1995).

McQuaid, Kim. "William Apes, Pequot, an Indian Reformer in the Jackson Era." *New England Quarterly* 50 (1977).

Meredith, Howard. "Native Images." *World Literature Today* 66 (Spring 1992).

Milbank, Dana. "What's in a Name?: For the Lumbees, Pride and Money." *Wall Street Journal,* November 13, 1995.

Morrison, Daryl. "Twin Territories: The Indian Magazine and Its Editor, Ora Eddleman Reed." *Chronicles of Oklahoma* 60 (Summer 1982).

Ortiz, Simon. "Toward a National Indian Literature: Cultural Authenticity in Nationalism." *MELUS* 8, no. 2 (1981).

Peyer, Bernd. "Samson Occom: Mohegan Missionary and Writer of the 18th Century." *American Indian Quarterly* 6, nos. 3–4 (1982).

Ruoff, A. LaVonne Brown. "Justice for Indians and Women: The Protest Fiction of Alice Callahan and Pauline Johnson." *World Literature Today* 66, no. 2 (Spring 1992).

Simard, Rodney. "American Indian Literatures, Authenticity, and the Canon." *World Literature Today* 66 (Spring 1992).

"The Spectrum of Other Languages: An Interview with Joy Harjo." *Tamaqua* 3, no. 1 (Spring 1992).

Starkloff, Carl K. "Religious Renewal in Native North America: The Contemporary Call to Mission." *Missiology* 13, no. 1 (January 1985).

Thomas, Robert K. "Colonialism: Classic and Internal." *New University Thought* 4, no. 4 (Winter 1966–67).

Tinker, George. "Columbus and Coyote: A Comparison of Culture Heroes in Paradox." *Apuntes* (1992).

Trigger, Bruce G. "Ethnohistory: The Unfinished Edifice." *Ethnohistory* 33 (Summer 1986).

Velie, Alan R. "American Indian Literature in the Nineties: The Emergence of the Middle-Class Protagonist." *World Literature Today* 66 (Spring 1992).

Warrior, Robert Allen. "Canaanites, Cowboys, and Indians." *Christianity and Crisis,* September 11, 1989.

———. "An Interview with Vine Deloria, Jr." *The Progressive,* April 1990.

———. "A Marginal Voice." *Native Nations* (March/April 1991).

———. "Reading American Indian Intellectual Traditions." *World Literature Today* 66 (Spring 1992).

Weaver, Jace. "American Indians and Native Americans: Reinhold Niebuhr, Historiography, and Indigenous Peoples." In Sylvia O'Meara and Douglas A. West, eds.,

From Our Eyes: Learning from Indigenous Peoples. Toronto: Garamond Press, 1996.

———. "Ethnic Cleansing, Homestyle." *Wicazo Sa Review* 10, no. 1 (Spring 1994).

———. *"Green Grass, Running Water." Publishers Weekly,* January 25, 1993.

———. "Native Reformation in Indian Country?" *Christianity and Crisis,* February 15, 1993.

———. "Original Simplicities and Present Complexities: Reinhold Niebuhr, Ethnocentrism, and the Myth of American Exceptionalism." *Journal of the American Academy of Religion* 63, no. 2 (Summer 1995).

———. "Poetry." *Native Journal,* January 1993.

———. "PW Interviews: Thomas King." *Publishers Weekly,* March 8, 1993.

———. "Trickster among the Wordies." *Christianity and Crisis,* August 17, 1992.

Weibel-Orlando, Joan. "Constructing American Indian Histories: On Myths and Meta-myths." *Journal of American Ethnic History* (Fall 1992).

Wiget, Andrew. "Elias Boudinot, Elisha Bates, and *Poor Sarah:* Frontier Protestantism and the Emergence of the First Native American Fiction." *Journal of Cherokee Studies* 8, no. 1 (Spring 1983).

———. "Identity, Voice, and Authority: Artist-Audience Relations in Native American Literature." *World Literature Today* 66 (Spring 1992).

Willard, William. "Pipe Carriers of the Red Atlantis: Prophecy/Fantasy." *Wicazo Sa Review* 10 (Spring 1994).

"Yellow Woman and a Beauty of the Spirit." *Publishers Weekly,* January 22, 1996.

Videos and Music

Canadian Broadcasting Corporation. "Interview with Robbie Robertson." October 14, 1994.

Cavanaugh, Linda, and Tony Stizza, prods. "Strangers in Their Own Land." Oklahoma City: Strangers in Their Own Land, Inc., 1993.

Curtis, Edward S. "In the Land of the War Canoes." Re-release of "In the Land of the Headhunters." New York: Milestone Film & Video, 1992.

Robertson, Robbie and the Red Road Ensemble. "Music for 'The Native Americans.' " Hollywood, Calif.: Capital Records, 1994.

Dissertations, Theses, Unpublished Papers

Akers, Norman. Notes to exhibition, Heard Museum, Phoenix, Ariz., January 1995.

Arnold, Philip P. "Wampum, the Land, and the Abolition of Grief." Paper read at American Academy of Religion Meeting, Philadelphia, November 20, 1995.

Aughtry, Charles E. "Lynn Riggs, Dramatist: A Critical Biography." Ph.D. dissertation, Brown University, 1959.

Baldridge, William. "Christianity after Colonialism." Unpublished paper, 1992.

Barrett, Herb. "The 'Storyteller' of Leslie Marmon Silko: A Commentary." Unpublished paper, Yale University, December 18, 1996.

Borst, Muriel. "More Than Feathers and Beads." Play presented at the American Indian Community House, New York, November 5, 1994.

Churchill, Mary. "Native Struggles for Freedom in the Land." Response at American Academy of Religion Meeting, Philadelphia, November 20, 1995.

Harjo, Joy, and Robert Warrior. "Tribal Aesthetics: A Conversation." Panel held at Stanford University, Palo Alto, Calif., January 17, 1996.

Jaimes-Guerrero, M. A. "Native Womanism: The Organic Female Archetype—Kinship and Gender Identity Within Sacred Indigenous Traditions." Paper read at American Academy of Religion Meeting, Philadelphia, November 20, 1995.

Jocks, Christopher Ronwanièn:te. "Combing Out Snakes: Violence in the Longhouse Tradition." Paper read at American Academy of Religion Meeting, Chicago, November 21, 1994.

Jones, Lucy. "The Land and the Spirit." Unpublished paper, Union Theological Seminary, January 22, 1996.

Jones, Peter. "Autobiography of Peter Jones." Microfilm. General Commission on Archives and History, The United Methodist Church, Drew University, Madison, N.J. N.d.

Swansburg, John, II. "In the Shadow of Rushmore: United States Government Misconduct in the Investigation and Continued Incarceration of Leonard Peltier." Unpublished paper, Yale University, December 22, 1996.

Treat, James A. "Native Americans, Theology, and Liberation: Christianity and Traditionalism in the Struggle for Survival." Master's thesis, Pacific School of Religion, 1989.

Warrior, Robert Allen. "Tribal Secrets." Ph.D. dissertation, Union Theological Seminary, 1991.

———. "William Apess: Recovering a Christian Native Nationalist Past." Paper read at Native American Religion Forum, School of Theology at Claremont, Claremont, Calif., August 11, 1995.

Weaver, Jace. "Natives and Community: Native American Literature as a Resource for Doing Theology." Lecture delivered at Union Theological Seminary, New York, September 1995.

———. "Zelophehad's Daughters: Indigenizations of Christ and the Possibility of a Native Theology of Liberation." Master's thesis, Union Theological Seminary, 1993.

Interviews

Bell, Betty Louise. February 18, 1996.

Colop, Moises. September 22, 1995.

Dudley, Joseph Iron Eye. June 10, 1994.

King, Thomas. January 27, 1993, and February 2, 1996.

McKinney, Jim. June 10, 1994.

Tonemah, Quanah. June 10, 1994.

Wantland, William. December 21, 1992.

Index